INSIGHT GUIDES

Created and Directed by Hans Höfer

TUSCANY

Edited by Rosemary Bailey

Principal Photography by Albano Guatti
and Patrizia Giancotti

Editorial Director: Brian Bell

Houghton Mifflin

APA PUBLICATIONS

The Stendhal syndrome is an affliction that appears frequently in this book – it has affected visitors to Florence and Tuscany for centuries, and its peculiar symptoms of fainting and ecstasy at the sight of overwhelming beauty are hazards for anyone writing or editing a book on Tuscany. Many of the following contributors were already victims and they bravely risked further attacks in the course of their research.

Project editor **Rosemary Bailey** first succumbed to the beauties of Tuscany while visiting friends in their villa near Lucca. She was badly bitten by mosquitoes and had to forgo a planned trip to San Gimignano and its famous towers. "I was obliged to spend the entire day sitting on the terrace reading Mary McCarthy's *The Stones of Florence*, contemplating a sublime view of vines and cypresses, surrounded by the scent of wisteria. That made me realise what a perfectly arranged place Tuscany was."

Bailey is a London-based writer and editor, specialising in travel writing and literary profiles. She has also edited Insight Guides to the *Loire Valley, Burgundy* and the *Côte d'Azur*. For this book, she explored the provinces of Pistoia and Massa-Carrara, describes the whimsical delights of Tuscan villas and gardens, and recommends a visit to one of the many health spas in the region.

Lisa Gerard-Sharp wrote a substantial proportion of this book, and proved extremely knowledgeable about all things Tuscan, from Etruscan grave robbing to the finer points of expatriate living in Chiantishire. She investigates the essence of the Tuscan

miracle, describes the importance of festivals in Tuscan life, and analyses modern Tuscany. She has also provided an informed and witty guide to the provinces of Siena and Livorno. Her love of Italy developed from "an infatuation with Masaccio's paintings and a doomed affair with a haunted Sienese farmhouse." Although based in London as a writer and broadcaster, she feels it is inevitable she will return to live in Italy where she previously taught English and edited programmes for RAI Television. Meanwhile, she was able to update this book thoroughly for this edition.

Tuscany was, of course, the birthplace of the Renaissance in art and architecture. Renaissance scholar **Russell Chamberlin** tackled the vital chapters on art and history, combining them with a detailed guide to Florence. "I first got hooked on the Italian Renaissance in Florence cathedral in the 1960s when I wondered why on earth the Florentines had dedicated an enormous mural portrait to a semi-bandit, the *condottiero* John Hawkwood. Tracking down the career of this mercenary soldier gave me the material for my first book – and I've never looked back, for we're still trying to unravel how and why the Renaissance came about." Chamberlin has written 27 books on European history and travel, and has been awarded a M.Univ (Master of the University) honorary degree by the University of Surrey in recognition of his work.

Architecture and travel writer **Paul Duncan** explored the provinces of Florence, Arezzo and Lucca for this book. He is especially good at spotting the perfect hidden fresco in a remote little church, which is what going to Tuscany is all about. He "specialises

Bailey

Gerard-Sharp

Chamberlin

Duncan

in discovering forgotten, unknown and ignored buildings and then writing about them." He has an MA in art and architectural history from Edinburgh University, writes for several UK magazines, and is a correspondent for *Casa Vogue* in Italy and Spain.

Wine is an essential aspect of Tuscany – and Chianti is still the most famous wine from the region. Wine writer **Maureen Ashley** explains why Chianti is no longer the only important Tuscan wine and she provides an invaluable guide to drinking and a succinct history of the wine industry. Italians happily serve wine to children and so she became an enthusiast at a tender age during childhood holidays in Italy. In 1984 she became one of the few women to qualify as a Master of Wine, and now specialises in writing about Italian wine.

Valentina Harris describes the simple pleasures of Tuscan food, and the history of olive oil. She has plenty of experience, having been brought up and educated in Rome and on her family's Tuscan homestead. She is an authority on Italian food, author of *Perfect Pasta* and *Regional Italian Cookery.* She still thinks of Tuscany as her real home, although she currently lives with her husband and two sons in a tiny Norfolk village.

Author **Barry Miles'** most recent book is a biography of American poet Allen Ginsberg. As well as a lifelong interest in art and literature, he has a passion for architecture and here he explores the Roman ruins of Tuscany and explains the importance of the Pisan Romanesque style of architecture and its spread through Tuscany and beyond.

Marco De Stefani and **Lorella Grossi** both live and work in Bologna where

Ashley

Harris

Grossi is an industrial heritage historian with the Bologna museum and De Stefani works as an economist. They spend as much time as they can in their medieval property in a tiny village in Grosseto; their enthusiasm and intimate knowledge of Grosseto and the Maremma provide an excellent guide to a still little known region of Tuscany.

Susan Zucker, who also contributed to the article on Grosseto, worked in London as a fashion consultant and writer before moving to Rome. She now lives in Grosseto.

Yvonne Newman, who wrote on Pisa Province, worked in Italy for the British foreign office, and now lives near Oxford.

Gabriella Ferranti compiled the exhaustive Travel Tips section for this edition. She lives in Siena and Chianciano Terme and is fully involved in Tuscan life, lecturing in law at Siena University while also working as a journalist, politician and director of a radio station. She particularly enjoyed compiling the restaurants section and reflecting on memories of traditional meals in Sienese trattorias.

T here is more than enough information in *Insight Guide: Tuscany* to send any visitor reeling with a heavy dose of Stendhal's syndrome, and you must excuse our writers if they occasionally get carried away by it all. However, none of them have gone quite as far as the Irish writer Sean O'Faolain, who described the Italians as "a race that of all the races of the world best knows what it is to devour life not only to the last crumb and drop, but to the eating of the cups and plates as well."

Buon appetito!

Newman

CONTENTS

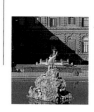

Preceding pages: view over Sienna; side door, Prato Cathedral; clockface.

CONTENTS

TRAVEL TIPS

THE TUSCAN MIRACLE

From the top of a village tower the Tuscan landscape lies below: the most civilised rural scene on Earth. Yet driving through southern Tuscany at night there is little sense of civilisation, still less of domesticity – even farm animals are kept indoors.

In the distance, a succession of small lights trail across the black countryside: tenuous links with separate, inward-looking communities. The spaces in between are remote, uncivilised. The blackness and emptiness of the countryside go back to medieval times and beyond; the "Tuscan miracle" only illuminates the cities.

D.H. Lawrence described Tuscany as where "men had been at their intensest, most naked pitch, here at the end of the old world and the beginning of the new". To Florentines, Michelangelo's *David* is the symbol of the ancient republic and the epitome of their own character. *David* is not just a study in naked intensity, but an awkward new spirit, struggling to be born out of marble. Emilio Pucci, the aristocratic fashion designer, used to visit *David* for inspiration: Michelangelo's grace of line inspired Pucci's designs in silk.

In giving birth to the Renaissance, Tuscany designed the modern world. In his painting, Giotto projected Tuscany into space. Brunelleschi crowned space with his Florentine dome, the greatest feat of Renaissance engineering.

Naked beauty: In the Carmine frescoes, Masaccio peopled space with recognisably human figures. His beautifully restored *Expulsion from Paradise* now reveals Adam and Eve in all their naked beauty. Gone is the medieval coyness; present is the palpable suffering of a couple who have lost everything. Even Michelangelo's version in Rome's Sistine Chapel does not plumb such tragic depths.

Florence's hospitals sometimes have the unusual task of reviving tourists who have

fainted not because of the heat but through over-exposure to unaccustomed beauty. However, the Tuscan miracle is not a frozen Renaissance portrait but a living procession of Tuscans at ease with their artistic setting and identity. Tuscans do have an innate aesthetic sense but the Tuscan tapestry is a rich weave which has been created by many different threads. Literary Tuscany is a strand traced through Boccaccio and Petrarch. Dante's verses adorn many Florentine walls and Tuscan squares. Republican Tuscany is best glimpsed through its fortified town halls

while humanist Tuscany is enshrined in poetry, sculpture and art, the fruits of patronage and craftsmanship.

Aristocratic Tuscany lingers in Medici palaces, villas and sculptured gardens, not to mention the ancestral homes of the Rucellai, Corsini and Frescobaldi. Bourgeois Tuscany parades along Florence's Via Tornabuoni, patronises the arts and restores family farms.

Peasant Tuscany traditionally takes a little of everything from the land: game, beans, chestnut flour, unsalted bread, olive oil, and, of course, the grapes needed to make Chianti and Brunello. Tuscan cuisine combines proportion and variety. Like the Tuscans them-

Preceding pages: bullfighters in the Campo, Siena; spiralling hysteria at the *Palio*; Chianti grape harvest; quintessential Tuscan landscape, Artimino; dusk over Fiesole. **Left,** *contrada* pride, Siena. **Above,** Masaccio's frescoes reveal the anguish of Adam and Eve in the *Expulsion from Paradise*.

selves, it is of good peasant stock. Variety on a small scale is also the secret of Tuscany's townscapes: from medieval hill-top towns to Etruscan villages; from *fin de siècle* spa towns to sophisticated mountain resorts; from the splendour of a Renaissance cathedral to a stark Romanesque church.

Architecturally, the cities are microcosms of all periods. Etruscan Maremma fades to Romanesque Pisa; Gothic Siena to medieval San Gimignano; and Renaissance Florence to Grand Ducal Chianti.

Nature tamed: The natural landscape is powerful, stretching from Carrara marble quarries to Maremma wilderness; from Livorno's rugged coastline to the mountainous olives' silver and the various greens of the growing crops appear an embroidered veil on a wilderness of bare geology."

With few exceptions, it is foreign poets who dwell on the cultivated tranquillity of corn, olives and vines. Tuscans are historically wary of space, preferring a safe, tribal existence in small towns to an alien, romantic notion of the countryside. Tuscan poets record the battles, the austerity, the protections of city life. *La campagna* was fit only for abbeys, monasteries, battles and exile.

Ambrogio Lorenzetti's *Città sul mare*, the first known European landscape painting, depicts an elaborate walled city against an austere backdrop. *Good Government*, the

Casentino. Much of the land appears tamed: the Chianti hills, the lush Mugello valley and "the Arno swirling past with its usual coffee-coloured foam" (Virginia Woolf).

Wooded Monte Amiata and the Sienese moon craters reveal another truth. Etruscans cultivated the land, Tuscans have tried to civilise it and foreigners romanticise it. A deep relationship with the land has always been present but it does not imply an ease with the land, still less a mastery. As the American writer Mary McCarthy noted, "The peculiar beauty of the Tuscan landscape is the combination of husbandry with an awesome and elemental majesty and silence; the

Sienese masterpiece, is idealistic in its portrayal of a cheerful, busy countryside. The pillaging and looting in *Bad Government* look infinitely more convincing. The "Tuscan miracle" therefore is, surprisingly, urban.

Unlike English towns, most Tuscan towns have been paved since the early 13th century. There are pavements through which no grass has ever grown. Given an urban heritage going back over two and a half millennia, Tuscany, even by Italian standards, is highly civilised. Tuscans prefer living in large villages or small towns today, echoing the Etruscan ideal, which was confirmed by the rural perils of medieval Europe.

Etruscan cities were conceived of as entities, settlements carved out of the countryside, never mere urban sprawl. When the civilisation disappeared, its imprint remained strong enough for D.H. Lawrence to record: "Because a fool kills a nightingale with a stone, is he therefore greater than the nightingale? Not he! Rome fell, and the Roman phenomenon with it. Italy today is far more Etruscan in its bones than Roman, and always will be."

This triumphant elegy is borne out by modern and medieval "Etruscans". Tuscans apparently feel no guilt about acquiring Etruscan treasures from local tombs. A family's ill-gotten Etruscan urns are treasured ances-

town was a small state with its own land, local government and traditions.

In claiming an urban identity, small places, which are really no more than villages, still feel like towns today and consider themselves as such. *Città* is a perception of status, not size. The concept of "town" has always cut across economic and social divisions within the community. Battles for independence have reinforced but not forged this cultural identity: it was always there.

The secret of Tuscan identity lies in each town's sense of completeness. Tuscan towns go against the current of modern homogeneity and internationalism; Florence is becoming more Florentine and Siena more Sienese;

tral relics, valued above Roman coins. And it was Etruscan settlements, not Roman grids, that provided the framework for the Tuscan townscape and identity.

In medieval Lucca and Florence, fractious nobles were often obliged to spend part of the year in town in order to instil a sense of belonging to something bigger than a warmongering tribe. The ideal of *civiltà* in the form of urban identity extended from the largest city-state to the smallest town. Each

inside image is more important than reality. Despite trade links, tourism and mass communications, Tuscan towns still feel spiritually self-sufficient. The town opens inwards to its inhabitants; everybody shares in its traditions and is regenerated. In the large cities this identity is maintained against enormous odds. Great passion and pride is attached to local traditions: to a Sienese bank manager, his role as usher for his *contrada* in the annual *Palio* may be more important than his career.

For a Tuscan, city life feels narrow, but it is also invitingly deep. For an outsider, the exhilaration lies in the city's confident sense of self. The English poet Elisabeth Jennings wrote that in such a setting as Florence,

It is simple to be a stranger,
To have a mind that is wide
To permit the city to settle between our
thoughts,
As between those hills, and flower and
glow inside.

Tuscans are iconoclasts who have believed in and broken many gods: Greek and Roman idols, Etruscan human sacrifices, Epicureanism. In Savonarola, the "mad monk" who railed against human vanity and excess, Florence gnawed away at Catholicism. *Campanilismo* (provincialism: literally, loyalty to one's own bell-tower), is a longer-held,

the art is the mystery of the miracle. The "Tuscan miracle" is more than the sum of its artistic parts. Even the notion of the "Tuscan artist" is a geographical expression, an outsider's label for Florentine, Pisan, Pistoian or Sienese artists. It is meaningless to compare Giotto's early Renaissance belltower in Florence with the Romanesque leaning tower of Pisa. While Pisan architecture practises sober restraint, Florentine goes for elegant experimentation.

As for art, Ambrogio Lorenzetti's wall frescoes show medieval Sienese chivalry while the *Macchiaioli* Impressionists paint a coherent picture of 19th-century Livorno. Even within Renaissance art, diversity is the

deeper faith and guarantees a future to local saints.

Cultured chemists: The miracle is rooted in the Tuscans' sense of place, family and craftsmanship. Olive Hamilton, speaking of a Lucchese, said: "It does not surprise a Tuscan that a chemist in our small town has written a two-volume work on the region from early Etruscan times." In this sense, even more than in the strictly artistic sense, Tuscans are highly cultured.

Dante and Petrarch excluded, Tuscany is steeped in visual rather than in literary traditions; art is the natural expression of identity. The full power and disturbing truthfulness of

norm. Piero della Francesca's mystical frescoes in Arezzo echo Masaccio's naturalistic Florentine frescoes: yet the alternative approaches of mysticism and realism represent the yin and yang of Renaissance art.

In Tuscany, the gap between an artist and an artisan is smaller than elsewhere in the world. To a picture restorer in Arezzo or to a weaver in Prato, the distinction is irrelevant. Adamo, the chief wine taster with Contessa Contucci's family firm, considers that after 30 years of drinking Vino Nobile he is both a master craftsman and an unsurpassed artist. Tuscan virtues are many, but they do not include modesty.

Questi primitivi is a term often applied to foreigners, southerners and Sardinians, in increasing order of scorn. During World War II, the American art historian Bernard Berenson was rebuked by a Florentine manicurist whose help he was seeking: *"O Signore, per noi tutti gli stranieri sono ugualmente odiosi"* ("Oh, Sir, for us all foreigners are equally hateful").

Chauvinism aside, Tuscans are polite, expect politeness in return and often criticise another Tuscan for being *mal educato*. If in doubt about what to say, such blandishments as *"è un posto meraviglioso"* ("it's a wonderful place") can be used indiscriminately, even in Livorno's mosquito-infested swamps,

industrial Poggibonsi or in the aptly-named Scrufiano.

A direct appeal to local pride can lead to unexpected gifts: the chance to meet Signor Parenti's "unique" donkey, "the only one within Florence's city walls" or to visit an abbey normally closed to the public. Even to watch a wealthy hotelier's joy in her grave-robbed Etruscan jewellery – "Why not? I'm Etruscan."

"Fare bella figura", literally "looking

Left, picking olives, as pictured by a 15th-century artist. **Above**, shepherd near Chiusi: peasant Tuscany takes a little of everything from the land.

good" or "making a good impression", stresses the importance of "face", which is a Tuscan's image in the community. Appearances are a touchstone of civilised behaviour. Indigenous Etruscan looks can be found in the streets of Chiusi or Volterra, "the full dark eyes, the pointed beard, long inquisitive nose and the Mona Lisa smile of a terracotta tomb figure" in the words of the English travel writer H.V. Morton. Tuscan looks are the product of perfect genetic engineering: classic Medici; luminous Sienese; austere Masaccio; cheeky Sodoma. A succession of invaders have also left Moorish, Spanish, German and Sardinian imprints.

Linguistic rivals: If Tuscans have a collective urban identity, the "pure" Tuscan dialect has helped in giving disparate towns a regional identity and national status. Modern Italian is the Tuscan dialect. Florence and Siena rival each other in claims for linguistic "purity", thus proving that city-state superiority is thriving, although the "purity" dissolves among country dialects.

Tuscans reveal themselves in their language. The Florentine proverb, *"Uomo senza roba è una pecora senza lana"* ("A man without clothes is like a sheep without wool") simultaneously indicates the vital importance of appearance and medieval Tuscany's original source of wealth. Tuscan includes colourful oaths such as *"porca miseria"* ("holy pork") and *"per cortesia"*, an expression of great civility.

There is also an old saying which confirms innate Tuscan wariness: "Keep away from sick doctors, dogs that don't bark, men that don't speak, people who go to mass twice a day and quarrels with those who are bigger than you are."

Certain images of the Tuscan miracle remain. *Città sul mare*, the city as bastion against the darkness; and, in Pienza, the *civiltà* that led a Tuscan Pope to construct a palace around a view, the first time the concept of a view entered European architecture. Two images of people interlock: the modern Tuscan holding her jewellery like a religious relic; and the ancient Etruscans, echoing through the centuries like the names of their own lost gods. While watching oxen slowly pulling a plough through olive groves and vineyards, Bernard Berenson recorded "a feeling that I was looking at what has been going on ever since civilisation began."

Modern Tuscans are proud of their Etruscan heritage and they feel no shame about stealing their own heirlooms; sadly, the ransacking of newly discovered tombs is rife. There are stories of farmers pretending to grow vegetables under cover while furtively digging up some ancient treasures. Most middle-class Tuscans have at least one item and a few conceal collections worthy of a museum. Many a wealthy dinner party ends with a showing of Etruscan treasures. A gold brooch is readily available for the price of a small Fiat. Pots are caressed with love. Jewellery is examined under a magnifying glass, its minute images of deities and animals admired and luxuriously enjoyed. This orgy of sensual indulgence is something the Etruscans would have loved.

As the freshest face in the ancient world, the Etruscans are often seen as a mythical people out of time. The Etruscans were "rediscovered" in the Romantic era and since then a "scholarly" Etruria and a "poetic" Etruria have been at variance. While Etruscologists have pieced together a picture of a complex urban civilisation with robust art forms, Tuscans see a myth shrouded in ritual sacrifice, an indecipherable language and delicate eroticism. Mystery aside, the colour and life of Etruscan art contrast with the cold marble perfectionism of the Greeks and Romans. This alone encourages Tuscans to speculate on racial continuity and to recognise themselves in the Etruscan rather than in the Roman civilisation.

Early immigrants: Etruscan origins are hotly disputed. The Romantics and latter-day writers believed that the Etruscans sailed from Asia Minor. However, Dionysius, writing as the Etruscan civilisation neared its end, held that the Etruscans were natives with an indigenous culture too deeply engrained to be Oriental. Most modern scholars believe that the Etruscans migrated from Eastern Europe over the Alps and represent the flowering of the early Italic tribes. What is clear is that between the 8th and 4th centuries BC "Etruria

Propria" flourished as a confederation of 12 city-states in central Italy. Northern Etruria, roughly equivalent to modern Tuscany, included Arezzo, Chiusi, Cortona, Populonia, Vetulonia and Volterra.

Etruscan seafarers and merchants first settled on the coast and began smelting iron ore from Elba and importing Oriental ceramics, glass and silverware. Greek naval supremacy meant an opening to Hellenistic culture: ships sailed to Corinth with honey, gold and bronze figurines and returned to Vetulonia and

Populonia with perfume and painted wine jars. The inland cities such as Chiusi and Volterra thrived on hunting, farming and internal trade.

Over the next two centuries, the Etruscans allied themselves to the developing Roman power and by the first century BC all the Etruscan territory was annexed. Although Etruscan and Latin coexisted, Etruscan culture was crushed and the region transformed into quiet Roman provinces. The Etruscan cultural role degenerated into the provision of soothsayers, musicians, dancers and fighters for Rome.

The original confederation had a complex

Preceding pages: the elemental majesty of the Tuscan landscape. **Left,** Etruscan tomb painting. **Above,** Etruscan tombs at Populonia.

urban and social structure: each city was originally run by a king, later by local aristocrats and finally by a priestly oligarchy. The lords owned large landholdings or navies and were served by serfs and slaves. Whereas the serfs were rewarded with agricultural plots, the slaves danced and sang for their supper. With urbanisation, an independent class of artisans and merchants emerged, often of Greek or Phoenician extraction. The granting of the same Roman citizenship to the middle classes as to the aristocratic priests and magistrates was a blow to the Etruscan princely tradition.

Since there is no extant Etruscan literature, our knowledge of the living Etruscans

aristocratic Etruscans had considerable freedom, social status and economic influence. They are depicted attending banquets without their husbands, riding covered wagons to their landholdings and playing flutes or lyres at funerals. According to Theopompus, a Greek contemporary, "The women often strip off in the presence of men" and "do easily give in to anybody". Their offspring were all fed, "ignoring their paternity".

Restless race: In art, the men are rarely still: they charge through games, boar-hunts, processions, journeys, dances, banquets and diving competitions. Even semi-recumbent on the sarcophagi, they look ready to fight the underworld single-handed. The "ordinary"

is oddly dependent on a reading of their funerary art for clues. We know them as they would like to be known, these idealised aristocrats elevated by Greek myths. In looks, they are certainly the Lawrentian "long-nosed, sensitive-footed, subtly-smiling Etruscans."

The women were depicted as pale while the men were uniformly reddish brown, either tanned by the sun or ritually painted. Friezes of serene married couples, tender lovers, absorbed wrestlers, erotic dancers, or grieving warriors reflect the fullness of Etruscan life.

In contrast to Greek and Roman women,

Etruscan is only glimpsed in passing: a prized blonde courtesan flits past dancing slaves; a serf clutching a plough mourns his dead master, perhaps a prelude to his own sacrificial death.

The Etruscans were called founders of cities by the Romans, expert at building cities of the living as well as cities of the dead. The *Libri rituales* prescribed the rites involved in selecting a sacred city site. The cities followed the contours of the land and sited the necropolis below the city walls and the living city above. If cities of the dead predominate today it is by accident and not by morbid design. Carrara marble was unknown so public buildings, built of wood and clay, did not survive. As the English novelist D.H. Lawrence said, the fragile wooden temples were "as effervescent as flowers". The tumbledown remains of a rare stone temple in Fiesole only hint at the vitality of the original building, once enlivened by friezes of dancers and mythical animals.

Pre-Roman stones: From what remains of the cities, there was enough to impress Roman and Renaissance architects. Volterra's Porta all'Arco is a deep gateway inspired by Mesopotamian architecture: its three faceless stone heads, perhaps deities, add gravity and protection to the city. The huge drystone walls at Saturnia, rebuilt to defend the

their owners. Death reflected life: the poor were often buried in shallow graves or their ashes put in small urns; the rich were buried in chamber tombs and stone sarcophagi decorated with pottery. Tombs, in every shape and form, can be seen in the Etruscan necropoli: "temple" tombs at Saturnia; melon-shaped tombs at Cortona; Oriental "trench" tombs at Vetulonia. At Sovana, "pigeon-hole" tombs are niches cut into the rock, while at Chiusi, a mysterious labyrinth reputedly conceals the sarcophagus of Lars Porsenna, mythical king of the Etruscans. Chiusi also contains early "well" tombs, those in which the ashes were placed in a shallow dish, perhaps covered by the dead

city against Roman incursions, are still standing. Pitigliano, a rough honeycomb hewn into the rocky tufa, is an Etruscan inland town with medieval finishing touches. Sovana also keeps the original town plan, complete with ancient sunken streets, *vie cave*, and a drainage system dug into the volcanic rock. Roselle neatly compartmentalises its sacred, industrial and residential areas.

But it is the tombs that remain as a cultural testimony to the power, wealth and beliefs of

Left, the Mistress of the Tomb: myth shrouded in ritual sacrifice. **Above**, the delicate eroticism of Tuscan dancers.

man's helmet, and placed in a small round grave. The tombs and mode of burial varied according to the local custom and period.

At the height of the Etruscan civilisation, large "chamber" tombs emerged, often containing frescoes. Although most of the tomb painting lies just outside modern Tuscany, some can still be seen in its natural setting at Chiusi. Painted by skilled craftsmen, the frescoes portray domestic scenes and outdoor pursuits as well as the sacred journey. In the shuttered tombs, a sense of the outside world is recreated through hunting scenes dotted with exotic birds and flowers.

The Etruscans were as vital in death as

they were in life but underneath the liveliness lay a deep fatalism, underscored by the hopelessness of predicting the unknown will of the gods. Locked into an unequal relationship, the Etruscans were bound to a treadmill of fear and appeasement. In keeping with primitive religions, natural forces were personified as gods of the sea, earth and rising sun. The Etruscans also reinvented Greek gods in their own image: Zeus, Hera and Athena were Tinia, Uni and Minerva. Oriental and Greek motifs coexisted: Egyptian sphynxes watched Etruscan winged demons pursue menacing Greek Furies. Despite Classical influence, their religion was far removed from Greek rationalism.

into the realm of the afterworld rather than surviving in the tomb itself. Until then, Greek myths had bolstered Etruscan legends and beliefs. This revelation, derived from the Greeks' experience, transformed the afterlife into a shadowy, demonic world without hope or human joy. As scepticism flooded in, the age of religious innocence gave way to the age of experience and Etruscan religion began to die.

In Etruscan funerary art, men and women are depicted differently. The man is often shown wearing his chains of office over his bare chest. He may hold an egg, container of the soul, or clutch the *patera*, a circular dish arguably symbolising the continuity of life.

Divination, human and animal sacrifice were used to stave off divine retribution. The Books of the Dead prescribe rules for interpreting thunder and lightning, animal entrails, and the flight of birds. But the central vision was one of a painful leavetaking or "death journey" to the underworld, hounded by demons. From there, if the gods had been appeased by sacrifice, the dead had the potential to become divine. In this painful leavetaking, some see a lingering race memory of the original journey from the Orient or Eastern Europe.

But from 4 BC onwards, the Etruscans became convinced that the dead person passed

The bejewelled woman is surrounded by a mixture of feminine and sacred symbols: perfume boxes and earrings to beautify; a pomegranate or pine cone to symbolise either sexuality or death; a mirror to reflect her physical and spiritual perfection. In effect, these were portraits which were commissioned to show to the gods the noble patrons at their best.

Etruscan art is essentially regional; Arezzo had a reputation for *Arretino*, fine red pottery, and for its metalwork. The famous bronze *Chimera* remains a magical illusion: a goat's head springs from a lion's back and is seized by the lion's tail, suddenly transformed into a serpent's mouth. Chiusi boasts canopic urns, cinerary urns with an idealised effigy of the deceased on the lid, while Cortona's Giacometti-like bronze figurines represent Etruscan deities. Volterra runs the gamut of Etruscan demonology and Greek mythology. The "cinerary urns" are in fact small alabaster sarcophagi featuring sea monsters, beaked griffins and sirens in addition to Ulysses, Iphigenia and Oedipus.

Mystery language: The Etruscan language is as mysterious as the Etruscan origins. Although the alphabet is borrowed from Greek, the language, read from left to right, is part of no known linguistic group and defies interpretation. Many claim to have

even by the 18th century, the sounds of most letters, names and gods had been identified and simple texts translated. Today, the core grammatical and phonetic structure is known and, by deduction, most of the 10,000 shorter texts can be read accurately. These texts are mostly funerary inscriptions and religious dedications. The one known book, a priest's manual which was discovered wrapped around an Egyptian mummy, has been only partially deciphered.

The art critic John Ruskin saw an unbroken line of tradition from the tomb paintings of the Etruscans to Giotto and Fra Angelico. Certainly, the Etruscan influence on the Romans was considerable. Apart from intro-

found a key text equivalent to the Rosetta Stone. In Marsiliano a writing tablet was found engraved with the Greek Euboic alphabet used as a model for Etruscan. The University of Perugia has created a database of 100,000 Etruscan words in an attempt to break the code.

Despite considerable progress, the unintelligibility of Etruscan is part of a glamorous myth. True, there are no external keys such as dictionaries or bilingual texts but

Left, fifth-century-BC Tomb of the Monkey, Chiusi. Javelin thrower with serving boy. **Above**, ruins of Etruscan city of Vetulonia.

ducing the purple toga, an abundance of gods and competent soothsayers to Rome, the Etruscans added a coherent set of religious, humanistic and regional values which outlived the Roman empire.

The Etruscans exerted a dynamic influence on Roman art before the original creativity was stifled by Classicism. Today, the Etruscan influence still emerges in modern art: Massimo Campigli's ochres and burnt browns are modelled on Etruscan landscapes, as are Paolo Busato's photographs. Tuscans still see the land as Etruria, untouched by the succession of Roman and Catholic empires imposed on it through the centuries.

The traveller leaves the airport at Pisa and pulls out into the traffic-clogged Via Aurelia, the main coast road between Rome and the north. A few feet below the trucks and buses, the honking drivers and exhaust clouds, lie the smooth stone slabs of the original Roman road, headed with military precision for the harbour of Pisae, which was once on the coast. Pisa is now 8 km (5 miles) inland, but the roads of Tuscany, as in so many other places, remain where the Romans put them.

Not all remaining roads are as busy. There is a surviving stretch of the Via Clodia, the Roman road from Rome to Saturnia; a straight march, a footpath between fields and overgrown hedgerows, leading from the baths at Terme di Saturnia up the steep hillside to Saturnia itself.

Further up the hillside, the flat paving-stones make a U-turn then follow the sheer town walls, built by the Sienese in the 15th century but incorporating both Roman and Etruscan sections. Finally the path reaches a long straight stretch which sweeps the traveller through the Porta Romana, and into the town. There the road continues straight on, passing a few shops, until the worn flag-stones disappear ignominiously beneath someone's garden wall.

Halfway town: Saturnia is a quiet little town, no more than a village, drowsing under the immense weight of its past. It was the Etruscan Aurinia, the main town of the Ager Caletranus, the intermediate zone between the great centres of northern and southern Etruria, which was under the control of Vulci just before the Roman conquest.

It came under Roman control as a *praefectura* in 280 BC and in 183 BC a Roman colony was founded there, attributed to the Sabatina tribe. The Romans re-named the town Saturnia after Jupiter's father. Surprisingly, there is very little to see: the Roman south gate, the end of the Via Claudia, is the most exciting thing there.

Roman towns in Tuscany were either built upon the foundations of Etruscan cities as

part of a continuous development, as in Volterra, Vetulonia or Arezzo, or else they were established as new Roman *colonia* on the ruins of Etruscan towns, or as new settlements. In the second century AD Appian described the colonies in his *Bellum Civile*: "As the Romans subjugated the people of Italy successively, it was their habit to confiscate a portion of land and establish towns upon it, and to enrol colonists of their own in the towns already on it. They intended these for strongholds…either to hold the earlier

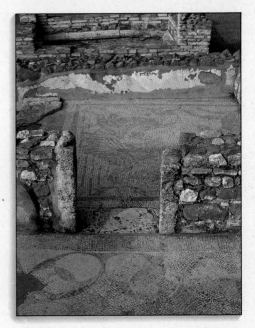

inhabitants in subjection or to repel enemy inroads."

Rome annexed Etruria in 351 BC and from the third until the second century BC, as part of the massive road building programme which was to transform Italy, four great Roman roads were built across the territory: the Via Aurelia, which ran up the western seaboard to Pisae and the naval base at Genua in Liguria; the Via Clodia, which stopped at Saturnia; the Via Cassia, built in 154 BC to connect Rome with Florentia; and the Via Flaminia, built in 220 BC to connect Rome to Umbria and the Adriatic.

It's hard to imagine the impact these giant

Left, *Primavera,* **a fresco from ancient Roman times anticipates the later style of Botticelli. Above,** **mosaic floor at Roselle, Grosseto.**

IMPORTANT DATES

800–500 BC: Etruscan civilisation flourished. Etruria Propria, a confederation of 12 states, included Arezzo, Cortona, Chiusi, Fiesole, Populonia, Roselle, Vetulonia, Volterra.

480–290 BC: Romans in power; annexed Etruria and founded colonies at Ansedonia, Roselle, Volterra, Luni and Lucca.

AD 200–600: Region invaded by Lombards, Goth and Franks.

AD 306: Constantinople becomes capital of Roman Empire; Byzantine period.

AD 476: Fall of Rome.

1000–1300: German emperors conquer Italy; constant warring between Guelfs (supporters of the papacy) and Ghibellines (supporters of the Holy Roman Empire).

1118: Consecration of Pisa cathedral.

1125: Florence begins its expansion with the takeover of Fiesole.

1265–1321: Dante Alighieri. *The Divine Comedy* is begun in 1314.

1266–1337: Giotto di Bondone. In 1334 Giotto begins work on the Florentine campanile.

1302: Giovanni Pisano executes the pulpit in Pisa cathedral.

1304–1374: Francesco Petrarch; his studies spark the resurgence of interest in antiquity.

1348: Black death strikes Florence, killing a third of the population.

1313–1375: Giovanni Boccaccio. His bawdy collection of tales, *The Decameron,* is set against the background of the plague.

1377–1466: Brunelleschi. His dome for Florence cathedral completed 1436.

1384: Arezzo is conquered by Florence.

1386–1466: Donatello. The sculptor is famous for the active poses of his revolutionary *Judith and Holofernes* and *David.*

1390: John Hawkwood, *condottiero*, becomes Captain General of Florence; inter-city wars fought by mercenaries.

1401–1428: Masaccio. The first of Florence's great 15th-century masters develops use of perspective.

1406: Pisa is defeated and becomes part of the Florentine state.

1420: Papacy returns to Rome from Avignon.

1434–1464: Cosimo de' Medici rules Florence.

1452: Alberti's *Ten Books on Architecture*.

1452–1519: Leonardo da Vinci.

1469–1527: Machiavelli. *The Prince* was written in 1513.

1469–92: Lorenzo de' Medici ruler of Florence

1475–1564: Michelangelo Buonarroti.

1498: "Mad monk" Savonarola is burnt at the stake for heresy in Florence's Piazza Signoria.

1527: Sack of Rome.

1555: Florence defeats Siena and incorporates its rival into the Florentine state.

1558: Benvenuto Cellini's *Autobiography.*

1564–1642: The Pisan Galileo Galilei discovers principles of dynamics.

1737: Death of Gian Gastone, the last male Medici; Tuscany falls to House of Lorraine.

1796: Napoleon's first Italian campaign.

1815: The Grand Duchy is absorbed into Austrian Empire.

1848: The War of Independence.

1858: Giacomo Puccini born in Lucca.

1859: Unification of Italy, initiated by Cavour.

1861: Proclamation of the Kingdom of Italy.

1865–1870: Florence briefly capital of Italy.

1915: Italy enters World War I on the Allies' side.

1922: Benito Mussolini comes to power.

1940: Italy forms pact with Germany and Japan, and enters World War II against Britain and France.

1943: Fall of the Fascists. Mussolini executed at the end of the war, in 1945.

1946: Italy becomes a republic.

1957: Treaty of Rome; Italy founder member of EEC (now the EU).

1966: Massive flooding in Italy: the Arno overflows in Florence and many works of art are damaged or destroyed.

1985: Great frost destroys between 50 and 75 percent of the olive trees.

1987: *Sorpasso*, the "overtaking". Italian economy outstrips British and French competitors.

1987: Terrorist bomb in Florence kills five and damages the Uffizi.

1994: Italy exchanges Proportional Representation for a first-past-the-post system. A right-wing government ushers in the Second Republic.

engineering projects must have had on the local inhabitants as surveyors and workmen spanned rivers with elegant stone bridges, built drains to prevent their new roads from flooding and, where necessary, cut through the hills themselves.

Etruscan roads were all designed to connect the interior with the coast, whereas Roman roads all led to Rome, thus the axis was turned 90°, from east-west to north-south. The new Roman roads purposely avoided the great Etruscan cities which slowly fell into decline, whereas the new Roman cities such as Pistoriae (Pistoia), a small town on the Via Cassia, grew in importance.

New colonies were founded at Ansedonia,

Fiesole, Roselle, Populonia, Volterra, Luni and Lucca. The cultural identity of the Etruscans was gradually absorbed into that of the Romans, a process which accelerated in 91 BC when Roman citizenship was extended to the Etruscans. The Romans learned many things from the Etruscans – principally the Tuscan arch which they developed as a central structural element in their buildings, relegating the classical columns of ancient Greece to a more decorative role.

Left, Francesco Petrarch: to his contemporaries a living representative of antiquity. Above, excavated Roman city at Roselle, Grosseto.

Using the arch, Roman architects and engineers built their extraordinary aqueducts and bridges. It was from the Etruscan kings that the Roman monarchy, and later the Republican magistrates, took their symbol of power: the *fasces*, an axe, surrounded by a bundle of rods, an eloquent symbol of the right to execute or scourge. (Sculpture depicting the *fasces* dating from 500 BC has been found at the Etruscan city of Vatluna, the Roman Vetulonia.)

The most complete remains in Tuscany are at Fiesole, Roselle and Cosa (Ansedonia); the best villas are near the coast, on Elba; near Porto Santo Stefano; and particularly on the Isola di Giannutri, near Grosseto, where the magnificent ruins of a villa with a number of intact slender columns overlook the Mediterranean. Most Tuscan cities have something to show, though sometimes a little detective work is required.

Roman colony: Ansedonia, the Roman Cosa, was founded as a Roman colony in 273 BC on the hilltop site of an earlier settlement, probably the Etruscan port of Vulci. The Roman city has been excavated and the site contains a main street, remains of a forum, a walled acropolis and, dominating the city on a southern hill, the ruined capitolium – a tripartite sanctuary for the triad of Jupiter, Juno and Minerva from which there are wonderful views out over the sea.

The city's 1.5 km (1 mile) of wall is virtually intact, as are many of its 18 guard towers, including the entrance at Porta Romana. The site is overgrown and many of the ruins are covered in brambles, giving it a melancholy atmosphere. Saplings are sprouting in the forum, returning the dead city to the earth. The lack of signposts and labels makes it easier to imagine the townspeople going about their daily routine.

Below the promontory is the silted up Roman port, and nearby, the Tagliata Etrusca (Etruscan Cut), which is not Etruscan at all but a drainage canal cut by the Romans to connect the port with the lake of Burano, to stop the lake and the harbour from silting up. The cleft in the rocks, the so-called Bagno della Regina (Queen's Bath), is not, as is sometimes claimed, a rock sanctuary, but part of the Roman drainage works.

Fiesole, possibly dating from the eighth century BC, is an Etruscan settlement overlooking the valleys of the Arno and the

Mugnone and has a superb view of what is now Florence. As Faesulae, it was a Roman military colony from 80 BC and later became the capital of Roman Etruria. The Piazza Mino da Fiesole is built on the site of the Roman forum.

The archaeological site is set on a hillside near the Duomo. There is a remarkably well preserved 3,000-seat Roman amphitheatre dating from 80 BC, which is still used for performances. Nearby are Roman baths and on the other side, the ruins of a Roman temple, both from the first century BC, and a 3rd-century BC Etruscan temple, set against the Etruscan city walls.

Detective work is necessary in Florence,

the Roman Florentia; the Roman grid-iron street plan is clearly visible in maps, with the Piazza della Repubblica following the outline of the old *castrum*. The perimeter of the amphitheatre, outside the city walls to the southwest, is still described by the little streets surrounding the Piazza S. Croce: the Via Torta, Via Bentaccord and the north side of the Piazza Peruzzi.

In Lucca, the original street plan is also still evident. Luca, as the Romans named it, began as a military colony in 178 BC (the last of the Roman colonies). The 10,000-seat amphitheatre was originally to the north of the Roman city, outside the walls. In time, it

was largely dismantled, and most of its remains are below street level.

During the Middle Ages, however, houses were built using the remaining walls of the amphitheatre, thus fossilising its outline and four main entrances. Fragments of its outside arcading are still visible from the surrounding lanes, incorporated in the outer walls of the houses. In the 19th century, the houses which filled the centre were cleared away to create the Piazza del Mercato.

Luni, called Luna by the Romans, was founded in 177 BC and was the springboard for the conquest of the Ligurian tribes in 15 BC. It was originally settled by 2,000 colonists, each of whom received 1.6 hectares (3.8 acres) of land. Originally on the coast, Luni became prosperous through shipping white Carrara marble from its fine harbour. The Roman city, its forum, a number of houses, and its amphitheatre have been excavated and today it is an important site for archaeologists.

Near-complete remains: Another extensive excavated site is at Roselle, the Roman Rusellae. The Etruscan city was taken by Rome early in the third century BC. It was originally an island, dominating the waters of the gulf. The ruins are satisfyingly complete, with a nearly intact circuit of Romano-Etruscan walls, a Roman forum, paved street, basilicas, villas, amphitheatre and baths.

Volterra was the Etruscan city state of Velathri. It became the important Roman municipality of Volterrae in the fourth century BC but was on the wrong side during the civil war and fell to Sulla in 80 BC. The Arco Etrusco has a Roman arched vault on massive Etruscan bases with three Etruscan basalt heads incorporated into the arch.

The ruins of the first-century BC Roman amphitheatre are situated outside the city walls to the west of the Porta Fiorentina. They are best seen by looking down on them from the city walls.

By creating the roads and major cities of Tuscany, the Romans left a permanent imprint on the landscape. A millennium later, the ruins of their great bridges, amphitheatres and city walls were the inspiration for the next great blossoming of Italian culture; Tuscany's coming of age, the Renaissance.

Above, remaining city walls at Cosa, Grosseto. **Right**, head of statue at Villa Garzoni, Pistoia.

"The City stands in the centre of the State like a guardian and a master. Towns surround her, just as the moon is surrounded by stars. The Florentine State might be compared to a round shield, with a series of rings surrounding a central knob. The central knob is the City itself, dominated by the Palazzo Vecchio, a mighty castle, the centre of the whole shield. The rings around it are formed first by the walls and suburbs, then by a belt of country houses, and finally by a distant circle of towns. Between the towns are castles and towers reaching the sky."

This was how a Florentine writer, Leonardo Bruni, described his city at the beginning of the 15th century. It was then at the height of its power, with many other cities and towns subject to it. Bruni's pride and love are obvious: his city is as beautiful as the moon and as strong as a shield. What he does not say is that all the other towns and cities in the state are held down by brute force. But Bruni probably thought that hardly worth mentioning: after all, that was what all other Italian cities were striving to achieve.

Power bases: Between the ending of the Roman Empire, in the 4th century AD and the beginning of the foreign invasions in the 16th century, after which all Italy became subject to foreign powers, the story of Italy is a catalogue of conflict between its cities, each of which was a sovereign state. Gradually, the larger absorbed the smaller. In the far south, Naples dominated the area from Rome to Sicily. In and around Rome, the Popes built up a power base. In the north, the great city of Milan swallowed up all its neighbours on the Lombard plain. And in Tuscany, a three-way battle was conducted between Florence, Pisa and Siena.

In the early stages the battles between the city-states were conducted by the citizens themselves, all able-bodied men between the ages of 15 and 50 sallying forth beyond their city's walls to fight the men of the neighbouring city. Even such a great poet and scholar as Dante took his part in these conflicts, fighting in the last battle between

citizen-soldiers which took place at Campaldino in 1289 when Florence finally crushed Arezzo. The blood-letting in that battle was so great that thereafter the cities began to fight out their differences with mercenaries, the *condottieri*.

Throughout the 14th century the *condottieri* held the balance of power. Commanding well-disciplined, well-armed companies numbering thousands of men, they sold their services to the highest bidder. The city which could afford them – and could control them

– dominated its neighbours. The extraordinary honour accorded these mercenaries is shown by the fact that, in Siena, Simone Marlini's great fresco in the town hall, *Guido Riccio da Fogeiano*, is dominated by a *condottiero*. In Florence, the Englishman John Hawkwood, who commanded the White Company, has a place of honour in the cathedral.

These wars between the cities were conducted, in theory, in the name of Guelf or Ghibelline partisanship. The Guelfs supported the papacy in its long battle against successive emperors. Italian politics had become so confused that the Holy Roman

Left, Florentine nobles. **Above**, Lorenzetti's *Bad Government* (1337-39).

Emperor was invariably a foreigner and, usually, a German. But the Ghibellines believed, while recognising that the emperor was merely a figure-head, that only with some kind of imperial control would peace ever return to Italy.

That at least was the theory. In practice, Guelf and Ghibelline were little more than battle slogans. When one party defeated its rivals in a city it would immediately fragment; in Florence, for example, when the Guelf party triumphed it promptly split into Black Guelfs and White Guelfs. Dante was one of those who, though a Guelf, was a "Black" and so was forced into exile when the "Whites" came to power.

Outside Tuscany, most city-states had fallen under the dominion of a single ruler: the Signor. The Tuscan republics maintained their independence far longer but eventually even Florence fell to a single ruler when the Medici transformed themselves into dukes.

Pisa subdued: While the Medici were still only private citizens, Florence was intent on subduing its two greatest rivals in Tuscany. It was inevitable that Florence should come into conflict with Pisa, because Pisa controlled the mouth of the Arno, Florence's lifeline. The Pisans made common cause with the great Ghibelline city of Milan, but Pisa was too close to Florence to fight off its powerful rival and in 1406 Pisa became part of the Florentine state.

Siena was at first more successful in resisting the Florentine embrace – but only by surrendering totally to Milan. Eventually, however, it too was absorbed into the Florentine state which had, under the Medici, become the Grand Duchy of Tuscany. This, in turn, came to an end with the death of the last male Medici in 1737. There then followed the long tussle known as the Tuscan Succession which eventually ended in 1815 when the Grand Duchy was absorbed into the Austrian Empire.

During the 1830s nationalist feeling began to grow and the *Risorgimento* movement was born, leading to revolution in 1848 and, finally, unification of Italy. From 1865–1870 Florence had a brief moment of glory as capital of a newly united Italy.

Right, Giorgio Vasari's *Foundation of Florence* (1563–65), on the ceiling of the Salone dei Cinquecento, Palazzo Vecchio.

One of the great myths of history provides a kind of Hollywood scenario for the "birth of the Renaissance", linking it to the fall of the Greek city of Constantinople in 1453, when scholars were supposed to have escaped, clutching their precious Greek manuscripts, to Italy. There, these manuscripts became a kind of magical seed, taking root, growing and bearing fruit almost immediately as "the Renaissance".

Of course, this is nonsense; like any other human phenomenon, the Renaissance had roots deep in history. Today, we know quite a lot about *how* the Renaissance happened, but we still do not know *why* it occurred at that particular time and, above all, in that particular place.

Contemporaries were equally puzzled. Writing in the 1430s, the scholar Lorenzo Valla said: "I do not know why the arts most closely approximating to the liberal arts had been in so long and deep decline and almost died out, nor why they have come to be aroused and come to life in this age."

Valla might also have added: "Why did it happen in Florence?" It was, of course, the political fragmentation of Italy which created the Renaissance, each little city-state contributing something unique to the whole. But the process certainly started in Florence, and the city dominated the cultural scene until the early 16th century.

The best book on Renaissance statecraft is by the Florentine writer, Machiavelli, and the best book on commerce by the Florentine Pegolotti. Art history owes everything to the Tuscan Vasari, and the whole course of art was changed by the Tuscans Giotto, Botticelli, Michelangelo and Leonardo da Vinci, to mention the most obvious.

Mystery to muse: Again and again over the centuries, attempts have been made to analyse the causes of the Florentine flowering, with reasons ranging from the poverty of the soil to the quality of the light. But it is no more possible to "explain" this than any other mystery of the human spirit.

Left, Sandro Botticelli's *St Augustine in his Study* (*circa* 1480), Church of the Ognissanti, Florence. **Right**, grain merchants in Florence.

The very word "renaissance" is a Florentine invention. In his book *Lives of the Most Excellent Architects, Painters and Sculptors*, first published in 1550, Giorgio Vasari, first of the art historians, remarks that the reader, "will now be able to recognise more easily the progress of [art's] rebirth (*il progresso della sua rinascita*)."

But what, exactly, did Vasari mean by *rinascita*? What was being "reborn"? Vasari was referring to a rebirth of the art and architecture of classical times; that is, before

Emperor Constantine transferred the seat of Empire to Constantinople at the beginning of the 4th century AD, causing Byzantium to become the centre of art and culture. A distinctive architecture, based on Roman models, using bricks and featuring domes and cupolas, was developed. Byzantine artists covered the interiors with mosaics, a Roman decorative form which they developed into a sumptuous art form; the thousands of glazed stone fragments catching the light in a way no fresco ever could, giving the images a shimmering, glittering presence in the semi-darkness – the "golden gloom" of Byzantium. The best examples in Italy are in

Ravenna, made in the 5th and 6th centuries, but the style prevailed in the 11th century in San Marco, Venice, and even in the 13th century in the magnificent Baptistry in Florence. It was the stiff formalised work of the Byzantine artists that Vasari, who dismissed them as "a certain residue of Greeks," was attacking, and which was completely overthrown by the new naturalism of the Renaissance artists.

Architects drew and measured the ruins of the Roman cities, rediscovering their building techniques and their rules of proportion: the "classical orders". Vitruvius's *Ten Books on Architecture*, the only surviving manual from classical times, was studied anew and became the basis, in the 15th century, for Alberti's treatise of the same name.

Reality in nature: Painting, which of all the arts is pre-eminently *the* art of the Renaissance, owed little to antiquity, though the great originality shown in the visual arts may be due partly to the fact that no Roman examples survived to be used as models. Renaissance artists broke new ground discovering perspective and observing the natural world which surrounded them. Nature meant little to the Greeks and the Romans, whereas one of the characteristics of the Renaissance artist was his ability to go back to first base. The 14th-century Florentine artist Cennino Cennini gave good advice to his fellow artists. "If you wish to draw mountains well, so that they appear natural," he wrote, "procure some large stones, rocky, not polished, and draw from these." The idea of a handful of stones standing in for the Alps or the Apennines might seem ludicrous, but it was a pointer to the new road the artist was taking, the road to reality in nature.

The classical world provided the inspiration for the artist to rise above the narrow medieval world, with its emphasis on theological studies. But, once started, he went his own way. What was reborn was an artistic sensibility but a re-cycled past.

Art historians divide the great period of transition into three sub-periods, using the logical Italian terms Trecento, (1300s) Quattrocento (1400s) and Cinquecento (1500s) instead of our rather confusing 14th, 15th and 16th centuries.

<u>Right</u>, Leonardo da Vinci's *Adoration of the Magi* (1481), Uffizi Gallery.

48

THE TRECENTO: THE ARTISTS' WORKSHOPS

Until the Quattrocento, the term "artist" had no particular significance, being virtually interchangeable with "artisan" or "craftsman". All were members of guilds, or *arti*: there was an *arte* for the shoemaker, no more and no less valid than the *arte* for the goldsmith, itself a subdivision of the immensely powerful Silk Guild.

The guilds extended their control, as a matter of course, over the decorative as well as the useful arts. Sculptors and architects were enrolled, logically enough, with the masons, and painters formed a sub-division of the apothecaries on the general principle that they had to have some acquaintance with chemistry to prepare their colours.

Far from resenting the obligation to join associations, painters and sculptors formed their own groups, or *compagnie*, created both within and across the boundaries of the larger guilds. The reasons were both social and technical. Socially, members could help each other, the group as a whole sharing both profits and losses. Technically, an increasing amount of work was done in co-operation, either on a kind of conveyor-belt system (two or three men might be engaged at successive stages in the shaping of a pillar, from rough hewing to final carving, or working side by side).

The growing popularity of the process known as *buon fresco* demanded such an approach. It had been introduced about a century earlier, and time had shown that it was the most permanent of all forms of mural art since the colouring became an intrinsic part of the plaster itself. (Michelangelo was to use the technique in the greatest of all works carried out using the process, the Sistine Chapel in Rome.)

The wall was first roughly plastered, and on this the master would make a rough outline drawing in charcoal. Over this outline was laid a layer of fine, smooth plaster, the *intonaco*. The outlines of the full-scale cartoon, as the original drawing was known, were punched through with a series of pin-

holes (often speedily done with a small spiked wheel known as a roulette). Charcoal was then rubbed through the holes, leaving the outline on the wet plaster as a series of dots. This technique is called "pouncing". For backgrounds, or when the master himself was doing the painting, the work was done from memory, with the original cartoon placed nearby. Only the amount of plaster that could be covered in one day's work was laid and, provided there was room, any number of men could work side by side from

the top of the wall downwards. It was a system which placed a premium on the skill of the individual at absorbing the style of the master – the man who had created the cartoon – so that, no matter how large the mural, the treatment was homogeneous.

In addition to these large, set tasks, the *bottega* (or workshop) would produce a variety of smaller articles for sale, either on speculation or on commission, ranging from painted scabbards and armorial bearings to holy pictures and statues. There was widespread demand for religious art which provided the bread and butter for hundreds of small *botteghe*. A peasant may have scraped

Left, Giotto's *Madonna and Child* (*circa* 1320–30). **Right**, *Madonna Enthroned* (*circa* 1280–85) by Cimabue, who discovered Giotto.

together a few lire for a picture; a parish priest might have a large sum at his disposal and commission a mural or even an altar piece: or a merchant who had made his fortune might be anxious to propitiate fate and show his piety.

The potential client had little interest in the identity of the craftsmen producing his order. But, if expensive colours were used (gold, silver, or blue made from the semi-precious lapis-lazuli), then the fact was clearly stated in the contract, along with the date of delivery of the finished piece. Commissioned work was almost invariably done on these written contracts which, in addition, usually specified how many figures were to appear in the finished painting, their activities and attributes. Religious paintings touched on the delicate area of religious orthodoxy and the wise craftsman ensured that his client stated exactly what he wanted.

Dour patron: A typical patron was Francesco Datini, a wool merchant of the little town of Prato, 16 km (10 miles) from Florence, whose story is told in Iris Origo's book *The Merchant of Prato*. After making his fortune, social and religious pressure prevailed upon him to decorate his house with religious paintings. He was superstitious rather than religious, indifferent to aesthetics, and he went about the business of commissioning holy pictures with the same dour eye for a bargain which made his fortune in wool.

In 1375 he was ordering from a *bottega* in Florence "a panel of Our Lady on a background of fine gold and a pedestal with ornament and leaves, handsome and the wood well carved, making a fine show with some figures by the best painter, with many figures. Let there be in the centre Our Lord on the Cross or Our Lady – whomsoever you find, I care not so that the figures be handsome and large, and the best and finest you can purvey and the cost no more than 5½ or 6½ florins."

Members of a *bottega* were usually contracted for three years, renewing or disbanding their company but always either reforming it or joining another. The practice began to die out at the beginning of the Quattrocento under new pressures – in particular, the dominance by a number of great painters who

Right, fresco in Palazzo Vecchio, from the workshop of Giorgio Vasari (1567–72).

52

could afford to regard members of the *bottega* virtually as their employees, and by the emergence of grand patrons such as the Medici.

The vast majority of the workers in these art shops are virtually anonymous. They were conscientious and skilled, rather than brilliant, but they formed the sub-soil from which the genius of the Quattrocento could flourish. The actual working pattern of the *bottega*, whereby a group of lesser men would paint the main body of a picture, leaving it to the identified master to put the finishing touches to it, would continue into the so-called High Renaissance of the Cinquecento, making it difficult and at times impossible for the most skilled art critic to say that such

joy, grief, anger. Contemporaries might be uncertain about why this great change occurred but there was a universal chorus of agreement as to who started it: Giotto di Bondone, according to Vasari, "restored art to the better path followed in modern times".

Born in Florence around the year 1267, tradition has it that Giotto was a shepherd boy until discovered by the great traditional artist, Cimabue, for whom the boy drew a perfect circle by freehand. Despite this supposedly rural experience, even in Giotto's work nature is formalised and in the background. It is the humans who occupy the foreground, vibrantly alive.

In Florence, Giotto's main work is in the

a painting is, beyond a doubt, the work of a particular famous artist.

First impressions: Any Italian art gallery arranged on a chronological basis will provide a dramatic shock for the visitor. The first section of the gallery will be endless stiff paintings of the Madonna and Child, or martyred saints. Eventually, the most religious visitor will tire of the monotony, drift on – and encounter a radical change.

Instead of a half-length painting of the Madonna clutching a large, fat, naked Child, or a statuesque representation of a saint liberally covered in gold, the eye encounters real human beings, displaying real emotion –

newly-restored Franciscan church of Santa Croce. His work (and, of course, that of the *bottega* that assisted him) covers the walls of the two chapels to the right of the choir. In a series of vivid vignettes they tell the story of the Finding of the True Cross, and the Life of Saint Francis.

Giotto died in 1337 and nearly a century would pass before his work was taken up by others. But, when the seed finally sprouted, it brought forth astonishing fruit.

Above, Florentine woodcut of banking scene, 1490. **Right**, portrait of Cosimo de'Medici, by Jacopo Pontormo.

THE MEDICI

The Medici were the most outstanding art patrons in European history because they combined a genuine aesthetic sense, which enabled them to detect new trends in culture, with great commercial acumen and ruthless political skill. Although the Medici were associated with Florence for over 400 years, from the mid-14th century, attention is always focused on two of them, father and grandson, who flourished in the 15th century. Cosimo de' Medici, who died in 1464, has been rather overshadowed by his glamorous grandson, Lorenzo Il Magnifico (the Magnificent), but it was Cosimo who brought about the fusion of business sense and aesthetic appreciation which made the Medici family so significant.

The family owed its fortune to banking. When the founder of the bank, Giovanni de' Medici, died in 1429, he left his son Cosimo the immense fortune of 180,000 gold florins. He also bequeathed him an appreciation of the new learning, because Giovanni himself had been a patron of the arts.

In many ways the Medicis might be regarded as the world's first capitalists, and among other grand ventures they financed several European wars. The florin, a monetary unit named after the city, only went out of use in Great Britain when the currency was decimalised in 1971, and it remains the currency in the Netherlands.

Cosimo kept very careful control of the family business while he jockeyed his way into political power. His grandson was frank as to the reasons why the Medici sought power: "It ill fares in Florence with any who possesses wealth without any share of the government." Both as political boss and as banker, Cosimo was the unofficial ruler of Florence by the time he died, at the age of 74, in 1464.

Cosimo poured out vast sums in subsidising the arts, calculated to be about 1,000 times more than they put in the public coffers through tax. In 1444 he built the first Renaissance *palazzo* for his family, typically commissioning the restrained Michelozzo instead of the more flamboyant

Brunelleschi, and it is here that the Renaissance came of age.

In the courtyard of the Medici *palazzo* were placed the statues of *David* and *Judith* that Cosimo's friend and protégé, Donatello (1386–1466) had been commissioned to create. The *David* (now in the Bargello Museum) was the first bronze work "in the round" to be seen in Europe for a thousand years.

Cosimo's son reigned briefly and uneventfully after his father's death, and in 1469 was succeeded by Lorenzo Il Magnifico. The subject of countless legends, his extraordinary character was an astonishing mixture of moods and talents. One day he would be drinking with rowdy companions in rough taverns: the next he would be deep in philosophical arguments with brilliant scholars. He was an ugly man, dark-skinned, heavy featured and with a harsh, high-pitched voice. But he was so charming that people forgot his physical appearance and described him as attractive Unlike his grandfather, he was not good at business and his prodigal support of the arts put the bank under severe financial strain.

The names of the artists whom Lorenzo encouraged are perhaps the greatest of the early Renaissance. Botticelli shared his childhood home; Leonardo da Vinci owed him his appointment to the Milanese court; the 15-year-old Michelangelo was given a home in his *palazzo*. Lorenzo was also a consummate statesman, holding Florence's place in the lethal cross-currents of Italian politics.

The early Medici were passionate republicans but, corrupted by power, the dynasty drifted towards despotism. Two of its members became popes: Leo X (who tangled with Martin Luther) and Clement VII, who resigned during the disastrous Sack of Rome of 1527. The family ruled as Grand Dukes of Tuscany until 1737, when the improvident and feckless Gian Gastone de' Medici died with no male heirs.

The last Medici, Gian Gastone's sister, Princess Anna Maria Luisa, left the entire Medici art collection to the state of Tuscany on her death in 1737, with the single proviso that it should all stay in Florence. This priceless work forms the backbone of the city's three main galleries, the Uffizi, the Pitti and the Bargello.

Florence was pre-eminent but not unique among Tuscan cities in the arts. Pisa was particularly noted for its work in sculpture, both in stone and bronze. In 1330, the Florentines had commissioned the Pisan Andrea Pisano to design and cast the first of the great bronze doors for their beloved baptistry. Almost a century before this, Nicola Pisano and his son Giovanni had created the great pulpits which were to sculpture what Giotto's work was to painting.

In Siena, Duccio di Buoninsegna, working around 1315, brought the stiff Byzantine art so criticised by Vasari to something near humanity. His pupil Simone Martini was deeply influenced by Giovanni Pisano, but also drew on French Gothic for the great *Maestà* in Siena's Palazzo Pubblico (Town Hall). In that same beautiful building, Pietro Lorenzetti created the immense fresco, *Good and Bad Government* between 1337 and 1379, which, in an allegory, provides a vivid illustration of the Tuscan countryside and the city of Siena of the period.

The Florentine dynamo: Brilliant though they were these artists were an end-product, the development of an existing trend. It is an undeniable fact of history that the great break-through took place in Florence, a moment so important that it can be dated to within a few years. Florence retained its dominance in art for barely a life-span because it exported so much of its native talent, ensuring the spread of Renaissance values and, with it, its own relative eclipse. But until the 1470s Florence was a kind of dynamo, providing light and energy for the entire peninsula.

In 1453 the scholar and polymath Leon Battista Alberti returned from many years exile and marvelled at the changes that had been wrought in his city. The dedication in his book *Treatise on Painting* is a tribute both to those who were making the change and the spell which Florence cast over its children. Movingly he describes how he came back to his city "beloved above all for its beauty" and singled out a small band of

artists for especial praise – "you, Filippo (Brunelleschi); our dear friend Donatello and the sculptor Nanni (Ghiberti) and Masaccio," all producing work, he declared, worthy of comparison with any of the masters of antiquity.

The process began about the turn of the century when the Florentine *Signoria*, or government, decided to refurbish the ceremonial centre of Florence – the group of buildings consisting of the cathedral, the campanile, begun by Giotto in 1334 and

finished after his death but to his design in 1359, and the octagonal baptistry.

This little black-and-white building had a special place in Florentine affections and when, in 1401, it was decided to offer a thanksgiving for the city's escape from plague, the baptistry was chosen to benefit. The wealthy Wool Guild announced that they would finance the design and casting of a second set of bronze doors for the baptistry that would be even grander than those of Pisano. The design for it was thrown open to competition.

Out of the many entrants, seven were chosen to live at public expense while each

Left, Brunelleschi's revolutionary cathedral dome. **Right**, Madonna and Child from Masaccio's *San Giovenale Triptych* (1422), Uffizi.

executed a panel on the same subject: the sacrifice of Isaac. Two of the entrants, the 23-year-old Brunelleschi, later credited as the creator of the "Renaissance style" in architecture, and the 20-year-old Lorenzo Ghiberti, produced work which caused considerable difficulty to the judges. Both the panels exist today, one preserved in the Museo dell' Opera del Duomo, the other in the Bargello Museum. Comparing the two, posterity finds it impossible to say which is "better". The *Syndics,* at a loss to choose, came up with a compromise, suggesting that the artists should share the work. Brunelleschi declined and took himself off to Rome, while Ghiberti began work on the doors, completing them 22 years later.

He was offered the commission to produce a second pair: these took him 27 years. During the almost half-century that he spent at work on the project, it is possible to see in his contracts the changing status of the artist. In the first contract he is treated essentially as an artisan, expected to put in a full day's work "like any journeyman". In the later contracts, he is treated far more as a free agent, permitted to undertake other commissions. Ghiberti, too, made explicit the change by boldly including his own self-portrait among the sculptures of the door.

Learning from the ancients: Meanwhile, in Rome with his friend Donatello, Brunelleschi was finding out just how the ancients had built their enormous structures. He was engaged in an entirely new approach to the past, examining originals rather than copies of copies. One of his discoveries – or possibly, inventions – was the *ulivella*. Intrigued and puzzled by the existence of regular-shaped holes in the huge stone blocks of the ancient buildings, he assumed that they had been made to allow the block to be gripped by some device, and designed a kind of grappling iron to fit. Whether or not the Romans had actually used such a device, it was extremely useful – a neat demonstration of the practical benefits to be gained by studying the past.

Brunelleschi returned to Florence at about the time that the *Syndics* of the Wool Guild, who also had the responsibility for the cathedral, were puzzling over the problem of completing it. Arnolfo di Cambio had begun it over a century before, in 1296, and it had been completed, all except for the dome, by 1369. Nobody knew how to bridge this immense gap which, for half a century, had been covered by a temporary roof.

In 1417 a special meeting was called to debate the problem and consider suggestions. One suggestion was to make an immense pile of earth and build over it. Mockingly, somebody suggested putting silver coins in the earth, which would speed its subsequent removal. Brunelleschi then put forward his own solution. He too was mocked for it because it dispensed with the wooden centering, over which architects traditionally built their arches and vaults, supporting their weight until the key stone was in place. But, in desperation, the *Syndics* offered him the job, and Brunelleschi accepted. He solved the problem by building a dome that was pointed in sections, supported by ribs with the lightest possible in-filling between them. He built two shells, an outer skin and an inner one, the first known use of the double shell dome, and one way in which the crushing weight of the dome, the problem which had prevented its construction, was considerably reduced. The work took 16 years, and was completed on 31 August 1436. This was the first Renaissance dome in Italy, the largest unsupported dome in Europe, bigger than the Pantheon in Rome which Brunelleschi had studied, bigger even than the great dome which Michelangelo raised a century later over St Peter's in Rome.

It was Brunelleschi's successor, the scholar Alberti, who first applied the classical orders to domestic architecture and created what we now think of as the Renaissance *palazzo*. Whereas Brunelleschi introduced the columns, pediments and cornices he copied from Roman ruins into his churches, there were no surviving examples of Roman domestic architecture for the 15th-century Florentines to copy. When Rucellai, a wealthy Florentine merchant, asked Alberti to design a palace for him, Alberti took as a model the Colosseum in Rome and applied its tiers of arches to the facade of a three-storey *palazzo*. Though it was the only *palazzo* he built, and though Brunelleschi's design for the Medici palace never got beyond the model stage, these two architects determined a type of building, the results of which can be seen today, from the City of London to New York; a system of proportion and an elegance of line which is still in use.

Brunelleschi's other major breakthrough was his use of perspective. Alberti described its effect to a generation for whom it appeared almost a magical technique. "I describe a rectangle of whatever size I wish which I imagine to be an open window through which I view whatever is to be depicted there." Donatello (1386–1466) eagerly used the technique in his bas-relief of *Salome offering John's head to Herod*. The observer is looking at a banquet where the diners are recoiling in horror from the offering. Beyond the banqueting rooms can be seen a succession of two more rooms, giving a remarkable and, for contemporaries, almost eerie sense of depth.

is also infused with religious awe. Beneath a *trompe l'oeil* classical arch stands the immense figure of God the Father, half supporting a cross on which there is an equally immense figure of Christ; below them are various saints and donors and a *memento mori* of a skeleton in a sarcophagus revealing an ancient warning: "I am what you are, and what I am, you shall be".

The huge figures stand out from the background and appear to loom over the observer. As a young man, Michelangelo used to stand before these calm and solid evocations of spiritual truth, copying them again and again to fix the style in his mind. Eventually, therefore, some essence of this ex-

A new perspective: Like the difference between Giotto's mobile, dramatic figures and their static, formal predecessors, perspective gave a new vista to civilisation. Its most dramatic form was that employed by the young Masaccio in the Church of the Carmine. Born in 1401 and dead by 1428, Masaccio, in his brief life, took up where Giotto left off and added to it the mysterious, potent ingredient of perspective.

His great painting of the *Trinity* in the church of Santa Maria Novella, is an intellectual exercise in the use of perspective that

<u>Above</u>, Ghirlandaio's *Birth of the Baptist*.

perimental period of the Renaissance found its way into the Sistine Chapel, that shrine of the High Renaissance dominated by Michelangelo's work.

The classical arch in Masaccio's painting is a pointer to a curious development which took place during the Quattrocento – the clothing of Biblical figures in a totally anachronistic way, either in classical Roman attire or in contemporary Florentine dress.

The frescoes which Domenico Ghirlandaio (1449–94) painted in the Sasseti Chapel in the church of Santa Trinità supposedly concern the prophecies of Christ's birth and the location should be Augustan Rome. But it is an Augustan Rome which bears a remarkably close resemblance to 15th-century Florence and the people standing round waiting for the awesome news are all citizens of Florence wearing their normal clothes. Lorenzo de' Medici is there, and his mother, the stately Lucrezia Tornabuoni, his children, friends and political colleagues.

In this odd approach to the past, ancient Hebrews, Egyptians or Romans appear in costumes that would not have seemed out of place in contemporary life. Apollo is usually depicted as a young dandy, Jesus Christ in the robes of a 15th-century scholar. In Verrocchio's *Tobias and the Angel* neither would have attracted much attention (except

for the Angel's wings) if they had been seen walking down the Via Tornabuoni.

Andrea del Castagno's *Last Supper* takes this theme to extremes. Supposedly working-class Jews sharing a frugal meal in a humble Eastern inn appear as upper-class Romans debating some interesting scholarly point while waiting for their banquet.

Mythological elements: The painters of the early Renaissance were preoccupied with technique. Their subject matter remained largely unchanged: religion was still the most important concern. But in the second half of the Quattrocento a new, exciting and somewhat disturbing element gradually began to

appear; the mythological and the allegorical.

The supreme practitioner in this field was Sandro Botticelli, who worked with Leonardo da Vinci in Verrocchio's workshop but developed in a totally different direction. His most famous painting, perhaps *the* most famous painting of the early Renaissance and certainly the most mysterious, is *La Primavera*, an allegory of spring, painted in 1478 and hung in the Uffizi.

Nine supernatural creatures are placed in an exquisite natural setting. Behind and above them are the trees of an orange grove. Their feet float just above a flower-spangled meadow. On the left, a young man is aiming at, or pointing at, something. Next to him a group of beautiful, grave-faced women are performing a solemn ritual dance. On the right is the only figure who seems to be aware of the observer: a stunningly beautiful woman with a provocative half-smile. (Who was she? That young woman appears again and again in Botticelli's paintings.) Beside her what appears to be an act of violence adds a discordant note: a bluish-green figure is leaning out of the trees and clutching at a startled girl.

In the background, but dominating the whole, is the most enigmatic figure of all: a pale woman whose expression has been variously described as frowning, smiling, gay, melancholy; whose stance has also been described in conflicting ways as dancing; as that of a consumptive; as pregnant; as offering a blessing. The figure itself has been firmly identified as Venus and just as firmly identified as the Virgin Mary.

What Botticelli was trying to do was to restate classical mythology in Christian terms while remaining true to the original – and true to his own quirky self. He later came into contact with the gloomy, savage friar Savonarola, who turned Florence into a Puritan reformatory in the 1490s. The Florentines eventually turned against Savonarola but the experience deeply influenced Botticelli. Almost overnight, he ceased his joyous mythological paintings, concentrating instead on orthodox religious subjects. Even here, though, one can trace the face of the beautiful young woman whose identity has tantalised generations of art historians.

Above, The city of Florence in the 15th century.
Right, Masaccio's *Trinity* (*circa* 1425).

In the 1840s, a group of high-minded British painters decided that art had gone too far down a mannered, self-conscious, academic path, and had lost its freshness and moral seriousness. They came to the conclusion that it must return to an earlier, more innocent period, and they sought the point when art seemed to have changed for the worse.

The point they landed on was some time during the career of Raphael (1483–1520), who died at the height of his powers. They elected to return to that form of art practised before the time of Raphael and it is therefore as Pre-Raphaelites that Burne-Jones, William Morris and the rest entered art history.

Even to the untutored eye, there is a profound difference between the work produced before and after the 1520s in Tuscany and elsewhere, most noticeably in Florence. Partly this was the result of an immense political crisis. Italy had become a battleground invaded again and again by warring foreigners. In 1527, a savage army composed partly of mercenaries, sacked Rome and held the Pope to ransom. Italy was never to recover from that experience which was the curtain-raiser for a period of foreign domination which would not end until the 1800s.

The glory goes elsewhere: Shortly after the Sack of Rome, the Medici Pope Clement VII clamped down on his native city of Florence, ending republicanism and preparing the way for the first dukedom. Meanwhile, in the world of art, the glory was departing from Florence as the impetus of the Renaissance shifted to Rome and Venice. From the middle of the 16th century, Florentine artists tended to be court artists, dancing attendance on the Medici dukes. Among them was Giorgio Vasari.

Until recently, Vasari's work as an artist was dismissed almost as contemptuously as his work as art historian was received enthusiastically. However, posterity owes him a debt of thanks, both as architect and as painter. Not only did he build the Uffizi for Duke Cosimo I, but in his paintings in the great

Salone dei Cinquecento, the parliamentary chamber of the Palazzo Vecchio, he created outstanding contemporary representations of the city and its surrounding countryside. Equally fine is his frescoed interior of Brunelleschi's dome, revealed in 1994 after a five-year restoration programme

The genius of Leonardo: The glory might be departing from Florence, but the sunset was stupendous. It could scarcely be otherwise with two such giants as Michelangelo and Leonardo da Vinci still working in the city.

Leonardo, born in 1452, trained in the *bottega* of Verrocchio, thus carrying the medieval systems on into the new era. One of Vasari's anecdotes claims that Verrocchio, on seeing his young apprentice's work, laid down his brush and never painted again. Unlikely though the incident is, the anecdote shows that Leonardo was recognised as being almost a freakish genius in his own lifetime.

An illustration of his restless, endlessly enquiring mind is shown by an incident on 28 December 1478 when, passing the Bargello, he noticed a body hanging from a window – one of the Pazzi conspirators. Taking out the notebook he always carried,

Preceding pages: cycle of olive oil production, 16th century. **Left,** Florence in the 15th century. **Right,** Michelangelo's *The Holy Family*.

he sketched the corpse, then meticulously noted in his mirror-writing: "Small cap tan coloured: doublet of black satin, black-lined jerkin, blue coat lined with black and white stripes of velvet. Bernardo di Bandino Baroncelli. Black hose." He gave no indication whatsoever of any emotion, whether pity or satisfaction.

Leonardo left Florence for Milan at the age of 30, shortly after that incident. He came back again in 1502 when he was commissioned by the *Signoria* to create the great mural, the *Battle of Anghiari* in the Council Chamber, returned to Milan in 1506 then finally crossed the Alps and became court painter to François I of France. His contribution to the history of ideas is incalculable but his physical contribution to Tuscan art history is relatively small. Typically, both the *Battle of Anghiari* and the *Adoration of the Kings* in the Uffizi are unfinished. And his two most famous paintings, the *Mona Lisa* (a portrait of a virtuous but otherwise undistinguished Florentine housewife) and the *Virgin of the Rocks*, are in Paris and London respectively.

Michelangelo Buonarroti is very different. His greatest creation, too, is outside Florence – the Sistine Chapel frescoes – but he did leave an enduring imprint upon his home city, in the form of the walls that gird it and the sculptures that grace it.

The next generation: Michelangelo was nearly a generation younger than Leonardo, born in 1475 when the Renaissance was approaching its apogée. His father was a poor but proud country gentleman who thoroughly disapproved of the idea of his son becoming an artisan or artist; in his mind there was no clear distinction. Michelangelo, too, was apt to be a little touchy on the subject. Although he served his apprenticeship in a *bottega*, that of Ghirlandaio, he later rejected the idea that he touted for trade, "I was never a painter or a sculptor like those who set up shop for the purpose."

One of Vasari's anecdotes describes how the young Michelangelo, then around 13 years old, made a drawing of the various tools in the workshop. His master, Ghirlandaio, was so impressed that, very generously, he drew Lorenzo de' Medici's

attention to the talented boy. As a result Michelangelo entered the princely Medici household, eating at the same table and studying with the same scholars as Lorenzo's own children.

During one of the bitter quarrels which punctuated the lives of Florentine artists, a bigger youth called Torrigiani (who, later, was to design the superb funerary monument of Henry VII in London's Westminister Abbey) broke his nose with a mallet. Michelangelo bore that disfigurement for the rest of his life.

He was just 18 when Lorenzo de' Medici died in 1492. Florence was plunged into chaos because Lorenzo's son, Piero, was

extravagant and unpopular and, after two years, the Florentines chased him out of the city. Michelangelo's relationship with the Medici made Florence a dangerous place and he took the road to Rome.

There he undertook the work by which he is best remembered. He also worked for the next 40 years on a task he never completed. This was the great tomb for his patron and taskmaster, Pope Julius II. The unfinished statues for this tomb, the famous *Slaves*, are now in Florence's Accademia gallery. In them it is possible to see, five centuries later, the sculptor's technique.

As in a *bottega*, the roughing out of the

Left, Renaissance zenith: Michelangelo's *David*.
Above, *Saint Ambrose* by Ghirlandaio.

figures was done by apprentices, the master himself giving the finishing touches. It is profoundly moving to see in some of them the shallow depressions surrounding the figure, made by the rounded head of a chisel which seems to be "freeing" the figure, as though it already existed and was simply encased in the stone.

Florence has many statues by Michelangelo; even though they are often unfinished, they always reveal the chisel strokes of a master. They include the famous *David*, and the statues of *Dawn, Evening, Day* and *Night* in the Medici chapel.

Universal man: In the Casa Buonarroti in Via Ghibellina are displayed some of the

sculptor's working drawings as well as a few of his earliest works. It was as a sculptor that Michelangelo Buonarotti saw himself, rather touchingly signing his letters "*Michelangelo scultore*". But he, too, is entitled to the accolade of "universal man" accorded to such as Leonardo. Although he is remembered as a painter and sculptor, he was also an engineer of very considerable skill and a poet of sensitivity and insight.

Michelangelo was just 25 when Benvenuto Cellini was born in 1500. Cellini admired his great compatriot so much that, when Torrigiani invited him to go to England, he turned down the offer, claiming he could not asso-

ciate with a man who had so disfigured hero. Or so he wrote in his remarkable au biography, and it is probably true enough f despite his many and manifest fau Benvenuto Cellini had a warm and gener nature.

Like so many of the artists of his time, was skilled in a number of crafts – he v improbably enough, a gunner. He playe role in the tragic Sack of Rome which, effect, brought the Renaissance to an e Acting as gunner in defence of the Vatic he assured his readers that the Pope promi him absolution "for all the murders tha should commit".

In Florence, his most famous work is t beautiful but curiously heartless statue *Perseus slaying the Gorgon*. The statue u to grace the Loggia dei Lanzi on Piazza de Signoria but, once it has been restored, it v be protected in a museum. But it is indicat both of Cellini and of the phase into wh the art of the Renaissance was moving, t his best known work would be the elabor golden salt-cellar which he made for Franç I of France.

The road to Rome: Raphael was a gen handsome young man who, remarkab seemed to have no enemies (thou Michelangelo made the occasional rem about him). He was not a Tuscan; he v born in Umbria in 1483 and received basic training in the workshop of Perugi working on frescoes in Perugia. In 15 however, at the impressionable age of 17, came to Florence where he drank at source, absorbing the works of Leonardo Vinci and Michelangelo.

He left Florence in 1508, attracted to Ro by the fiery Pope Julius II, who was plann a tremendous series of architectural emb lishments to the Vatican. There the you Raphael easily proved himself. He pain the series of rooms known as the Stanze de Segnatura and, under the Medici Pope I X, was placed in charge of archaeologi excavations in Rome itself.

Thus, the last true artist of the Renaissa introduced into the mother city of Eur that passionate search for the past which triggered off the Renaissance in Flore nearly two centuries earlier.

Dante placed the action of his great epic *The Divine Comedy* at Easter, 1300. Machiavelli died in 1527, just before the Florentine Republic came to an end. These two dates provide useful boundaries for a brief survey of the literature of the Renaissance. In a crowded field, three towering figures provide some orientation. Dante, Petrarch and Machiavelli follow each other chronologically and, because each caused, as well as recorded, great changes, it is possible to plot the course of the Renaissance through them.

Dante made the bold decision to write his epic in Italian, the language of the marketplace and the tavern, instead of the dead language, Latin. The Latin works upon which Petrarch prided himself have long been forgotten, and it is his lively letters, so modern in their description of everyday life and people, which are prized today. And poor Machiavelli – the dogged, disappointed, courageous Florentine bureaucrat whose name was to enter most European languages as a synonym for all that was deceitful and devious, as though he were responsible for what he described, laid down the blueprint for modern politics.

Cast into exile: Born in 1265, Dante was an exact contemporary of Giotto, whose work he admired for its originality. But where Giotto sensibly kept out of politics, Dante involved himself wholeheartedly and was exiled for his pains during one of Florence's perennial upheavals. He never returned to Florence, eventually dying in Ravenna in 1321. Today, Florence annually sends a gift of oil to light the lamps on his tomb on the anniversary of his death.

The Divine Comedy, dealing with the great mysteries of religion, had a profound effect on Italian thought. Everybody today knows at least one line, in translation, from the inscription over the gate to Hell:

Per me ci va nella città dolente
Per me ci va nell' eterno dolore
Per me ci va fra la perduta gente
Lasciate ogni speranza voi ch'entrate

Preceding pages: Giorgio Vasari's *Assault on Pisa*. Left, Dante painted by Andrea del Castagno. Right, Boccaccio by Andrea del Castagno.

(Through me is the way into the city of sorrow
Through me is the way to eternal sadness
Through me is the way among the lost people
Abandon all hope you who enter)

Today historians ransack the *Comedy* to identify historical figures (most of them in Hell where Dante tended to consign his enemies). It is a vivid story with a meticulous chronology and philosophers and theologians still debate its significance.

Francesco Petrarch, though a Florentine, was born in Arezzo, where his parents had been exiled during the same feuds that caused Dante's expulsion. He actually met Dante, and was a lifelong disciple, but his own interests lay in the classical past. Petrarch was one of the first to hunt down and discover the lost classical literature without which the Renaissance – the "re-birth" – could not even have begun. He travelled widely, had an enormous circle of friends and kept in regular contact with them through his letters.

It was as much through these letters as through any formal work that the "new learning" was disseminated. But Petrarch also shared, with his English contemporary Chaucer, the dawning awareness that the humble and the humdrum were just as legitimate literary subjects as the noble and the extraordinary. In poetry, he devised the sonnet form which took his name – Petrarchan – and which was to have a great influence on the poets of Elizabethan England.

Niccolò Machiavelli was born in 1469, nearly a century after Petrarch's death. Viewed from almost any angle, his life looks like a failure. As a career diplomat, rising to be Secretary of the Republic, he never wielded real authority. As a convinced republican, he was obliged to spend his later years currying

favour with the now openly despotic Medici.

His personal appearance and habits were totally at variance with the personality that comes across in his political writings. There he is ice-cold, logical, in total command. In real life he was shabby, lecherous and adulterous. Something of that dual character is evident in his portraits: his expression is almost hangdog, furtive, yet with an inner, self-mocking integrity.

He was, despite all appearances, an idealist. His notorious book *The Prince* was only one of a large output, which includes a delightful comedy, *Mandragola*, still staged today. Altogether, there are few writers who

have been so misjudged as this republican who wrote the classic textbook on the practice of tyranny.

Town chroniclers: One great class of Italian literature of which there is virtually no equivalent in other countries is that of the urban chronicles. Almost every city had some devoted citizen carefully recording history as it happened, some achieving the status of true literature. In Florence the outstanding chroniclers were the Villani brothers, writing in the first half of the 14th century. In Siena, at about the same time, Donato di Neri and his son were compiling the *Cronaca Senese* while in Pisa Giovanni Sarcambi not only made a lively literary record but also illustrated it with exquisite little line drawings that bring the times to life.

Although innovations in literature were less spectacular than in art and architecture, there are a number of outstanding "firsts". Francesco Guicciardini wrote the first true History of Italy and Giovanni Boccaccio (1313–75) produced Europe's first novel. *The Decameron* is a bawdy, jolly collection of tales told by 10 young aristocrats who retreat from the plague which struck Florence in 1458. Staying in a country house they while away the time telling erotic stories and poems, and poking fun at the wily ways of the clergy

The Decameron opens with a detailed and grisly description of the plague which has become a classic in its own right; many of the stories themselves are so vulgar that they are often toned down considerably in translation. All demonstrate Boccaccio's well-honed skills as a story-teller.

Finally there were the truly Renaissance figures who expressed themselves in all the arts, including literature. There is Michelangelo's poetry, and Benvenuto Cellini's swash-buckling *Autobiography*. Cellini, a brilliant sculptor, part-time soldier and, by his own account, murderer, was also a superb writer. He wrote a heart-stopping account of the problem of casting the exquisite *Perseus*, a bronze sculpture destined for the Loggia dei Lanzi. Cellini records that, at a crucial moment, he ran out of metal and had to throw in the family pewter in order to complete the statue.

"A man who has not been to Italy is always conscious of inferiority," said Dr Johnson. But many English writers had already beaten Dr Johnson to Florence. In 1737, Sir Horace Mann, Minister to the Grand Ducal Court, announced: "If I could afford it, I really would take a villa near Florence but I am afraid of it becoming a cheesecake house for all the English."

A century later, *Inglese* was a generic term for all foreigners. A hotel porter might say: "Some *Inglesi* have arrived but I don't yet know whether they are Russian or German." Given the hordes of foreign writers in Tuscany, the manager might have welcomed Dickens, Dostoyevsky or Heine.

The poet Shelley pronounced Tuscany a "paradise of exiles" tempted by art, adventure and escape from persecution. But the exiles' motives were as varied as their prose styles. Henry James preferred real Tuscans to "one's detested fellow-pilgrims", while Leigh Hunt expressed the accepted Romantic view. "Florence has more convenience for us, more books, more fine art, more illustrious memories, and a great concourse of Englishmen." A healthy climate, picturesque peasants, cheap villas and an abundance of servants decided the issue.

Gloomy view: In the 18th century, travellers tended to be leisured aristocrats or eccentric dilettantes. Tobias Smollett, the misanthropic English writer, found nothing to admire in Tuscany. Reflecting the prejudices of his class, he failed to appreciate the entrepreneurial nature of the Tuscan aristocracy, finding it undignified for "a noble to sell a pound of figs or to take money for a glass of sour wine".

He abhorred the Tuscan practice of *cicisbei* (18th-century "toy boys") and generally considered the Tuscans immoral and treacherous. Little of Tuscany finds its way into his picaresque novels, while his *Travels Through France And Italy* are tales of unmitigated gloom. The irascible Smollett died unrepentant, thanks to a surfeit of cold baths, goat's milk and opiates.

The Romantic poets brought a much-needed enthusiasm to Tuscany. But even the Romantics thought of material comforts: the exiled Lord Byron travelled "lightly" with seven servants, five carriages and additional furniture carts. Once in Florence, the patrician republican identified with Dante's exile, later alluded to in *Childe Harold's Pilgrimage*. Byron threw himself into Renaissance art and was "dazzled, drunk with Beauty" in Santa Croce.

With equal passion, he condemned the

Medici Chapels as "fine frippery in great slabs of various expensive stones, to commemorate fifty nobles and forgotten carcasses". His novelettish affair with Contessa Teresa Guiccoli gave him an exceptional entrée into Tuscan provincial society and enabled him to boast that he had not "Florenced and Romed and Galleried and Conversationed" but had "been amongst all classes, from the *conte* to the *contadino*".

His friend Shelley devoured Pisan landscapes and Livornese seascapes but had little interest in the natives. As his wife Mary said after his death, "We lived in utter solitude". *Ode To The West Wind* was inspired by the floating leaves and autumnal chill in Florence's Cascine Park:

Drive my dead thoughts over the universe
Like withered leaves to question a new birth.

The poem *To A Skylark* was composed after a dramatic storm near the his house in Livorno. In Bagni di Lucca, Shelley washed away his remaining northern European inhibitions. "My custom is to undress and sit on the rocks, read Herodotus until the perspiration has subsided, and then to leap from the edge of the rock into the fountain." When Shelley drowned near La Spezia, Byron and Leigh Hunt cremated him on the beach with offerings of wine, oil and frankincense.

Tuscany soon became a pilgrimage for the later Romantic poets such as Tennyson and Wordsworth. "Emotion recollected in tranquillity" was the keynote: neither poet particularly enjoyed Tuscany at the time, yet both later idealised their experiences, as in Tennyson's execrable verse:

O love, what hours were thine and mine,
In lands of palm and southern pine.

The Stendhal Syndrome: Although officially a diplomat in Florence, Stendhal spent most of his time absorbing Renaissance frescoes and planning his novel, *Le Rouge et le Noir*. As with Byron, the Santa Croce Effect sent Stendhal reeling: once outside, "I walked in constant fear of falling to the ground." This aesthetic sickness, now known as the Stendhal Syndrome, struck the future art critic John Ruskin. In Giotto's campanile, the "panorama of snow and marble" filled him with "wild, sickening yearning – the desire of the moth for the star".

Unfortunately, the literary effect of sublime beauty often brought this human moth's prose to the ground with a thud. As he matured, Ruskin's critical judgement matched his passion until he became, in Harold Acton's words, "a bishop of aesthetic taste". Towards the end of his life, Ruskin's taste became more melancholic and quirky. He declared that "the dead are Italy's real inhabitants" in a vain bid to keep the modern world away from his Tuscan museum.

Henry James felt that Ruskin's discordant

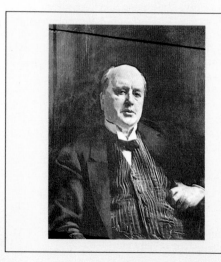

Top: Lord Byron, Robert Browning, Elizabeth Barrett Browning. **Middle:** Samuel Johnson, Percy Bysshe Shelley, Mary Wollstonecraft Shelley. **Bottom:** Henry James by John Singer Sargent, D.H. Lawrence, Virginia Woolf.

and dictatorial views prevented a visitor from appreciating the joy of Tuscan art in a changing Florence. "*Be artistic yourselves!* is the very natural reply the young Italy has at hand for English critics and censors." James was one of the few foreign writers able to see through Tuscany's literary and artistic veil. His *Portrait of Places* gives an opinionated but sensitive portrait of the region in the 1870s. "Beautiful works of art *[are]* the mere stock in trade of an impecunious but thrifty people."

Thin disguises: If Tuscany only appears indirectly in his novels, it is because James succeeded in transforming his experiences into real literature; he did not want to be

night on its feet, and there's a terrible deal of singing".

The most romantic mid-Victorian couple were undoubtedly the poets Elizabeth Barrett Browning and Robert Browning. Robert brought his wife to their Florentine *palazzo* because of her poor health. There he cunningly used local Chianti to wean Elizabeth off her long addiction to laudanum. According to Virginia Woolf, Elizabeth "tossed off a tumbler and slept the sounder".

Elizabeth attributed her improved health to the spiritual powers of the Tuscan climate rather than the wine and her husband's lively erudition was stirred by Tuscan architecture, Mannerist painting and botany.

identified with the dilettante scribblers of "Little Tuscany". In *The Aspern Papers*, James included the Shelley Circle – in disguise, of course.

George Eliot also subtly transformed her Tuscan experience. Although her novel *Romola*, set in Renaissance Florence, is an unsuccessful pastiche, *Middlemarch* has a key Tuscan episode in which the puritanical "English" character battles with the life-giving "Italian" character.

Dostoyevsky, exiled in a delightful spot beside the Pitti Palace, found little Tuscan inspiration for *The Idiot*. He complained that "the population of Florence spends the whole

Elizabeth tolerated her husband's mild liberalism, but she herself was a fervent believer in Italian Unification. In essence, Browning loved the Florence of the past and Elizabeth loved the Florence of the future. Apart from their relationship, work and the house, neither lived much in the present nor had a burning desire to meet the natives. Both were inspired by a mythologised Florence, "When Galileo stood at night to take the vision of the stars." Their 15th-century *palazzo*, redecorated in Victorian style, is a literary museum and a haunt of writers.

This century brought E.M. Forster, with his ironic analysis of the resident English community at play. Forster's *Room With A View* is justly famous for its portrayal of the heroine's encounter with alien culture and passions. Lost in Santa Croce without a *Baedeker*, Lucy panics and mistakes a Machiavelli monument for a saint. But gradually "the pernicious charm of Italy worked on her, and, instead of acquiring information, she began to be happy".

In her *Diaries*, Virginia Woolf looked at the Tuscan people with a cool appraising eye: "They seem stunted, dried up; like the grasshopper and with the manners of impoverished gentle people; sad, wise, tolerant, humorous." Along with many other writers on Tuscany, she sees her own image re-

Tuscan novel, he wrote: "I reckon here men for a moment were themselves, as a plant in flower is for the moment completely itself. Then it goes off. As Florence has gone off."

War story: World War II prevented further literary flowering, but in *War In Val D'Orcia*, Iris Origo, an Anglo-Florentine, painted a dramatic picture of the Tuscan battlefield. As a young woman, Origo was part of Lawrence's artistic circle but her instinctive understanding of the Tuscans set her apart.

Soon after the war, the Welsh poet Dylan Thomas came for the first time and was entranced: "The pine hills are endless, the cypresses at the hilltop tell one all about the length of death, the woods are deep as love

flected in the landscape, "infinite emptiness, loneliness, silence..."

D.H. Lawrence, living in his "grave old Tuscan villa" in Scandicci, thought he was communing with the original Etruscans rather than with his farmer neighbours. "The curious, fine-nosed Tuscan face, with the half-sardonic, amber cold eyes. Their curious individuality with their clothes worn so easy and so reckless." His philosophy dominated the landscape. In *Aaron's Rod*, his most

and full of goats." He led a hedonistic life, vegetating in the sun and devouring asparagus, strawberries and wine at only 20 lire a glass which induced constant alcoholic stupor; "drinking chianti in our marble shanty, sick of *vini* and *contadini* and *bambini*".

Tuscany continues to befuddle the minds of visiting writers. While inspiring the writer's life, the region often has a disturbing or numbing effect on literary output. The portrayal of Tuscany in contemporary foreign novels too often lacks credibility. Although Tuscans are no longer portrayed as peasants or forces of nature, there is still "no foundation in natives" in literary Chiantishire.

Left, Adolfo Tommasi's *Villa di Belvedere a Crespina*. **Above**, Torre del Largo Puccini: "emotion recollected in tranquillity".

Since the glories of Rome and the Renaissance, Italy has written little history. The head of Italy's Bureau of Statistics likens modern Italian history to a muddle, "a happy ant-heap where everyone is running about and no one is in control". The alternative is the "strong man" view of recent history, as expressed in the Florentine saying, "whose bread and cheese I eat, to his tune I dance". But, while Rome danced to martial music, Tuscany sometimes starved or burned.

Tuscany has been buffeted rather than enriched by its recent past. Well-kept war memorials in shabby towns attest to the loss of two generations, one abroad and one at home. Look at Asciano, a village dwarfed by its Carabinieri stronghold, built by Mussolini and still used to maintain order. Visit Montisi, where for the price of a drink, locals will describe the German bombing of the village tower, a story complete with sound effects, gestures and genuine sorrow. Ask Florentines why the medieval houses on the south side of the Arno are lost forever.

Bold flourish: The welding of Tuscans into Italians started promisingly enough but the end-result is still only to be seen abroad or at international football matches. Piazza della Repubblica, built in 1865 to celebrate Florence's brief spell as Italian capital, remains a bold flourish of nationhood. But when the capital was transferred to Rome, Tuscan allegiance remained in Tuscany.

Unification, under the leadership of Cavour, a French-speaking Piedmontese, was seen as a foreign threat to the *de facto* sovereignty of Florence and the smaller city states. Defenders of the Risorgimento, the Movement for Italian Unification, appealed to nascent patriotism. Critics of unification cited Dante's pleas to Tuscan liberty before both sides settled down to start subverting the power of the new rulers.

Unification represented a missed chance for Italy. By failing to help shape a national identity, Tuscans also fell victim to the clearer vision of a "strong man". Even before World

War I, Mussolini was making inflammatory speeches while a weak parliament practised the art of "timely resignation", a ploy used ever since to stage-manage a new coalition.

Although the pre-war Tuscan economy thrived under weak government, it was no match for growing social pressures and a deepening gulf between society and state. With few real policies, one of the last liberal governments blundered into World War I. Italy's unpopular late entry cost Tuscan lives and support. The pyrrhic victory was exacer-

bated by a power vacuum, economic problems and a revolutionary working class. Benito Mussolini, from neighbouring Emilia, wasted no opportunity in proclaiming, "Governing Italy is not only impossible, it is useless", before proceeding to govern it impossibly but fairly usefully for 20 years.

By 1922, the corporate state was literally under construction. The economic benefits lasted until 1929 but the aesthetic effects linger on in functionally "improved" cities all over Tuscany. Florence Station, from which trains presumably ran on time, was the first Functionalist station in Italy. At the outbreak of World War II, most Tuscans

Preceding pages: leafy country Roman road. **Left,** *Fare bella figura*: young bloods pose in front of Arezzo cathedral. **Right,** Siena *Palio*.

were cautiously neutral. Mussolini, despite having signed the Pact of Steel with Germany, only entered the war in 1940, after the fall of France. By 1943 the north was under German control but the Allies were progressing northwards from Sicily. Allied bombing, German entrenchment and an emerging Tuscan Resistance transformed Tuscany into a battleground.

Anti-fascist cells had been secretly set up by the communists and Catholics in key towns under German and neo-Fascist control. Florence was split: while it was the intellectual centre of the Resistance it also harboured strong fascist sympathisers. Even after the city was captured by the Allies, individual fascists held out, firing from the rooftops. Surprising loyalties emerged: while the director of the British Institute was a known fascist sympathiser, the German consul risked his life to protect Florentines who had been denounced. After the liberation he was granted the freedom of the city.

Florence was liberated in August 1943 but Mussolini and the German forces survived the winter behind the so-called "Gothic Line" in the Apennines. Apart from Florence, the partisans were very active in the Monte Amiata area; also in the Val d'Orcia where Iris Origo, an Englishwoman married to an Italian *marchese*, sheltered many refugees and prisoners of war in her villa, La Foce.

Writing about it at the time, she said, "In the last few days I have seen Radicofani and Cortignano destroyed, the countryside and farms studded with shell holes, girls raped, and human beings and cattle killed. Otherwise the events of the last week have had little effect upon either side; it is the civilians who have suffered."

Nor were the Allies blameless. The modernity of Grosseto, Livorno and Pisa owes much to Allied bombing in 1943. The British War Office reports naturally exonerated the Allies: "No damage of any significance is attributable to Allied action [in Florence]." The Allies issued their troops with booklets listing buildings to be protected but baulked at Florence: "The whole city of Florence must rank as a work of art of the first importance." According to one report: "The great monuments, nearly all of which lie north of the river, escaped practically undamaged because, though the enemy held the northern bank against an advance, our troops deliberately refrained from firing upon them."

Feats of Allied bravery included the penetration of enemy lines via the Pitti Palace-Uffizi passageway, a secret route used by the Medici in similar crises. Florence nevertheless lost bridges, streets, libraries, churches, *palazzi*, paintings, and Tuscan lives. But in contrast to the "mutilated victory" of 1919, Italy lost the war but won the peace. Massimo Salvadore, a supporter of the partisans in Florence, saw the war as character building: "Without it [we] would surely have sunk into a morass of low politics and intrigues." That was still to come.

The political scene: Tuscans often compare their political system to the Leaning Tower

of Pisa, an object of curiosity precisely because it defies appearances and does not fall down. The belltower is also an apt symbol of *Campanilismo*, attachment to one's region.

True Tuscans are provincial, conservative and independent. Since World War II, they have tended to vote for right-wing governments nationally but for left-wing councils locally. Until recently, this meant Christian Democracy at national level and communism at regional level. On the surface, this appeared a rather curious recipe for success.

Given the level of national opposition to communists in government, the Communist Party evolved an aggressively pro-regional-ist stance. The reward was the "red belt" across central Italy, run by left-wing coalitions since the first regional elections in 1970. Red Tuscany formed the central strand between Emilia Romagna's model economy and rural Umbria. Despite the transformations in the "new Italy", the "red" regions survive under broad left labels as some of the most efficient of regional governments.

Not that a Tuscan communist ever fitted an easy stereotype. She could wear Ferragamo, own a hotel and a BMW but go to work on a *motorino*. Although Catholic and conservative, she voted socialist in national elections and was fearful of seeing the communists in government. Her cousin ran his own com-

the talk was of summer villas, the accountant's bill and wine.

The Tuscan Left believes in a broad but increasingly secular church. Civic culture, regional pride and fierce individualism form the real faith. The power of the Left is as much a reflection of regional hostility to Roman centralisation as an espousal of social-democratic principles. Even in "red belt" Tuscany, the region's most popular newspaper is the right-wing but regional *La Nazione*, not the left-wing but national *La Repubblica*. How could a Roman product compete with a Florentine/Sienese masterpiece?

Crisis? What crisis?: By the early 1990s, over 50 post-war governments had come and

pany and had a Filipino maid but socialised with his workers. While failing to declare all his profits, he was scrupulous about implementing guidelines on reduced working hours. He attached more value to "personal culture" than to politics. Apart from family and local roots, the couple shared nothing except political disaffection.

Communist *Festa dell'Unità* celebrations epitomised a Tuscan political conscience on holiday. As elegantly dressed locals ate *bistecca alla fiorentina* and downed Galestro,

Left, convent schoolgirls of a former age. **Above**, 19th-century Florence.

gone and "ungovernability" was again a common cry. To many, the crisis lay not in Italy's flawed institutions but in its flawed administrations and moral torpor. Senior party leaders tended to die in office; governments suffered from predictability, not instability; from opportunism, not lack of opportunity. The Christian Democrat party (DC) saw itself as the natural party of government and dominated coalition governments until its downfall, amidst allegations of corruption. Most of its traditional coalition partners, including the Socialists (PSI), were also charged with institutionalised corruption.

Partitocrazia, the party system, supplanted

democracy. The long arm of the party stretched from government to public corporations, industry, banking, the judiciary and the media. The reality of party power was genuinely subversive: the fostering of an "old boy network" based on *clientelismo*, political patronage. However, the public were slow to realise that a system they tacitly condoned concealed far greater evils. *Tangentopoli*, or "Bribesville", was the name given to the political corruption scandals that erupted in the early 1990s, followed by a resurgence in terrorism.

Florence literally exploded in May 1993, after a terrorist bomb attack beside the Uffizi killed 5 people and damaged priceless paint-

tation to a largely first-past-the-post system, modelled on British lines. This change was so momentous that Italians refer to it as the Second Republic.

These watershed elections were won by an alliance spearheaded by the media magnate Silvio Berlusconi. The right-wing government was elected on an anti-corruption ticket, with promises of privatisation, business competence, new jobs, new faces and an end to the old regime. While some Tuscans voted for various left-wing groupings, including the reformed communists, many were won over by the glossy image and optimism projected by Forza Italia, Berlusconi's party.

Yet any government should take heed of

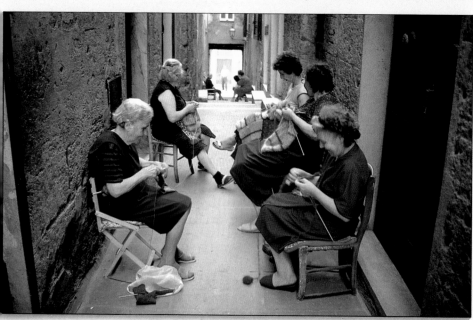

ings. The atrocity was seen as a challenge to the state, and blamed on collusion between the Sicilian Mafia, the secret services and the political old guard. Florentines responded in anger and generosity, with the Uffizi staff working without pay to reopen the gallery. With the exception of the Vasari Corridor, the rest of the building and most of the paintings were restored by 1995.

Mani Puliti, the "Clean Hands" campaign, ushered in *glasnost* and the attempted reform of a discredited political system. As a result, a third of *deputati* (MPs) were investigated for corruption. The 1994 general elections saw the switch from proportional represen-

Tuscan scepticism. Historically, Tuscans see leaders, even faceless ones, as a threat to liberty. When Lorenzo de' Medici was on his deathbed, Savonarola reputedly said, "Lastly you must restore liberty to the people of Florence" – whereupon Lorenzo looked scornful and died soon after.

Tuscans still balance their love of liberty against fears of political instability. The continuing preference for left-wing councils can now be seen as a sign of conservatism rather than radicalism. In Tuscany, the former communists (now the PDS) may have changed their name but not their spots. This hedging of bets is in keeping with the Tuscans' desire for regional independence. Moreover, if threatened by a central government that is out of touch with local concerns, Tuscans will instantly retreat into regionalism. In the end, provincialism rides roughshod over national politics.

Economic realities: The quality of life in historic town centres is excellent and Tuscans are not prepared to jeopardise it for more heavy industry. Topography also helps preserve the past: hill-top towns cannot expand so development is restricted to the plains or, in Florence's case, to new suburbs or satellite cities, such as Novoli and Firenze Nova. The grand urban plan, already underway, is for commerce and public offices to move out

when the Italian economy outstripped its British and French rivals. Tuscany's contribution was to slip smoothly from a rural to an industrialised society.

Since then, the recession has taken its toll, reinforced by public spending cuts and the loss of public confidence. In the early 1990s most public sector work came to a halt: the new moral climate meant that few civil servants dared sign contracts in case they were accused of taking bribes. Recently, despite unemployment, Tuscany appears to have recovered faster than many regions in Italy.

Luckily, Tuscany's traditional industries show no signs of going out of fashion. Prato is living proof that the cloth trade was not just

to these north-western suburbs, leaving the city centre free for culture.

In recent times, the Italian economy has moved slowly but finished fast. Tuscany followed this pattern with a late Industrial Revolution in the 1880s and a slow post-war recovery in the "long boom" of 1958–63. High labour costs in the 1960s and energy costs in the 1970s slowed down progress. Strikes, housing crises and outbreaks of terrorism did the rest. But in 1987 came the much-publicised *Sorpasso*, or "overtaking",

a 12th-century fad. Although its textile industry was fully mechanised in 1850, Prato feels like a closed shop run by rich Ghibelline merchants. It has become a highly skilled industry while remaining a collection of family businesses. After Florence and Livorno, Prato is the largest city in Tuscany and, as a sign of its prominence, was elevated to provincial status in 1993, a final escape from the Florentine Guelf yoke.

Nor did the great Renaissance families all die out. Strozzi is still an important name in Florentine banking and business circles, as are Frescobaldi and Antinori in the wine and food trade. Florentine design genius emerges

Left, Pitigliano street showing the narrowness and depth of urban life. **Above**, *carabinieri* at play.

in the styling of Ferragamo, Gucci and Pucci.

Many popular medieval industries are still minor classics: in Siena, Nannini's spicy *panforte* comes complete with its 15th-century recipe. In Carrara, the marble cutters are proud to tell you that Michelangelo selected marble from quarries that now produce a nice line in bathroom suites. The traditional craft industries are thriving: alabaster chess sets from Volterra; gold jewellery from Arezzo; glassware from Empoli. Tuscany also exports terracotta vases, della Robbia style ceramics, antiques and leather goods. Sales of Tuscan textiles, clothes and leather fell after Italy left the ERM in 1992 but subsequently became more buoyant.

Such small and medium-sized firms are in the dynamic private sector of the Tuscan economy. The managerial class consists of *padroncini*, "little bosses", drawn from the independent and affluent *borghesia*, strong in manufacture, the crafts, the retail trade and tourism. Tuscans have a civilised approach to tourism because they take leisure seriously. Given the vast "black economy", such *padroncini* are probably running a hotel by day and a restaurant by night.

By contrast, the public sector has a high profile but low prestige. Until recently, IRI, the Institute for Industrial Recovery and ENI, the state energy company, ran the region without either energy or industry, from shipbuilding at Livorno to iron and steel works at Piombino, the last of the Etruscan iron settlements that lined the coast for 3,000 years. However, privatisation programmes have been drawn up and these state umbrella companies are due to be privatised by the end of the 1990s, including banking, telecommunications, service and investment sectors.

It is easy to see Tuscan agriculture as a victim rather than a beneficiary of economic growth: a mass exodus from the land occurred between 1951 and 1971. Although large-scale wheat and cattle farming have drawn many farmers back to the fertile Val d'Arno and Val di Chiana, traditional Tuscan farming is labour-intensive and relatively unmechanised.

But four decades of industrial development have not erased three millennia of rural settlement. The Romans perfected the mix of grain and tree crops and this *coltura promiscua* is still characteristic of Tuscan farmscapes. The olive groves at Lucca date

back to Roman times and Elban wine was linked to Etruscan bacchic rites. Contrary to popular belief, most wine-growing is small-scale, with vineyards set on terraced slopes unsuitable for other crops. Although Chianti is the wine best known abroad, it is less valued by Tuscans than sweet Vin Santo, rich Brunello, amber Vernaccia or the sandalwood Vino Nobile di Montepulciano.

For this continuity of land use, Tuscans have to thank their medieval system of *mezzadria* or sharecropping, which brought security of tenure to the peasants. Although *mezzadria* contracts were officially banned in 1978, the old patron-client relationship continues to exert a significant pull. Mean-

while the "exodus from the land" is giving way to the "flight from the city" as urban Tuscans appreciate the attractions of old farmhouses in upland settings. Part-time farming, property inheritance, gentrification and the dramatic increase in second-home ownership are winning a new population.

Tourism or traffic: However, the days of cheap, unconverted country homes have long since gone. Tuscans protest at the influx of rich German and British residents but the foreigners reply that they have restored entire villages such as Sovicille, near Siena, or Bugnano near Lucca, for future generations. In turn, Tuscan land-owners have become more astute about tourism: *Agriturismo* (farm stays) are increasingly popular, both as a way of making the farm pay and as an opportunity to reinvest profits in the restoration or conversion of family property.

The government is now promoting the countryside, medium-sized towns and the revival of the *centro storico* or historic town centre. The region's harmonious blend of craft, service and manufacturing industries makes Tuscany a model economy. Its cultural heritage and natural beauties also make it a highly desirable tourist destination.

Although tourism has been boosted by the opening of Florence's Peretola airport and the increase in flights via Pisa, Tuscans have

mixed feelings about the influx of visitors. In 1994, following the controversial example of Venice, Tuscany's historic towns first raised the issue of restricting the number of visitors or imposing a tourist tax. Tourists are guilty of not staying long enough or spending enough, particularly "East European day-trippers". While Siena, San Gimignano, Pisa, Arezzo and Cortona may be grateful for contributions to their coffers, many within their local councils regard the move as counter-productive.

Left, the Tuscan nose. **Above**, portrait of Lorenzo de' Medici, a classic family profile.

For residents and visitors alike, traffic is a blot on the horizon, particularly in Florence. The *Vigili Urbani* complain that their 600-strong force was designed to police 400,000 residents, not the summer population of 7–8 million. Noise and air pollution harm major buildings and modern sensibilities. In the historic centre, pollution from exhaust fumes has been reduced by a controversial but much modified traffic ban. Grumpy residents complain that enforcement is arbitrary, that the scheme harms commerce and Florentine freedoms, and that the restrictions on traffic in the centre merely lead to the clogging of the *viali*, traditionally Florence's arteries. To the average visitor, the first impression is of motorbikes: there are arguably more *motorini* than in any other Italian city.

Work in progress: According to UNESCO, Italy possesses over half of the world's cultural treasures so it is fair to assume that in Tuscany, the holder of the lion's share, a number should be undergoing restoration at any one time. In Italy, 90 per cent of restoration work is funded by the private sector. In Florence, the harrowing Masaccio frescoes in the Carmine Church were restored by Olivetti while Cassa di Risparmio, the Tuscan bank, recently restored the Gozzoli frescoes in the Palazzo Medici-Riccardi, as well as a clutch of works in the Uffizi. Monte dei Paschi, the oldest bank in the world, naturally protects its Sienese artistic heritage.

After restoration, statues are rarely returned to their outdoor sites, but protected in museums. Art historians approve but architects believe that the substitution of copies for the originals changes the relationship between the city and its artefacts. Princess Corsini has decided views on restoration: "Unlike the French, we Florentines never accept restoration to the original state: time passes and it's quite normal that this should show on the work."

The most impressive recent restorations include the Simone Martini *Maestà* in Siena and the Piero della Francesca fresco cycle in Arezzo. In Florence's Duomo, the magnificent restoration of the frescoes inside Brunelleschi's dome was completed in 1994, with work on the south and central facade finished in 1995. The Leaning Tower of Pisa has been closed since 1989 but if Tuscans can set their political house in order, there must be salvation for a mere toppling tower.

The doyen of Anglo-Florentine society, Sir Harold Acton (1904–94), called his adopted home, "a sunny place for shady people". The name "Chiantishire" is redolent of the dullness and domesticity of the English provinces. It is not by chance that Tuscany is twinned with Kent, the Garden of England and the guardian of Englishness.

Chiantishire is an archipelago of foreign islands. In the Chianti hills German shepherdesses tend errant sheep; bucolic Swiss cheesemakers produce pecorino cheese; French winemakers have abandoned Beaujolais for Brunello, while Ireland's Guinness family drink their estate wine instead of beer. Meanwhile the English literary set paces rural lanes and olive groves. Somehow the novelist Muriel Spark fails to encounter Peter Porter reciting his poetry, Miriam Margolyes rehearsing her latest part, Germaine Greer analysing the socio-sexual scene or John Mortimer pulling them all into a Chiantishire novel.

Everyone out of the mainstream feels at home in Chiantishire. All residents have in common is a firm avoidance of their native land and an antipathy towards their fellow countrymen. Art lovers are there to follow the Ghirlandaio trail while their offspring are enrolled on Renaissance "painting by numbers" courses in Florence. Art historians are there to remind Tuscans that, despite Michelangelo's useful contribution, Ruskin, Burckhardt and Berenson invented the Renaissance, and with it Tuscan tourism.

Academics on sabbatical enjoy a mental convalescence from real life. The literati scribble in the belief that beauty and art are contagious. Hedonists abandon a long British winter for drunken November lunches on the terrace. Scholarly eccentrics finish off theses about the help given by English Florentines to Mussolini's Blackshirts, topics inappropriate to communist Tuscany. Foodies are simply there to add Tuscan antipasti to their repertoire.

Each major town has its own foreign fanclub mimicking Tuscan city-state rivalry. It usually takes 10 years for an incomer to become an Anglo-Florentine, but this "citizenship" can take a month if one is famous,

rich, beautiful or related to Harold Acton. Every year up to 10,000 British and 15,000 Americans try to complete the transformation in Florence alone. While Florence and Siena have captured the intellectual high ground, real Chiantishire blooms best in the countryside. The location is inevitably one of Tuscany's 200,000 isolated farms, often bought from a smart *contadino* who has left a hand-to-mouth existence for a luxury town house. Iris Origo, the Anglo-Tuscan writer, noted the transformation of the farm's stone

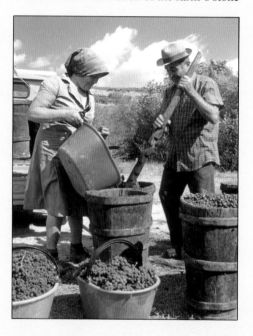

fireplace and marble floors into a chintz sitting room with framed prints, library books and "a fragrance of home-made scones and freshly-made tea. But no Italian can warm the tea-pot properly, my dear."

For the incomer, there are three golden rules: to eulogise the countryside, to be self-sufficient and to interact well with the natives. Enter the typical Chiantishire family with their light skin, straw hats, dark glasses, blazers and white linen trousers. When they arrive, their farmhouse, set at the end of a rough dirt track, is furnished with rustic minimalism. After unpacking the stocks of Irish linen, Lipton's tea, Colman's mustard, paint-brushes and mosquito-repellent, they admire the converted stables and go to sleep on the stone benches, formerly ox stalls. A night of discomfort effects a change of heart.

The first week is spent waxing lyrical about the chiaroscuro quality of Tuscan light, the silvery olive groves, the Matteo di Giovanni fresco in the local church, the clarity of the water. The only problem is that the Medicean well runs dry whenever the lavatory chain is pulled. Chopping wood with a rusty axe is not easy but they persevere…

The third week is spent in bed recovering from a mystery virus caught from bacteria in the well water. Gianni's rough *rosso dei Cacciaconti* provides much relief. The lights keep flickering if the refrigerator and the grill are on simultaneously. The washing machine fails in sympathy. A freak summer storm transforms the dirt track into a mud bath and, on the way to the *alimentari* shop

Preceding pages: the vintage Chiantishire hills. **Left**, making *vin santo*: "There's no point in Italy when it's not being picturesque." **Above**, mental convalescence from real life. Giovanni Fattori's *Valerio Biondi at Castiglioncello*.

via the communal wash house, the car gets bogged down. Cold and hungry, they despairingly eat unripe olives and burn damp olive branches. As time passes, language is less of a problem: they now pick up some *acqua* and Earl Grey in the *supermercato*, but return home to find local hunters threatening the baby for getting in their line of fire.

After a year, they have the social system worked out: they buy overpriced wine from the impoverished local marchese, and individual carrot tops and mouldy funghi from the peasants. An understanding with the shopkeepers allows them to be cheated often but never by large amounts: in return, Anita will take phone messages, Gianni will hold the mail, Marco will no longer let the car tyres down, and the hunters will stop taking pot shots at the baby. In exchange for regular supplies of Johnny Walker whisky, the carabinieri will curtail their dawn raids in search of drugs or irregularities in the family's residence permits.

They now speak Italian in private but revert to loud English in front of the *contadini*. Quintessentially English, the wife reminds her husband to "put the *scarico* out for the dustmen, dear". Deep down, she knows there are no dustmen and that her husband will dump it over the nearest hill like all the other villagers. The local stream is usually full of indestructible blue plastic bags. Life is full of unexpected joys: the family is invited to join the locals in the olive harvest and to feast on *bruschetti* drenched in freshly-pressed olive oil. In the butcher's, the *macellaio* now laughs at her pathetic jokes: "A bird in the hand is worth two in the bush," she says as she takes a sparrow instead of the quail she had tried to buy.

The gulf between the residents and their visitors grows. They are quietly triumphant when English guests accuse them of "going native". Visitors are aghast at relying on faulty electricity, polluted well water and crafty shopkeepers. One quotes a character in a John Mortimer book, *Summer's Lease*, who proclaims: "There's no point in Italy when it's not being picturesque." But the English, like Michelangelo, accept the agony with the ecstasy.

The wicker-covered Chianti flask called, as it happens, a *fiasco*, is rarer these days in Italian restaurants than red-and-white check tablecloths. This emblem of the early days of Tuscan vine culture has been superseded by an elegant square-shouldered bottle, reflecting the upgrading in quality of one of Italy's best-known wines.

If you order wine in a bar or restaurant in Tuscany, you will almost certainly be served the local *vino da tavola* (table wine) in an unlabelled jug or bottle. It is always drinkable and often very good. Now however, Tuscany is much more conscious of its standing as a producer of higher quality DOC (*Denominazione di Origine Controllata*) wines and increasingly you will find a sophisticated list of superior Tuscan vintages.

Nevertheless Tuscany *is* still Chianti. Of this there is little doubt – to the chagrin of producers of the region's other fine wines. But Chianti passed through a stormy period in the late 1970s and 1980s which caused many to despair of its ever being able to live up to its image. The problems stemmed from the laudable, and at first successful, attempts to control standards of wine production in this extensive area.

Winning formula: The heart of the Chianti district stretches in a large oval between Florence and Siena and there are branches extending west towards Lucca and Pisa, south to Montalcino, southeast to Montepulciano, east to Arezzo and past Pontassieve, and north past Pistoia. The heartland is called **Chianti Classico**, and it is over this territory that concern for the quality of the wine has longest been evident.

The first move was in the mid-18th century when Barone Bettino Ricasoli, who later became the second prime minister of united Italy, laid down the formula for making the wine. It involved a blend of four grape varieties in specified proportions, two of which were white.

It also reaffirmed the traditional practice of *governo*, which involves keeping some

grapes back during the harvest and leaving them to dry gently so that, when the main body of the wine has finished its fermentation, the reserved grapes can be added to the vat. This provokes a second fermentation, said to make the wine softer and rounder, but which mainly makes it livelier and ready to drink sooner.

The control of Chianti went a stage further in 1924 when a consortium, the Consorzio Chianti Classico, was founded to control production. It confirmed the Ricasoli blend and added stipulations on minimum alcohol, minimum ageing and so on. Membership was voluntary but as the consortium offered producers advice and promised efforts to stamp out the burgeoning amount of wine from outside the region calling itself "chianti", most of them joined.

To signify that a bottle was "Consorzio-approved", a special sticker was placed round its neck. These stickers carried the symbol of the Consorzio, a black rooster (*gallo nero*), and the name Gallo Nero soon became synonymous with Chianti Classico. Soon afterwards the satellite Chianti zones – Montalbano, Colline Pisane, Colli Senesi, Colli Aretini, Rufina and Colli Fiorentini – banded together to form their own *consorzio*, Chianti Putto, which took as its symbol a *putto* or cherub.

Once it became part of the European Community, Italy had to develop a country-wide wine law. In line with EC regulations "quality" wines were designated *Denominazione di Origine Controllata* (DOC), which distinguished them from their "lesser" brethren, called just *vino da tavola*. In Chianti the law more or less followed what the *consorzi* had already specified. By the 1970s, Chianti producers were hemmed in by tradition, national law and *consorzio* rules, to making wines in one specific way.

The problem was that this approach did not produce the quality or style of wine they wanted. The best quality grape of Tuscany is Sangiovese, but producers were restricted to using between 50 and 80 percent of it; white grapes and *governo* make for a light wine for early drinking, but they wanted a fuller wine that would age well. The solution was approached in typical Italian fashion. There were those who perpetuated the image of quality while lowering standards, cutting corners and engaging in a sales war that resulted in the price of Chianti dropping so low that its production was either fraudulent or loss-making.

There were others who decided to ignore the law and made high-quality Chianti as they believed it should be made, with whatever grapes they reckoned worthwhile. There were those who made much less Chianti and put their efforts into producing fine wine untrammelled by legal constraints; they gave each a *nome di fantasia* (invented name) and sold it as *vino da tavola,* but at a suitably high

ing a profitable use for all those white grapes he was no longer putting into his Chianti.

Salvation came in 1984 when Chianti joined the élite that was entitled to call its wines DOCG, the G standing for *e garantita.* This change presented an opportunity for the revamp of the regulations that was so needed and it was willingly, if somewhat argumentatively, embraced.

Since 1984 Chianti has been improving beyond recognition. It was, though, too late to prevent firm establishment of a plethora of individually named, costly *vini da tavola,* dubbed "supertuscans". The wine list of any restaurant in central Tuscany will certainly include Chianti. It will probably also contain

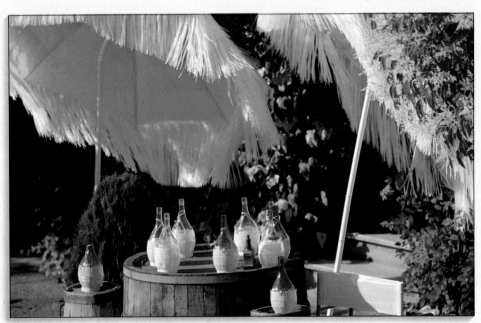

price. There were also just a few who soldiered on trying to make the best Chianti they could within the law.

Finding out exactly what each producer was doing required more than a little detective work. All swore their Chianti was both excellent and legal. To discover what was really happening required interpreting the glint in their eyes, and probably deferring the investigation until they felt more confident of their interrogator – perhaps over lunch.

One great give-away was always the emergence of a white wine. Tuscany is predominantly a red wine zone and new whites nearly always signified that the producer was find-

one or more names like Coltassala, Flaccianello, Mormoreto, Tavernelle, Tignanello or Le Pergole Torte.

Superior clone: These are often wines made solely with Sangiovese, or Sangioveto, a superior clone. Sometimes they are a blend of Sangiovese and Cabernet Sauvignon, the French grape which gives excellent results in Tuscany. They are occasionally made solely with Cabernet. The only way to divine their constituents is to scan the back label (which may not reveal all) or to ask.

To add a little spice to the quest for good drinking, a single name on a wine list will not necessarily signify a "supertuscan". Numerous estates have a particular vineyard whose wine, when kept separate, is always better than the rest. Each is labelled with its vineyard name as well as its official designation: Chianti or Chianti Classico. Tuscans are expected to know that Montesodi, for example, is a particular *cru* (single vineyard wine) of Chianti Rufina from the Frescobaldi estate. So the one word is often all that is put on the list. In shops, where the label can be scanned, life is easier.

The general, but not infallible, rule of thumb is that Classico is better than non-Classico. A good non-Classico producer can always outclass an average Classico estate. On the better, more matured, wines the label

sudden rainy squall can turn perfectly ripe concentrated bunches of grapes into a rotting mass.

Even when the harvest is successfully completed, there is little time to relax. A year's livelihood and several years' reputation is tied up in the large vats of bubbling grape juice and they require constant attention and monitoring. Producers with rings round their eyes are far more likely to have been up all night attending to their wine than carousing. A regional celebration is anyway impossible because the vintage, which can last three weeks or so, starts and finishes at different times in different zones.

Then there are the **Vin Santo** grapes to

will state *Riserva*, which indicates the wine has been aged at least three years, mainly in oak. For easy drinking, lively Chianti non-*Riserva*, informally called *normale*, comes into its own.

One would have thought that the harvest of a wine of such renown would be commemorated by great celebrations, but this is rarely the case. The vintage is a nerve-racking period and nail biting is seen more often than singing and dancing. In late September and October the weather can be erratic and a

Left, the traditional Chianti bottle, the *fiasco*. **Above**, figurine of fun.

guard. Vin Santo ("holy wine") is a dessert wine made all over Tuscany from white Trebbiano and Malvasia grapes. Once picked, they are dried slowly, weather permitting, either hanging up, lying on straw mats, or in shallow stacked crates. Six weeks to four months later, raisin-like, they are pressed and the small amount of concentrated, sweet juice that results is put into small barrels. There it slowly ferments and matures, untouched, for a number of years.

Most Vin Santo is sweet, but some is dry. Nearly all of it is rare, expensive and often a real treat. It is served at the end of a meal with *biscotti secchi*, hard almond biscuits which are to be dunked in the sweet golden wine.

Red wine in Tuscany is still inextricably linked with Chianti, but it shouldn't be. It really ought to be linked with the Sangiovese grape. Chianti, well diffused though it is, is not Tuscany's only red wine; Sangiovese is far and away the predominant grape of the entire region, despite occasional outcrops of Cabernet Sauvignon. There are several clones of the grape planted: Sangioveto, Sangiovese Grosso, Sangiovese Piccolo, Prugnolo, Brunello and so on. A fierce debate rages constantly about which are superior and which are similar.

Brunello is found around the town of Montalcino, south of Siena. The wine,

Brunello di Montalcino, is one of Italy's best, though it only dates back to 1870. It was the result of a firm conviction of Ferrucio Biondi-Santi, then only 20 years old, who put his beliefs into action, and his descendants have kept the name Biondi-Santi in the forefront of the wine's reputation. Lack of tradition can be a disadvantage – but there are advantages too. One of Brunello di Montalcino's prescribed characteristics is a long minimum ageing period (four years, three and a half of them in oak).

This was felt by some to be too long for all but the grandest wines, which then need to mature longer in the bottle. So a younger wine, **Rosso di Montalcino**, was swiftly created in the same style. The two co-exist comfortably and the risk of discontented producers "bending" the law has been avoided. Chianti's traditions could never have accommodated such flexibility.

The Prugnolo clone of Sangiovese predominates further east and produces **Vino Nobile di Montepulciano** around the town of the same name. Vino Nobile may be best described as a half way house between Brunello di Montalcino and Chianti Classico. Like both these wines it has been decreed DOCG, giving Tuscany three of the first five wines in Italy that have been so elevated.

White, too: Whites very much take second place. They are light, simple and pleasant but generally, despite continual improvements, could not be described as "great". Most are based on Trebbiano and Malvasia grapes and are named after the locality of their origin; many (like **Galestro**) have resulted from the need to use the white grapes no longer needed for Chianti production.

The main exception is the dry, elegant, but quite full-bodied **Vernaccia di San Gimignano**, of which Michelangelo apparently said: "It kisses, licks, bites, thrusts and stings." The grape name Vernaccia crops up in a few parts of Italy but each bears no relation to the others: Vernaccia seems to imply no more than a "local" grape.

The other exception was the great fashion of the 1980s: the French variety Chardonnay. More and more producers turned over one or more plots to the grape, many invested in small, new oak barrels from France, called *barriques*, to mature the wines, and whoops of delight could be heard all over Tuscany as the results started appearing.

For most red Tuscan wines, including Vino Nobile di Montepulciano, 1990 was a good year. Both 1990 and 1993 vintages were notable for Chianti, while 1988, 1990 and 1993 were exceptional years for Brunello di Montalcino.

Traditionalists who believe that all good things in Tuscany should be Tuscan in origin either had to let the excitement pass them by – unthinkable – or else retire to the libraries to try to prove that Chardonnay was planted in Tuscany long ago after all.

Above, wine festival to sample the new vintage. **Right**, freshly picked green olives.

LIQUID GOLD

Tuscany's olive oil has long been famous for its quality and excellent flavour and texture. The humid, temperate climate of the Tuscan hills is especially suitable for growing olives and the silvery gnarled branches of the trees, hung with white nets before harvest, are as characteristic a sight as vines or cypresses.

The oil produced is so good that *bruschetta*, a quintessential Tuscan dish, consists simply of a slice of bread, toasted, rubbed with garlic and trickled with thick, green olive oil of the best possible quality. Tuscans are passionate about olive oil; they believe it is the most important cooking ingredient, and that its flavour and strength fundamentally affect the final dish.

They are immensely proud of their oil, too; wherever you go locals will claim that *their* olive oil is the very best available. It is possible to become quite a connoisseur; there is a restaurant in Grosseto, *Enoteca Ombrone*, which has a cellar of olive oils, stocking over 40 varieties, and you can sample and compare them all at the table.

Olives are grown all over Italy. As a general rule, the flavour of the oil becomes heavier and stronger further south. In the north it is at its lightest and most delicate. Even within the boundaries of Tuscany itself, the oils can vary enormously in sweetness, fruitiness, flavour and colour from deep green to light gold. An olive oil from Siena or Florence may appear quite different from the produce of Lucca or Grosseto.

In Tuscany the olive harvest begins in November or December and the olives are picked and processed during the following weeks. Some olives are picked while green, but usually they have turned almost black before they are picked for oil. Olives should always be picked by hand if possible. To make sure that not a single one is lost, the ground underneath the gnarled trees is covered in fine nets so that the olives fall down into them and can be gathered up more easily.

The technique of picking olives is not unlike milking a cow. The end of each small branch is held firmly in one hand while the other hand pulls downwards and strips off olives, leaves and twigs to let them fall on to the ground. It is a long and laborious task, but the machine has yet to be invented which can accomplish the job so well.

There is an immense feeling of pride and love connected to the pressing of olive oil; it is the food element which comes closest to maternal milk for its composition of fats and vitamins.

After the olives are picked, they are taken to a local mill where they are pressed, traditionally by stone, nowadays more commonly using steel rollers. The initial "cold pressing" produces the very best and most expensive oils; thereafter the mash is pressed using heat which produces a greater yield but inferior oil. Quality is measured by acid content, the finest oil being *Extra Vergine* with an acid level no higher than one percent, followed by *Soprafino*, *Fino* and *Vergine*.

Olive oil, like wine, is alive, with different characteristics depending on the year it is made and the area where the olives are grown. It goes rancid quickly and should therefore be used within a year of its pressing. Also, it absorbs smells and flavours very easily, which means it must be stored with some care – and away from anything which has a strong smell.

Tuscan cooks use olive oil all the time, brushed on to meat for grilling and roasting, raw to dress salads or to pour over warm vegetables or potatoes, trickled into soups and stews before serving, and for deep frying sweet cakes and fritters. The quality of oil chosen depends on what it is to be used for; richer oils are more suitable when the flavour is likely to dominate the dish.

A few excellent oils worth seeking out are Extra Vergine di Scansano, Extra Vergine di Macchiascandona, Extra Vergine di Montalcino, Extra Vergine di Seggiano cru Querciole, Extra Vergine del Chianti, Extra Vergine di San Gimignano cru Montenidoli, and Extra Vergine Badia a Coltibuono.

Although Tuscany was only the sixth largest producer of Italian olive oil in 1994, the quality of Tuscan oil is outstanding. In recognition of its superiority, Tuscan oil is accorded DOC status, as if it were a wine. Unfortunately, the costs of superior Tuscan oil are often comparable with those of superior wines.

What is immediately striking about Tuscan food is that, no matter what you are eating or where you are eating it, it is always very rustic, very simple, designed to nourish the soul and the spirit as much as the body. Tuscan cooking is never elaborate or excessive; there are no fussy decorations, complicated reductions of sauces or subtly blended flavours. But there is a basic, honest simplicity about their dishes which have made them popular for centuries the world over.

Tuscany produces its own inimitable versions of Italian staples: pasta dishes with gamey sauces of hare, wild boar, even porcupine; *polenta* with fresh *funghi*; rabbit or roast baby goat. But along with a particular attitude to food, Tuscany also has many dishes and delicacies unique to the region.

Hearty stews: Tuscans are known as *Toscani Mangiafagiolii* – bean eaters, because the versatile pulse is used so much in local specialities – adding a velvety smooth texture as only well-cooked beans can. Rich thick soups and hearty bean stews are served in rustic terracotta pots, often enhanced by a trickle of thick green olive oil which is added at the table.

Tuscan cooks favour cooking methods that can be carried out on a large scale and preferably out of doors – the spit or grill over an open wood fire is something you will come across in courtyards behind chic Florentine restaurants or in the garden of countryside *trattorie*. Fresh herbs like sage, rosemary and basil, are used, as they grow, in abundance.

The most important Tuscan meat dish is the excellent *bistecca alla Fiorentina*, a vast tender, juicy and succulent beef steak – preferably from cattle raised in Val di Chiana. It is brushed with one drop of the purest virgin olive oil and grilled over the glowing embers of a scented wood fire of chestnuts or vine branches, then seasoned with salt and pepper before serving. In good Florentine and Tuscan restaurants in general, you will be able to see the meat raw before you order.

Preceding pages: Tuscan cooks. **Left**, slicing *porchetta* in Greve di Chianti. **Right**, *cinghiale* (wild boar), hams and salami.

Another famous Tuscan meat dish is *arista alla Fiorentina*, consisting of a pork loin which is pierced all over and the holes filled with chopped rosemary and ground pepper. The origin of this dish goes back to the 15th century. At the Ecumenical Council of 1430 in Florence, the Greek Bishops were served this dish at a banquet and pronounced it *"aristos"* which in Greek means very good. The name stuck and it has become a feature of Tuscan cuisine ever since. It is a particularly useful dish to cook because it keeps

very well for several days and is even better cold than hot.

Local ham can include wild boar meat, and there is a salami flavoured with fennel called *finocchione*. Soups are made of the ubiquitous beans, and include *acquacotta*, a vegetable soup with an egg added before serving, and *pappa al pomodoro*, a thick soup of bread and tomatoes.

The coastal province of Livorno produces the delicious *cacciucco*, an immense seafood and fish soup claimed to be the original *bouillabaisse*. The story goes that the soup originated in the port after a tremendous storm that left a widowed fisherman's wife desperately trying to feed her many children.

The children were sent from house to house, begging for something to eat. As the fishermen had nothing else to give, the children came home with handfuls of mussels, a few shrimps, half a fish and some fish heads. The clever mother put them all in a pot, added herbs and tomatoes from her garden and created the glorious *cacciucco*. While *zuppa di pesce* can be eaten all over Italy, *cacciucco* can be eaten only in Livorno and surrounding areas.

During the Renaissance, food had its place among the arts along with painting, sculpture, poetry and music. Many extraordinary dishes were created around that time; menus

When she left Florence to marry Francis I of France, she took many of her recipes and ideas with her. There are many Italians who claim that it was largely through her efforts that the French learnt to cook at all! To this day, the origin of rich hare stew, called *lepre in dolce e forte*, with candied lemon, lime and orange peel, cocoa, rosemary, garlic, vegetables and red wine, is contested by both Italian and French cooks. It is still called *dolce forte* in French.

The cheeses available in this region are plentiful and varied. There is a delightful overspill of cheeses from neighbouring Emilia Romagna including, of course, the King of Cheeses, *parmigiano Reggiano*. It is

at Florentine Renaissance banquets abounded with dishes such as pasta cooked in rose water and flavoured with sugar, incredible candied fruit and almond confectionery, the famous hare stew called *lepre in dolce e forte,* and many more.

Frozen delights: Caterina de' Medici was responsible for much of the renewed interest in the creation of original dishes. A keen gourmet, she encouraged her cooks to experiment and was responsible for the introduction of ice-cream to the northern regions from Sicily, where it had been eaten for decades thanks to the Arabs who brought it over from North Africa.

used extensively to complement Tuscany's marvellous pasta dishes and soups.

Other cheeses made locally include *marzolino*, a ewe's milk cheese made in March when milk is most plentiful in the Chianti valley; *mucchino*, cow's milk cheese made in and around Lucca by the same procedure as *pecorino*; *Brancolino* from the town of Brancoli; the delectable *formaggette di Zeri*, made with half ewe's and half cow's milk in Massa Carrara; and all the local rustic *cacciotte* and *ricotta* made with cow, goat and ewe milk. Hunting is a popular local sport (though tourist participation is discouraged) resulting in plentiful supplies of *cinghiale* (wild boar) and numerous small birds, from sparrows to quail.

Sweetmeats: Siena is famous for the *Palio*, for its ethereal Gothic beauty, and for its incredibly wide selection of pastries and sweetmeats. *Cavallucci* are delicious little hard biscuits which are usually served at the end of a meal and dipped into glasses of sweet Vin Santo.

Panforte has been made here since the 15th century and is sold the world over, an Italian Christmas speciality, unmistakable in its brightly coloured octagonal cardboard box. It is a very light, rich, sweet cake of candied fruit, nuts, spices, honey and sugar, sandwiched in between sheets of rice paper.

the borders with Emilia Romagna they bake a delicious apple cake, the *torta di mele*.

Pistoia produces the pretty *corona di San Bartolomeo* for the feast of St Bartholomew on 24 August, when mothers lead their children to church wearing this cake necklace around their necks for a special blessing from the saint. Prato has *biscottini di Prato* made from almonds, eggs, flour and sugar, delicious dipped into the fragrant amber-coloured local Vin Santo. In Livorno they make gorgeous light, golden buns called *bolli*. A speciality of Lucca is a ring-shaped plain cake called *buccellato*, and an unusual sweet tart of spinach and chard with pine nuts. Florence is famous for *sticciata* – a type

Ricciarelli are delightful, diamond-shaped almond cakes, also saved for the Christmas celebrations, along with the delicious, golden rich rice cake called *torta di riso*. The local *pasticcerie* are filled with these and many other delectable varieties.

In other areas of the region, different specialities appear. At Castelnuovo della Garfagnana they make a wonderfully simple cake of chestnuts called *torta garfagnina*; on

of rich, sweet bun flavoured with Marsala and orange flower water.

But the pride of place amongst all Toscana's sweet specialities is the incredible *zucotto*, a sponge cake mould with a filling of almonds, hazelnuts, chocolate and cream. Once eaten, it is never forgotten. It is called "small pumpkin" because the segmented cake looks like a bright yellow pumpkin.

Mountain harvest: Chestnuts are a staple of the region, particularly in mountain areas, where they are made into flour, pancakes, soups and sweet cakes like *castagnaccio*, flavoured with rosemary and pine nuts.

In the autumn, when the rains fall, the hills

become a target for family outings. On the mountain sides and along the roads there are little groups of people equipped with baskets and sticks, searching for the harvest of chestnuts and *funghi*. The wild mushroom season is awaited impatiently, as the spoils are highly prized both for their pungent flavour and the price they will fetch in the market.

There are many different varieties of wild mushrooms, growing in abundance amongst the trees in the hills – the type of mushroom found will depend very much upon the type of tree it is growing next to or under – but the most sought after is the perfect *porcine (boletus edulis)* which grows to enormous size and thickness. These are often served simply grilled with olive oil and salt – just like a steak.

Horror stories: You need to be an expert if you decide to go mushroom picking. Each year during the season the newspapers are filled with horror stories about families poisoning themselves with their own hand-picked mushrooms and it is easy to make a dreadful mistake. Some local authorities have passed laws preventing people from picking the mushrooms unless they have paid for and been issued with a licence.

Yet, despite the restrictions imposed by the licence, the dangers of picking the wrong thing, and the shortness of the season, wild mushrooms are widely available at restaurants, in the markets and at roadside stalls from late August to early October. The wild mushroom season coincides with the beginning of the wine harvest, the olive oil harvest and the snail season. It is a time of plenty, when a great deal of eating and drinking is enjoyed throughout the region.

Tuscany has everything to offer the visitor in terms of food. There is a rich selection of fruit and vegetables from the wide, prolific countryside, and a fantastic bounty from the sea – everything from red mullet to mussels, sweet and tender beef and pork, excellent oil with which to cook and dress it and superb wines with which to wash it down. To finish off there are hearty cheeses and divine cakes and desserts.

This is not the region to seek out complicated or intricate dishes. The food of Tuscany is a pure and simple art.

Right, aubergines, peppers and grapes in the market in Pescia, a town noted for its flowers.

Festivals are Tuscany's richest theatre, ranging from the simple *sagra* (feast) to the most complex Italian festival of all, the *Palio*. In a sophisticated festival, scenes of high drama or contemporary relevance can recall a pagan or medieval past, succumb to Bacchic indulgence or soar to mysticism and magic.

Even the most ordinary festival reveals an unbroken tradition, a curious competition or a rustic delicacy. There are *feste* in honour of fire and water, *ravioli* and wine, historic football jousts, saints and witches. Every conceivable animal is celebrated, from the thrush to crickets. Even the Virgin's Holy Girdle is worshipped.

It is difficult to avoid such small festivals in Tuscany. Any of the following signs suggest the unfolding of a secret rite: a parish church decorated with banners and snapshots of horses; huddles of town dignitaries plotting in corners; agile boys tossing flags; and a trestle table set for 200. Inevitably, the table is piled high with stodgy chestnut *polenta*; wizened old men are "helping" uncork the local wine.

Just for fun: In the background, yesterday's motorbike daredevil is today's Renaissance courtier in harlequin tights. Somewhere, a mechanical donkey fails to start but the fireworks explode anyway. Ask anyone what the festival is "about" and the innocuous reply will be *allegria*, "fun".

But *allegria* belies the seriousness of intent. Festivals are a distorting mirror to Tuscan life, projecting the rawness and romanticism of civic pride onto a citizen's individualism. Even if there is no overt competition, each participant expects the finest horse, the most lavish costume, the biggest bonfire or the longest *contrada* procession.

This expectation usually crystallises around the *contrade*, cities within a city. These emerged in the 12th-century "communes" when a particular square, church and fountain became associated with a local area and character. The *contrada* spirit, particularly marked in Siena, Arezzo and Lucca

provinces, inspires most of Tuscany's festivals. Without such passion, many would have degenerated into tourist displays. With it, the survival of *palio* and *giostra* rivalries is ensured.

In Siena, the archetypal *contrade* city, each of the 17 *contrade* has its own organisation, church and even museums housing the *Palio* memorabilia. These announce births, marriages and deaths: marriage is celebrated with a flag-waving display and funerals are attended by a *contrada* page.

Children are enrolled at birth and membership is for life.

Children learn *senesità*, the city's proclaimed values of freedom, friendship and altruism. They are also gently indoctrinated in *contrada* folklore, *Palio* triumphs and disasters. The boys practise the noble arts of flag-waving, drumming and nobbling the enemy *contrada*'s horse, while girls learn how to cook *risotto* for 100 *contradaioli* on feast days. Both sexes absorb *contrada* values: stealth, diplomacy and single-minded victory. At its highest, the *contrade* spirit fosters individual excellence and a striving towards collective perfectionism. Even the

Preceding pages: watching and winning the *Palio*. **Left**, in full rig for the *Palio*. **Right**, *buttero* winner in a Maremma horse race.

humblest *palio* races reflect local *contrade* traditions and are not a mere parody of the Sienese model. Asciano and Querceta always race donkeys rather than horses. Likewise, Livorno's *palio marinaro*, a regatta along the atmospheric canals, is a natural choice for a sea-faring city. Jousts or *giostre* are a rougher variant on the *palio* theme.

Belligerent beginnings: The origins lie in medieval fist fights and the jousts are still a safe way of reliving and relieving ancient rivalries. There are moments when the *giostre* have the fervour of a war ceremony, or the finality of a farewell service for crusaders. Although the buffalo races and bullfights have now died out, real or mechanical fal-

quiet while rival fans stamp, whistle, scream and wave. The guiding spirit is completely anti-Olympiad: winning, not taking part, is definitely what counts.

Arezzo runs an elaborate *giostra* with a more complex scoring system and greater rewards and punishments. The winner receives a gold lance, adulation from one *contrada* and hatred from the three losers. A knight missing the target can be knocked off his horse by a savage "cat-of-three-tails".

Each *contrada*, ensconced on its own side of the Piazza Grande, is engrossed in the accompanying procession which is a contradictory mix of medieval costume and modern sentiment. As Archibald Lyall wrote of

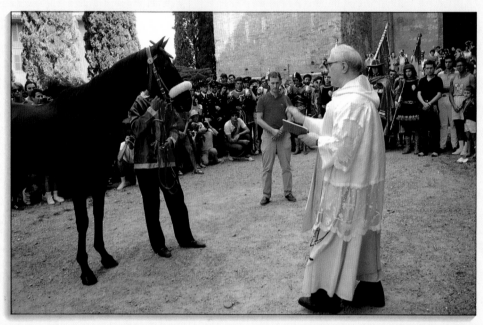

cons, bears, donkeys and horses still "joust" regularly.

Two dramatic jousts at Arezzo and Sarteano re-enact local feuds, disguised as the ritual savagery of medieval crusaders. The jousts centre on charges at a dummy representing the "Saracen". In Sarteano, a cortege circles into the medieval square and bows to the *notabili*, the stand packed with local dignitaries. The segregated members of the five opposing *contrade* explode in a riot of drumming and banner-waving. In turn, the knights try to hit and carry off the ring on the Saracen's shield. As each knight gallops up to the Saracen, supporters are

Arezzo, "Beautiful ladies ride in the procession, their make-up by Elizabeth Arden and their costumes out of the Duc de Berry's book of hours." The religious festivals range from simple homage to obscure saints, to Grassina's elaborate "Way of the Cross", a re-enactment of the ascent to Calvary and the crucifixion. Prato's "Display of the Virgin's Holy Girdle" is certainly the oddest.

According to legend, Doubting Thomas could not accept either the resurrection or Mary's assumption until he found roses in Jesus's empty tomb and then saw the Virgin in heaven removing her girdle for him. The girdle eventually reached Prato Cathedral in the 12th century via Thomas and the Holy Land crusades. *Pratese* merchants, conscious of their priceless relic, display it five times a year to incredulous crowds.

Flaming dove: The fullest religious festival is Florence's "Exploding Carriage", *Lo Scoppio del Carro*, celebrating the resurrection and the success of the First Crusade. On Easter Day, citizens excitedly squeeze into the Piazza del Duomo to catch a glimpse of a mechanical dove or a miracle. The essential elements are: a tense wait for an uncertain fire, intense children who believe in magic, and a suspension of adult disbelief that a firework dove is the Holy Spirit.

The ritual began when Pazzino de' Pazzi

to the city and successive popes made more opulent carriages. The present one, dating from 1700, resembles a Japanese palanquin on wheels. In a moment of inspiration, Leo X added the dove to the ritual.

As High Mass in the Duomo comes to an end, children outside eye the magic box of flowers and fireworks and will it to explode. Inside the Duomo, children gaze at the firework dove suspended on a wire above the high altar. At the intoning of the *Gloria*, the dove, fizzing with sacred fire, swoops through the open doors and ignites the triumphal carriage. Amid the chiming of bells, shrieks and fireworks, the dove fizzles out, its mechanical miracle accomplished.

returned from the First Crusade to Florence in 1305. Legend has it that he was the first to scale the walls of Jerusalem and seize a piece of the Holy Sepulchre. Every year, these precious chips are taken from San Miniato to the baptistry where a spark from the stones lights the holy fire. The fire, carried in procession to the cathedral, is later used to ignite the dove.

Six white oxen drag the creaking, gilded carriage into the square. De Pazzi had the first simple *carro* built to bring the holy fire

Left, benediction for the *contrada* horse, Sienna.
Above, drums add a beat to the festival noise.

Although today's participants are more likely to be shopkeepers than peasants, the sense of relief is just as great. The liberated crowds spill over the Ponte Vecchio, wander to lunch near the Boboli Gardens or watch the foolhardy dive into the river. The atmosphere is one of exhilaration. A successful ritual means a joyous release of tension.

The simplest and most dramatic festival is held in Monte Amiata. Abbadia di San Salvatore's *Fiaccole di Natale* or "Christmas Torches" is a mountain festival built around towering, conical bonfires. Originally a pagan mid-winter festival, its medieval roots lie in the vigil kept by villagers and shepherds as they waited for Midnight Mass on Christmas Eve. Carols, storytelling, feasting and fires helped to drive away the cold. In the gathering of shepherds, the long wait, the ritual worship, the cold of the mountains, there are echoes of Bethlehem.

Today, pyramids of fire are still used to rekindle memory and collective faith. The fire-making is a male art and village boys compete in building the most graceful fire to adorn their local piazza. The surrounding forests, in common ownership since 1300, symbolise local pride and the fires are a seasonal thanksgiving. The bonfires of chestnut wood from Monte Amiata illuminate the town hall, squares and alleyways. Torchlit processions and dancing to mandolins only die out with the fires at dawn. The dying embers signal the explosion of the winter sports season: skiing, nature trails and New Year balls.

Pork and beans: Despite their pagan, religious or seasonal labels, many festivals are really a pretext for gastronomic delights. One tiny village near Florence holds a festival to celebrate the broad bean harvest in early May. Radicofani unashamedly holds a *Ravioli Festa* while Montale and Montalcino ennoble and eat the thrush in *Sagra del Tordo*. The celebrations are not limited to locals: casual visitors are also welcome to enjoy a dip in the pot. If the beans, thrush or white truffles do not appeal, *porchetta* (roast pig) is usually on sale.

But for uninhibited merrymaking there is nothing to equal *Carnevale*, a pagan spring carnival with a Christian veneer. Arezzo, San Gimignano and Piombino compete with allegorical or *Commedia dell'Arte* floats followed by processions of harlequins, courtiers, jesters and popes. Viareggio's pre-Lenten carnival offers an unequalled display of political satire and burlesque. It is the time to discover the masked desires of close friends and colleagues.

The last word belongs to Horace Walpole, writing in Florence in 1740, "The end of carnival is frantic bacchanalia; all the morn one makes parties in masque to the shops and coffee houses and all the evening to the operas and balls. Then I have danced, good gods! How I have danced!"

<u>Right</u>, triumph and unbearable happiness at the end of the Siena *Palio*.

PLACES

Sometimes the delights of Tuscany all become too much, and a curious disease afflicts visitors, known as the Stendhal Syndrome. It manifests itself in sensitive visitors so overcome that they sometimes faint away completely. Stendhal recorded his own experience: "The tide of emotion which overwhelmed me flowed so deep that it scarce was to be distinguished from religious awe. As I emerged from the port of Santa Croce, I was seized with a fierce palpitation of the heart; I walked in constant fear of falling to the ground." Wagner was similarly affected, bursting into tears at the sight of the Duomo in Siena.

Tuscany has always been a favourite destination for travellers and pilgrims. But there is a risk of becoming so surfeited by the richness of the artistic inheritance of Tuscany that you may find yourself exclaiming with Mark Twain: "Enough! Say no more! Lump the whole thing! Say that the creator made Italy from designs by Michelangelo!"

The English poet Laurie Lee fled to the hills after a visit to Florence. "I'd had my fill of Florence," he wrote, "lovely but indigestible city. My eyes were choked with pictures and frescoes, all stamped one on top of the other, blurred, their colours running. I began to long for those cool uplands, that country air, for the dateless wild olive and the uncatalogued cuckoo."

The truly wonderful thing about Tuscany is that its artistic riches are fully matched by the radiance of nature, and the grace of the people who live there. As E.M. Forster observed, "The traveller who has gone to Italy to study the tactile values of Giotto, or the corruption of the papacy, may return remembering nothing but the blue sky and the men and women who live under it." And there is nothing wrong with that.

Preceding pages: the band takes a break; vineyards in Badia a Passignano, Chianti; campanile and rooftops of Florence.

ROMAGNA

Vignola
Bologna
Castelecchio di Reno
Alfonsine
Lugo
Ravenna
Minozzo
Sasso Marconi
Castel S. Pietro Terme
Adriatic Sea
FRIGNANO
Pavullo nel Frignano
Imola
Necrópoli Etrusca (Etruscan Tombs)
Faenza
Forlì
Cesenatico
M. Cimone 2165
Lago di Suviana
Firenzuola
Brisighella
Torre di Ceparano (Tower)
Méldola
Cesena
Rimini
Abetone
S. di Bocca di Rio
Modigliana
Predappio
Santarcangelo di Rom.
Lima
MUGELLO
ALPE DI S. BENEDETTO
S. MARINO
Bagni di Lucca
Pistóia
Borgo S. Lorenzo
Mercato Saraceno
Pescia
Prato
M. Falterona 1654
Bagno di Rom.
M. Fumaiolo 1408
MONTEFELTRO
cca
Montecatini Terme
Ombrone
Fiésole
Eremo di Camaldoli
La Verna 1128
Urbania
ertosa di Pisa
Fucecchio
Scandicci
Firenze
Pontassieve
Poppi
Bibbiena
CASENTINO
Arno
S. Croce s. Arno
Empoli
Impruneta
PRATOMAGNO
VALTIBERINA
Sansepolcro
Apecchio
edera
Castelfiorentino
S. Casciano in Val di Pesa
Greve
VALDARNO
S. Giovanni Valdarno
Città di Castello
Pietralunga
Casciana Terme
Certaldo
CHIANTI
Montevarchi
Arezzo
S. Gimignano
Poggibonsi
Canale Maestro
Umbertide
Volterra
Tévere
Saline di Volterra
Casole d'Elsa
Siena
Monte S. Savino
Cortona
Lago Trasimeno
Perugia
COLLINE METALLIFERE
Monteroni d'Arbia
V. DI CHIANA
di Castagneto-noratico
Larderello
Monticiano
Asciano
Cornia
Monterotondo Maritt.
Arbia
Abbazia di M. Oliveto Maggiore (Abbey)
UMBRIA
Vincenzo
Massa Maritt.
Montepulciano
Marsciano
mbino
Roccastrada
Montalcino
Chianciano Terme
Chiusi
Follonica
Bruna
Paganico
Chiana
Todi
Necrópoli Etrusca (Etruscan Tombs)
Ombrone
Abbadia S. Salvatore
Castiglione della Pescaia
S. Fiora
Acquapendente
Orvieto
Lago di Córbara
Grosseto
Terme di Saturnia
Tombe Etrusche (Etruscan Tombs)
Amélia
M. di Uccellina
PARCO NATURALE D. MAREMMA
Albegna
Manciano
Lago di Bolsena
Montefiascone
Narni
OLA DEL GIGLIO
Porto S. Stefano
Orbetello
635
M. Argentario
Castro (Castle)
Marta
Bagno d. Bussele
Rovine di Ferentium
Montalto di Castro
Tombe Etrusche (Etruscan Tombs)
Tuscania
Viterbo
Vignanello

TOSCANA

129

THE CITY OF FLORENCE

In a country of spectacular sites, the site of Florence is outstanding. Viewed from the surrounding hills, the city seems to be floating in a bowl which, at dusk, is tinged violet. The honey-coloured walls and myriad, rose-coloured roofs of the city combine to make a unity which is dominated by a single, vast building, the cathedral. It is by far the biggest building for miles around, with its roof and dome in the same subtle colour-range as the surrounding smaller buildings above which it seems to float like a great liner among tugs.

There are few towers or spires. Giotto's multi-coloured campanile next to the cathedral, plain in outline but intricate in detail, and the thrusting tower of the Palazzo Vecchio, elegant and sombre, soar above a generally low profile. The overall impression is not that of a city, composed of tens of thousands of units, but of one single, vast building, a majestic palace.

This is symbolic of Florentine history: unity in diversity, a mansion occupied by a single family. Frequently there are family quarrels: members are even prepared to make common cause with foreigners to get the better of a neighbour, but they are still one family in one abode.

Close contact with the city can be at first disconcerting, even disappointing. The first impression is claustrophobic. The streets are narrow, hemmed in by towering, plain buildings. There is no delicate filigree, as in Venice, or cheerful baroque, as in Rome, to tempt the eye.

Some of the buildings resemble 19th-century warehouses, grim structures erected at a time of social unrest and so discharging the primary function of fortresses. In any case, Florentine taste runs to the understated, the restrained, the prudent, as befits a race of farmers.

But gradually, the visitor comes to terms with a city which, though sharing basic characteristics with the larger family of Italian cities, is a unique mixture. The banning of traffic from the historic centre has given Florence back to pedestrians. The streets, instead of being conduits for lethal streams of fast-moving metal, are again part of the city's fabric, simultaneously discharging the role of stage-set and communication link. The visitor is free to wander, and stop, and wander again, absorbing all the city has to offer.

Overwhelming riches: It is perfectly possible to spend a lifetime studying Florence. Scores have done so in the past; scores will do so in the future. For the visitor to attempt a comprehensive survey on one single visit will simply invite fatigue, then boredom. The monuments and localities which figure in the following bird's-eye view are chosen on a necessarily arbitrary basis. Some, of course, automatically select themselves; others have been included because they can stand as an example for their class as a whole, or illustrate some particular point of the Florentine story.

The city has been grouped into four sections: starting with the area around the Palazzo Vecchio; followed by the

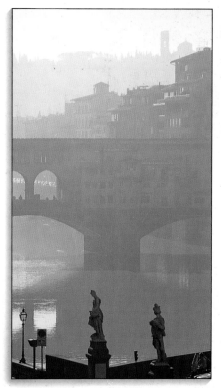

Left, the Duomo. **Right**, River Arno.

Florence

500 m

area around the Cathedral; and then by three important religious foundations, (which, for reasons which will be explained, have been grouped together in the narrative though physically scattered around the city). The final section is the River Arno and beyond. Nearly all the places are within easy walking distance of one another.

As Florence is a small town, it is possible to walk its entire width, from the Porta Romana in the south to the Porta San Gallo in the north, in half an hour or so. During World War II, an aircraft dropped a stick of three or four bombs to the west of the town on a line running roughly north-south. Had the pilot corrected his course by a fraction to take him over the centre, then that small stick of bombs would have taken out almost everything we imagine when we think of Florence.

The civic heart: Of all the great Italian city squares, Florence's is the most perversely irregular. There's nothing in the **Piazza della Signoria** of the harmony which makes Venice's San Marco a vast, unroofed hall. There's nothing here of the grace of Siena's curved Campo, or the simple majesty of Rome's Capitol. Instead, buildings follow each other around the perimeter of the Piazza in no particular order.

Tucked uncomfortably on one side is the **Palazzo Vecchio**, the seat of government for the past six centuries. Next to it is the elegant **Loggia dei Lanzi**, crammed with statues, which doesn't seem to relate to anything in particular. The huge fountain in the centre is the subject of amiable mockery by the residents of Florence themselves, and no two buildings in the Piazza seem to have the same facade.

With a despot's love of order, Duke Cosimo I tried to impose an artificial unity on the square, and Michelangelo even came up with a scheme to continue the shape of the Loggia all the way round. Happily, such schemes came to nothing – happily, because the Piazza della Signoria is a perfect illustration of Florentine "unity in diversity".

Despite the absence of an overall plan, despite the bristling individuality of the buildings, the Piazza as a whole does come together. How little it has changed over the centuries can be seen by comparing the contemporary painting of the execution of Savonarola in the Piazza in 1498 with the square today.

The narrow platform in front of the Palazzo Vecchio sums up the function of the Piazza della Signoria. The platform is all that remains of the original *Ringheria* – literally, the "haranguing place", where orators could address the assembled citizenry.

The statues upon it are not simply decorative, but have profound political significance. Here stood the *Judith and Holofernes*, returned here in 1919 after many migrations, but now housed for safety in the Palazzo itself. Here is the **Marzocco**, the lion symbol of the city which prisoners were forced to kiss. Michelangelo's immense statue of David is a copy of the first, commissioned in 1501 to mark another important change in the constitution.

Nearby is the statue of the first Medici duke – and the first Medici to so aggran-

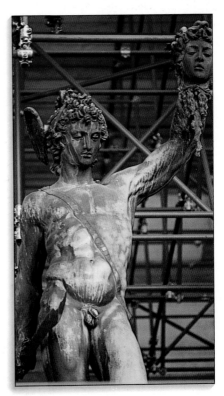

Cellini's *Perseus* during restoration of the Piazza della Signoria.

dise himself – Cosimo I. The **Loggia dei Lanzi** (named after the *landsknechts* or mercenaries employed by Cosimo) used to have a statue of Perseus holding the head of the Gorgon (*see page 68*). Cellini was commissioned to do this work by Cosimo – perhaps as a riposte to the *Judith*. Perseus is being restored prior to his move to a museum.

The Palazzo Vecchio itself, begun in 1299, has changed its name many times over the years, each change signifying a change in the city. Originally, it was the Palazzo dei Priori, the priors being the heads of the guilds who formed the government. In the 14th century it became the Palazzo del Popolo, then the Palazzo dei Signoria when the government of the city fell into the hands of commercial magnates (*Signori*). It became the Palazzo Ducale when the first Medici duke moved into it from the old family *palazzo* and finally, when he moved out to his splendid new home on the other side of the river, it became simply the Palazzo Vecchio.

Its interior belies that grim exterior. The flower-bright courtyard, with its copy of an enchanting fountain by Verrochio, is a delight. The portentous **Salone dei Cinquecento** was built for the Republican *Council of 500* introduced by Savonarola in 1496. It was transformed into a throne room for Cosimo I by Vasari, who produced vast, rather tasteless but historically fascinating frescoes lauding the exploits of the Medici. Finally it served as the first parliament of a united Italy when Florence briefly became the Italian capital in 1863.

Although the Palazzo still functions as Florence's town hall, most of the historic rooms, including the Medici suite and the grim little cell where Savonarola was held before his execution in the Piazza below, are usually open to the public.

Adjoining the Piazza are the immense galleries of the **Uffizi**, running round the entire **Piazzale degli Uffizi** to link up with the Loggia dei Lanzi back in the Piazza della Signoria. Mental indigestion is an inevitable hazard in any Italian tour. It achieves acute form in Florence,

acutest of all in the Uffizi. The only possible cure is avoidance, to fight down the temptation to look at every picture.

Since the terrorist explosion nearby in 1993, most rooms have reopened but some works are being restored and others have been moved out of chronological sequence. Only the famous Vasari Corridor remains closed "indefinitely". It is a triumph of Florentine spirit that over 80 percent of the works are currently on display.

The overall scheme of the gallery is chronological, thus making it possible to pick out groups or periods. Which to choose can only be a matter of opinion and personal taste.

The Uffizi does present an unrivalled opportunity to follow the development of Renaissance art from Cimabue (whose *Virgin in Majesty* was painted when Giotto was still a little boy) onward through to the mannered works of the late Cinquecento.

Chronologically, the Palazzo Vecchio is the second city hall of Florence. Its predecessor, the **Bargello** (in Via del

Hanging the washing out over the city streets.

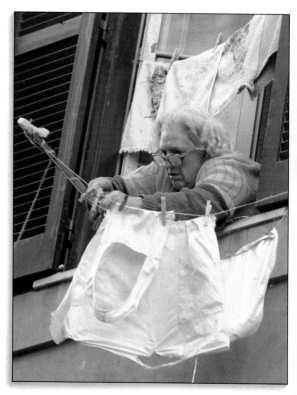

Proconsolo) was built 50 years earlier, in 1250, as the seat of the chief magistrate, the *Podestà*. The office of *Podestà* was common in all medieval republics and was an attempt to check the endlessly warring factions within a city. He was always a foreigner – that is, from a city at least 80 km (50 miles) away – appointed for one year only but given supreme power in that year.

The Bargello was therefore, in effect, police headquarters – reflected in its forbidding exterior. The elegant, but grim, courtyard was frequently the scene of public executions. Here they followed the curious custom of painting the effigies of criminals with details of their crime, sometimes in doggerel verse. The Bargello is now a museum specialising in sculptures; it has a rich collection with works by artists like Brunelleschi, Michelangelo, Cellini, Donatello among many others, but it is not nearly as bewildering as the Uffizi.

Four centuries of history: Just west of the Piazza della Signoria is a loosely associated group of three buildings which takes you across some four centuries of Florentine history, from the embattled Middle Ages to the era of ducal control. The **Palazzo di Parte Guelfa** (just off the Via del Terme) was the headquarters of the all-powerful Guelf Party which, after the defeat and expulsion of the Ghibellines, completely ruled the city. The Palazzo was built in the 13th century, but subsequently enlarged many times – an indication of its expanding status in Florence.

The **Palazzo Davanzati** in the Via Porta Rossa is the earliest example of a patrician's home adapting to a more comfortable and safer age. Built about 1330, its painted walls and ceilings are excellent examples of Trecento work serving to soften and brighten domestic architecture, turning a fort into a home.

Nearby, the lively **Mercato Nuovo** belongs to another world. "Nuovo" is only relative, for the elegant covered market was built around 1550. It is still a popular shopping place, particularly for visitors looking for some genuine memento (high quality leather goods,

Brunelleschi's dome needs a good head for heights

for example) instead of tacky souvenirs. Here is the **Porcellino**, the amiable bronze boar, whose snout is polished to gleaming gold by the rubbing of visitors who touch it as a means of ensuring a return to the city on the Arno.

The religious centre: It is characteristic of the Florentines that the main artery of their city, the street which links the two great monuments of the Palazzo Vecchio and the cathedral, does not bear some grand impressive name. It is still known as the Street of the Hosiers – Via Calzaiuoli – after the trade of the stocking-knitters who were concentrated here. It still specialises in footwear. The guilds were concentrated in this area: on the left of the street is **Orsanmichele**, the guild church. Its exterior is an open-air art gallery: each guild made itself responsible for one section and commissioned an artist to decorate it.

The enormous size of the **cathedral** (it can hold 20,000 people) is emphasised by the smallness of the square in which it is placed, and the narrowness of the streets which enter it. At no point can one take in the whole: instead there are a series of glimpses – blinding, multi-coloured glimpses, for in decorating the exterior the Florentines departed from their usual restraint, and indulged themselves in a riot of coloured marble.

Despite the cathedral's dominating presence, the little **baptistry** in front of it easily holds its own. The Florentines particularly revered the baptistry, the oldest building in the city. It was built on, or reconstructed from, a seventh-century building sometime between the years 1060 and 1120 and served as the cathedral of Florence until 1228 when it was relegated to the role of baptistry.

Dante was among the eminent Florentines baptised there (he nearly drowned in the great font) and the wealthy Wool Guild (*Calimala*) lavished vast sums on its interior. In particular, they commissioned the superb Venetian mosaics which decorate the interior of the cupola.

The *Calimala* then turned their attention to the three great doors, first commissioning a Pisan to create bronze doors for the south entrance, then initiating a competition for the other two doors, which was won by Lorenzo Ghiberti. There is no mistaking the second pair, which took Ghiberti 27 years to create and which Michelangelo described as the "Gates of Paradise", for there is always a little knot of people standing staring at them. But the present panels are newly-installed copies. The original panels are in the **Museo dell'Opera del Duomo** while the competiton panels are in the Bargello.

The two doors are divided into 10 panels, each representing a scene from the Old Testament. Round the panels are heads representing the Sibyls and the Prophets. To get an idea of the incredible detail, and the precision to which Ghiberti worked, look for his self-portrait. It is half-way down on the right-hand side of the left-hand door and, though only a few inches high, is a perfect portrait – a little, balding man peering knowingly out, rather like an inhabitant from another dimension looking into our world.

It took the Florentines over 400 years

The old streets are paved and narrow.

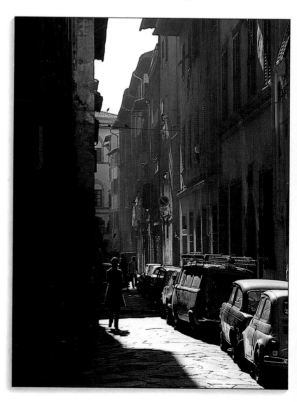

to decide just what kind of facade they wanted for the west front of the cathedral – the side immediately facing the baptistry. Again and again both artists and the city fathers came up with some scheme which satisfied nobody (when the first Medici pope, Leo X, visited his native city in 1515 they even erected a cardboard front for it). The present front was designed in 1887 and has inevitably come in for criticism.

After the multi-coloured splendour of the freshly restored exterior, the interior of **Santa Maria del Fiore** (the cathedral's official name) comes at first as a disappointment. Many of the treasures have been removed and are now in the Museo dell' Opera del Duomo (on the eastern side of the Piazza). The overall colour scheme of the interior is muted, rather muddy, coming to life only at the time of religious festivals when immense crimson banners are hung on the walls and pillars.

But the relative lack of architectural detail allows the eye to pick out the remaining treasures which highlight the city's history. High on the wall immediately to the left of the entrance are two large murals of soldiers. The right-hand one is of an Englishman, John Hawkwood, a mercenary soldier or *condottiero* who first attacked Florence for his paymasters and then became the city's Captain-General in 1375. It was intended to erect a monument to him, but thriftily the Signoria settled for this clever *chiaroscuro* imitation which gives the impression of a three-dimensional monument, painted by Uccello in 1436.

Further along the same aisle is the painting *Dante Declaiming the Divine Comedy* by Michelino. On Dante's right in the painting are Hell and Purgatory (the latter looking rather like a wedding cake) while on his left is a contemporary view of the city's major monuments, looking as they do today. For years readings from the *Comedy* used to be given in the cathedral during Lent, a fact which would doubtless have given Dante wry amusement, and in 1465 this painting was commissioned to mark the second anniversary of his death.

The Duomo behind a forest of TV aerials

The cathedral's greatest treasure is the *Pietà* by Michelangelo, which is now in the museum. He sculpted it for his own tomb in 1550, though it was never finished. It is entirely different from his earlier, and perhaps more famous *Pietà* in St Peter's in Rome; where that is all calm, resigned acceptance, this is simply the utter defeat of death.

In the nearby **New Sacristy**, Lorenzo the Magnificent took refuge on Easter Sunday morning in 1478 when the Pazzi Conspirators wounded him and murdered his brother Giuliano during High Mass. (One of the murderers was later hanged from a window of the Bargello and Leonardo da Vinci painted the dangling corpse, carefully noting the clothes it was wearing.)

If you have a head for heights, ascend to the gallery of the **dome**. It is not for vertigo sufferers, for the gallery is narrow and the balustrade low, but only here can Brunelleschi's stupendous achievement be fully appreciated. It was originally intended to cover the interior of the dome with mosaic, which would have emphasised its soaring majesty; instead Vasari was commissioned to cover it with bold allegories, which were restored in 1994.

Memories of the Medicis: A few streets to the northwest of the cathedral is the heartland of Medicean Florence. Here is the **Medici Palace** and the church of **San Lorenzo** with the Medici tombs. The main facade of the palace is on the Via Cavour, one of the few streets in Florence to have changed its name – it was known as the Via Larga at the time of the Medici.

The palace (now known as the **Medici-Riccardi** from the name of the family to whom the Grand Duke Ferdinand sold it in the 17th century) is dignified but not ostentatious. It still has the look of a fortress about it, particularly in the facade of the ground floor with its massive blocks of "rustic" masonry. It is today the Prefecture of Florence but the Medici chapel and the Medici Museum are open to the public.

The museum contains various mementoes of the family, including the **Statues in the Piazza della Signoria.**

poignant death-mask of Lorenzo, but it is the chapel which contains one of the brightest jewels in the Medici crown, the newly-restored *Procession of the Magi* by Benozzo Gozzoli, painted in 1469. This painting has been reproduced again and again, for it breathes the essential spirit of the Florentine Renaissance in its mixture of real figures of identifiable people, historical re-creation and sheer delight in colour.

The immense procession, winding its way through a delightfully improbable landscape, is led by a handsome, richly dressed youth on horseback – the young Lorenzo. Behind him comes his grandfather, Cosimo, soberly dressed, attended by a black servant. Other members of the family are in the group – which includes the painter himself, with his name inscribed on his hat. In the distance is the Medici country Villa Cafaggiolo – and a couple of camels to remind the observer that the picture is set in the Middle East!

Franciscan church of Santa Croce.

To go from this painting in the chapel to the **New Sacristy** in **San Lorenzo**, which Michelangelo designed, is to go from dawn to sunset. This is not simply because the colours in the Sacristy are muted, or that it is a mausoleum for the Medici. It is because Michelangelo created his incomparable commemorative sculptures in bitterness and defeat, mourning that the republic he worshipped had been destroyed by the Medici pope Clement VII. Under this pope's orders, he was executing memorials not to the great Lorenzo the Magnificent, his old patron, but to a worthless young man who was a nephew of the Pope and another insignificant member of the younger generation.

The two tombs are graced with the extraordinarily symbolic figures of *Dawn*, *Dusk*, *Night* and *Day* conveying to the observer an unforgettable feeling of uneasiness, of sadness, of loss. In one of his sonnets, Michelangelo put these words into the mouth of *Night*:

Sweet is sleep to me and
even more to be of stone,
while wrong and shame endure.
To be without sight or sense

is a most happy chance for me.
Therefore do not rouse me.
Hush! Speak low.

Black and white friars: The three great buildings of Santa Maria Novella, San Marco and Santa Croce are widely separated in the city. **Santa Maria Novella** is the first major building encountered by a visitor coming in by train. When first built, it was in vineyards outside the city walls. **Santa Croce** is on the far eastern side of the city, a little beyond the Palazzo Vecchio, while **San Marco** is in the north.

They are grouped together here because they illustrate a truth about Florence, in the absence of which even the most splendid buildings lose something of their significance. The truth is that religion was a driving force probably even stronger than commerce or the desire for self-aggrandisement, a force that on more than one occasion nearly drove the city to destruction.

Santa Maria Novella and San Marco are Dominican foundations, Santa Croce is Franciscan, and the difference between them illustrates the two sides of the Latin character. The Dominicans, taking after their harsh, intolerant Spanish founder, were great persecutors of heretics. They delighted in the Latin pun on their name – *Domini canes* – the "hounds of the Lord," symbolised in paintings and stained glass by black and white dogs. The Franciscans, on the other hand, followed the precepts of their founder, Francis of Assisi, and achieved their objectives not by fire and sword, but by persuasion and love.

The church of **Santa Maria**, begun in 1246, is the most important example of Italian Gothic, the style which preceded the Renaissance. Designed by Dominican monks, though dignified and indeed majestic, it reflects their gloomy preoccupations: striped like a tiger, the family chapels are sombre and overwhelming, their murals little more than illustrations of sermons. The **Spanish Chapel** carries this to extremes, with its murals dedicated to the 13th-century theologian, Thomas Aquinas, who was, of course, a Dominican.

The Spanish Chapel now lies within the cloister museum adjoining the church, as do Uccello's frescoes. In the church itself are Masaccio's *Trinity* and the chapel is frescoed by Fra Filippino Lippi and Ghirlandaio.

Decorations in the church were carried out well into the Renaissance, with work by Brunelleschi among others, so there is a lightening of the spirit. But the overall impression is a somewhat gloomy one, with a rather threatening air. It was in Santa Maria, incidentally, that Boccaccio's seven young maidens met in the spring of 1348, where they were joined by three young men and launched the comedy of *The Decameron.*

Ironically, the convent of **San Marco** was almost entirely rebuilt with money provided by Cosimo de' Medici – ironically, because San Marco became the headquarters of the friar Girolamo Savonarola, who was the greatest and most determined enemy of Cosimo's grandson, Lorenzo. Cosimo engaged his own favourite architect, who had designed the Palazzo Medici, to build San Marco and eventually spent more than

Feeding the birds outside Santa Croce.

50,000 florins upon it, as well as presenting it with a magnificent library.

Bonfire of the vanities: Savonarola was Prior of San Marco from 1491 until his execution in 1498. During those eight years he totally dominated Florence, nearly succeeded in overthrowing the Medici and presented a challenge the papacy. The vivid portrait of him by Fra Bartolommeo, which can be seen in San Marco, shows a man with a forceful but ugly face, a great beaked nose and burning eyes.

Contemporary reports of his sermons show that they were only average in content and delivery. It was their burning sincerity which moved his audience, coupled with the fact that his prophecies of damnation seemed to come true with the French invasion of Italy, and occupation of Florence in 1494.

The Florentines, ever responsive to novelty, responded to this harsh, austere retainer. When he ordered them to cleanse their bodies and homes of the Devil's frivolities, they burnt their precious ornaments on a vast bonfire in the Piazza della Signoria. The great pile represented not only a fascinating cross-section of contemporary art, but also a substantial cash value, and a Venetian merchant, who happened to be present offered 22,000 florins cash for the objects. The Florentines responded by throwing his own portrait on the pile before setting light to it.

There was, naturally, a strong reaction. Just a year after that triumphant *auto-da-fe*, Savonarola's power crumbled. The people abandoned him to the powerful enemies who had been waiting for this moment. He confessed that he had been deluded and his visions false. They hanged him, with two of his disciples, in the Piazza della Signoria and burnt the bodies afterwards.

The **Convent of San Marco** is now a museum. The prize exhibits are, perhaps, the murals of Fra Angelico, himself a Dominican but one who brought a delicacy to his work quite at variance with the austere tenets of that order. Each of the friars' cells is graced by one of his murals and at the head of the stairs

Souvenir stall.

is the most famous of them all, the *Annunciation*, where he almost achieves the impossible in showing how a young girl receives the news that she is to be the Mother of God. Savonarola's cell is laid out as he knew it, complete with desk and elegant, but decidedly uncomfortable-looking chair.

The great **Piazza** in front of Santa Croce was a particularly favoured place for such large-scale activities as horse races and tournaments. It was here that Lorenzo de' Medici held the most sumptuous tournament of all on the occasion of his marriage.

"To follow the custom, and do like others, I gave a tournament on the Piazza Santa Croce at great cost," he recorded complacently. "I find that about 10,000 ducats was spent upon it." The square is now dominated by a statue of Dante, whose monument was erected within the church.

Santa Croce, begun by Arnolfo di Cambio in 1294 and with the lightness and elegance associated with Franciscan churches, is the pantheon of Florence.

And, indeed, of Italy since so many of the country's illustrious dead now rest here. The tomb of Michelangelo is here, designed by Vasari and invariably with a little bunch of flowers laid upon it. Here also are the graves of Ghiberti and Galileo; of Machiavelli, who died in 1527. Among these great Italians is a solitary Englishman, John Catrick, Bishop of Exeter, who came on an embassy from King Henry V in 1419 and died in the city. And crowning all are the frescoes of Giotto. Santa Croce's 500th anniversary in 1994–95 was designed to coincide with the conclusion of a major restoration programme.

Across the river: The Florentines look upon their river with decidedly mixed feelings. It has brought wealth but it has also brought danger for it is entirely unpredictable.

In summer it can shrink to nothing more than a trickle along a dried-up bed. As Mark Twain put it: "It would be a very plausible river if they would pump some water into it. They all call it a river, and they honestly think it is a river, do

Entertainer outside the Palazzo Vecchio.

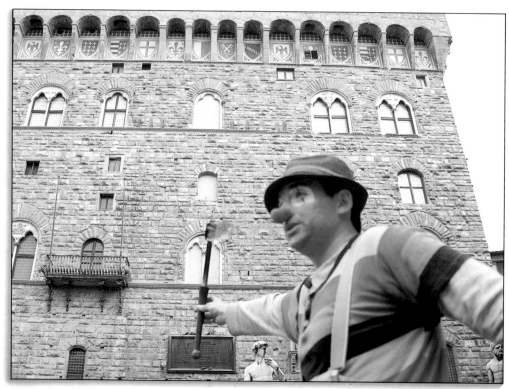

these dark and bloody Florentines. They even help out the delusion by building bridges over it. I do not see why they are too good to wade."

In winter, however, the Arno becomes a raging brown torrent. As recently as 1966 it flooded the city, causing great damage—probably the worst flood since the great inundation of 1330 destroyed the ancient Roman bridge.

The present bridge, the **Ponte Vecchio**, was erected by Taddeo Gaddi some time after 1360 and has become virtually a symbol of Florence itself. Fortunately, the Germans spared it when they blew up every other Florentine bridge in their retreat to the north during World War II. It bears, therefore, the same appearance that it has borne for six centuries. Even the goldsmiths and jewellers who throng it today were first established there in the time of Duke Cosimo I.

It was for this same Medici that Vasari built the extraordinary gallery that runs from the Uffizi to the Pitti across the Ponte Vecchio, making a physical as well as symbolic link between the two centres of Medicean power. In his film, *Paisà*, Roberto Rosellini shot an unforgettable sequence of the fighting that took place along this gallery during the German retreat, which caused damage so severe that the gallery has been closed until recent years.

Opposition to the Medici: The part of Florence beyond the river, the **Oltrarno**, has a character all of its own. It was not even a part of the city until an expansion of the walls in the 12th century encompassed it. Here the nobles gathered in the 14th century to make their last stand against the victorious populace who would henceforth run the city until the Medici grip tightened.

Here, in the 15th century, was centred the opposition to the Medici, spearheaded by the Pitti family. It was they who built the **Pitti Palace**, the most grandiloquent of all Florentine buildings which, by the irony of history, eventually became the seat of government for the Medici dukes themselves.

The Pitti Palace flaunts itself, a vast

Benozzo Gozzoli's *Journey of the Magi* (1459–61) fresco in the chapel, Palazzo Medici-Riccardi.

cliff of golden-brown stone enclosing on three sides an equally vast *cortile*, the whole being the antithesis of Florentine restraint. The visitor, crossing that arrogant, shadeless approach on an Italian summer's day, might well feel that there is a lot to be said for Florentine restraint.

The Pitti was built after 1440 to the design of the Medicean architects Brunelleschi and Michelozzo, but it was specifically planned to eclipse Medicean grandeur. According to Machiavelli, Luca Pitti had no scruples about laying his hands on public funds to build his palace, and even offered asylum to criminals who could either pay or work.

The Medici, however, triumphed over Luca Pitti; he was pardoned, but ruined, and the palace was still unfinished when his descendants sold it to the Medici in 1549. It was then completed to an immense design and in due course became one of the royal palaces of the kings of Italy.

It is today a museum and art gallery on probably an even greater scale than the Uffizi, with its magnificent art collections, and sumptuously decorated rooms, including the recently opened State Apartments.

An excellent antidote to the overwhelming splendours of the Pitti are the enchanting **Boboli Gardens** attached to them. Begun by Duke Cosimo in 1549, they are not only an attraction themselves with their fountains and grottoes and shady walks, but provide exquisite views of Florence from gradually rising ground. The grottoes have statues by Bandinelli and Giambologna, and there is a 17th-century amphitheatre behind which is Neptune's pond with a bronze statue by Stoldo Lorenzo.

The **Via Romana**, which runs past the Pitti Palace, goes to the **Porta Romana**, providing an artery from the centre of the city, via the Ponte Vecchio, to the outside world. The gates of Florence were more than a means of entry and exit. The larger ones, like the great Porta Romana, built in 1328, were both a garrison and a customs post, collecting dues on all the goods that came into the city whether they were silks from far

Boboli Gardens, dating from the 16th century.

Cathay or farm produce from just down the road.

The 14th-century writer Franco Sachetti tells a tale of a farmer who tried to smuggle eggs, hidden in his baggy breeches. Tipped off by the farmer's rival, the gate guards courteously insisted that he should be seated.

The southern section of Florence outside the remainder of the city wall is doubly poignant; it was here that the republic of Florence came to an end in 1529 when the combined armies of Pope Clement VII and the Emperor Charles V besieged the city. The area is a reminder, though a rapidly fading reminder, that Florence is a country town. A brisk walk along Via di San Leonardo, for instance, will take you from the very heart of the city out into vineyards, olive groves and maize fields.

The Ponte Vecchio and Ponte San Trinità span the Arno.

Threading its way through this rural scene is the last remnant of Florence's **city wall**, golden-brown among the green. Michelangelo acted as defence adviser during the last, frantic days of the republic.

The story goes that he hid in the belfry of the Church of San Niccolò when the city capitulated, but gave himself up when Pope Clement offered to pardon him if he would complete the work on the Medici tombs.

And here, just outside the walls of Florence, is the great set piece, the city itself, viewed from the **Piazzale Michelangelo**. You can get to it from the Porta Romana along the enchanting Viale dei Colli, constructed in the 19th century, or else by climbing up from the river, past the Porta San Niccolò, taking the winding paths through the gardens to the Piazzale.

Another 19th-century construction, adorned with bronze copies of Michelangelo's statues, the Piazzale is the one place no visitor should miss. From it is visible the entire panorama of the city, looking much as it would have done in the time of the Medici, despite the vast convulsions of the intervening centuries. Towering above it is **San Miniato al Monte**, one of the loveliest Romanesque churches in Tuscany.

A DAY IN THE LIFE OF THE CITY

Restless Florence wakes up to the soothing whirring of the Pulizia Stradale water machines. At 6am abandoned cars are towed away from the Piazza del Duomo so that the street cleaning can begin. The bars gradually fill with a democratic mix of Florentines enjoying a coffee, brioche and a glance at *La Nazione*'s entertainments page. Just before 8am, students gather around Piazza San Marco in the vain hope of squeezing into an inadequately small lecture hall.

In fine weather, students and executives alike weave into work on *motorini*, far easier to park than cars. Thanks to a partial ban on city centre traffic, Florence is becoming a pedestrian's paradise and a driver's nightmare, at least during the day. The traffic may all run in the opposite direction once Florence's satellite city is built: its part-sponsor, Fiat, should ensure adequate parking.

As the early cool turns humid, the air-conditioned shops near Via Tornabuoni open their elegant doors for business. Even for those who choose to patronise home-bred designers, the choice is dazzling: under a Raspini coat, a sombre Coveri suit can be paired with Ferragamo shoes, a Pucci headscarf and a Gucci bag and belt. By eleven, the smart morning coffee crowd surges into Giacosa.

Those with *tanto da fare* (lots of work to do) opt for repeated trips to more plebeian establishments where local or international affairs can be picked to pieces over an *espresso* or four. Over in Via Cavour, the *funzionari* (civil servants) from the provincial administration may be swapping insults over more *espressi*. Outside the post office, the senior citizens are gathering by the newsstand to while away the morning in idle but impassioned debate.

The peckish sneak into nearby *Cantinetta Antinori* for an early rustic lunch in palatial surroundings. Like most of the Florentine nobility, the Antinori are no longer *rentiers* but entrepreneurs, consolidating empires in wine, food, fashion or crafts. To the Tuscan aristocracy, their produce is sacred: when a foreign neighbour accidentally damaged a few Antinori olive trees, the family sued.

On a warm day, office workers are inspired only by an ice cream in the shade while overheated tourists swelter in the midday heat of the Ponte Santa Trinità. The Ponte Vecchio is left to *giovanotti* hunting for naive foreign art students. Florentines with more than an hour to spare voluntarily double their daily travelling time by heading home for *pasta* and *riposo*, the latter variously interpreted as anything from watching TV cartoons to simply sleeping. At the tail end of the rush come hordes of starving school children: no packed lunches here since the school day finishes at 1.30 pm.

For those who are stuck in town, lunch is a *pasta primo* at the counter or a *crostone ai carciofi* eaten in a *birreria*. In Giubbe Rosse in Piazza della Repubblica, employees, entrepreneurs and local politicians grab a quick *ravioli* in a restaurant which was once the haunt of *Risorgimento* revolutionaries and later became a salon for Futurist painters.

Around two o'clock, disconsolate tourists discover they have just missed both Michelangelo's and Donatello's statues of *David*, plus everything in San Marco. The centre by now is semi-deserted; the only shop still open is the *Upim* department store.

Fortunately not all culture comes to a halt in the afternoon: colourful street banners advertise the latest exhibitions. Art lovers are drawn to the magnificent sculptures of nudes and horses at the Marino Marini museum or to the latest photographic exhibition at the Rucellai's frescoed *palazzo*. Florentine cultural influence may have declined of late, but the city is still a major displayer of works of art.

The third rush hour gets under way. In sleepy Oltrarno, gallery attendants and shopkeepers wake up over a coffee and a conversation about the next Florence-Juventus football clash. If business is slack, Santa Croce leather workers and San Frediano silversmiths abandon shop and head likewise for the nearest bar.

By early evening, people watchers are already sipping *aperitivi* in Rivoire, the elegant bar on Piazza della Signoria. A furious battle recently divided Florentines. The *Comune* wished to recover the Piazza with grey paving stones, while traditionalists favoured the *Cinquecento* red herringbone design. The late-lamented Emilio Pucci led the campaign, arguing against "a sad grey stone blanket" but the council won.

After seven o'clock, the city again becomes a traffic hazard. Piazza della Repubblica is the first stop on the youth circuit of *pizzerie*, *gelaterie* and noisy video bars. Workers head home to Campo di Marte or Sesto, bank managers and retailers to Bagno a Ripoli, while wealthy entrepreneurs and designers return to Bellosguardo or the slopes of Fiesole. Around nine, the streets empty as Florentines disappear into cramped *trattoria*, discreetly elegant *ristoranti* or the white minimalist interiors favoured by Tuscan *nouvelle cuisine*

and music seasons. Although based on a conservative repertoire, Florentine theatre combines foreign classics and Florentine favourites in the Teatro Verdi and Teatro della Compagnia as well as in the grander Teatro Comunale. As for opera and ballet, Florence is no longer considered a "cold piazza". In Fiesole, summer crowds gather to see international opera and ballet companies perform in the atmospheric Roman theatre. In the city below, students flock to Forte di Belvedere's open-air film festival.

Film buffs and inveterate clubbers scan *Firenze Spettacolo* to see what is on. On a good night, there is Latin American music at Teatro Tenda, rock at Auditorium Flog or Zubin Mehta conducting a *Requiem Mass* by Verdi. Less "cultural" but equally active are the Viali, the streets which

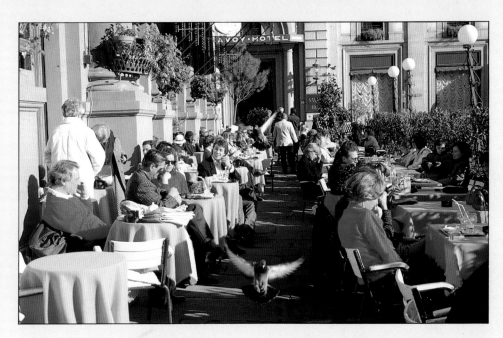

restaurateurs. After dinner, bustling Via Calzaiuoli attracts impromptu mime artists, puppeteers and comedians. A tatty cardboard box signals a new delivery of fake Lacoste T-shirts or African trinkets sold by Senegalese students.

Since Florence is a large garrison town, Florentine evenings need to accommodate hordes of homesick soldiers prowling the streets. After failing to find civilian companionship or thrills, they congregate in the Central Post Office and make sad calls home to Naples or Milan.

Natural culture vultures, Florentines of all classes buy season tickets to the theatre, opera

replaced Florence's town walls. Driving along them at night, try to avoid the inside lane or you may find yourself in a queue for a transvestite rather than the traffic lights. Happily married Florentine men occasionally prefer the services of a luscious transvestite to those of the distinctly mundane female prostitutes. But the recent influx of Eastern European prostitutes is seen as a threat by both camps.

By this time the *giovanotti* are watching a light show or eyeing the American students at the Space Electronic disco; Florentines drink a final Fernet Branca *digestivo*, the *borghesi* at home and the yuppies at a jazz club or at Dolce Vita in Piazza del Carmine. Arty eccentrics linger on at Garga's *trattoria* where poems and paintings are created late into the night.

Preceding pages: pavement artist, Piazzale Michelangelo. **Left**, Florence's elegant shops. **Above**, *aperitivi* in the Piazza della Repubblica.

FLORENCE AND PRATO PROVINCES

The province of Florence is full of towns and villages perched on steep, cypress-covered hills. Below them, straggling down to the bottom of the valleys, are the vineyards that have been producing some of the most famous wines in Italy since the Renaissance – red Chianti and Carmignano and white Malvasia and Trebbiano.

This delightful legacy from the past is almost as important as the historical and artistic heritage of the people this region which was the most advanced in Europe throughout the Middle Ages and the Renaissance era.

North of Florence: The best place from which to observe the mountains of the Mugello is a seat in the Roman amphitheatre at **Fiesole**. These mountains to the north of Florence once provided hideouts for ruthless medieval barons who occasionally descended into the valleys from their fortified lairs to sack and pillage. At first Fiesole could fend for itself. But in 1125 it was the Florentines who attacked the city and completely destroyed it, leaving only the Duomo and the bishop's palace. In its heyday as one of the chief towns of the Etruria Propria, secure on its hilltop, it could claim to be the mother of Florence itself; now it is little more than a highly refined and slightly subdued suburb, protected from the urban sprawl surrounding Florence by the steep hill on which it stands.

From Florence the Via Bolognese, the SS65, climbs up to Fiesole past villas built on sites which are desirable for their magnificent views down into the valley to Florence, and for the cool breeze, the lack of which makes Florence itself so unattractive during the hot summer months.

On the Via Vecchia Fiesolana is the **Villa Medici** which was built, by Michelozzo between 1458 and 1461, on Cosimo il Vecchio's instructions for his youngest son, Giovanni . The villa was favoured particularly by Lorenzo Il Magnifico who entertained his humanist friends here.

Today the interior of the villa no longer retains its original decoration; much of it was swept away in 1772 and replaced with the English Chinoiserie style by Robert Walpole, Earl of Oxford. But the terraced gardens retain their original lines; these can be visited though the villa is closed.

The road climbs on up to Fiesole's centre, the lively main piazza, named after Mino da Fiesole, a Quattrocento sculptor and a native of the town. Bars and *pizzerie* surround the Duomo which contains some of the best examples of Mino da Fiesole's works – the tomb of the Bishop Salutati and an altar front in the Capella Salutati. The **Duomo** itself dates from 1024 to 1028 and contains frescoes and sculpture by lesser known, though excellent, artists.

On the west side of Piazza Mino da Fiesole is the 11th-century bishop's palace and the Seminary, both with fragments of the Etruscan acropolis wall in their garden, and to the east is the Palazzo Pretorio. The Piazza itself was once the site of the Roman Forum and a road leads from it to the Roman Amphitheatre which was excavated in 1911.

Behind the Duomo, in Via Duprè, is the tiny **Bandini Museum** containing an art gallery with a fairly wide and representative selection of paintings from the early and middle Renaissance, as well as some School of della Robbia terracottas.

The route to Fiesole passes through the village of **San Domenico**. Apart from its magnificent view of Florence, it is well-known for its monastery and church of San Domenico di Fiesole. Both contain important remains of an art collection much vandalised during World War II. In the first chapel on the north side of the church is *Madonna with Angels and Saints* by Fra Angelico, who lived in the monastery; in the chapter house is his *Crucifixion*.

The Via Badia leads to the **Badia Fiesolana** which was the cathedral of Fiesole until 1028. The present building was left unfinished in 1464 and it incorporates the facade of a smaller Roman-esque church embedded into it. This earlier facade is an excellent example of the Florentine Romanesque style which uses as surface decoration layers of green and white marble. There is a tiny open piazza in front of the church where you can sit and admire the view of Florence.

On the northern side of Fiesole, on the road that winds through the olive groves to Olmo, is a turning on the right to **Settignano**. It is probably easier to reach this village, straggling around its hillside, from Florence via the Lungarno del Tempio, though the road from Fiesole is more diverting, with delightful views of the Tuscan countryside – rows of cypresses, oak woods and old terraced olive groves vanishing into the hot, blue, afternoon haze.

Settignano has been home to many illustrious people. At the Villa Buon-arroti, Michelangelo spent his youth. At the **Villa I Tatti** lived Bernard Berenson (1865-1959), the American art historian who restored the villa to house a large collection of Renaissance paintings eventually inherited by Harvard

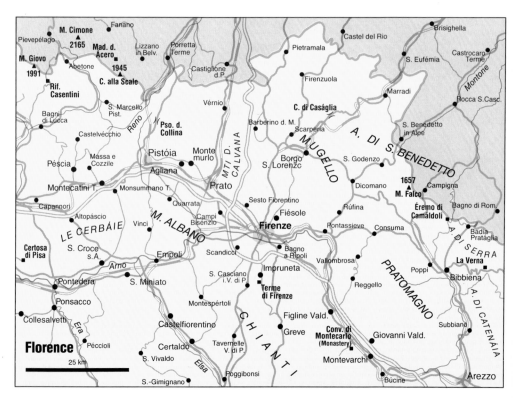

University. Other well-known residents of Settignano included Desiderio da Settignano, an important Renaissance sculptor, Tommaseo, D'Annunzio and Eleanora Duse.

A fine Renaissance villa which survives here with most of its original garden intact is the 15th-century **Villa Gamberaia**. The inspiration for this remarkable building was Pliny and it was consciously modelled on descriptions of his own Tuscan villa. It also exploited descriptions of the ideal garden as advocated by Alberti, on whose advice it was thought best to build a house on a light, airy and breeze-swept site.

All around are small wayside shrines and broken-down fences; buy a bottle of the local farm wine, some bread and a hunk of *pecorino* cheese and spend a lazy afternoon looking down at the view over the village.

Settignano is also richly endowed with ecclesiastical treasures: **Santa Maria** has a 16th-century pulpit by Buontalenti and a white terracotta *Madonna with the Child and two Angels* by Andrea della Robbia; and **San Martino a Mensola** contains a triptych by Taddeo Gaddi.

The SS65 from Fiesole climbs northwards to Pratolino and to the **Parco Demidoff**. At one time the park (in fact, a vast garden) contained the Villa Pratolino, later named the Villa Demidoff, which was built in 1569 and demolished in 1820 as a misguided economy measure.

Practically nothing of the gardens of the former Medicean villa survive except for Giambologna's massive statue, *The Apennine*. This huge stone monster was once an important feature in an arrangement of watercourses and fountains which lead down the hill behind the house.

Today the garden is wild and unkempt and in dank corners under thick undergrowth can be found the remains of stone terraces, broken statues and old urns. Be warned: the custodian here keeps strange hours, so check the opening times in advance of a visit.

The Mugello Valley: Situated above Pratolino is the Servite monastery of

Romanesque facade of Badia Fiesolana.

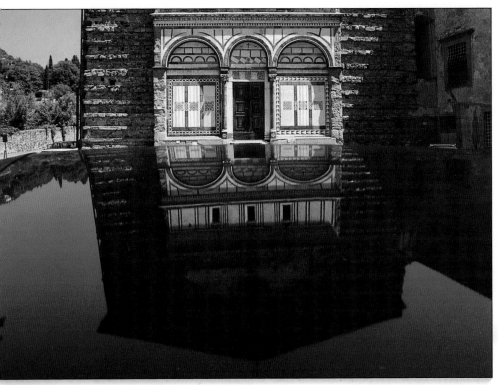

Monte Senario. Built in 1233 it was a retreat for wealthy Florentines who had renounced the material world, preferring to live a contemplative life of fasting and prayer. Magnificent views over the valley to the Sieve make the isolation of the local hotels more attractive.

The **Mugello** has great associations with the Medici; it is the region from which they originated and it is one of the regions on which they lavished a lot of attention. In 1451 Cosimo di Medici had Michelozzo alter the old fortress of **Cafaggiolo** in **Val de Sieve**, creating a country retreat. He did the same at the old Castello del Trebbio, slightly further to the south.

The run-down appearance of the exterior of **Villa Cafaggiolo**, which has lost one of its towers, hides a magnificent interior Most of the interior is used for the storage of hay, a strange use for such an important building. It also suffers today because of the siting of a sliproad to the Bologna–Florence motorway just in front of the building. How the mighty have fallen.

Castello del Trebbio, by contrast, has a much more satisfactory existence. It has been extensively restored and more than any other 15th-century Tuscan villa, retains the feudal atmosphere of a Medici villa. Large parts of the gardens are still intact – due to the remote siting of the villa on a hill in the middle of a large private estate. (The gardens are open on weekdays, but the interior can only be visited on the first Tuesday of each month.)

Facing Villa Cafaggiolo, high on a thickly wooded outcrop, is the Medici fortress of **San Martino**, built in 1569 by Lanci and Buontalenti to enable Cosimo I to defend the Florentine state. Today this massive pentagon-shaped castle at the end of a rough track outside San Piero di Sieve is completely derelict. As with Cafaggiolo, a minimum of effort would be needed to restore and repair this building, part of which is open to the public.

Just north of San Piero di Sieve is **Scarperia**, a pristine little town, its clean streets and tidy houses the epitome of

Statue of Giambologna's *L'Appenino* in Villa Demidoff.

civic virtue. Its spotless monuments are rarely visited, yet there is much to see. **Palazzo Pretorio** in the main street is one of the finest examples of 13th-century civil architecture in Tuscany.

The outer facade, decorated with the coats-of-arms of local notables, carved in stone or worked in della Robbia terracotta, faces the Oratorio della Madonna della Piazza in the small rectangular piazza. The latter is a tiny, darkened room in which, over the altar, is a *Madonna and Child* by Taddeo Gaddi.

At the bottom of the main street, near the entrance to the town, is the **Oratorio dei Terremoti** which contains a fresco also of the *Madonna and Child*, said to be by Filippo Lippi. An air of calm hangs over its monuments which gives the visitor a chance to contemplate the paintings and the architecture in silence and without distractions.

A turning on the left of the southern approach to Scarperia wends its way through dense woodlands to the remote **Bosco ai Frati** convent. This Franciscan retreat retains the peace and solitude of the Franciscan ideal that places like Assisi lack; no touring hordes, no postcard sellers, only the peace and quiet offered by a church and its convent in a clearing in the woods.

These buildings were restructured by Michelozzo around 1440 for Cosimo il Vecchio. They house a little-known, large wooden crucifix, gessoed and painted by one of the greatest masters of the Italian Renaissance, Donatello.

West of Florence: Prato, to the north-west of Florence, exactly half-way between Florence and Pistoia, has recently been promoted to provincial status, a fitting tribute to the third largest city in Tuscany and long-time rival of Florence. The city possesses an extraordinary relic: in the Duomo, in Piazza del Duomo, is what is believed to be the girdle of the Virgin Mary. The legends surrounding this relic have been celebrated by Agnolo Gaddi, whose frescoes cover the walls of the Chapel of the Holy Girdle and there is a sculpture by Giovanni Pisano with a statue of the *Madonna and Child* on the altar.

Remnants of demolished Villa Demidoff, Pratolino.

Outside the Duomo is the Pulpit of the Holy Girdle, designed by Donatello and Michelozzo, where on Christmas Day and several other holy days in the year the girdle is exhibited to the faithful (*see pages 118–119*).

The daily activities of Prato are more prosaic than this, however: today the city is renowned for its textile manufacturing industries. Although the trade has made contemporary Prato a rich city, it was already an important centre for textiles in the 12th century and its magnificent monuments are evidence of its former great wealth.

The small, ancient centre of Prato, enclosed within its medieval walls, contains – apart from the Duomo – the **Church of Santa Maria delle Carceri** behind the **Castello dell'Imperatore**. It was begun by Giuliano da Sangallo in 1485 in a Brunelleschian style – an attempt on this architect's part to emulate the great Duomo of Santa Maria del Fiore in Florence. The Castello was built by Frederick II Hohenstaufen in the first half of the 13th century and is unique in Tuscany, taking as its model the Norman castles of Apulia (Puglia).

In the Via Rinaldesca is the **Palazzo Datini** (*circa* 1350), former home of the man who invented the promissory note and founder of the city's riches in the wool trade in the 14th century. His story is told in *The Merchant of Prato* by Iris Origo. Further north in the Piazza Commune is the **Palazzo Pretorio**, Prato's seat of government in the days of its independence and now housing the Galleria Comunale.

To the west of Florence along the Pisa-Florence highway, the first major stop is **Empoli**. The main piazza in this country town is named after Farinata degli Uberti who made a speech to the Ghibelline Parliament in 1260, saving the town from destruction after the Battle of Montaperti. As a result Empoli retains at its centre, around the church of Sant'Andrea, its earliest buildings, some dating back to the 12th century.

Like so many other Tuscan towns it has a great quantity of religious paintings, now housed in the **Museo della**

Hunters seek *cinghiale* (wild boar) and birds.

Collegiata, a collection which ranges from Masolino to Pontormo.

A few miles west of Empoli is **Fucecchio**, another typical ancient Tuscan town the core of which is surrounded by more modern outskirts. A variety of its buildings, including Castruccio's Tower, are worth visiting.

From Empoli, it is fairly easy to visit two important Medici residences, the **Villa Poggio a Caiano** in the town of **Poggio a Caiano** and the **Villa of Artimino** just outside the hilltop village of **Artimino**.

Poggio a Caiano is one of the most magnificent buildings of the 15th century. It was converted by Giuliano da Sangallo for Lorenzo de' Medici between 1480 and 1485, and from its position above the town it dominates the surrounding flat countryside, which of course was Lorenzo's intention. The entire building sits on a continuous loggia which surrounds the house and which supports the *piano nobile*. Lorenzo's son, Giovanni, who eventually became Pope Leo X, continued the building

work, commissioning from the della Robbia family a frieze for the entrance pediment.

Some of the internal decoration is proof that the Florentine leader and his circle were very conscious of modelling themselves on the ancients. Two of the main rooms have scenes from Roman history painted by Andrea del Sarto and Pontormo, into which have been injected matching scenes from the history of the Medici family.

In the 19th century the gardens were converted according to the fashionable English style. They were given romantic temples, an aviary, fountains and a mock-Gothic ruin. Most recently, the villa was used as a country residence by King Umberto of Italy and the few remaining furnishings date from then.

It was also the scene of the ghastly double murder of the Grand Duke Francesco and his wife in 1587. Now the huge bare rooms are sad and desolate and the villa has been converted into a somewhat tawdry museum.

The walled village of **Artimino** is

Coaxing a new-born lamb to its feet.

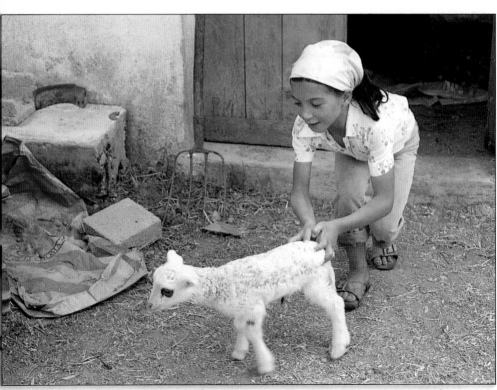

about 11 km (7 miles) away from Poggio a Caiano. Its huge villa was built by Bernardo Buontalenti as a hunting lodge for Ferdinand Medici I in 1594. It stands on a rise connected to the village gates by a tree-lined avenue. Inside is a small Etruscan museum. The heady vapour that hangs over Artimino itself emanates from the many small local wine *fattorie*, seemingly the only means of support in this remote and rustic place.

Half a mile down the hill on the other side of Artimino is the Etruscan cemetery from whose stones the nearby church of Pian di Rosello was built in the seventh century.

From Artimino a tortuous road leads via Carmignano to **Vinci** on the southern slopes of Monte Albano and to the village of Anchiano, the latter the alleged birthplace of Leonardo da Vinci. The entire *raison d'être* of Vinci is to celebrate its most famous son.

The medieval castle of the **Conti Guidi** houses the **Museo Leonardiano**, a museum which exhibits a vast selection of mechanical models built to the exact measurements of Leonardo's drawings. There is also the **Biblioteca Leonardiana**, devoted to the documentation of his life and work. In **Anchiano**, near his rustic birthplace, is another museum featuring the more prosaic mementoes of his life.

Valdarno: To the east of Florence, off the SS70 which goes to Consuma, is a narrow pass which climbs tortuously up the western slope of the Pratomagno hills to the monastery of **Vallombrosa** – 292 metres (958 ft) above sea level in the central Apennines. Founded by San Giovanni Gualberto in the 11th century, this monastery, the first house of the Vallombrosan Order, is surrounded by magnificent woodland of oaks, pines and firs, many of which were planted by the monks themselves.

By the time Gualberto died in 1073 the Vallombrosan Order, part of the Benedictine Rule, was spreading all over Italy. Its power became so great that in 1866 the Order was suppressed and today only four monks remain to say the offices of the church.

Restaurant on the Chianti road.

In the vicinity of Vallombrosa are Romanesque churches worth visiting – **San Pietro** in **Cascia**, **Sant'Agata** in **Arfoli**. There is also the tiny village of **Saltino**, handy in the winter for the ski runs of **Monte Secchieta** which lie above Vallombrosa.

The Chianti: In 1716 a decree issued by the Grand Duke of Tuscany defined the boundaries of the area known as Chianti and established the laws governing the production and sale of wine. Chianti wine became popular in the 15th century, and within 200 years it had become well known.

Today this region is the world's oldest wine-producing league. The Chianti Classico area includes the communes of **Barberino Val D'Elsa**, **Impruneta**, **Greve**, **San Casciano** and **Tavernelle Val D'Elsa**.

Closest to Florence in this area is the town of **Impruneta**, an important sanctuary in the early medieval period when a shrine was erected here to house an image of the Virgin Mary, which was supposed to have been the work of St Luke and believed to be capable of performing miracles. This shrine, the **Basilica di Santa Maria**, with its terracotta tabernacle by Luca della Robbia in Michelozzo's Chapel of the Cross, underwent numerous alterations throughout the centuries, until finally it was badly damaged by a bomb in World War II.

Subsequent restoration and repair to this and to other pre-17th century buildings have meant that Impruneta has retained a great deal of its early character, though without the patina of age. Brunelleschi insisted that the tiles for the roof of the Duomo in Florence be supplied by Impruneta, which is still important as a centre for terracotta production. Vases, bricks and roofing materials are still made here.

South of Impruneta, in the centre of the Chianti area, is **Greve** whose annual September Mostra Mercato del Chianti (Chianti Classico Fair) in Piazza Matteotti attracts much attention. Fairs have been held in the marketplace since the Middle Ages and today the market also does an excellent trade in the Chianti's other main products – extra virgin olive oil, traditional boar sausage and a variety of local handicrafts.

San Casciano in Val di Pesa, another quiet old Chianti town a third of the way along the highway connecting Florence and Siena, is enlivened every February by a Carnival. The town's reputation today rests solely on the great quantity of art works held by the Collegiata Church, the Convent, the Church of St Francis and the Church of the Misericordia – paintings by Simone Martini, Ugolino di Neri, Taddeo Gaddi and Fra Bartolomeo.

The Valdelsa: Because the town of **Castelfiorentino** in the Valdelsa is split between two sites, it has two centres. The older of the two has its origins in the Middle Ages and is located around the Piazza del Popolo.

But now the town's former beauty is somewhat lost among the sprawling modern outskirts while the hill town of **Certaldo**, further to the south, has been saved from being swallowed whole because its upper part, **Certaldo Alto**, is fairly inaccessible. It straddles the summit of a steep hill and is reached by a narrow winding road. Consequently the integrity of the medieval townscape has survived virtually intact. It consists of nothing more than a central street, off which are a series of alleyways.

It is built predominantly of red brick and its claim to fame is that Boccaccio, author of the *Decameron,* came here towards the end of his life and died here in 1375. What is thought to have been his home was restored in 1823, bombed during World War II, and has now been rebuilt and can be visited.

The differences between Certaldo Alto and Certaldo Basso are marked by the silence of the former where, on summer afternoons, the only sounds are footsteps and the distant music of a radio. The town is crowned by the 15th-century Palazzo Pretorio, the front facade of which is studded with terracotta coats of arms. Exploration around the back of the town will reveal the early gateways, the portals of which are still intact and which lead down to steep, narrow approach lanes.

PISTOIA

Pistoia is the smallest province of Tuscany, sandwiched between Lucca and Florence and fought over for centuries by both. It is part fertile plain and part mountains, bordered in the north by the Apennines where Abetone, a popular ski resort, is little more than an hour's drive from the city of Pistoia.

The other major town in the province is Pescia, cradled in the plain of the Valdinievole and famous for its flower production. The province is also important for railway construction, embroidery, furniture making and shoe manufacture. Here too is Montecatini Terme, an elegant international spa town.

Pistoia (population 94,500) is only 37km (22 miles) from Florence and rather unfairly neglected as a result. Its historic heart is a delight which makes it well worth negotiating the surrounding industrial suburbs, and it has enough good hotels tucked away in the medieval streets, as well as excellent restaurants and elegant shops, to make it an attractive alternative base.

If you stay in a hotel in the centre of Pistoia be sure to get a sticker which entitles you to park; cars are otherwise banned so leave yours near Fortezza di Santa Barbara and walk 10 minutes or so to the centre.

The citizens of Pistoia take great pride in their many historic monuments and churches but there is little in the way of the more tawdry tourist trappings. There are shops as glamorous as in Florence or Lucca and the traffic could compete with any town in Italy; but when dusk falls, the lamp-lit shadowy streets of Pistoia still have an authentic medieval atmosphere. Church bells peal, Franciscan monks stride along in their unmistakable brown habits and rope belts, and the stone slabs outside the shops are laid out with goods for sale just as they were in the Middle Ages.

Pistoia was originally a Roman town, founded as a staging post on the Via Cassia, but it was razed to the ground in AD 400 by the invading Longobards. It flourished as an important banking centre during the Middle Ages when most of its important buildings were constructed, but it suffered during the wars between Florence and Lucca, eventually falling under the dominion of Florence. The word pistol apparently derives from Pistoia, named after the daggers known as *pistolese* which were worn by the local soldiers.

The impressive trapeze-shaped walls with bastions and four gates that still encompass the centre of the city were built by the Medici during the 15th century. Happily, the central **Piazza del Duomo** is banned to traffic and, when not full of bustling market stalls (Saturdays and Wednesdays),it is a good place to quietly take stock of Pistoia's riches. (You can pick up a city map from the tourist office in the Palazzo dei Vescovi in the Piazza.)

The **Cathedral of San Zeno** is originally fifth century but was rebuilt in the Romanesque style in the 12th century with a splendid facade of green and white marble stripes. A marble porch

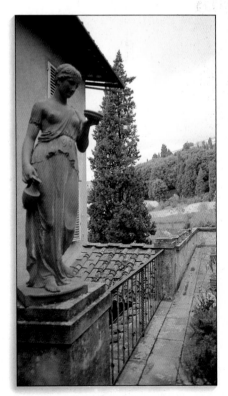

Preceding pages: Villa Garzoni and gardens at Collodi; San Giovanni Fuorcivitas, Pistoia. **Left**, 12th-century Romanesque facade of the cathedral of San Zeno, Pistoia. **Right**, terrace of a Tuscan country villa.

was added later and decorated with an exquisite blue and white Andrea della Robbia bas-relief.

Inside are many medieval frescoes and Renaissance paintings, the tomb of the poet Cino da Pistoia, and – most glorious of all – the massive silver altar in the chapel of San Jacopo (Saint James), decorated with bas-reliefs and statues over a period of two centuries by many different artists, including Brunelleschi. It is a priceless work and usually the chapel is kept locked, so ask the sacristan if you want to take a closer look. Next door, above the tourist office, is the **Cathedral Museum**.

Beside the Duomo is the soaring campanile, originally a watchtower, to which have been added three tiers of green and white Pisan arches reflecting the Duomo facade. Opposite is the 14th-century octagonal **baptistry** of San Giovanni in Corte, designed by Andrea Pisano. It has the most wonderful high brick ceiling and a huge font of many different coloured marbles.

The Piazza is completed by a number of fine Renaissance palaces, including the **Palazzo del Podestà** which is still the city's law court. Opposite is the **Palazzo del Comune** (Town Hall) built in the 13th and 14th century with a harmonious facade of arches and delicately pointed windows, decorated with the ubiquitous Medici crest and a grim black marble head.

Inside is a courtyard and sweeping stairway and sculptures by celebrated modern artist Marino Marini, many of them based on his favourite theme of riders and horses. At the foot of the stairs is his *Rider Miracle* from 1953. Upstairs in the first and second floor rooms is the impressive art collection of the new **Museo Civico**, which includes a rare 13th-century painting of St Francis, a number of 15th-century altarpieces from churches in Pistoia and many delightful polychrome wooden sculptures, such as the 15th-century *Angel* by Francesco di Valdambrino and an exquisite 16th-century *Madonna and Child*, as well as works by many more recent artists.

Octagonal baptistry of San Giovanni in Corte.

To the north of the Piazza Duomo in Piazza Giovanni XII is the **Ospedale del Ceppo**, named after the offering boxes in which alms for the poor were collected. It was built in the 14th century and still functions as a hospital. Above the portico is a brilliantly coloured majolica frieze by Giovanni della Robbia which is well worth observing in detail. In rich blues, greens, yellows and browns it depicts the *Seven Acts of Mercy*: worthy citizens handing out food to the poor, comforting prisoners and the sick, washing the feet of dusty travellers and ministering to the dying. The figures are realistic, and sometimes even humorous, despite the gravity of their occupations.

Pistoia has a large number of churches, many of great architectural interest, some with notable art works – in particular the Pisano pulpits, which are the great pride of the town. A few of the churches are neglected or under restoration, some are closed, some so badly-lit it is impossible to see anything, and some have been so altered and embellished that their interest lies mainly in the way they reveal the different styles and tastes that have emerged over the centuries.

Most are within easy walking distance of each other and a rewarding selection could be visited in a morning's tour, bearing in mind that most will close at midday until three or four o'clock. Alternatively, just drop in whenever you happen to pass one.

Sant'Andrea in the Via Sant'Andrea, is flanked by an enormous spreading pine tree. It has an arcaded facade and reliefs above the central door. Inside is a richly painted wooden ceiling and narrow nave well-lit from the upper clerestory. Here is one of the famous pulpits by Giovanni Pisano, created in 1298 and modelled on the Nicola Pisano pulpit in the Pisa Duomo. The sharply carved marble reliefs border on the melodramatic in their depiction of the life of Jesus and the Last Judgement. In the right of the nave hangs a wooden crucifix, also by Giovanni.

San Bartolemeo in Pantano, in the Piazza San Bartolomeo, is one of

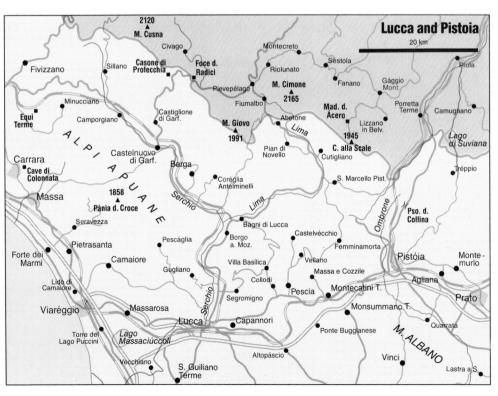

Pistoia's oldest churches, built in the 12th century with a five-bay facade and rich in marble carvings and reliefs; those above the door are based on Roman sarcophagi. Inside there is a reconstructed pulpit by Guido da Como (1250) with marble reliefs showing Christ's nativity, the whole massive construction resting on the backs of men and lions carved out of marble.

In the Via Cavour is the 12th-century church of **San Giovanni Fuorcivitas**, thus named because it was built outside the city walls. It has an elaborate green-and-white striped marble facade and walls in the Pisan style, and inside is light enough to afford a good view of some fine works of art. These include the pulpit created in 1270 by Fra Guglielmo da Pisa, a water stoup by Giovanni Pisano and a touchingly beautiful white glazed terracotta of the *Visitation,* by Luca della Robbia.

The church and monastery of **San Domenico**, in the Piazza Garibaldi, is an example of 13th-century Gothic style and a good illustration of what not to do to a church. Its original windows have been filled in and new ones inserted, and huge paintings have been unaccountably chopped about. But inside are a number of colourful original frescoes and works claimed to be by Rossellino and Bernini.

Opposite San Domenico is **Cappella del Tau**. This former chapel now functions as an artistic monument, containing many darkly dramatic Gothic frescoes on its walls and vaulted ceilings, including a fine fresco of *The Fall.*

Other churches worth including in a visit to Pistoia are Santa Maria del Grazie, San Francesco, San Paolo, and Santa Spirito. But at almost every turn there is *some* architectural find which will enrich a meander through the narrow streets, from a fine *palazzo* to a simple carving over a doorway.

The main shopping streets, with excellent clothes, shoes, leather and jewellery stores, are the Via Cavour, Via Cino, Via Ateo Vannucci and Via Orafi, and it is here that the evening *passeggiata* takes place. In July the *Giostra dell'Orso*

Majolica frieze of *Seven Acts of Mercy* by Giovanni della Robbia, Ospedale del Ceppo.

(Bear Joust) is held in the Piazza del Duomo, a colourful costumed display of a joust between 12 knights and a bear, though the bear is now a prosaic wooden model. About 5 km (3 miles) outside the town, in Via Pieve a Celle, is Pistoia's famous zoo, set in a large pine forest.

The spa towns: West of Pistoia, and most easily accessible via the A11 autostrada are the spa towns, the grandest of which is **Montecatini Terme**, famed throughout Europe for its elegance and luxury. It was rebuilt by the Grand Duke Leopold of Tuscany in the 18th century and has since become a company town with whole avenues of huge spa buildings dispensing waters to drink and treatments ranging from baths and inhalation to the famous mudbaths. You can stroll through the magnificent parks, or sip the waters in marble pavilions – or, of course, you could commit yourself to a complete cure.

Montecatini Alto is the original medieval fortified town above the thermal springs, and can be reached by funicular railway or by road. Although full of

wealthy tourists in high season, it is still a charming and restful place to visit, with a shady walk of chestnut trees around the lower terrace of the village and panoramic views over the plain of the Valdinievole.

The main square, **Piazza Guiseppe Giusti**, has large open cafés. Little remains of the original fortress, although its walls and towers are being restored. It is surrounded by a quiet little park of pine trees with a moving war memorial of cannon and barbed wire. The adjacent church of St Peter has Romanesque origins, but has been hideously restored with its columns and exquisitely carved capitals barely visible for sheets of cheap marble veneer.

Monsummano is the birthplace of the poet Guiseppe Giusti (1809–1850) and the site of a particularly extraordinary spa, a thermal grotto, Grotta Giusti, where the steam treatments are actually taken deep in underground caves.

Driving north of Montecatini along the N633, you arrive at **Marliana** via a stunning mountain road that winds

Pistoia City

500 m

TAKING THE WATERS

Spa treatment in Italy is available on the country's National Health Service, and many Italians are firm believers in the benefits of taking the waters. The spa cure has remained virtually unchanged for hundreds of years, since Papal couriers used to carry the waters to Rome, and Ugolini di Montecatini wrote his treatise on mineral waters in the 14th century.

The initiates bathe in the spa waters, inhale them, steam in underground grottoes, or merely stroll, sipping elegantly, in the marble halls of spa towns such as Montecatini Terme.

Tuscany is the location of a large number of different spas, ranging from open-air hot springs used by local people to luxuriously equipped and medically regulated residential establishments. Most can be visited for a few hours or a day and make a very pleasant diversion during a holiday; but less dilettante practitioners would recommend taking a full cure, which can last for a week or 10 days and is regarded very seriously. The most appealing aspect of it is that you don't really need to have anything wrong with you to take a cure, and it is an excellent restorative way to spend a vacation.

There is plenty of medical evidence for the physical benefits of mineral waters taken externally and internally; thermal treatments are prescribed for skin problems, digestive, urinary and gynaecological ailments, rheumatic problems and respiratory diseases, but it is the concept of the complete cure that is so attractive. All the spas are in the middle of beautiful countryside, surrounded by parks, mountains and lakes and an essential part of the treatment is calm and rest and long gentle walks.

Like the Ancient Romans before them, whole families or groups of friends go off to the spa together, all equipped with voluminous towelling bathrobes and plastic slippers. At Saturnia, near Grosseto, is a newly developed spa on an original Roman site. Now modern Romans come over from Rome for the day to take the waters.

There are large swimming pools, waterfalls and fountains for drinking, all overhung with the acrid smell of sulphur. Visitors spend the day bathing, sitting in deck chairs and snoozing in the sun. Floating in the water are large clumps of slimy green seaweed which the truly dedicated smear over their face and body.

In summer it can be an enervating experience since the water here is very warm; perhaps the best time to go to Saturnia is in winter when it is quiet and the pools steam gently in the frosty air, the cold providing a welcome contrast to the warm waters.

Montecatini Terme is by far the most splendid of all the spas, famed throughout Europe along with Marienbad or Baden-Baden, and frequented since the 18th century by the grand and leisured, from European royalty to Hollywood stars. It comprises whole avenues of huge spa buildings dispensing waters to drink and treatments from baths and inhalation to the famous mudbaths.

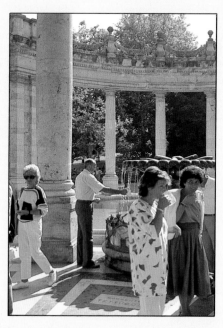

The Leopoldina pavilion is the most magnificent, a baroque 1920s edifice of rose marble, with fountains gushing the healing waters and an orchestra playing. Glamorous women sip coffee and eat pastries served by formally attired waiters, and romantically pale *Death in Venice* types waft through the marble columns, glass in hand.

The different waters, prescribed for varying ailments, are dispensed with great formality from elaborate brass taps over marble basins worn smooth with use. It is recommended to drink the waters in the morning on a empty stomach, preferably while walking.

But the most bizarre spa treatment must be the Grotta Giusti, near Monsummano Terme. The spa offers a complete range of treatments from thermal baths to hydro-massage but the hot thermal springs themselves are deep underground, fed by an eerie green thermal lake. White hooded figures shuffle down a rocky winding passage of stalagmites and stalagtites into a dimly lit cave where rows of chairs and shrouded sweating wraiths look like a scene from a Fellini movie. The further you descend the hotter it gets and the different levels are appropriately named Purgatorio and Inferno. No wonder the composer Giuseppe Verdi called it the eighth wonder of the world when it was discovered in 1849.

steeply upwards through chestnut trees and olive groves with views of a much darker and more rugged Tuscan landscape. Marliana has the remains of a castle, and a campanile from which there are magnificent views.

A little further on is **Vellano,** a hilltop fortified village, which is well worth exploring. It is still a working village, little changed since medieval times, although there are now washing machines along with the stacks of wood for winter tucked beneath the ancient portals. As you climb the little twisting streets to the campanile, the town becomes more ruinous, but every tiny piece of land is cultivated, and pumpkins and courgettes sprout among the ruins. It's a handy place to break for lunch as Vellano has a number of good family restaurants with windows overlooking the valley slopes and olive terraces.

Pescia itself is best known for its flowers with the largest flower market outside Holland, specialising in carnations, gladioli, lilies and chrysanthemums. The market itself, now in a vast new building, can be visited but it is necessary to get there early because it is all over by 8 am. Pescia is a prosperous town, surrounded by nurseries, greenhouses and olive groves as well as acres and acres of flower gardens.

Elegant villas, sheltered by cypresses, are visible in the hills beyond Pescia, many of which can now be visited or even rented as part of the current drive towards "agri-tourism". The town itself, most of which is 13th-century in origin, is divided by the River Pescia, and at its centre is the Piazza Mazzini, dominated at one end by the Oratory of the Madonna di Pie di Piazza, which dates from the 17th century. It has a finely carved wooden ceiling, richly embellished with gold leaf by Giovanni Zeti, and there is a delightful little painting beneath the altar showing Pescia as it looked in the 17th century.

At the opposite end of the Piazza is the Palazzo Comunale with its fortified tower, still used as the town hall. On the other side of the river is the 17th-century baroque cathedral which still re-

Left, sipping the waters in the marble halls of Montecatini Terme. **Below**, visitors to Montecatini at the turn of the century.

Bagni di Montecatini - Piazza Umberto I

tains its 14th-century bell tower but has a modern facade.

Pescia's most prized works of art are the earliest known paintings of St Francis, to be found in the church of San Francesco in the Via Battisti. Buonaventura Berlinghiero painted them in 1226, only nine years after the saint's death. In the church of Sant'Antonio are frescoes by Bicci di Lorenzo. In the hills above Pescia is the Convento di Colleviti, a peaceful Renaissance monastery, accessible by footpath from Pescia.

Just to the south of Pescia are two villages worth visiting, though they are in dramatically different states of repair. **Uzzano** is a pretty hill village with winding streets, but it is not in good shape and many of the houses are in danger of imminent collapse. However, it has an interesting gateway and a curious church right at the crest of the hill which has a rose window and an elaborate Pisan doorway.

Buggiano, by contrast, has been carefully though not over-restored, many of its stuccoed houses painted with a coral red wash. If you head towards the church and campanile you will find a very fine *palazzo* where a proud caretaker will appear and show you round for a small consideration. The building has massive oak beams and lovingly preserved frescoes on the walls, and houses a store of documents from the town which date back to 1377.

The village of **Collodi** is famous for the magnificent Villa Garzoni and its gardens and for the Parco di Pinocchio. The village itself, once part of Lucca province, was the scene of fierce fighting during the wars between Lucca and Florence. Today it is a peaceful place, straggling up the hill behind the Villa Garzoni, with only a few ruins of its original fortifications remaining. It is worth climbing up the winding stone steps of the pretty streets to be rewarded with wide-ranging views of the plain below. In the church of San Bartolomeo are wooden sculptures, 15th-century frescoes and terracotta statues.

The **Villa Garzoni** can be visited; access is through the 18th-century neo-classical gardens, which are enchanting. Fountains and flower beds are laid out in an elaborate formal pattern with parterres and pools, behind which is a complicated series of interconnecting stairs and terraces leading to waterfalls, hidden statues, grottoes and a maze. To the left the path takes you through a bamboo grove, up to the great wooden doors of the villa itself, and through into the inner courtyard.

Within the 17th-century villa are grand reception rooms, bedrooms and galleries decorated with flowery frescoes, polished terracotta floors and charming, if faded, furnishings.

But the most appealing room in the house is undoubtedly the kitchen with its huge fireplace, cast-iron cooking utensils and well-scrubbed pine table, where Carlo Lorenzini wrote *Pinocchio,* using the pen name of Collodi. The local people are very proud of their little wooden hero and find it irksome that so many people believe that the famous puppet was created by Walt Disney.

Proper tribute is paid in the nearby

Statue of Fame in the garden Villa Garzoni, Collodi.

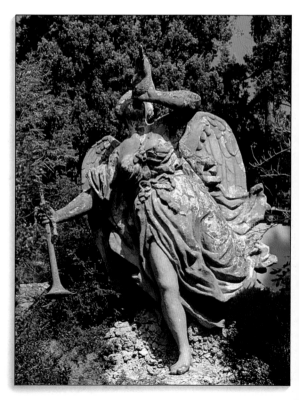

Pinocchio Park, which is full of bronze monuments of *Pinocchio* characters and a square of mosaics by Venturino Venturi depicting familiar episodes from the story. There is also a good restaurant on the site, the Gambero Rosso, designed by modern Italian architect Giovanni Michelucci.

Mountain pursuits: The drive up into the mountains to the north of Pistoia, the **Montagna Pistoiese**, is stunningly beautiful, with sunlight slanting through tall slender birch trees. Its beauty is perhaps at its most intense in autumn when the colours of the trees rival those of New England, but winter sports enthusiasts will prefer it with a good covering of crisp snow.

The main town of the Montagna Pistoiese is **San Marcello Pistoiese,** functioning primarily as an administrative centre and tourist base. It is traditionally known for the *Mongolfiera*, or hot-air balloon, which is launched every year on 8 September to mark the end of the summer. According to local legend, if the balloon rises higher than the bell tower, there will be a good harvest. Near to San Marcello, at Mammiano, is a spectacular suspension bridge, a footbridge 220 metres (720 ft) long connecting the village with the road across the rushing waters of the River Lima.

Cutigliano, further down the valley, is a typical mountain village, quiet and peaceful with the all-pervading scent of woodsmoke in the air and surrounded by fir trees. Limited skiing and a cable car service is available, but the more dedicated will probably prefer the facilities at Abetone. Cutigliano has a surprisingly grand 14th-century Palazzo Pretorio with numerous shields emblazoned on the facade, including the ubiquitous Medici coat of arms. Opposite is a quiet village loggia, with arcading and stone seats.

Abetone, about 90 minutes' drive from Pistoia, is 1,400 metres (4,660 ft) above sea level and is the most important ski resort in central Italy, with ski lifts, cable cars and chair lifts to a wide range of *pistes*, catering for intermediate and advanced skiers. It has two ski schools and a wide variety of accommodation, as well as cinemas, clubs, discos, swimming pools and ice rinks. It is a centre for international skiing with competitions including "Pinocchio on skis", a mini-Olympics for children which takes place every April.

In the summer this is a good centre for climbing and walking expeditions in the surrounding forests of pine and chestnut trees – one of Puccini's favourite pastimes. *Rifugi*, or mountain shelters, are dotted around the area, supplying basic shelter and sometimes restaurants as well. Abetone is also well supplied with mountain restaurants which command wonderful views of the dramatic landscape and supply hearty food and restorative drinks. A local speciality which should be tried is the *Grappa di mirtilli*, a strong spirit made from mountain bilberries.

Abetone is basically a mountain pass, not a town, and has little else in the way of cultural attractions. Two pyramid-shaped milestones in the centre of the town mark the original border between Tuscany and Liguria.

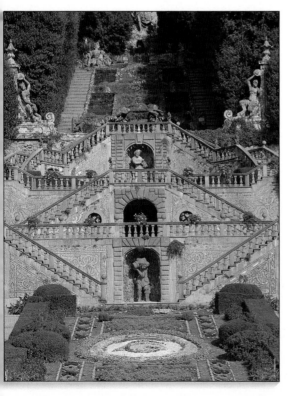

Terraces and waterfall in the Villa Garzoni gardens.

MASSA-CARRARA

Massa-Carrara is the northernmost province of Tuscany bordering on Liguria. It has been part of Tuscany only since the middle of the 19th century and is very different from the archetypal image of the Tuscan landscape.

Inland, Lunigiana is a little-known region of pine-covered mountains, craggy ravines and remote castellated villages. The coast is a predictable, over-developed continuation of the Versilian Riviera, but overshadowed by the marble industry. The beaches are dominated by the majestic marble peaks of the Apuan Alps glittering deceptively like snow in bright sunshine.

The towns of Massa and Carrara have both prospered as a result of the marble trade, although the resulting industrial development has blighted great swathes of the surrounding area. **Marina di Massa** is a popular resort with fine wide sandy beaches interspersed with groves of pine trees and a promenade of pretty pastel-shaded holiday villas. The ribbon of development extends up to and beyond **Marina di Carrara**, where the beach is divided by the sight and sound of the mighty port out of which ships carry marble all over the world.

Massa is a busy modern town but has a well-preserved medieval centre, built by the Dukes of Malaspina who ruled Massa for three centuries, holding sway over the entire region. The core is the Piazza degli Aranci, edged with orange trees and presided over by the elegant 17th-century Palazzo Cybo Malaspina, with airy courtyard loggias where cultural events are staged in summer.

Beyond a cluster of narrow winding streets stands the Duomo at the top of a wide flight of steps. It was begun in the 13th century but now has a baroque interior and a modern marble facade. The crypt, where the Malaspinas were entombed, is a museum.

Massa is dominated by its magnificent **Castello**. Beyond the narrow old streets of the town, walk on up through leafy lanes past decaying villas dotted over the mountainside. The walls of the old fortress provide marvellous views and welded onto it is a graceful Renaissance palace, its delicate marble pillars and frescoes providing a powerful contrast to the grim towers of the original castle. After World War II it was used as a prison but is now slowly being restored as a cultural centre.

Disaffected air: The main evidence of the marble quarries in **Carrara** is the river of white mud that flows though the town, which has a dusty, disaffected air about it. It is very much a working town, not a monument to marble and there are few fine marble statues to be seen. Even the **Duomo** – with distinctive features like its 14th-century rose window, Pisan-style facade and, inside, the 14th-century statue of the *Annunciation* – is in serious need of cleaning.

The interesting sights are within a few streets of one other and are adequately signposted. Worth visiting is the **Accademia delle Belle Arti**, a 16th-century Malaspina residence built around an older medieval castle. To

Massa-Carrara
15 km

view the galleries you need permission from the director but a brief reconnoitre will reveal splendid marble bas-reliefs on the walls, and sculptures from the Roman site of Luni as well as a Roman altar found in the marble quarries.

In nearby Piazza Alberica are two imposing 17th-century *palazzi* and here every July there is a massive symposium of work in marble. Carrara also holds a biennial sculpture exhibition and an annual International Marble and Machinery Fair.

Marble workers: Of particular interest in Carrara are the marble ateliers, of which there are a number in the Piazza XXVII Aprile. Atelier Niccoli is full of marble craftworkers and sculptors, hair protected from dust with newspaper hats, all intently carving and drilling to produce a huge range of marble statues, friezes and ornaments.

The quarried marble was originally dragged down to this square by oxen, "pulling as though to break their hearts under the tyranny of the stones," as Edward Hutton described it. Later the huge blocks were brought by train and truck from the nearby quarries. The marble caves are fascinating to visit; you can either take a guided tour or, better still, drive up there yourself and just wander around, following signs for **Cave di Marmo**, and taking the obvious safety precautions.

The fine-grained, pure white marble for which Carrara is renowned has been quarried here since Roman times, and has supplied artists from Michelangelo to Henry Moore with raw material. It is still the world's most important source of marble.

There are 300 quarries scattered throughout three steep valleys, the **Colonnata**, **Fantiscritti** and **Ravaccione**. Here the villages cling on to sides of mountains which have been sliced away like chunks of cheese. Dusty little houses have washing flapping from the windows, tomatoes and beans lovingly planted in any available crevice, and little marble exhibits carved by the quarry workers themselves.

Hutton, writing earlier this century,

Marble polishing in Carrara.

captures the drama of the caves, "...glens of marble that lead you into the heart of the mountains, valleys without shade, full of a brutal coldness, an intolerable heat, a dazzling light, a darkness that may be felt."

There are extraordinary views down into the quarries where the marble has been excavated deep into the ground. Precarious-looking staircases are strung across the sides, and massive trucks look like dinky toys as they trundle across the smooth marble surface far below. Modern equipment such as wire saws and compressed-air drills substitute for a time when marble blocks of 25 tons were transported manually on rollers lubricated with soap, and two men took an hour to saw through one centimetre of marble.

There is a marble museum, the **Museo del Marmo**, on Viale XX Septembre between Marina di Carrara and Carrara. Displays include many varieties of marble and granite and geographical and historical exhibits, but no information is available in English.

Just on the border of Tuscany before heading inland is **Sarzana,** a bustling market town which has been colonised by artists and is being carefully restored. There is a large market in the Piazza Matteotti which is surrounded by arcades of Romanesque arches sheltering smart little cafés.

Finally, in a scruffy area off the Via Aurelia north of Carrara, there is **Luni,** the original Roman settlement from which marble was shipped. There is an amphitheatre and museum, and excavations have revealed columns, capitals, mosaic floors and tomb fragments.

Land of a hundred castles: Luni gave its name to **Lunigiana**, "the land of the moon", an almost undiscovered part of Tuscany which sees few tourists and makes little provision for them. It has always been a main trading route, however, and its many castles were built to extract tolls from pilgrims and merchants by the powerful Malaspina family who controlled the region.

Lunigiana was in the front line of fighting at the end of World War II, and this has left its mark. Since then there has been inevitable rural depopulation with many people emigrating to the United States. Now an enlightened attitude to tourism promises new hope for the area, villages and castles are being restored and the roads are in good repair. There are enough hotels, pensions and local restaurants to make a visit comfortable but its attractions are unlikely ever to generate mass tourism. This means that its inhabitants will not grow rich, but it will probably help preserve the charm of the area.

It is a mountainous region of steep winding roads, deep wooded valleys and unpolluted, rushing streams. On the lower slopes of the hills vines and olives grow. Higher up are forests of oak and the chestnut trees which have provided a staple of the local diet for centuries, and there are deer and wild boar (*cinghiale*) in abundance.

The terrain ranges from the busy, productive flat valley of the River Magra to the profound silence of deep river gorges. Narrow valleys are dotted with tiny villages, quiet except for the sound of cowbells, dogs barking and the occasional gunshot.

The region is famous for its Romanesque churches and intact medieval villages as well as its castles, many of which are in the process of restoration through government grants. A number have been taken over by artists and sculptors and are used both as private homes and cultural centres.

The inhabitants of Lunigiana are proud and insular, in rural areas still growing most of their own food and wine and olives and regarding all other produce with some suspicion. They will buy in grapes from Chianti, making the wine themselves rather than buy an unknown finished product from foreigners.

Lunigiana is becoming a popular area for property hunters, although the locals still find it hard to understand the fascination of a ruined farmhouse. One English purchaser, deciding that the farmer's cowshed spoiled his view, offered to buy it along with the farm. But the farmer wanted more money for the shed **Villa near Sarzana.**

184

than for the farm; the house was his grandparent's, falling down and no use to him, he explained, but the cowshed was his livelihood!

Fosdinovo is the first fortified village you arrive at as you drive towards Aulla on the winding road from Sarzana. Its little piazzas are shaded by huge chestnut trees and the steep twisting streets are dominated by the magnificent castle. It is one of the best preserved castles in the region, despite being damaged by Allied fire during World War II. The Germans had a command post there, exploiting its superb strategic position with views from all sides.

It was constructed by the Malaspina family between the 13th and 14th centuries with a complicated network of corridors and loggias. Beautiful frescoed walls and ceilings and furniture have been restored; it is sometimes used for cultural events and is one of the few castles with an interior open to the public on a regular basis.

Aulla itself is the gateway to the region, where the rivers Magra and Taverone meet, but much of it is war damaged. Of the 10th-century Abbey of San Caprasio only the original apse survives. **Brunella**, the *fortezza* of Aulla, broods over the town. It was originally built in the 15th century as a defensive rather than a residential castle with walls 3 metres (10 ft) thick, narrow windows and vaulted ceilings. It was restored earlier this century by Montagu Brown, the British consul in Genoa, and now houses a natural history museum. It is accessible up a steep driveway off the main Via Nationale from Aulla, and surrounded by a large park of holm oaks and purple heather.

Fivizzano is a few miles west of Aulla along the 63 road, a busy attractive market town full of elegant Renaissance palaces and with a distinct air of pride in itself. The young people of Fivizzano are prominent in the movement to revive folk traditions, with colourful flag-waving performances, dancing and mock duels, and they travel all over Tuscany giving demonstrations.

Nearby is the enchanting castle of

The hills of Lunigiana.

Verrucola, a completely fortified settlement on the banks of the river which has been superbly restored. Little red-roofed houses and narrow medieval streets cluster around the fortified square keep, with geraniums spilling from window boxes and gardens full of courgettes, beans and tomatoes crammed right down to the river's edge.

The castle is thought to date back as far as the 11th century and is distinguished by its two separate fortified towers, erected when the town was divided between two rulers. The castle and the 15th-century church with its peaceful arched loggia can be visited at some periods of the year.

To the northwest of Fivizzano is **Licciana Nardi**, an 11th-century fortified town. Much of the town wall is still visible with narrow passageways running through immensely thick walls into the village. In the Piazza del Municipio the 16th-century castle dominates the square, and is joined to the graceful baroque church by a small bridge spanning the narrow street. There is a small market held once a week in the leafy main square.

Above the nearby Taverone river are the hill villages of **Bastia** and **Cisigliana**, a good base for walking, with high meadows and wonderful views out to sea, perfect for picnics and mushrooming. Bastia has a 15th-century square-bodied fortress, with cylindrical turrets at the corners, built by the Malaspina and now privately owned.

Along the valley from Licciana is **Crespiano** with a Romanesque church, Santa Maria Assunta di Crespiano, so old that it was *restored* in 1079.

Comano is an important base for walking and riding, and nearby is the Castello of Comano, a ruined malevolent-looking tower surrounded by a tiny farming community, with ducks and chickens wandering the streets, and steep steps up to the tower.

At the end of the valley is **Camporaghena**, the last outpost before the Apennines, where there is a sad war memorial in the church. When German soldiers came hunting escaped prison-

Springtime wisteria blossom.

186

ers of war and partisans, the priest rang the church bell as a warning and was summarily shot for his brave deed.

Monti is a tiny village with a particularly charming domesticated castle, complete with geraniums, lace curtains and even a street number on the door. It is well restored with its original gateway, keep and towers and is still apparently used as a summer residence by a surviving member of the Malaspina family. The church of Santa Maria Assunta di Venelia has an apse in *pietra serena* (the local grey "sacred stone") dating from the 12th century.

Pallerone is most famous for its crib, which can be seen in the church on request. It is an extraordinary clockwork nativity scene which changes from night to day and has a huge cast of busy clockwork characters, the Holy Family, angels, millers, blacksmiths, and fishermen. It is touching, sentimental and very Italian.

A 16-km (10-mile) drive south of Fivizzano will bring you to **Equi Terme,** a popular spa resort, smelling strongly of sulphur, with waters that are claimed to have radioactive properties. If you follow the path through the old village tucked into the mountain gorge, you will reach a bridge and a waterfall and the high-roofed caves called Buca del Cane, because the remains of paeleolithic men and dogs were found here. Guided tours of the caves are available at certain times.

Close to Aulla is another fine castle, **Podenzana,** a well-proportioned, triangular white building, massively restored in the 18th century after an explosion in the powder room. The castle is at the top of a steep hill and nearby is an excellent local restaurant, *Gavarina d'Oro*, which specialises in the regional dish of *panigacci*, small chestnut flour pancakes cooked over an open wood fire and served with creamy cheese and home-cured meats.

Quiet villages: Along the main road (SS62) up the Magra valley between Aulla and Pontremoli are many fascinating villages and castles, all within just a few miles. Few of the small vil-

Left, covered village street in Filetto. **Right**, woman doing embroidery in Filetto.

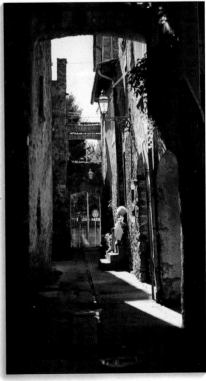

lages have facilities such as shops, restaurants or even bars, so if in need of refreshment try Villafranca or Bagnone.

Villafranca in Lunigiana lies in a strategic position near a ford over the River Magra and has some remaining medieval streets. But its 12th-century castle is in ruins, destroyed during World War II, and only parts of the keep and outer walls remain. The church of San Francesco has a terracotta of the School of della Robbia, and there is an interesting Ethnographic Museum in an old water mill near the river, which specialises in exhibits of typical local rural activities such as weaving, crafts and woodwork.

Bagnone is a large attractive town of Renaissance palaces, wide streets and cool shady arcades with many little bars and cafés. A honeycomb of houses, arches and passageways leads down to the river bank and tiny gardens. The 15th-century village of Bagnone is clustered on the hillside above, surrounding the cylindrical tower of the Castello and a fine 15th-century campanile. There is

an exquisitely carved wooden pulpit in the church of Santi Nicolo da Bagnone.

Nearby **Filetto** is a delightful, totally symmetrical, square-walled village with a tower at each corner. Almost every street is linked by covered overhead passages or bridges. Originally a defensive structure, it is now quite cosy, with cats snoozing in corners and village women sitting on the steps sewing and gossiping. Filetto has two piazzas overlooked by palaces, also connected with the rest of the town.

Malgrate and **Filattiera** are also worth a detour and nearby, next to the main highway, is a magnificent Romanesque church, **Pieve di Sorano.** The nave is ruinous and has been turned into a cemetery but in the main apse is a very simple and beautiful little chapel.

Mulazzo was headquarters of a branch of the Malaspina family which had territories to the west of the River Magra; their arms are emblazoned over a fine arched doorway which guards the steep steps up to the town. Fragments of the original walls are left and in the upper part of the town the narrow streets widen into charming little squares which are overlooked by elegant loggias and their inquisitive inhabitants.

The town of **Pontremoli** was originally divided into two halves to separate the warring factions of the Guelfs and Ghibellines, and the Castruccio Fortress, built in 1332, cuts the town in two. There are many rich medieval town houses and the Church of the Annunziata has a 16th-century octagonal marble temple by Sansovino. To the north is the **Castello del Piagnaro** which was part of the original fortifications, and now houses the Archaeological Museum with its unique collection of *menhirs*, prehistoric and Bronze Age stone monuments. Pontremoli is also famous for its travelling booksellers and awards the Bancarella literary prize each July.

At almost every turn there are more medieval villages, more castles, more breathtaking views. One of the best ways to see this rich and varied region is to take the little train between Aulla and Lucca on its slow journey through the mountains.

Left, Romanesque church of Pieve di Sorano, near Filattiera. Right, crushed grapes and new wine on offer in Malgrate.

LUCCA

To the west of Lucca province is "Tuscany by the Sea", a broad strip of land between the sea and the Apennines which contains a rich playground of villas and hotels. To the north is the steeply mountainous Garfagnana region, popular in the past for its variety of spas – a more remedial kind of playground – now more or less forgotten and hardly ever visited by tourists.

The city of **Lucca** (population 92,500) has a more realistic outlook on life, with its renowned olive oil industry and increasingly important wine production.

Driving west along the A11 towards Pisa and the sea, you could be forgiven for thinking that Lucca was one Tuscan city which doesn't merit inspection. Yet to miss Lucca is to miss one of the least appreciated Italian – let alone Tuscan – cities, with its wonderful tree-topped walls, its enchanting Gothic and Romanesque churches, but above all the ease with which life is lived. More perhaps than Siena, its ambience is "*simpatico, molto simpatico*", making it one of the best places to bring a comprehensive tour of Tuscany to an end.

The city **walls** were built at the height of the 16th-century revolution in warfare, when the nature of fighting moved from the offensive to the defensive. Largely inspired by Michelangelo's designs for the defence of Florence, the walls of Lucca are the only major city walls in Italy to have survived 19th-century destruction and are an excellent place to conduct *passeggiata* at dusk and to catch the last glimpse of the sun before it sets behind the Pisan mountains.

With its well-kept chestnut trees, already a part of the Luccan walls in the late 17th century, it is not surprising to discover that this continuous, circular avenue was to be the model for the larger-scale Tuileries in Paris.

For the people of Lucca, however, the walls represent a fierce fight to preserve their independence. Until the 11th century, Lucca had been the capital of Tuscany. Then for 400 years it defended itself against an ever more belligerent Florence and, even though the Florentines won the title of capital of the region, Lucca never ceded its political and economic autonomy. It remained an independent republic, apart from a brief period of Pisan rule, until the Napoleonic invasion of 1799.

At the other end of the historical scale, Lucca was the most significant Tuscan town in Roman times. The legacy of this history is seen in a plan of the city with its grid iron pattern of streets – so typical of any Roman habitation – and more obviously in the elliptical Piazza Amfiteatro around which houses were subsequently built. Caesar, Pompey and Crassus, the three most influential figures in the last years of the Roman Republic, met here in 56 BC to patch up their differences and to grant Rome a few more years of Republican rule.

The wealth of Lucca, like Florence, was based on banking and, from the late 14th century, its extensive silk industry. As early as the 12th century, bankers

Preceding pages: Lake Massaciuccoli at Torre del Lago. **Left,** the promenade at Viareggio. **Right,** Via Fillungo, Lucca.

from the "*banchi grossi*" were plying the waters of the Mediterranean or travelling north to Bruges, Antwerp and London, buying and then selling silk and woollen cloth. Successful bankers, like the Guinigi family, built substantial city homes. To demonstrate their prosperity some of them erected towers, although only one of these, the Torre Guinigi, remains, distinguished by the oak trees sprouting from the top.

The Guinigi were not the only ones visibly to display their wealth by creating towers. A picture hanging in the **Villa Guinigi,** home of Lucca's principal art gallery, shows that the city was once, like San Gimignano, a forest of towers, and it illustrates just how wealthy late medieval Lucca was.

Villa Guinigi, not far from the Palazzo Guinigi, originally lay outside the medieval city walls. Among its treasures, which date mainly from before 1475, is a wonderfully pious *Madonna and Child* in bas-relief. The artist was Matteo Civitalli, a contemporary of Donatello and Lucca's most renowned sculptor.

Walking back into the centre of the town – walking is the only way to see Lucca unless you adopt the Luccans' preferred means of transport, the bicycle – you'll pass the delightful extended **Piazza di San Francesco** with the simple facade of the church at one end and the 17th-century column with the Virgin Mary on top. If the area immediately around the column suggests a picaresque scene from an opera, one's senses are being led in the right direction: Lucca was the birthplace of Puccini, who is commemorated with a plaque outside his house in Via di Poggi.

But Lucca's chief attraction is its particularly interesting and beautiful churches. **San Michele**, built on the site of the old Roman forum, has one of the most spectacular Pisan Romanesque facades in Italy. The four storeys of intricate arcades rest above some splendid examples of blind-arcading, and the delicate motifs and allegories carved above each arch are especially noteworthy.

The **Cathedral of San Martino**, if

you haven't got waylaid in *Il Giglio* – an attractive restaurant with excellent freshwater fish close to San Martino – is also splendid, enhanced by its tower and the particularly attractive piazza in front of it. The facade was built in the 12th century, and the Gothic interior took 100 years to complete. So Romanesque and Gothic are combined and work surprisingly well together.

Inside there is the mysterious 13th-century labyrinth, symbolizing Life, and Lucca's masterpiece, the tomb of Ilaria del Carretto by Jacopo della Quercia. To stare at her face is to be transfixed by a sense of quietude and devotion rarely felt in any other sculpture.

The church of **San Frediano** is at the north end of the Via Fillungo, a street redolent of the city's medieval past and a popular place for shopping. It is rare to find a mosaic on any church, let alone a Romanesque one, but represented here is the *Annunciation of the Virgin*. Inside, the church is supremely simple, practically austere. There is also an intricate and unusual font.

Round the corner is the **Palazzo Pfanner**, which was built in 1667 and is currently being restored. With its large 18th-century garden and its well preserved staircase, it is a perfect contrast to the medieval and religious architecture that so dominates the centre of the city. The critic John Ruskin was so inspired by the architecture of Lucca that he declared that this was where he "literally *began* the study of architecture". He wrote, "Absolutely for the first time I now saw what medieval builders were and what they meant."

Just outside Lucca are even stronger contrasts: the Villas **Mansi** and **Torrigiani**. Mansi, with its statues and busts dotted above windows, in niches, on pediments, looking almost like candles from a distance, is close to fantasy, so ornate is the baroque decoration. Villa Torrigiani is less beautiful, but has a strong patrician feel. Both the villas are set in large open parks.

The Versilia: This coastal region of Italy has always attracted the attention of scholars, poets, writers and artists. It

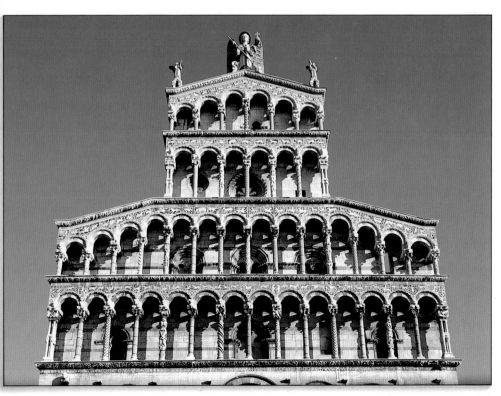

Pisan Romanesque facade of San Michele, Lucca.

VILLAS AND GARDENS

The idea of a country retreat, so popular in Tuscany today, originated with the Romans who built *villa suburbana* where they could escape to the peace and quiet of the countryside, usually only a few miles from the city. The villas were either working farms, which supplied the townhouses with produce, or were planned purely for pleasure. They would be visited for a day's outing and many did not even have bedrooms.

In the 15th century the idea of the country villa was revived by the Medici, who commissioned magnificent residences and elaborate gardens, modelled on classical ideas. In 1452 Leon Battista Alberti laid down in his *Ten Books on Architecture*, the essential ingredients for a truly well-appointed country retreat: it had to be on a slope, full of light and air, with rooms grouped round an inner hall, "the harmony and concord of all the parts achieved in such a manner that nothing could be added or taken away or altered except for the worse".

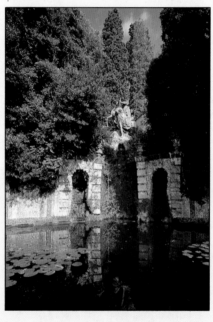

Some are relatively simple structures, with gardens more lavish than the house; others are more extravagant, with whimsical additions, colonnades, domes, even mock antique ruins and statuary. Often they were copied by visiting Europeans, who applied principles intended for the sunny Mediterranean to more northern climates, with romantic but chilly results.

The Medici villa at Fiesole, which has been described as "the first true Renaissance villa", was designed by the architect Michelozzo for Cosimo the Elder between 1458 and 1461. The villa was favoured particularly by Lorenzo Il Magnifico who entertained his humanist friends there. The design of the hanging gardens, in particular, was very influential and the villa commands a superb view of Florence.

The villa at Poggio a Caiano, near Pistoia, was converted by Giuliano da Sangallo for Lorenzo dei Medici between 1480 and 1485 and it dominates the surrounding countryside. It is characteristically Palladian in style; strictly symmetrical, with a classical temple front of colonnades and pediment added to the villa facade. In the 19th century the gardens were converted according to the fashionable English style, with romantic temples, an aviary, fountains and a mock Gothic ruin.

The 15th-century Villa Gamberaia in Settignano, near Florence, has retained most of its original 18th-century garden and was considered by Harold Acton to be "the most poetic garden in Tuscany" with its fountains, statues, geometrically planned pools and parterres, secret grottoes, bowling alley and manicured arcades of clipped yew and cypress.

The area surrounding Lucca is rich in villas: the patrician Villa Torrigiani, the baroque Villa Mansi and the Villa Reale at Marlia are all surrounded by beautiful parks and are open to the public. Marlia was created by the Orsetti family who were responsible for the gardens, and it was substantially re-modelled by Elisa Bacciocchi, Napoleon's sister. There is a lush park of shrubs, with a lake, which surrounds the formal Italian gardens. Box parterres lead to shady damp grottoes, a large fishpool adorned with swans, a garden of lemon trees in terracotta pots, fountains and – most wonderful of all – the *teatro di verdura,* an outdoor theatre sculpted from yew, a supreme example of the art of topiary.

Both the house and gardens of the baroque 17th-century Villa Garzoni, near Pescia, can be visited. The neo-classical gardens, which were laid out during the following century, are particularly extraordinary: fountains and flower beds are designed in an elaborate formal pattern with parterres and pools, behind which is a complicated series of interconnecting stairs and terraces leading to waterfalls, hidden statues, grottoes and a complicated maze. To the left the path takes you through a bamboo grove, over a rickety bridge to the adjoining villa, which was built in the 17th century by the Garzoni family from Pescia, fleeing Ghibellines who found refuge in Lucca.

Most of these villas are still in appreciative private hands, and often the gardens can be visited even if the house is closed to the public. Wandering through fragrant shrubbery and cool grottoes, past whimsical statues and fountains, can be recommended as an especially delightful diversion on a hot Tuscan summer's day.

is the area west of Lucca, squeezed between the Apuan Mountains in the east, the sea and the mouth of the Cinquale River in the north, and Lake Massaciuccoli in the south.

The flat landscape covered in pine trees has lost a lot of its earlier rustic and remote appeal now that it has been developed and built on so heavily. The sea can be reached only if you are prepared to pay an entrance fee and actually want to lie on a sunbed among rows of others, on sand carefully raked and flattened for your added comfort.

Viareggio is the oldest of the coastal towns in the Versilia. Its origins are Roman and in the Middle Ages it was most important as a sea landing for the Republic of Lucca. In the 19th century, as the capital of the Versilia, it was reputed to build some of the best boats ever launched on the Tyrrhenian Sea.

It was also in the 19th century that areas were established along its coast where men and women could bathe separately – though today it is a popular mixed bathing resort.

Today Viareggio is best known for its February Carnival. Vast hangars at the end of the Viale Marco Polo are set aside for the preparation of floats which are built to a specified theme and which are usually spiced up with political satire and irony. The whole town joins in and there are football matches, masked balls and fireworks.

To many English visitors however, Viareggio is best known as the place where, in 1822, the drowned corpse of Percy Bysshe Shelley was washed up after a particularly lethal squall out in the Tyrrhenian Sea. The poet and a friend were on their way from Leghorn (as they called Livorno) to La Spezia. The two bodies were eventually cremated south of Viareggio, near the mouth of the Arno.

Viareggio reached its heyday at the turn of the century and there are a number of buildings of this period remaining in the town, such as the **Bagni Margherita** on the seashore, as well as a great many huge *art nouveau* hotels located on the seafront boulevard. During the summer months there is a very lively atmosphere here; not many foreigners tend to visit and the stretch of coastline going towards Forte dei Marmi is well-known as the playground for the *Milanese*.

Many different factors have helped make Viareggio so popular. It has a wide sandy beach, there are plenty of trees and originally the promenades along the seafront were quiet places to stroll and relax. Nowadays strollers dice with death if they attempt to cross the main seafront road and it can be extremely difficult to find a patch of beach that hasn't been colonised by a bathing establishment.

Puccini's lakeside retreat: Just south of Viareggio, along the Viale dei Tigli, is **Torre del Lago Puccini**. The approach to this lakeside resort passes through one of Viareggio's two pine forests of which this one, the **Macchia Lucchese** or the *Pineta de Levante*, is the most beautiful.

On **Lake Massaciuccoli** at Torre del Lago Puccini, is Giacomo Puccini's villa in which were written all his operas except *Turandot*. The area has been rather over-popularised but when Puccini first came here it was a peaceful backwater where he was able to indulge not only in composing but in his other favourite pastime, which was shooting birds and animals. His villa displays his musical instruments as well as his guns. Puccini, his wife and his son are all buried in the nearby chapel and Torre del Lago holds a festival of his operas each August in his memory. The lake, and some of the neighbouring wetlands, form a nature reserve.

Continuing north from Viareggio, the resorts fall into line in quick succession. **Lido di Camaiore** is slightly more downmarket than the other places further north but then access to the beach is easier – being virtually free of pay-as-you-enter stretches of sand. From this part of the shore it is easy to reach **Camaiore** (to the Romans, *Campus Major*), which is about 7 km (4 miles) to the east. The town has an interesting range of architecture, of which the 8th-century **Badia dei Benedettini** with a

Torre del Lago Puccini.

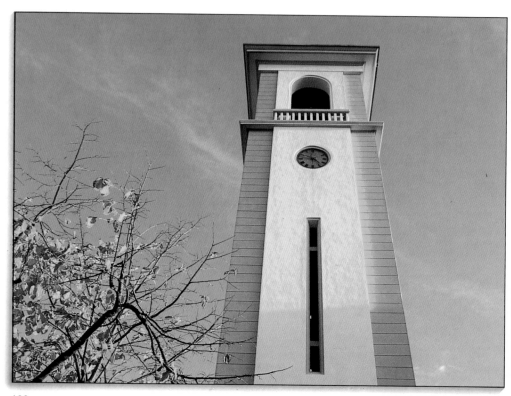

monumental 14th-century portal and the Romanesque **Collegiata** are the most important.

From Lido di Camaiore the subsequent pocket of watering holes are collectively known as Marina di Pietrasanta. **Pietrasanta** itself is about 8 km (5 miles) inland from the sea; its name, "Holy Stone", refers to the town's chief product, marble.

Not much happens in Pietrasanta today except for the celebration of the town's main product. It is the Tuscan centre for stone sculptors who come here in droves to work the marble in the privacy of rented studios – private or commercial. Each year the town hosts large sculpture exhibition which is held in the Consorzio Artigiani, and in the old Istituto d'Arte is a permanent exhibition illustrating the various ways of working marble. A fine white dust covers everything in Pietrasanta, even the wine glasses in the bars of the Piazza Carducci.

Sunset at Forte dei Marmi.

While this town has some of the loveliest monuments in the Versilia, including the 13th-century **Duomo** and the 9th-century **church of SS Giovanni and Felicita**, the **Marina** down below on the shore is bland and unexceptional. The two are joined by a tree-lined avenue which reaches the Marina at Fiumetto. The Marina is really a series of former villages – **Fiumetto**, **Tonfano**, **Montrone** and **le Fucette** – and each offers something different. Fiumetto has a pretty park with an ancient bridge in it, the "Ponte dei Principi".

But the gem of the Versilia today is **Forte dei Marmi**, still further to the north. Here the rich old villas of the late 19th century are still occupied as private residences, some *art nouveau*, some ornate and ugly, all forming a suitable backdrop to lives of the utmost luxury. The Agnellis, owners of the Fiat car conglomerate, have houses here. So do holidaying industrialists from Turin and fashion magnates from Milan, and the number of expensive sports cars seen cruising the streets at the hour of *passeggiata* in the early evening is directly proportional to the number of

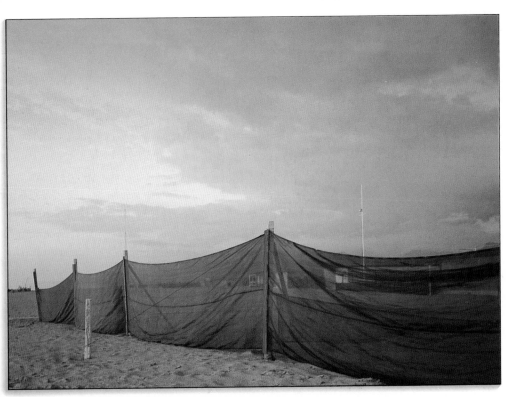

bullet-proof vests required by the drivers and their bodyguards.

Forte dei Marmi grew up around a fort built in 1788 by Leopold I of Tuscany, the remains of which still survive in the main square of the town. The shops and cafés around the square still manage to retain something of a small-town atmosphere even if they do sell some of the most expensive items that money can buy.

There are no high-rise buildings, unlike Lido di Camaiore. The highest things are the pine trees in the gardens of the villas, and in the back streets there is still the quiet and solitude that artists, writers, poets and scholars found here in the late 19th century.

Patches of beach are freely accessible while the remainder is made up of smart bathing huts and tropical-style bars with palm-frond roofs, perched on the fine pale grey sand. Here the shore slopes gently into the calm water and bathing is very safe.

In most Italian towns, life is led conspicuously out in the streets – shopping, walking or simply sitting about in cafés. At Forte dei Marmi it happens on the beach. Along the sand at the water's edge there is an endless parade of nearly naked bodies strolling languidly up and down in the sun, chatting or simply sporting a fine figure.

Many of the holidaymakers stay in villas over the road from the beach, behind high wooden fences that shield private gardens with swimming pools from prying eyes. These people cross the road in the morning and late in the afternoon simply to stroll; swimming in the sea is out, that's what the private pool is for and at lunchtime the beaches are deserted.

Fortified Garfagnana: The landscape changes dramatically east of Pietrasanta. On the other side of the Alpi Apuane (Apuan Alps) is the **Garfagnana** region, through which runs one major road once very popular with travellers wanting to avoid the risk of catching malaria in the formerly mosquito-infested Versilian lowland by the sea.

The centre of the Garfagnana is the

The beach at Forte dei Marmi, gem of the Versilia.

town of **Castelnuovo di Garfagnana**, about 64 km (40 miles) north of Lucca. This fortress town once controlled the route from Genoa to Lucca and Pisa and was under the rule of the Este family of Ferrara until Italian unification. The town also had strategic importance during World War II; it suffered badly during this period and a great deal of its town centre was destroyed.

But the Duomo survived and so did the town walls which surround the church of San Michele, which contains a 14th-century *Madonna* by Giuliano di Simone da Lucca. The **Rocca**, or governor's palace, which dates from the 12th century, is now the town hall.

In the Rocca, in the 16th century, lived Ludovico Ariosto, the epitome of the Renaissance man – successfully combining his talents as a poet with the functions of soldier and statesman. The Este appointed him governor of the district, a post which he evidently hated and some of the murkier passages in his *Orlando Furioso* may have been influenced by his time at Castelnuovo.

Just north of the town of Castelnuovo, at the foot of the pass which leads up through the rugged heart of the Garfagnana, are the thermal springs of **Pieve Fosciana** which produce radioactive water. This is just another variety of the therapeutic springs, with which the area is prolifically endowed. The treasures of Fosciana are displayed in the church, including a terracotta *Annunciation* by Luca della Robbia.

Continuing over the pass for about 18 km (11 miles), the first stop is **San Pellegrino in Alpe**, where there is a museum of peasant life of the Garfagnana. But **Barga** to the south is by far the most interesting town in the district. The passing of time forgot to take Barga with it and today there is a curious silence in the lanes and alleyways behind its walls.

The Romanesque **Duomo** contains a 13th-century marble pulpit carved by a sculptor from Como called Guido Bigarelli. The pillars supporting the pulpit rest on the backs of lions while the inlaid decoration and the panels of

The hills of Garfagnana, painted by Adolfo Tommasi.

the pulpit itself, on which are scenes from the scriptures, ensure that this work ranks among Tuscany's finest early Renaissance altars.

However, the real tourist attraction of the area, apart from the July/August opera festival which is held annually at Barga and the house and tomb of the poet Giovanni Pascoli at Castelvecchio Pascoli, are the subterranean caves at **Grotta del Vento**, near the village of **Fornovolasco**. Nearly three-quarters of a mile (1.2 km) of caverns wend their way through the ground, surrounded by stalactites and stalagmites, every inch of it looking like a stage set from a horror movie.

The cold clammy atmosphere is very slightly repugnant, but compelling nevertheless, and an added theatrical dimension is obtained by the use of coloured lights and echoes. Each visitor must be part of a guided tour because it is fairly easy to lose one's way as only a fraction of the caves are lit.

The terrain is steep and barren and offers the possibility of excellent, but rather dangerous, walks. The caves themselves are only open at certain times (from April to September).

San Romano in Garfagnana is an interesting town on the way to Bagni di Lucca. It has a large medieval castle and stunning views across the Alta Garfagnana, whose barren beauty is best appreciated with a visit to the nearby **Parco Naturale Demaniale dell' Orecchiella**. This is the preserve of rare flowers, wild boar and deer and all around are the grandiose peaks of the Alpi Apuane.

Near this spot, in a valley where the rivers Lima and Serchio meet, is the spa town of **Bagni di Lucca**. The town has always been known as a source of hot spring water, which contains sulphur and salt. It was very fashionable around the year 1800 when Byron, Shelley and Elizabeth Barrett Browning visited it, but since then it has been quietly forgotten. It has retained, however, an air of quiet respectability and faded elegance and is worth a visit.

In the 19th century the bathhouse was in the Palazzo del Bagno, which is now in a rather neglected state. There are 19 springs in the town as well as two steam vapour grottoes which easily sustain temperatures of up to 47°C (118°F). The open season for the springs lasts from May to September and they are good for anyone suffering from arthritis and rheumatism.

From Bagni di Lucca the road continues along the banks of the River Serchio to **Borgo a Mozzano**, a hamlet well-known for its Medieval Ponte della Maddalena. The other name for this hump-backed bridge, which spans the Serchio, is *Ponte del Diavolo* because the devil is supposed to have built it for the villagers in return for the first soul to cross it on its completion. The crafty villagers cheated the devil by sending over, by night, a pig with which the devil had to be content.

In reality, this bridge, with arches of five different sizes, was built by Countess Matilda of Tuscany (1046–1115). Her generosity was also responsible for the construction of the Romanesque churches of Diecimo, Pieve di Brancoli and Villa Basilica.

Left, cooling off in the shade. **Right**, cypresses marching down a Roman road.

PISA

The Leaning Tower draws tourists to Pisa like a magnet, many of them pausing to appreciate the religious architecture, others to enjoy the glorious art and history of this Tuscan city.

Once a thriving Roman port, Pisa's harbour silted up in the 15th century and it now stands on the Arno river, 10 km (6 miles) from the coast. Great sea battles were fought during the Middle Ages, with the city-state of Pisa becoming first allies then rivals of a number of other states including Genoa, Lucca, Venice and Florence. At its height, Pisa's power extended to Sardinia, Corsica and the Balearic Islands.

During World War II the city was heavily bombed and has been working ever since to restore its buildings. Pisa is halved by the gently curving River Arno, its steep stone banks coloured by floating green algae. Elegant 16th-century *palazzi* along the banks hide the less imposing buildings and general decay in the narrow streets and alleys behind. Two-horse carriages lazily clip-clop along the quiet banks in the middle of the day, when most Pisans are taking their siestas.

The **Church of Santa Maria della Spina** sparkles in the distance. The statues on the sides were carved by followers of Giovanni Pisano, while the central statue of the *Madonna and Child* came from the workshop of Nino Pisano. The chapel once guarded what was believed to be a (*spina*) thorn from the crown of Jesus but that relic, plus the original statues, are now housed in the National Museum.

Crossing the original city bridge, Ponte della Citadella, the Via Nicola Pisano leads to the **Campo dei Miracoli** (Field of Miracles), probably the most perfect assemblage of religious buildings anywhere on earth.

The secret of enjoying Pisa is to see the monuments for the first time from the right place. For the **Leaning Tower**, the first sight should be through the archway of the Porta Santa Maria, otherwise known as the Porta Nuova. When the sun is shining, the whiteness dazzles; when raining, it glistens.

The best time to visit Italy's most famous landmark is in the early morning, before bus-loads of tourists arrive. The air is fresher then, the heat not too intense, and it provides a magical introduction to the historic buildings.

Visitors come from all over the world to marvel, if only once, at the phenomenon of the 12th-century campanile or Leaning Tower. In 1989 the tower was closed in response to the increasing tilt. Since then, international teams have vied with one another to suggest scientific solutions – and have been deluged with weird and wonderful advice from the general public. Until one of the Anglo-Italian schemes is successfully implemented, the tower's tempting 294 steps must remain untrod.

The tower was begun in 1173 by Bonano Pisano, the designer of the bronze south transept doors of the cathedral, but almost immediately began to tilt because the alluvial subsoil was

Preceding pages: Roman amphitheatre at Volterra. Left, Leaning Tower of Pisa.

unable to take its great weight. When last measured, it was leaning 5.5 metres (18 ft) from vertical.

Various proposals have been made to stop the tower leaning any further: removing the belltower which was added in 1350 and is about 5 percent of the total weight of the tower; inserting steel girders; injecting concrete under the foundations – and even dismantling it and starting again.

Major Duomo: The **cathedral**, built between 1068 and 1118, is one of the major monuments in Italy. The beautiful white marble facade, the model for the Pisan Romanesque style, is set with mosaics, inlaid marble and glass stones. The tomb of Buscheto, the architect of the building, is on the left of the facade which was designed by Rainaldo and built in the early 12th century. The central bronze doors, designed by Giovanni da Bologna in 1602, gleam from the caresses of thousands of fingers stroking the figures carved on them: a lizard, the head of Mary, the naked baby Christ, the pointed head-dress of an attendant, the back of a dog, two frogs, the head of a woman, a pointed helmet, the round upturned hat of a guard, and four noses on the faces of heads in the friezes.

The main entrance to the cathedral was intended to be through the bronze transept door of the Porta di San Ranieri, near the Campanile. These panels of the life of Christ date from 1180 and show the Greek and Roman influences in the work of Bonano Pisano.

On entering the cathedral the visitor is immediately drawn to the height of the nave, with its ornate golden coffered ceiling, rebuilt after a fire in 1596. Hanging in the centre on a long corded chain is "Galileo's lamp". The bronze chandelier with its balancing *putti* (cherubs), supposedly helped Galileo to understand the theories of movement of the pendulum.

The nave, 95 metres (312 ft) long, is supported by 68 Corithinian columns. The interior is impressive, not only for its huge spatial effect but also for the originality of its black and white striped marble walls.

Pisa cathedral seen from the leaning tower.

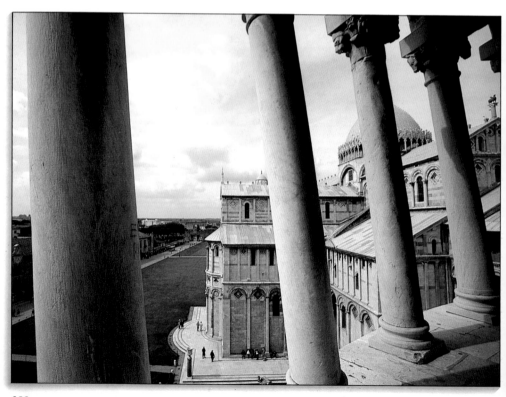

The magnificent pulpit, sculpted by Giovanni Pisano between 1302 and 1311, was damaged by fire and removed in 1599, and not reconstructed until 1926. The five detailed reliefs show scenes of the birth of John the Baptist, the life of Christ and the Last Judgement. The six supporting columns are decorated with lifelike statues of biblical figures. The pointed arches draw the eye to a lighted stained-glass window depicting the Virgin Mary.

Across from the Rainaldo facade is the third building of the cathedral complex – the **baptistry**, begun in 1153. It is unfortunate that time and pollution are beginning to take their toll. Statues and busts by Giovanni Pisano, his father, Nicola and Arnolfo di Cambio are being removed from the second tier to the Museo dell'Opera del Duomo while the four massive doors already have wooden replacements.

The spacious interior, with its eight stained glass windows, holds in the centre the 1246 octagonal font of Guido Bigarelli da Como, decorated with squares of ornate black, white and russet oriental design.

The carved **pulpit**, by Giovanni Pisano, has, around the centre column, which is supported by three sculptures, six others – each alternate one resting on a lion's back. The five exquisitely sculptured panels depict scenes of the nativity, the message to the shepherds, the Adoration of the Magi, the presentation of Jesus in the temple, the crucifixion and the Last Judgement.

A visit to the baptistry is not complete without a guide or chorister singing a single note which echoes several times over around the building, lifting even the most atheistic spirit. "Go by night into the Baptistry, having bribed some choirboy to sing for you, and you shall hear from that marvellous roof a thousand angels singing round the feet of San Raniero," the English writer Edward Hutton noted earlier this century

The fourth element of the cathedral group is the **Campo Santo**, the "sacred field", a cemetery consisting of cloisters surrounding a field of earth taken

Kiss of Judas, detail from the cathedral doors.

THE PISAN STYLE

In 1062, in a sea battle fought off Palermo, the Pisan navy won an overwhelming victory over the Saracens of Sicily. The next year, the Pisans used their fantastic spoils to begin work on the foundations of a mighty cathedral. It was designed by one Buscheto (or Buschetus) in what became known as Pisan Romanesque – a style which spread across the country and greatly influenced the early Tuscan Renaissance. Its distinctive marble stripes and arcading are to be found all over Tuscany, pre-dating Gothic and Renaissance additions.

The cathedral was consecrated in 1118. It was soon joined by a baptistry, a bell tower (the celebrated Leaning Tower) and the Campo Santo, making it the best example of grouped cathedral buildings in the world and a grand and lasting monument to the splendour of the Pisan republic.

Stylistically the buildings showed many influences, but all were faced with marble panelling and featured arcades and colonnades. The blind arcades – a row of filled-in round arches – on the outer walls of the cathedral were very distinctive, as were the four tiers of arcading on the facade, designed by Rainaldo, with a facing of alternating dark and light marble. Marble arcades, filled-in or left open to make a colonnade or gallery, became the style manual of the Pisan school. Another distinctive element at Pisa is that the curved tympana at the top of the blind arches contains an inset square diamond. These are all features of the Pisan style.

The facade of San Paolo a Ripa d'Arno (begun in 1210) in the city of Pisa itself is a good example, as is Santa Maria della Spina (1325), also in Pisa. This church has different layers of marble facing striped like a zebra – a feature to be found on many Pisan school churches. In addition to stripes, the different tones of marble are often used to make other geometric patterns, squares and circles in combination with the arcading and windows. Sometimes the stripes are all that remain after a facade has been rebuilt.

An excellent example of the Pisan school is the cathedral at Lucca, San Martino, which has a fine Pisan Romanesque facade by Guidetto da Como, dated 1204, and an almost exact imitation of the first three tiers of colonnades on the cathedral facade at Pisa. There are more columns and arcades surrounding the apse. Other examples in Lucca include San Michele in Foro (begun in 1143), which is surrounded on all sides by blind arcading, including the base of the bell tower. The four ranges of galleries on its amazing facade dwarf the nave which was intended to be raised. The arcading on the facade has the characteristic insert square panels, as has Santa Maria Forisportam (late 12th century), which was based directly on the cathedral at Pisa. More colonnades can be found on San Pietro Somaldi (rebuilt 12th century) and on the apse of San Frediano (1112).

The influence of the style spread far beyond the Pisan republic itself and can be seen in the blind arcading on the facade of the cathedral of Troia in Apulia (1093), San Giusto at Bazzano in the Abruzzi, and the cathedral of Massa Marittima which was begun in 1228 in the Pisan Romanesque style with blind-arcading across the lower part of the facade.

Parts of the cathedral of Genoa (1199) are Pisan-influenced and the church of San Giovanni Fuorcivitas in Pistoia displays three stages of purely Pisan arcading along its flank, complete with square insert panels and exuberant green and white zebra stripes. Next door, across an alley, there are more zebra stripes embodied in a commercial building that was clearly originally part of the San Giovanni Fuorcivitas group. Pistoia has many Pisan Romanesque churches including Sant'Andrea and San Bartolomeo in Pantano. And Santa Maria della Pieve in Arezzo (1216) has three ranges of colonnading on its Pisan Romanesque facade.

The style also influenced a number of churches in Sardinia – in particular, San Gavino at Porto Torres (1111). Looking for traces of striped marble or a row of small columns giving a complex interplay of light and shadow among the pointed arches of Italian Gothic is a rewarding exercise, and a particularly pleasant occupation while seated, with a cool drink, outside a café on the *piazza* of a Tuscan village.

from the Hill of Calvary by the crusaders. A fire bomb in 1944 destroyed most of its celebrated frescoes. However, the most famous, *The Triumph of Death,* as well as those depicting *Hell* and the *Last Judgement* were saved from the conflagration and are now on display in a room off the north cloister.

The **Museo delle Sinopie** is housed in what was one of the wards of the "New Hospital of Mercy" (Ospedale Nuovo di Misericordia), which was built between 1257 and 1286. *Sinopia* is the name for a preparatory design which was carried out directly on to walls on a special kind of rough plaster, known as *arriccio.*

After preparing the outline of the design, the painter would gradually cover over and paint various parts of it, using a different kind of plaster which was richer in lime (*grassello*) until he had finished the whole work, so the sinopias were destined to disappear for ever.

The fire which followed the bombing of the Campo Santo destroyed some of the frescoes and left the others in so precarious a condition that it was necessary to remove them – but that was how the immense sinopias lying beneath the frescoes came to light and were salvaged, and now carefully restored.

Last on the itinerary of the Piazza is the **Museo dell'Opera del Duomo** – the Cathedral Works Museum, housed in the former chapter house. The exhibits are all from monuments in the cathedral square. The main items of the collection can be seen on the ground floor; these are sculptures dating from the 11th, 12th and 13th centuries and are evidence of the artistic currents present in Pisa when, as a republic, it was at the height of its power.

The precious objects in the museum collection – the cathedral treasure and plate – are to be found in Room 9 and in the seminary chapel, together with some very old ecclesiastical garments, dazzling rich silk robes, heavily embroidered in white, gold, red and black. Here too is Giovanni Pisano's famous *Madonna and Child* in ivory. There is also a fragment of a famous belt that once

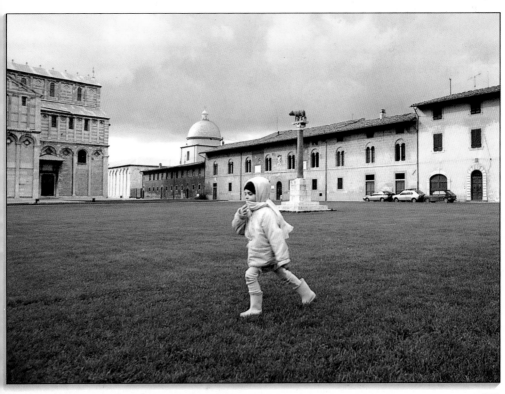

was the length of the cathedral perimeter, encrusted with enamelled plaques, gemstones and silver crosses.

The archaeological section displays the Etruscan and Roman material looted from the ancient settlements of Pisa and Volterra to decorate the city's new buildings. In Room 1 the 12th-century sculptures taken from the cathedral allow a full appreciation of the artist's work and a clear diagram shows where the fragments originated in the facade.

Another unusual art form, in Room 13, is wood marquetry, or intarsias, of which Cristoforo da Lendinara was the greatest master of the 15th-century school of inlaying that was to develop in the Po valley. His two intarsias are, together with Guido da Seravallino's six panels of animal figures, one of the favourite themes of the Pisan intarsia workers.

From the Museo dell'Opera del Duomo the Piazza dei Cavalieri is a short walk, but the best viewpoint for this spectacular square is opposite the Palazzo dei Cavalieri at the exit from Via San Frediano. From here the whole of Vasari's glorious 16th-century facade may be appreciated. From six niches above, the Grand Dukes of Tuscany gaze down over the central steps and the fountain topped with Pietro Francavilla's sculpture of Cosimo I.

Vasari (1511–74) designed the tower of the **Church of Santo Stefano dei Cavalieri** where trophies and spoils of war are displayed. In 1606 Giovanni de' Medici added the marble facade and placed the knights' emblem above the great doorway.

The large, irregular square is sometimes called Piazza dell'Orologio, the name originating from the porcelain clock above the archway which has cool, stone benches beneath it. In 1284, when the Pisans lost the Battle of Meloria, the Podestà, Count Ugolino, suspected of treachery, was starved to death in the Palace of the Clock.

From the Field of Miracles, you can follow the banks of the Arno as far as the Piazza Garibaldi. From here it is a short walk along the river to the **Museo**

Nazionale di San Matteo. Pisa's National Museum is housed in the converted ex-convent of the Sisters of Saint Matthew, and is renowned for its panel paintings with gold backgrounds, including one of Saint Paul by Masaccio, wooden crucifixes, altar-pieces and medieval Islamic and Pisan pottery.

There is a collection of antique armour used in the *Gioco del Ponte* (a medieval tug-of-war), which comprises breastplates, helmets, and other pieces dating from the 15th and 16th centuries. There are also many wooden shields, painted with the colours of the city quarters, which are used in the fight and during the parade.

The contest takes place each year on the last Sunday in June, together with the Historical Regatta and other celebrations. The historical procession which precedes the pageant is composed of 750 people in medieval costume. A crowd of about 100,000 gather along the banks of the Arno to watch this spectacular event each year.

The pretty road out of Pisa to the coast

Dining al fresco.

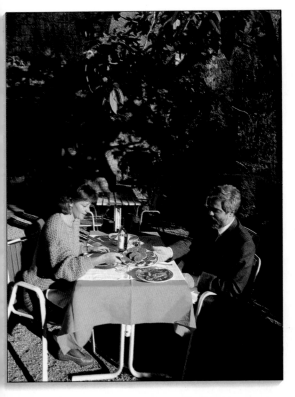

pauses here and there at railway crossings as it follows the River Arno to the sea. It passes the San Piero a Grado Basilica where legend has it that Saint Peter landed when he reached Italy.

At **Bocca d'Arno** the hanging trawl-nets from fishing boats and the rods of silent fishermen evoke the atmosphere captured by artists like Nino Costa and Gabriele d'Annunzio.

On both sides of the mouth of the Arno the coastline boasts miles of sandy beaches. Beyond the river mouth is the regional park of San Rossore, with its busy race-course and enchanting woods. Just in front of the former Royal Estate, lies the seaside resort of Marina di Pisa with its variety of architectural styles. Concerned newspaper reports of the pollution on this part of the coast are probably true, since industrial waste from the Arno and the sewage of seaside towns fill the Tyrrhenian Sea at this point, but the beaches are kept clean.

Natural barrier: A kilometre or so down the coast at **Tirrenia** is the remaining stretch of Mediterranean pine forest – the one place where no building has been allowed on the shore. The evergreen trees act as a natural barrier against the *libeccio*, a strong southwest wind. Thanks to the trees, the strong wind is reduced to a light, scented breeze of pine and juniper which cools the air on hot, summer days.

As a much larger resort than Pisa di Marina, Tirrenia offers luxury hotels and homely boarding houses. Night clubs, restaurants and sporting facilities for golf, tennis, horse-riding, underwater fishing, windsurfing, sailing and rowing are enjoyed by Tuscans but few foreigners take holidays along this coast. Each year colourful regattas and boat races are held and the training centre for the Italian National Olympics is based in Tirrenia.

Midway between Pisa and Lucca, at the foot of the Pisan mountains, is the spa town of **San Giuliano Terme**. The Palazzo Termale (spa building), set in private grounds guarded by high walls is a national health hospital.

Olives, chestnuts and pines grow in the surrounding fertile countryside and wild horses roam the hills. A number of ruins are dotted among the valleys and at Capoluogo in the Caldaccoli region are eight stone arches remaining from the aqueduct built by Mediceo di Asciano in 1592.

Monastic retreat: Set in lush green countryside, **Certosa di Pisa** (the Charterhouse of Pisa) was founded in 1366. From the end of that century modifications and additions were continually made until the final touches to the interior decoration were finished in the early 18th century.

The Carthusians were one of the new strict orders who believed that the increasing prosperity of the Cluniac orders was accompanied by a decline in religious observance. Their architecture reflected this; the monks lived in separate cells within a main enclosure, and took their name (anglicised as Charterhouse) from La Grande Chartreuse in Dauphiné. The centre of monastic life was the Great Cloister of which the Certosa di Pisa has a particularly fine example.

Artists and craftsmen worked on the frescoes of the church walls from 1701–1703; Angelo Maria Somazzi from Livorno added fine stucco work to the church, chapels, guest quarters and boundary walls and in 1718 workmen from Carrara carved the marble and renovated the church facade. In 1981 a part of the Charterhouse was allotted to the University of Pisa to house the Museum of Natural and Regional History.

Entering **Cascina** past fields of sunflowers, grapevines and maize, the roads are lined with plane trees. Cascina is proud of its solid stone walls, dating from 1142, which are depicted in Vasari's energetic painting of the Battle of Cascina, now hanging in the Palazzo Vecchio in Florence.

The town is centred round the production of wooden furniture. At the end of the arcaded main street, Corso Matteotti, there is a large factory with *MOSTRA DEL MOBILI* displayed in huge letters and containing a permanent furniture exhibition. Yet most of the workshops are tucked away in the pretty

Umbrella pines, dusk.

side streets, which are usually festooned with seasonal flowers.

Leaving the Mostra and walking up Corso Matteotti, the tiny chapel of **Suore di Carmelitane di Santa Teresa** is on the left. It has beautifully detailed frescoes depicting the creation of the sky and the earth, the expulsion of Abel, the Tower of Babel and St John the Baptist. The nearby Church of the Saints Casciano and Giovanni, dating from 970, is a graceful arched building with a starkly simple interior.

Casciana Terme, less than 40 km (25 miles) from Pisa, lies 160 metres (525 ft) above sea level and is surrounded by flourishing vineyards, olive groves and peach orchards. The beautiful hillsides and the mild climate create a relaxing atmosphere for visitors.

The town exists solely for the spa, which is open from April to November, and the pace of life is leisurely, if somewhat clinical. The powers of the thermal waters have long been appreciated and attract people seeking a break, as well as those "taking the cure".

In 1870 Poggi designed the large spa building, but a bomb destroyed it in World War II, leaving only the facade and the hall intact. In 1968 the building was completely re-built around the remains of the original structure.

The country around Casciana Terme is good for walking, especially in the nearby pine woods of Pineta della Farnia. The village of **Colle Montanino di Ceppato,** which has a 1,000-year-old tower, and **Pariascia,** which has a fortress, are also both within easy reach and a visit to the **Sanctuary of the Madonnina Dei Monti** might serve to restore the spirit. At **Crespina** and **Fauglia** are several magnificent 19th-century villas as well as the church of **Chianni** and the nearby **Lari Castle,** which is heavily adorned with medieval coats of arms and family crests.

A few minutes' drive from Casciana is the co-operative wine cellar Enoteca di Terricciola, well-stocked with local wines and those from other parts of Italy. The area around Casciana Terme is known for the production of Chianti

A curious onlooker.

Colline Pisane, while the Arno valley from Santa Croce to Cascina and south of San Miniato produces Bianchi San Torpe. The third local wine-producing area is around the town that bears its name – Montescudaio.

Ancient town: In a stillness not usually associated with Italian cities, rests the ancient town of **San Miniato**, whose origins go back to Etruscan and Roman times. It is set on the top of three hills, 192 metres (630 ft) above sea-level, and gazes out upon magnificent views. On one side stretches the large plain of the River Arno with the Apennines towering over the Pisan, Pistoian and Florentine mountains. On the other side, what Carducci described as "the wavy gracefulness of the hills" continues to San Gimignano and Volterra.

The nature and history of the town has always been closely linked to its geographical position, equidistant from the important cities that played a decisive historical role: Pisa, Florence, Lucca, Pistoia, Siena and Volterra.

High on the hillside are the two towers of the **Rocca** which was rebuilt in the 12th century by Frederick II. Torre di Federico, as it became known, was destroyed in World War II but has been faithfully reconstructed. Dante recounts that it was from this tower that Pietro della Vigna leapt to his death and as punishment was turned into a gnarled and twisted tree.

The oldest tower of the fortress, the Torre di Matilde was restructured as a belltower when the **cathedral** was added, with its Romanesque brick facade and later restructuring. The oldest building in San Miniato is a church constructed by the Lombards in the 8th century.

The church of **San Francesco** originates from AD 783 but was completely rebuilt in 1276. It is a magnificent example of a Franciscan building. The remains of a 15th-century fresco depicts Saint Christopher with the Child Jesus. The church, to which a convent was later added was in a state of constant transformation until the 16th century. By using bricks made from local clay,

The rocca at San Miniato.

the medieval construction and decorative traditions were maintained.

The **Diocesan Museum of Sacred Art** (Museo Diocesano d'Arte Sacra) in the old sacristy of the cathedral exhibits art and sculpture including works by Lippi, Verrocchio and Tiepolo.

Many local traditions are still maintained. On the feast of St John, when winnowing is over, bonfires of ears of corn and cloves of garlic are lit on all the hills surrounding the town, to keep ill-luck away. From the middle of September to the end of Christmas is the season for white truffles (*tuber magnatum pico*). The Association of Trufflers of the San Miniato Hills issue a map showing where to find the aromatic plant, which is dug out of the ground with a type of pole called a *vangheggia*. On the last Sunday in November a huge market and exhibition is mounted to display the catch of the season.

Majestic position: One of the most important towns in Tuscany is **Volterra**, which has a richly layered history with abundant evidence of its 3,000 years of civilization. It commands a beautiful, windswept and majestic position on a steep ridge 545 metres (1,780 ft) above sea level between the valleys of the Era and Cecina rivers. Walking round the ancient defensive walls is an excellent way to view the town and the Roman remains and the wide sweep of countryside below.

Volterra was the Etruscan city-state of Velathri, one of the confederation of 12 city-states which made up Etruria. It became an important Roman municipality (Volterrae) when Rome annexed Etruria in 351 BC. It followed the new faith of Christianity and at the fall of the Roman Empire in AD 476, it was already the centre of a vast diocese.

Although predominantly medieval, the town still cherishes abundant evidence of the Etruscan period, including the massive stretches of the city wall. The **Porta all'Arco** (the Arch Gate), is the best preserved Etruscan gateway in Italy, dating from the 4th century BC with sides of huge rectangular stone blocks and three mysterious carved stone

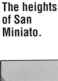

The heights of San Miniato.

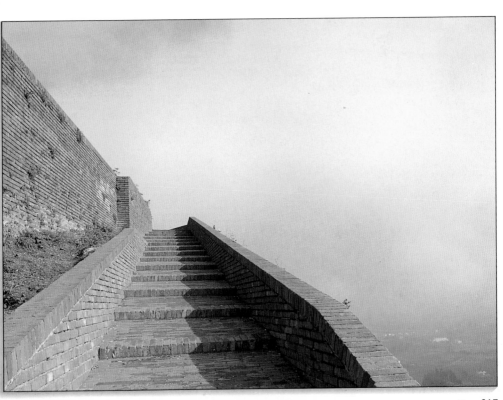

heads above the gateway. The Acropolis in the Enrico Fiumi archaeological park on the Plain of Castello shows various periods of human settlements from prehistory to the Middle Ages; also preserved are a large number of hypogea, vases and cinerary urns.

The traditional craftsmanship in alabaster is a legacy from the Etruscans who made great use of it from the 5th century BC onwards for their beautifully sculptured urns. Alabaster is one of the most typical products exported from this region, and it is sold at many of the local workshops.

Examples of Roman artefacts include the remains of the **theatre** in Vallebona, which was started under Augustus but completed during the rule of Tiberius, and which has recently been excavated and partly reconstructed. There are also baths, an enormous rectangular water cistern, a number of sculptures and mosaic flooring.

Evidence of the Middle Ages is demonstrated, not only in Volterra's urban structure but in its buildings, the most important of which are in the **Piazza dei Priori**. Here is the tall, 13th-century Palazzo dei Priori, whose facade with its iron flag and torch holders is decorated with coats of arms of the Florentine magistrates; to the right of the square is the Palazzo Pretorio, with its crenellated Torre del Porcellino (Tower of the Little Pig), the name adopted from its decorative bas-reliefs of wild boar.

Family towers: There are other structures of great architectural interest including the towers of the Buonparenti and Bonaguidi families united by a high arch; the house-towers of Toscano in the small square of the church of San Michele in the Via Guarnacci; the 12th-century cathedral which houses works of art from the Middle Ages to the Renaissance; the baptistry, an octagonal building dating from the 13th century, streaked with Volterran stone, with an elegant marble doorway; and the church of San Francesco and the adjacent chapel of the Croce di Giorno which was decorated with frescoes by Cenni di Francesco in 1410.

Volterra cathedral with Romanesque facade.

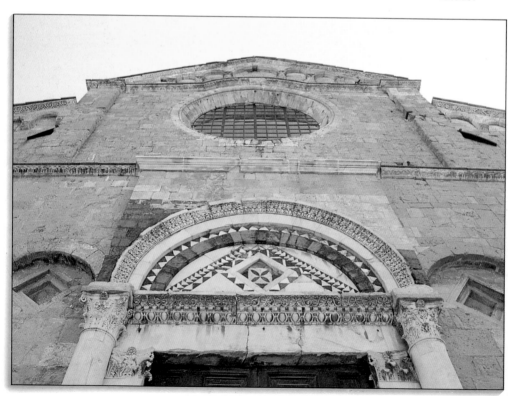

The Renaissance buildings such as the Palazzo Minucci-Solaini, blend gracefully with the medieval Volterran houses. The conventual complex of San Girolamo has a splendid *Annunciation* by Benvenuto di Giovanni and some della Robbia terracotta statues.

Volterra has three major museums; the **Guarnacci Museum** is one of the most important museums in Italy for its Etruscan exhibits, and is particularly notable for the outstanding collections of alabaster, terracotta and travertine cinerary urns, decorated with many different motifs and sculpted in a great variety of styles.

The Art Gallery and Civic Museum of **Palazzo Minucci-Solaini** houses valuable paintings of the Sienese and Florentine schools of art. Among the works of Taddeo di Bartolo, Benvenuto di Giovanni, Donato Mascagni and Baldassare Franceschini are such notable paintings as the *Annunciation* by Luca Signorelli and the *Christ in Glory* by Domenico Ghirlandaio.

The most famous painting in the collection is the *Descent from the Cross* by Rosso Fiorentino (1494–1540), a work of considerable importance and innovation because of the stylisation of the figures and the striking tragedy of the composition. The **Museum of Sacred Art** has many ecclesiastical vestments, a collection of gold reliquaries, church bells, illuminated manuscripts and some 13th-century sculptures of the Sienese school of art.

The countryside around Volterra is one of gentle, undulating hills, interrupted in the west by the wild and awe-inspiring spectacle of abrupt crevasses known as the **Balze** (the crags). This is a natural phenomenon created by the continual erosion of layers of sand and clay. Repeated landslides over the centuries finally destroyed the Etruscan and early Christian remains.

Neighbouring **Lardarello** is an area at the centre of the borax industry. The landscape is dominated by borax *fumaroles*, machinery which harness the volcanic energy of hot springs to generate electricity.

Defensive city walls of Volterra.

LIVORNO

Livorno Province is sweet wine, Elba, sandy beaches, Napoleonic myths and a few unfortunate industrial ports. With barely enough Renaissance art to enliven an overcast beach holiday, Livorno should be on the defensive. In fact, the province is as varied as its famed fish soup, *cacciucco*.

The fishy ingredients, a little of everything in the right proportions, apply to Livorno's seascapes. Captured in moody canvases by the Tuscan Impressionists, the rocky northern coast is as dramatic as the southern coast is soothing. The mainland stretches from wild, marshy Maremma to the rugged, hilly interior, or the Elban mountains.

Livorno is no architectural desert: a coastline of Pisan watchtowers and Medicean fortresses hides the occasional Roman villa or Etruscan necropolis. Inland, the neglected hilltop villages inspired equally romantic verse from Carducci, Livorno's greatest poet. Livorno is rich in Romanesque and baroque architecture but the lone sanctuary or homely red-painted farmhouse are truer to the province's individuality.

Livorno City: The city, which used to be called Leghorn in English, owes its existence to the silting up of Pisa in 1530, and the Livornese joke that, unlike their rivals, the Pisans, they will never be so careless as to let the sea slip away from them. In 1421 the Florentines paid the Genoese 100,000 florins for Livorno, a vast sum for such a malaria-infested and mosquito-ridden village.

It was the enlightened Cosimo I who transformed Livorno into the greatest Medicean port in 1575. Cosimo was aided by Buontalenti whose plan for the "ideal city" envisaged the present star-shaped port with its five bastions.

Grand Duke Ferdinand employed Robert Dudley, the great naval engineer, to build the harbour walls and administer the port. Dudley benefited from Livorno's status as an "open city" with free trade, tax exemption and shelter from persecution.

As late as the 19th century it was an enterprising yet patrician city. Cosmopolitan salons, elegant avenues, Renaissance and baroque villas made it a fashionable port of call for the "Grand Tourists". But after 80 bombing raids in World War II, Livorno resembles a modern necropolis.

Except for the oyster beds laid down by Cosimo, the Medicean port is unchanged. The crumbling red-brick **Fortezza Vecchia** is a patchwork of Livornese history: Antonio da Sangallo's and Buontalenti's masterpiece has Roman remains in its vast Medicean dungeons; 14th-century Pisan walls enclose a small Medicean house and are topped by a Romanesque tower.

The **Fortezza Nuova**, built in 1590, completed the Medicis' ambitious fortifications. The murky canals encircling it once led to Pisa. Now restored, the New Fortress is home to conferences, festivals and children's romps through the palm trees and gardens.

Between the fortresses is **Venezia**, an ill-lit, seedy area not unlike working-

Preceding pages: ships departing from Livorno. Left, the Tuscan archipelago.

class Venice. The canals are lined with 17th-century *palazzi, crumbling* warehouses, fish stands and workshops.

The area comes alive in July with the *Carnevale Marinaro,* more of a water pageant than a race. Escorted by swimmers in carnival masks, bedecked boats follow the maze of canals between the two fortresses and sail under the main square, Piazza Repubblica. Visitors soon realise that the city lives on commerce, not tourism. A baffling one-way street system and gruff hotel and restaurant service reflect the fact that most tourists spend only one night here on their way to the islands, the hills or to Florence.

Livorno is often described as a *città particolare,* an unusual city, and it is hard to visualise it as a medieval town or an elegant seaside resort. Unless fascinated by naval engineering and military history, most visitors cannot bridge the gap between Livorno's glorious past and ordinary present.

The rocky west coast: Most of the city's artistic and literary pretensions lie in **Ardenza** and **Antignano**, now elegant coastal resorts. On the outskirts of Livorno, Villa Maria houses the Museum of Contemporary Art and is particularly good for 1930s art, especially Ottone Rosai's lyrical landscapes and shadowy depictions of fascism.

Villa Fabbricotti houses a gallery to the "Macchiaioli Movement", the Italian counterpart to Impressionism. While a fuller collection exists in Florence's Pitti Palace, Lega, Signorini and Fattori are well represented.

This area was home to much of what the Livornese called "Leghorn's British Factory". In 1819, after the tragic death of their son, Percy and Mary Shelley moved to Villa Valsovana, now a depressing building in the suburbs. The sea views and the dramatic summer storms revived the poet enough to enable him to work on his blank verse drama, *The Cenci,* and to write his famous *Ode to a Skylark.*

Mary Shelley's description of the villa reflected standard Romantic happiness: "The peasants sang as they worked beneath our window during the heat of a

The harb at Livor

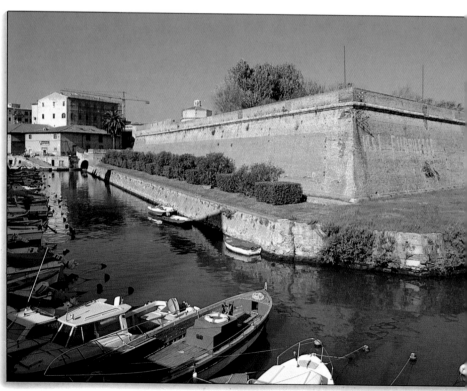

very hot summer; and at night the water wheel creaked and the fireflies flashed among the hedges." Byron, living at Villa Dupouy in Ardenza, was a frequent visitor when not working on *Don Juan*. Ardenza is now a fashionable coastal resort flanked by palms, box hedges and Liberty villas.

From prosperous Antignano, once a mere creek at the foot of the Montenero hills, a road or rickety cable car climbs to the **Sanctuary of Madonna di Montenero**, the patron saint of Tuscany. For those who dare look, there are views of Livorno, Elba and even Corsica. Between 1345 and 1774 the original shrine was transformed into a church.

The church is always full of votive offerings from relics to crutches and gold hearts to handwritten promises. Beside the sanctuary is a deep series of watery grottoes. Outside, elixirs are on sale to gullible visitors from beyond the Madonna's parish. Once the ritual stroll and religious observance is over, the locals head for **Castiglioncello**'s fish restaurants with a clear conscience but

without elixirs. Dried cod, red mullet and a spicy version of bouillabaisse are best eaten at inland rustic *trattorie*, or cheap dockside bars, not at exorbitant resort restaurants.

Out of season, the high coastal road from Ardenza to Castiglioncello is a delight, with spectacular views of the wildest coastline in the province. The coast becomes progressively more rugged as Ardenza's hills of neat dwarf oaks give way to rocky creeks cut into deep pine woods.

The road winds past Medici castles, watchtowers and even follies. **Castello del Boccale**, encircled by gulls and rocky paths to the shore, is a Medicean fort converted into a villa. At **Calafuria**, an isolated Medicean tower and distorted rock formations provided the Macchiaioli painters with a dramatic setting. But their favourite spot was **Romito**, a Grand Ducal castle later occupied by the French in 1799. It looks like a whimsical folly, a miniature bandstand perched over the sea.

After exposed Romito, the coastline

Ship painting, Livorno.

becomes wild and wooded. As **Quercia-nella** comes into view, pine woods run down to the water's edge; small coves, shingle beaches and a narrow harbour struggle for space.

The Lucchese, proud of their flat golden sands, wonder how the Livornese can neglect their own sands below **Cecina** in favour of **Castiglioncello**'s fashionable rocks. But the Livornese place adventure over comfort, just as they prefer a living city to a museum city, modern art to Renaissance art, "ver-nacular" theatre to classical theatre, the Risorgimento poet Carducci to Floren-tine Dante. The cunning Livornese also know that there are sandy bays tucked into the rocks.

Cosimo's fort, built on the pine-clad promontory, was designed to keep the pirates at bay but since the 19th century has drawn all the great Italian Im-pressionists. In the 1930s Castiglion-cello was popular with film stars and, although now less chic, it is still one of Marcello Mastroianni's haunts.

Rural Maremma: Ignoring **Cecina** and the vast **California** beach, take the in-land road towards Bibbona and the real Maremma beyond. Quiet lanes trace through marshy countryside dotted with red farmhouses and occasional herds of placid white Maremman cattle.

The Grand Dukes drained the swamps in 1828 but the reclamation was only completed in fascist times. The neatly parcelled countryside is a result of the 1950 land reforms designed to break up the *latifundia*, the old feudal estates. Expropriated land was irrigated and ploughed but also divided into uneco-nomical strips, each linked to a coopera-tive or to a local farmer. Unconsciously, perhaps, these paternalistic reforms drew on fascist models of land settlement, creating a landscape of visually tran-quil, pastel-coloured homesteads but doing nothing to stem the painful drift away from the land.

Bibbona is a higgledy-piggledy me-dieval village traditionally linked to Volterra. One of its simple churches, Santa Maria delle Pietà, has the odd inscription, *Terrible Est Locus Ist* –

Coast road at Castiglioncello (1880), by Adolfo Tommasi.

either written after a touch of Livornese fever or because the church is built on a precarious slope.

Nearby is the **Oasi di Bolgheri**, a nature reserve and bird colony. It is a place apart, neither sea nor land. The "Oasis" is home to moorhens, wild ducks, herons, egrets and migratory birds which might end up as Bolgheri roast duck or thrush *alla Carducci*.

From Bibbona it is a short drive to the tiny chapel of **San Guido** and to medieval **Bolgheri**, the land beloved by Giusè Carducci, one of Italy's finest poets. So potent is his work that Tuscans still tend to see the intensely green valley through Carducci's brooding eyes. The landscape is a shrine to a poet loved as much for his revolutionary fervour and commitment to national unity as for his melancholic verse.

San Guido and Bolgheri are linked by a magnificent avenue of cypresses, almost 5 km (3 miles) long, planted in 1801 by Camillo della Gherardesca. In Carducci's celebrated poem the tall flowing trees are *quasi in corsa giganti giovinetti*, "galloping young giants" or ranks of upstanding Tuscan soldiers waiting in double file for inspection.

The flatness beyond the trees is broken by low farmhouses, olive trees and the village vineyards. The gateway to the village is the ancient door to the Gherardesca castle. The poet's home was in the village as was the home of his first love, Maria Banchini. A square called Piazza Bionda Maria recalls his poem, *If Only I'd Married You, Blonde Maria*, a lament which sounds marginally more poetic in Italian.

Lines of Carducci's verse in Bolgheri are as common as Dante inscriptions are in Florence. Busts of Carducci are available at the local shop, sold alongside bottles of Sassicaia, one of Italy's most costly wines, which comes from the Marchesi Incisi estate.

For the resolutely cheerful there is an austere cemetery where the poet's beloved "Nonna Lucia" is buried, "her white solemnity dressed in black" and the only provider of solace in his dismal childhood. For the faint of heart,

Geraniums in the afternoon sunshine.

Bolgheri's excellent wine will dispel Carducci's ghost.

Castagneto Carducci was once a Gherardesca stronghold and a scene of more childhood misery for the young Carducci but is an attractive hilltop village in its own right. Superficially, little has changed since the Gherardesca lords drained the land, planted the vines and encircled the castle with high stone walls. From its rocky balcony, the town surveys pine forests, plains, golden beaches and two castles. On summer evenings the town is popular with *borghesi* families tempted by the views – and the aromas of sizzling sausages, roast pigeon and hare.

Sassetta, a bird's nest of a village, was once accessible only to local warriors who thrived on feuds and a diet of game. The area was damned in Dante's *Inferno* as "an impenetrable thicket without paths, leafy patches or apple trees". Since then, Sassetta has sat on its mass of red marble and waited for visitors to penetrate the deep chestnut woods.

Despite the serenity, few have visited its medieval Castello, parish church and alleyways. The locals are no longer ferocious except towards their traditional enemy, Monteverdi Marittima, with whom they share a patron saint, Sant' Andrea, but nothing else. It is a hardy, self-sufficient community with a tradition of weaving, embroidery and pipe making. An injunction on the wall sensibly tells visitors, *Lavorate in città, Ristorative a Sassetta,* ("Work in the city, rest in Sassetta").

Thrush hunters: The *sagra del tordo* is a celebration of the thrush in a place where hunting is both a religious cult and a hobby, carried out in all seasons, legally or otherwise. The last Sunday of October heralds a torchlit procession, a *palio* in costume, and a banquet of roast thrush served with chestnut-flavoured *polenta*. The village displays signs of token tourism: a Zona Climatica board publicises the fresh climate while the summer "information office" is run by eager children.

From Sassetta a winding road through olives, oleanders and woodland leads to

Cypress copse after the harvest.

Suvereto. The well-preserved villages have much in common, including the same line in advertising. A battered sign encapsulates the region's charm: *La Mattina al Mare, il Pomeriggio ai Monti* ("Mornings at the Sea, Afternoons in the Mountains").

Suvereto was the first "free commune" in Maremma and is proud of its 13th-century Palazzo Comunale with its intact loggia and crenellated tower. The early Romanesque church of San Giusto combines decorated Byzantine portals with a Pisan facade. Many churches and houses are decorated with the local red, brown or grey variegated marble which has been quarried since medieval times.

Suvereto's urban design, based on rising concentric circles, is simple but effective: each level corresponds to a street, from San Giusto to the towering Rocca above. The steep ascent winds through a rabbit warren of covered passageways. The fortress itself was the scene of a great royal funeral in 1313: Harry VII of Luxembourg died at the Battle of Buonconvento in Siena prov-ince but was embalmed here and buried in Pisa.

The sedate village pours on to the streets for the evening *passeggiata* and, in season, for the *sagra del cinghiale*, a wild boar feast combining food, folklore and spectacle. Early December signals flag-waving displays and crossbow competitions between the rival *rioni* or districts. It all culminates in a feast dedicated to the "King of the woods". The boar is washed down with the Ghimbergo wine which locals claim is "as simple and honest as the people of Suvereto".

This area is **Val di Cornia**, an enchanted region of gently wooded hills, hot springs, lush valleys and old quarries. Wild orchids and anemones grow on the rocky outcrops while a mix of myrtle, broom and yellow saxifrage cover the slopes.

Up towards **Monte Calvi**, the "Macchiaioli" artists liked to paint the cork trees: the contrast of the fragile leaves and gnarled branches occupied them for days. Wildlife often trotted

19th-century village life, also by Adolfo Tommasi.

into the picture, particularly white Maremman oxen and sad-eyed Chianina cows; today it is more likely to be foxes, porcupine and foolish wild boar.

At **Montioni**, a village and spa southeast of Suvereto, Elisa Bacciocchi, Napoleon's sister used to bathe nude in the hot springs. Pauline, his favourite sister, used to scandalise the Elban natives in much the same way.

The ancient baths at **Caldana Terme** are even more impressive than those at Montioni. Both the natural lake and pool contain ferrous sulphates and natural radioactivity "guaranteed to restore youthful vigour in one session."

In spite of its name, **Campiglia Maritima** is a small market and mining town set in the hills. As a "free" commune it was fought over by the Florentines, Pisans and Sienese, all of whom have left heraldic traces on the town walls, four gateways and imposing Rocca. Coats of arms surmount the Gothic arches of Palazzo Pretorio.

The Romanesque church of San Giovanni has an equally turbulent past. When San Fiorenzo's relics were found nearby, Piombino and Campiglia disputed ownership. A test was devised to establish the saint's posthumous sense of home: the relics were put on a cart and the oxen, left to decide where to go, trudged uphill to the saint's present resting place. Naturally the oxen were *Campigliese.*

Campiglia's mineral past is never far from the surface. Apart from viewing the permanent mineral display, visitors can visit a working quarry in **Madonna di Fucinaia**. The Campigliese boast that their marble contributed to Florence's Duomo is to be taken with a Tuscan pinch of salt: claiming ownership of national monuments is a common regional habit.

Just outside town is the **Rocca San Silvestro**, the centre of a site quarried since Etruscan times. Recent excavations have revealed traces of copper, lead, silver and tin and a minerological park is planned to show the historical development of Tuscan mining.

Although mining is an important cultural tradition, food plays a bigger role in the local economy. The simple peasant dishes reflect Campiglia's traditional poverty and dignity. Many dishes were imported by the so-called *Lombardi,* seasonal workers from the Emilian or Pistoian hills.

These shepherds and woodcutters lived in tenements near the swamps but came inland in the evenings to mix with the locals. In exchange for kindness and dinner, the Lombardi introduced those in the Val Di Cornia to chestnut *polenta,* rice soups and *raviolini.*

Local game, sausages and *funghi porcini* were easily incorporated and Campigliese cuisine has never looked back. The dynamic Suvereto and Campigliese tourist offices will suggest restaurants and *Agriturismo* farm stays where these delights can be sampled.

The Etruscan coast: For sightings of flamingoes sheltering under umbrella pines, the **Rimigliano** nature reserve hugs the coast between San Vincenzo and Populonia. If the coast beckons, San Vicenzo's metallic sands and endless bungalow colony can be sacrificed

Windswept bay of Baratti.

to Populonia's Etruscan city. The Etruscans considerately had themselves buried by a pine-fringed beach, reason enough to visit the only Etruscan city built on the coast.

Behind the sweep of **Baratti Bay** lies **Populonia**, the last of the 12 Etruscan cities to be founded. The ancient city was divided into two parts: the "acropolis", the religious centre clustered high around the village; and the maritime and industrial centre around the bay. The necropoli cover the slopes between the two centres. When the Maremma revealed its treasures in the 19th century, the contrast between the desolate marshes and the sophisticated tombs stirred locals and scholars alike.

Thanks to its proximity to Elba and to the metal-bearing Campigliese hills, Populonia became a rich industrial city, often called "the ancient Pittsburgh". While Elban iron ore was smelted and then traded within the Etruscan League, minerals from Campiglia were shipped to Corsica, Sardinia and France.

Populonia's secure industrial base meant that, unlike most Etruscan cities, it flourished from the 9th century BC to the Roman age without economic or political upheavals. In the ancient "industrial zone", excavations have uncovered a blast furnace and sophisticated metal-working equipment dating back to the 6th century BC. Foreign slave labour was used to dig water channels, operate the furnace and mint coins. In the 6th century BC Populonia was the first Etruscan city to mint gold, silver and bronze coins, often featuring a lion's head. Since the main tombs were used continuously, all periods and tomb types are represented; early oriental "trench" tombs; cylindrical "chamber" tombs; "temple" tombs and tiny "niche" tombs. Sadly, many tombs lie buried or collapsed under the weight of ancient slag heaps. Others have been looted, some recently.

Every few years a new tomb reveals tools, silver coins and bronze jewellery, often designed by resident Greek goldsmiths and gem cutters. Most of the tomb contents are now in Florence but a

Etruscan tombs at Populonia.

tiny Etruscan museum in Populonia contains sacred objects found in the unlikely "Tomb of the Harpy".

From Populonia there are smoky views of **Piombino** but the most typical first view is from a hot traffic jam on the way to Elba. Sprawling iron and steel works continue Populonia's tradition. Piombino has been ruled by the Pisans, the noble Appiani family, the ignoble Cesare Borgia and, most effectively, by Elisa Bacciocchi, Princess of Piombino and Lucca and Napoleon's sister.

As befits a city which was once the capital of a tiny state, vestiges of old Piombino remain in Piazza Verdi's town walls and in the heavily restored Palazzo Comunale and fortress. Best seen on foot, the city's genteel, dilapidated charm lingers on in quiet squares and Art Deco bars.

The Island of Elba: Known to the Etruscans as *Ilva* ("Iron") and to the Greeks as *Aethalia* ("Soot Island"), **Elba** has exploited its mineral wealth for more than 3,000 years. As the European powers occasionally took an interest in the island's attractive strategic position, waves of Romans, Pisans and Genoese were followed by Spanish, Turkish and French invasions.

In 1548 Duke Cosimo I fortified the capital and named it "Cosmopolis" after himself. His great military architect, Giovanni Camerini, designed the star-shaped defensive system and the two defensive forts, Forte della Stella and Forte Falcone.

However, **Portoferraio** is inextricably linked to that other great modern imperialist, Napoleon. He made his official home in two converted windmills above the charming Forte della Stella. Under the terms of the Congress of Vienna in 1814, Elba became a principality of the fallen sovereign.

Napoleon's great empire shrank to his faithful "old guard", pragmatic mother and libertine sister Pauline. Most Elbans were proud to have him improve the administration, build new roads, develop the mines and expand the fleet. The foreign commissioners rightly feared the "Eagle" might spread its wings

Evergreens enrich the landscape.

and after nine months Napoleon flew, with the connivance of the Elbans.

On the eve of his escape, he sent for the island governor and reputedly confided, "I am leaving my mother and my sister in your care to show you how much I trust you. I am also placing in your charge this country which means so much to me". He escaped with 1,000 troops, the Elbans' affection, his sister's diamond necklace and his mother's curt blessing, "Go and fulfil your destiny."

His **Palazzina dei Mulini** was lined with silver and books from Fontainebleau and furniture from Elsa's house in Piombino. Most of its charm lies in the period furnishings and Italianate gardens. His country villa, **San Martino**, set amid woods and vineyards, was purchased with one of Pauline's handy diamond necklaces. There is a fine garden shaded by evergreen oaks and terraced vineyards. The 17th-century **Misericordia church** displays one of Napoleon's bronze deathmasks and a requiem mass is still said for him on 5 May each year. Napo-

leon used to say, "When I die, the world will heave a sigh of relief," a sentiment not shared on Elba.

To the east of Portoferraio is Elba's iron heart. Most minerals are concentrated around **Rio Marina** where open cast mining, polishing and jewellery making still exist. Surrounded by hills rich in ferrous oxide, the whole port has a pinkish hue, including the 16th-century tower of San Rocco.

Most of the minerals are ferrous, including black lodestone, yellow pyrites and blackish-red ilvaites. Semi-precious stones are also worked, including green quartz, black onyx and pink or pale green beryl. More than 700 exhibits are on display in the Museo Mineralogica.

Inland, **Rio Nell'Elba** is a strange, rather wild village perched on a couple of ledges among desolate mountain slopes. Seemingly untouched by tourism, its misfortunes can perhaps be traced to its destruction by Barbarossa's pirates and abduction into slavery of the entire population.

Many of the rocky beaches are min-

Farmhouse in the Maremma.

eralogical treasure hunts. A line of parked cars signals hazardous tracks down steep cliffs to the sea. From Rio to Cavo in the northeast, the road cuts through woods and moorland. Paths trail through gorse, heather and the wild flowers of the maquis.

The spectacular drive westward from Portoferraio to Marciana Marina passes a number of popular beaches including Le Ghiaie, noted for its multicoloured pebbles, and **La Biodola**, considered the chicest sandy beach on the island. There, serried lines of deckchairs contain bronzed Florentine villa owners dressed in Valentino swimwear.

At La Biodola and **Procchio**, a more egalitarian paradise, the rocky ocean bottom means clear, sediment free water. Between Procchio and Marciana Marina is "La Paolina", a rock named after Napoleon's sister whose passion for nude sunbathing still scandalises the natives today.

Marciana Marina has made a smooth transition from fishing village to elegant resort. Set amidst magnolias,
palms and oleanders at the end of a long valley, the resort narrowly avoids picture-postcard beauty. The thin, pastel-coloured houses in the old quarter are reminiscent of those on the Ligurian coast. On 12 August the port explodes in a firework display in honour of Santa Chiara, the patron saint.

Marciana Alta, perched above, is the island's best preserved medieval town. Chestnut woods frame the red-tiled rooftops, narrow alleys and crumbling Pisan fortress. The local "Antiquarium" displays Etruscan sacred objects as well as Roman oil lamps and ivory statues found in shipwrecks.

From Marciana, a cable car lurches over crags and chasms to the summit of **Monte Capanne**. Even in the height of summer this wooded mountain area is quiet and breezy. Hot springs and old hermit caves often come in sociable pairs. Depending on the season, patches of orchids, snapdragons and helianthemums are as common as the cedars and chestnuts above. Even the coastal vegetation is more exotic than in the

Herbs, flowers and sun-dried tomatoes overlook the woods of the Maremma.

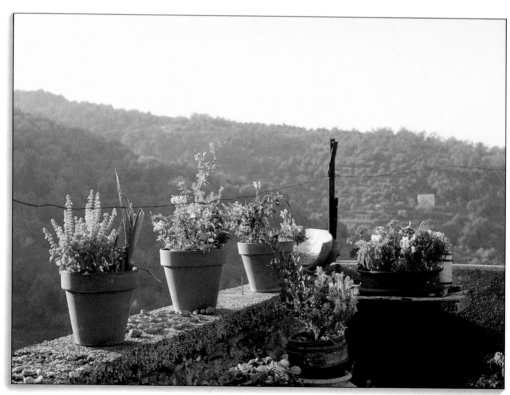

east; eucalyptus and magnolia rather than vines or rough maquis.

From Marciana to **Marina di Campo** in the south, the high road winds past the neglected village of **Poggio** to **Monte Perone** nature reserve, vineyards and the plains behind Marina. With its expanse of golden sands, Marina is a loud, rather tacky resort near the airport.

However, two dusty medieval villages nestle in the hills behind. Fortified by the Pisans in the 12th century, **San Ilario** and **San Piero in Campo** conceal Romanesque churches and hermitages. A tangy *panzanella* or crisp *crostone* blows the cobwebs away.

Capoliveri is a traditional inland village with a Roman and Medieval past as dramatic as its location high on the southern promontory. Carved into the iron mountain of **Monte Calamita**, Capoliveri is also an old mining village. The black, iron-bearing lodestone still plays havoc with the compasses of passing ships but is ideal for the production of sweet red Aleatico, said to be Napoleon's favourite wine.

Often independent, Capoliveri was the only village to reject Napoleon in 1814. The story is that only the intercession of a local beauty saved the village. It soon became part of Napoleon's hunting estate and is still noted for its dishes of woodcock, pheasant and hare.

The hills are covered with heath, fern and juniper; the scent of thyme and rosemary are never far away. Roads from the hills to the sea often turn into cart tracks but are worth pursuing unless specifically marked *strada privata*; this is often the only access to the loveliest beaches.

Innamorata is a sandy inlet linked to the romance between a nymph and a fisherman. Believing her lover drowned in a shipwreck, the nymph drowned herself; he survived and asked the gods to turn him into a seagull so he could seek her out.

From the village there are views of **Pianosa**, **Montecristo**, **Gorgona** and **Capraia** islands. Inaccessible Pianosa and Gorgona are prisons, now filled with Mafiosi caught after the 1991–94 crime blitz. Montecristo is a nature reserve; Capraia is a miniature Elba without its history or architecture.

Capoliveri also surveys fashionable **Porto Azzurro**, the main town on the east coast and once part of the Spanish protectorate. The vast Forte Longone, built in 1603 as a Spanish naval base, is now a top security prison. Visitors can buy crafts from the prison shop, the scene of a mass break-out in 1987. Forte Focardo, its sister fortress across the bay, has uninviting ramparts running down a sheer cliff.

By day, the port is an uninspired seafront with slightly tacky side streets. In the evening, it is a place for a leisurely *passeggiata*, designer shopping and people watching. It is also the place for seafood specialities: a *cacciucco* of octopus, scorpion, dogfish and prawns; *riso nero*, "black rice" with cuttlefish or squid – perhaps followed by *schiaccia briaca* ("drunken cake"), made with hazelnuts and Aleatico wine.

Distinctive wines: There is also dry Elba Bianco, sweet Moscato, a heady white, or Elba Rosso, similar to Chianti. The distinct flavour is due to the iron, phosphorous, arsenic and natural radioactivity in the fertile soil. After enough Elban wine, one's impressions of Porto Azzurro are of harbour lights, cheerful bustle and gently bobbing boats.

Behind Porto Azzurro is the most mystical spot on the island, the remote sanctuary of **Madonna di Monserrato**. It was built in the Toledan style by a Spanish governor, Ponce de Leon, in 1606. A steep, rocky track leads high up the mountain to the tiny red-domed church balanced among the crags. Despite mountain goats cavorting on impossible ledges, the place has great solemnity. There are few visitors and the only sound is of the water running down a conduit in the mountains.

The Spanish facade and belltower find echoes in the Black Madonna inside, which is a copy of an early Spanish painting. Every September, an Elban pilgrimage celebrates the *Festa della Madonna* with a walk past ravines and isolated grottoes to the church. At the foot of the hills is a rustic restaurant with service as leisurely as an Elban Sunday.

GROSSETO

Grosseto is the largest and least known of the provinces of Tuscany, yet it has some of the most beautiful coastline in the entire region. The landscape is varied, ranging from the flat plains around Grosseto, now drained, to the thickly wooded peak of Monte Amiata, capped with snow throughout the winter months, to the smooth hills bordering the province of nearby Siena.

The coastline has an unrivalled mix of Mediterranean flora and fauna along its wide sandy beaches, or on promontories descending to the sea and lagoons. Three areas (Monti dell' Uccellina, Monte Argentario and Monte Amiata) have been converted into nature parks, perfect for trekking, bird-watching, canoeing and horse-riding.

The region is dominated by the marshy plain of the **Maremma**, "the swamp by the sea", described by Salvatore Battaglia in the *Grande Dizionario della Lingua Italiana*, as "a generally flat coastal zone, a swampy and insalubrious plain adjacent to the sea, formed following the stagnation of watercourses blocked at the mouth by the existence of coastal sand-bars". Until quite recently travel books tended to warn visitors away from the area, but the marshes have now been successfully reclaimed and it has become a popular tourist spot, especially for nature lovers.

Etruscan influence: Evidence of Roman and Etruscan settlements in the area is considerable. One of the most important Etruscan cities, Vetulonia, is close to Grosseto, as are the once-prosperous Roman and Etruscan settlements of Cosa and Roselle.

By medieval times the coastal plain had become quite unsafe and unhealthy, partly due to the plundering of Saracens from the sea, partly because of the malarial swamps. In the early 14th century the whole area fell under the power of Siena. Towards the end of the 16th century, Grosseto became part of the Grand Duchy of Tuscany, until the formation of Italy in 1860.

The capital of the province is a relatively recent city by Tuscan standards. **Grosseto** was built as a fortified citadel only around AD 950, when the Saracens looted the former capital, Roselle, less than 10 miles away. The city has expanded beyond its walls only in the last part of this century, to provide housing for its 50,000 inhabitants. Mainly because of its unhealthy climate, Grosseto was for a long time no more than a military citadel, and was never as big as Massa Marittima or Pitigliano. Only during this century has it become the largest city in the area, but it is still primarily an administrative centre with practically no industry.

The old town of Grosseto is quite small, contained within an ancient six-sided citadel created by the Aldobrandeschi family in the 11th century, and surrounded by brick walls added by the Medici in the 15th century.

There is a 14th-century **Duomo** on the main square, at the end of the traditional *corso*, where all the best shops and a café are to be found for the pleasure of late afternoon strollers.

The Duomo, dedicated to San Lorenzo, was built towards the end of the 13th century on a church constructed about 100 years earlier. It is a mixture of Romanesque and Gothic styles, with a rose window and three magnificent doors with Romanesque arches in the main facade. There is an adjoining 15th-century campanile in *cotto* bricks, as well as a museum displaying a *Madonna dell' Uccellino* of the Pietro Lorenzetti School, and a *Madonna delle Ciliege*, which is considered a Sassetta masterpiece.

Next to the Duomo in the Palazzo del Licio is the **Museo Archeologico**, one of the richest museums in the area; it has an excellent collection of pre-Etruscan, Etruscan and Roman artifacts.

The recently restored museum displays cinerary urns, vivid terracottas, pottery and coins. This is the place to pick up maps of the key archeological sites where the finds were made: Roselle (7 km/4 miles north of the city),
Vetulonia (17km/10 miles north of the city); Talamone, Pitigliano and Saturnia to the south.

There is an important archeological site at nearby **Roselle**, with a nearly intact circuit of Romano-Etruscan walls, a Roman forum, paved streets, basilicas, villas and baths. **Vetulonia**, which was originally the Etruscan city of Vatluna, has remains of Roman houses and a Mithraeu, and is due to reopen to the public in 1995–96.

The coast: Grosseto is in the middle of a flat plain formed by the Ombrone river and is about 17 km (10 miles) away from the sea. Many Grossetans have a second home along the nearby coast, either in modern and congested **Marina di Grosseto** or in the more snobbish and quieter **Principina** hidden in a beautiful forest of maritime pines.

Some prefer **Castiglione della Pescaia**, an old fishermen's village where they can keep a sailing boat, ideally located at the foot of rocky mountains north of Grosseto. This is a famous coastal resort. The harbour, crowded **The marshy plain of the Maremma.**

with both fishermen's and tourists' boats, is believed to be the Etruscan *Hasta*, or *Portus Traianus* in Roman times. Overlooking the port is the Rocca Aragonese with its mighty walls and towers dating back to the 14th century.

Slightly north of the same promontory lies exclusive **Punta Ala**, an almost private resort situated between maritime pines and the finest sand; it has good hotels, golf clubs, horse-riding and polo facilities. The water here is nearly always calm, thanks to its sheltered position. A little further along the coast, before Follonica, is a lovely quiet bay, **Cala Violino**, so-called because of its squeaky musical sand.

Massa Marittima is about 24 km (15 miles) inland, despite its maritime name. It is one of the most astounding Tuscan cities, perched on top of a high hill on the edge of the Colline Metallifere, or "ore-bearing mountains", which divide the province of Grosseto from Siena. It was the most important town in the Maremma until the 17th century when the land silted up, and was originally called Massa; but the name of Massa Maremma or Massa Marittima has been introduced to distinguish it from Massa in Massa-Carrara province.

Massa Marittima was built around the 10th century, after the decline of ancient Populonia (*see page 231*), which was too exposed to plundering from the sea. It was known for its copper and silver mines even in Etruscan times, and the rich variety of metals available was a major factor in the economic development of the city.

The affluence of medieval Massa Marittima is apparent in its rigorous town planning, and in the concentration of public buildings (*palazzi*) around the cathedral. In the main piazza are Palazzo Vescovile (seat of the bishop), Palazzo Pretorio (seat of the governor, now also an interesting museum), Palazzo del Comune (town hall), Zecca Cittadina (the mint), Fonte Pubblica (public fountain) and Palazzo dell' Abbondanza (the public granary).

The **cathedral** (Duomo) is an example of Pisan Romanesque architecture

Cathedral of Massa Marittima.

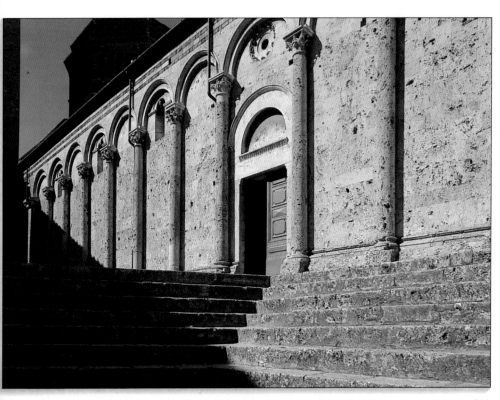

with marvellous reliefs of *Madonna delle Grazie*, ascribed to Duccio Di Buoninsegna (1316) and the *Arca di San Cerbone* (St Cerbone's ark), a masterpiece of the Sienese school of sculpture, dating back to 1324. There is a 4th-century sarcophagus in the cathedral and St Cerbone (who died in AD 380) is buried in the crypt.

A memorable experience – and a lot easier to see than Siena's *Palio* – is the traditional *Balestro del Girfalco*, every last Sunday in May and every second Sunday in August. Here the three *terzieri* of Massa (old city, new city and the outer *Borgo*) struggle for victory in a shooting contests using mechanical falcons with ancient crossbows.

There is a mining museum, located in the Palazzetto delle Armi, and it is also possible to visit a real mine, a network of tunnels very near the city.

The **Colline Metallifere** is rich in metal ores, and was the focus of the Industrial Revolution in the area, but by the end of the 19th century mining and related industries were already in decline and now these mountains are a remote and lonely region. The ancient mines and factories now in ruins present a surreal picture, hidden away in thick forests littered with strange heaps of coloured metals.

The South: Beyond the river Ombrone, the **Monti dell' Uccellina** nature park covers about 20 km (12 miles) of the coastal mountains and the marshland around the mouth of the river Ombrone. The park is entered at **Alberese, Marina di Alberese** or **Talamone**, a walled coastal resort. Its most noticeable peculiarity is the tradition of *butteri* – the only Italian cowboys. They actually won a challenge with Buffalo Bill at the end of the last century; to commemorate the event, an annual rodeo is held in August, which brings American cowboys to Alberese, a small village in the heart of the wild coastal prairie.

Other local festivals include the *Torneo del Buttero*, in Alberese, the *Sagra del Cinghiale* (boar fair) in Montepescali, and the *Sagra del Gnocco* (a culinary speciality) in Batignano, the

One of the famous *butteri* (cowboys) of the Maremma.

Sagra della Gastronomia (gastronomic fair) in Manciano and the *Sagra della Trippa* (tripe fair) in Montemerano.

Activities within the nature park include canoeing along the Ombrone river, sailing along the coast, trekking or riding across the mountains, visiting the noble ruins of San Rabano and the many towers on top of the mountains overlooking the sea, each with its story of marauding pirates and hidden treasures, going back to the times of the Saracens and Spanish galleons.

South of Monti dell' Uccellina is **Monte Argentario**. This promontory was once an island. The name of Argentario comes from *argentarius* (money-lender), since it was owned by Roman money-lenders in the 4th century. The island became attached to the mainland by two long sandbanks, containing a lagoon. The main city of the area, Orbetello, is sited on a peninsula which projects into the lagoon from the mainland.

From 1556 until 1815, Monte Argentario was politically detached from the Grand Duchy of Tuscany, existing as a separate state, under Spanish rule. It encompassed the whole promontory and the existing ports of Orbetello, Porto Santo Stefano, Porto Ercole, Talamone and Porto Azzurro, in the island of Elba, and many Spanish fortifications still remain here.

This complex landscape is a beautiful region for walking, with a wide variety of flora and fauna, and you can see magnificent sunsets and views as far as Corsica from the peak of Argentario.

Among the fortunate inhabitants of these hills are the *Passionisti* monks. In keeping with the monastic traditions of central Italy, the monks reserve some cells for pious guests, and even after a short visit the traveller may leave with a precious memento: *Amaro dei frati dell' Argentario*, a special liqueur produced by the monks.

Rocky coast: The coastline is rocky and precipitous with breathtaking descents to the sea beneath. The most easily accessible beach is the Feniglia, but it is also very popular and therefore

Walls of Massa Marittima.

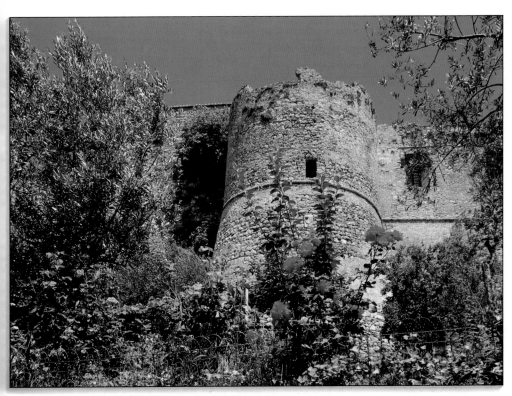

is often crowded. (It was also where the riotous genius Caravaggio died on his way back to Rome in 1610.) There are many other hidden coves and beaches, but a boat is needed to reach them; it is an ideal location for scuba diving and underwater photography.

Porto Santo Stefano is now the most important harbour in the area, and little fishing boats nestle against huge yachts in the crowded harbour. Although scarred by World War II bombing, it is still a picturesque town with many boutiques, bars and excellent *gelaterie*. For many years, Susanna Agnelli, of Fiat's Agnelli family, has been the mayoress of Porto Santo Stefano. One of her main achievements has been to slow down the rapid tourist development.

Orbetello, the state capital, stretches along a very narrow peninsula, surrounded by Spanish walls built over the previous Etruscan fortifications. The city still has a maritime atmosphere, in spite of being now almost 5 km (3 miles) from the sea. The individuality of Orbetello is reflected in its cuisine, with a

mixture of three traditions: seafood, freshwater fish from the lagoon, like the exquisite *anguilla fumata* (smoked eel), and game such as wild boar from the hillside and surrounding marshes.

The Islands: On the southern side of Monte Argentario, **Porto Ercole** has a 16th-century Spanish fortress on the hill overlooking the harbour. From Porto Ercole, a small ferry-boat offers day-trips to **Giannutri**, a tiny, virtually un-inhabited island 22km (14 miles) away where one can imagine pirates finding refuge long ago. On the island are the ruins of a Roman villa which belonged to the Domizii Enobarbi family during the first century. The villa has columns and mosaics, baths and a private pier.

Santo Stefano has a ferry connection with the fascinating island of **Giglio**, half an hour's sail off the coast. The island, the second largest in Tuscany after Elba, has an impenetrable coastline with only one easy port, Giglio Porto. Heading up into the hills, among vineyards producing grapes for the very strong, distinctive local wine, *Ansonaco*, Giglio Castello dominates the landscape. It is a fortified settlement, with arches and dark passages, and stairs carved from the rock.

Giglio has a number of sandy beaches and is covered in typical Mediterranean vegetation: aromatic herbs and plants, and orange and lemon groves. It is ideal for sailing, swimming and all water sports, but because of this and because it is close to Rome, it is very popular and is better visited out of season.

Returning to the coast, there are the important Roman remains of **Cosa**, built on top of what was originally an Etruscan settlement. The city has been excavated and the site contains a main street, a forum, a walled acropolis and capitolium from which there are magnificent views out to sea; the site is somewhat overgrown and has a melancholy air.

Below the rocky promontory is the silted up Roman port and the **Tagliata Etrusca**, the Etruscan Cut – which is in fact Roman, built as a canal to drain Lake Burano.

Inland from Monte Argentario is

Skiing on Monte Amiata.

Capalbio, one of the first towns on the hills bordering Latium (the region in which Rome is situated). It is the heart of the Maremma and famous for its brigands. One notorious *bandito*, Domenico Tiburzi, a local Robin Hood, was executed in 1896. There was disagreement over whether he could be buried in consecrated land and eventually a typical Italian compromise was reached: he was buried at the edge of the cemetery with his head in sacred ground, the rest of his body outside.

Capalbio is much appreciated by Roman intelligentsia, who have bought up every corner of the village as a fashionable summer refuge from the capital. Nearby is the magical **Tarot Garden** (Giardino dei Tarocchi, Pescia Fiorentina) created by French sculptor Niki de Saint Phalle, and inspired by the symbolism of the tarot. Open in summer, this park displays fantastic, brightly coloured figures covered in mirror and mosaic, glinting in the sun.

Capalbio Scalo is a few hundred metres from Lake Burano, where there is a lake and small nature park, a favourite stopping place for thousands of birds migrating from the former Yugoslavia to North Africa. Bird-watching (seagulls, coots, pheasants and blackbirds, among others) is the main attraction for visitors, but the flora is also very varied, with cork-oaks, holm-oaks, lake reeds and junipers.

Across the densely wooded hills north of Capalbio is the flat plain of the River Albegna, now completely drained, which leads to the **castle of Marsiliana**, once an Etruscan town and now the only property left to the Corsini family, who originally owned the entire area. Most of these swamps were expropriated by the state, drained and then distributed to small landowners.

Not far from the coast, **Magliano in Toscana** still has intact city walls, built in the 15th century. Both civil and religious architecture show a strong Romanesque influence, with Gothic and Renaissance additions. A perfect example of the blend of styles is San Giovanni Battista, a Romanesque church, with

Church and farmhouse, Monte Amiata.

Gothic side windows and a Renaissance facade.

A few miles inland, **Scansano**, now a quiet town with a separate fortified section (*oppido*) on top of a modest hill, used to be the summer capital of the province, when all administrative powers were moved from malarial Grosseto during the hot season.

Travelling eastwards across hills and moors inhabited by *butteri* and their cattle you arrive at **Saturnia**, about 32 km (20 miles) from the coast. Saturnia is a quiet little town, drowsy under the immense weight of its past. It was the Etruscan Aurinia, and then came under Roman control in 280 BC.

The atmosphere here is so attractive that a number of northern Italians have settled in the area and run speciality shops in the village, which is centred around a large oak-ringed piazza. Saturnia and surrounding villages have some notable *trattorie*.

Through the old Porta Romana, half hidden by vegetation, you can walk about 3 km (2 miles) down the hill along the old Roman road to **Terme di Saturnia,** a modern spa, where you can experience the healing waters coming from the earth beneath the distant Monte Amiata. You can swim in the thermal pools or in the hot waterfall at Cascate del Gorello, on the Montemerano road.

This southern part of Tuscany is in the process of gentrification and many Romans and foreigners living in Rome buy property here. One reason why the area is so attractive is that for centuries it has been neglected by the main traffic routes, one on the coast along the Roman Via Aurelia, and one inland along Roman Via Cassia, both going north from Rome. The old Via Clodia, between the coast and Via Cassia, almost disappeared, cutting out important Saturnia and other towns like Sovana, Sorano and Pitigliano – all of which are well worth including on a holiday itinerary.

The most important town in the area is **Pitigliano**, which in the mid-18th century was one of the main cities in southern Tuscany. After a drive along a particularly tortuous road, Pitigliano

Pitigliano has wine and oil cellars cut out of caves.

rises up before you, a spectacular sight. It has the distinct shape of a crib, built on a hill of volcanic tufa with wine and olive oil cellars carved out of caves in the hillside.

The town is centred around a magnificent fortified **Palazzo**, built by the Orsini in the 16th century. Palazzo Orsini is a separate citadel, linked to the town by a vast, arched aqueduct and close to the new **Etruscan museum**.

Pitigliano used to be called "little Jerusalem" because it was a refuge for Jews fleeing from religious persecution in the Papal states. Even today the Jewish section of the city – 60 narrow streets crossing two main ones – is still quite distinct. Tiny streets and winding alleys intersect and the backs of the houses form a sheer drop to the valley below. It is one of the few places in Catholic Italy where you can find kosher wine or turkey "ham" (*billo*), another Jewish speciality. *Bianco di Pitigliano* from the tufa wine cellars is also well-known.

Sovana, a few miles away, is a tiny village rich in history. There is an important Etruscan necropolis as well as Roman ruins hidden in the surrounding woods, but a local guide is recommended, rather than trying to find your own way around.

No visit to this area would be complete without a walk in the old streets of **Sorano,** which is also built on a tufa outcrop. Unfortunately some of the buildings have begun to collapse into the steep valleys around the city, but the great majority of Sorano can be seen without danger.

Visible from every corner of the province on a clear day, particularly in a snowy winter, is **Monte Amiata**, the highest peak in Tuscany south of Florence. It is a dormant volcano, with hot geysers on its slopes and underground waters that supply the spa at Saturnia. Monte Amiata is a paradise for mountain trekkers, and a refreshing escape during the hot summer months.

The third main town in the area, **Santa Fiora,** is particularly delightful, and has exceptional works of art in the 12th-century Santa Fiora and Santa Lucilla churches, including ceramics by Andrea and Luca della Robbia.

Arcidosso was the birthplace of David Lazzaretti, "The Prophet of the Amiata". In the 19th century Lazzaretti created a revolutionary social and religious movement with its headquarters on **Monte Labro**, a lonely peak which forms part of a nature reserve where deer, chamois and wolves roam, and protected trees, shrubs and wildflowers grow. The best time is autumn, when the crowds have left and the wild mushrooms appear.

Local dishes: Maremmana cuisine is not particularly sophisticated but it is unique. Dishes peculiar to the region include *prosciutto di cinghiale*, boar ham; *acquacotta*, a celery and tomato soup, served on top of a slice of stale bread scented with garlic and garnished with a poached egg; *scottiglia*, a mixture of various meats, such as boar and *capriolo* (deer), cooked with fresh olives; local *pecorino* cheeses, Monte Amiata chestnuts, *anice* biscuits and *ricotta* cheese. Good local wines include *Morellino di Scansano*, *Bianco di Pitigliano*, and *Ansonaco di Argentario*.

Narrow streets in "Little Jerusalem".

SIENA

The approach to **San Gimignano** on the old Lombardy-Rome pilgrim route is justly famous. After speeding through sprawling Poggibonsi, the loveliness of the road as it curves around Monterrigioni's perfect walls to the many-towered town is even more marked. The seasons lie in wait: emerald green wheat and yellow rape seed are only a prelude to golden summer corn, parched olives and autumnal burnt sienna.

The local poet Folgore, nicknamed "Lightning" for his speed of thought, celebrated much the same landscape in the 14th century. The famous San Gimignano towers come into view behind olives, cypresses and vines.

Apart from the fact that only 13 of the original 76 *belli torri* are left, Folgore would feel at home. Not that "home" conjures up the atmosphere of daily terror, the hazards of rocks and scalding pitch tossed from great heights.

The 12th- and 13th-century towers were designed as keeps by the *magnati*, or nobles, during the internecine Guelf-Ghibelline feuds. The original conflict between the Ghibelline Salvucci family and the Guelf Ardinghelli family degenerated into more localised disputes between rival factions. As height meant prestige, power and status, towers were as big as the nobles' egos.

Earthy pleasures: Folgore was lucky enough to be writing in a period of relative wealth and peace. He has left sensuous descriptions of the city's earthy pleasures. In winter, "the silk sheets, sugared nuts, sweets and sparkling wine, clothes from Douai" all helped fortify citizens "should the *sirocco* blow". As for wealth and foreign influence, there were "*ambiente palafren, destier di Spagna e gente costumata alla Francesca*" ("nimble horses, chargers from Spain and persons dressed in the French vein").

Unfortunately the arrival of the Black Death in 1348 put an end to silk sheets in San Gimignano until this century. The diminished population fell under Florentine control and this important city became an economic backwater, bypassed by the Renaissance.

While more advanced cities were exchanging towers for *palazzi* as feudal lords became civilised by communal life, San Gimignano destroyed nothing and built nothing. The city's misfortune has made it the best preserved medieval city in Tuscany.

The Romanesque **Collegiata**, framed by towers and fortified *palazzi*, does not have the status of a cathedral because there is no longer a bishop. Inside, Benozzo Gozzoli's fresco of a plump St Sebastian in agony deserves a glance. The radiant aisles are dedicated to two cycles of Biblical frescoes painted concurrently by two 15th-century artists.

Bartolo di Fredi's Old Testament frescoes on the north aisle are vivid, intimate and full of careless violence. *The Parting of the Red Sea* is an animated jumble of flying and floating bodies, like a happy Hieronymus Bosch. There is a childlike but lively narrative in all the frescoes. For people raised on too

Siena map: La Sterza, Castelfiorentino, Firenze, Impruneta, Bagno a Ripoli, Saline di Volterra, Volterra, Certaldo, Terme di Firenze, Cécina, S.-Gimignano, MTI DEL CHIANTI, Greve, Reggello, Pomarance, Poggibonsi, Figline Vald., Conv. di Montecarlo (Monastery), Soffioni, Colle d. V. d'Elsa, Radda in Ch., COLLINE METALLIFERE, Monteriggioni, Montevarchi, Giovanni Vald., Siena, Castelnuòvo Berardenga, Monticiano, Monteroni d'Arbia, Monte S. Savino, Arezzo, Roccastrada, Asciano, Abb. di M. Olivéto Magg. (Abbey), DI CHIANA, Canale Maestro, Buonconvento, Paganico, Sinalunga, Cortona, Montalcino, S. Quirico d'Orcia, Terme di Montepulciano, Ombrone, Chigiano, Abb. S. Antimo (Abbey), Pienza, Castel del Piano, Montepulciano, Chianciano Terme, Tombe Etrusche (Etruscan Tombs), Castiglione del Lago, Lago Trasimeno, Abbadia S. Salvatore, Chiusi, **Siena**, 25 km, Piancastagnáio, Città d. P.

many words and too little religion, it is fun trying to work out the significance of the Biblical stories through a pictorial narrative. Among Barna di Siena's New Testament frescoes, one odd section depicts an underwater Christ with two angels; and in *The Last Supper* the disciples appear to be eating a baby seal. The New Testament portrays a more civilised world than the Old, since no one except Jesus suffers.

The variety of Biblical animals is astonishing: expressive camels, dogs and sheep often have more emotional resonance than the human subjects. As in Siena Cathedral there is a ceiling of faded stars to complete the magic. This was perhaps Barna di Siena's last view as he fell off his scaffolding and died.

In **Santa Fina's Chapel** off the south aisle, Ghirlandaio's frescoes of the local saint are rather too flowery. Legend has it that when she died in March 1253, violets sprang up on her coffin and on the towers.

In *Where Angels Fear to Tread*, E.M. Forster, writing of a thinly disguised

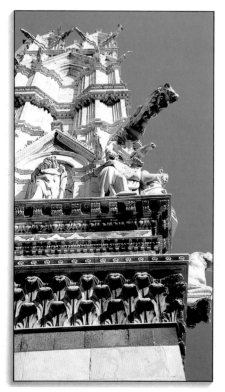

San Gimignano, described Santa Fina's starvation and death at the age of 15 as a feat "which shows how much is within the reach of any school girl". As the violets still flower on the tower every March, perhaps Santa Fina has the last word. In the baptistry loggia is an *Annunciation* by Ghirlandaio (1482), as always an admirable colourist.

Also in the **Piazza del Duomo** is the crenellated Palazzo del Popolo, housing the **Museo Civico** with its countless Sienese "masters" and "schools of". On the second floor, the Camera del Podestà contains domestic and profane scenes by Filippuccio. Amongst the gentle erotica is a picture of a semi-nude couple wearing wooden nightcaps and similar expressions. The nearby **Piazza della Cisterna** is a lovely triangular square with a 13th-century well and medieval *palazzi*.

If many of San Gimignano's palaces are elegant and architecturally diverse it is because "any immigrant who behaved well for a decade could build within its walls". The English writer James Bentley's explanation accounts for the profusion of Florentine, Sienese, Lucchese, Pisan and even Moorish styles.

The final visit should be a short walk along the city walls to the 14th-century fortress. This semi-derelict **Rocca** has views over tiered gardens and olive groves winding down to the "Vernaccia" vineyards. As you leave, do not be surprised by the smell of sulphur – it is only Monte Amiata doing her stuff again.

Shady city: From its striped marble cathedral to its tunnelled alleys, brilliant Campo and black-and-white city emblem, **Siena** is a *chiaroscuro* city. In its surging towers it is truly Gothic. Where Florence is boldly horizontal, Siena is soaringly vertical; where Florence has large squares and masculine statues, Siena has hidden gardens and romantic wells. Florentine art is perspective and innovation while Sienese art is sensitivity and conservatism. Siena is often considered the feminine foil to Florentine masculinity.

Approached by night, Siena's towers resemble "firebrands that are the last to die in the ashes of the night". Federigo **Siena's cathedral.**

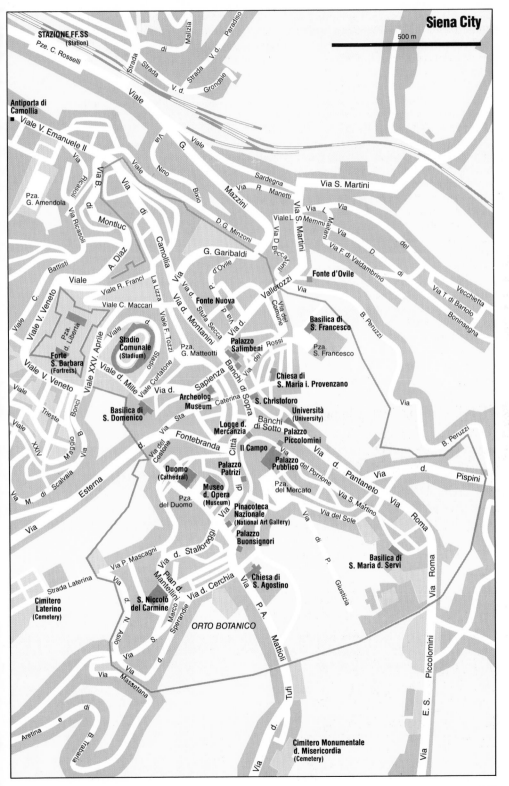

Siena City

500 m

STAZIONE FF.SS
(Station)
Pze. C. Rosselli

Antiporta di
Camollia
Viale V. Emanuele II

Pza.
G. Amendola

Montluc

Viale

Battisti

A. Diaz

Camollia

Viale R. Franci

La Lizza

Viale C. Maccari

Viale F. Tozzi

Viale XXV. Aprile

Stadio

Viale d. Mille viale Curtatone

Via d.

Stadio
Comunale
(Stadium)

Forte
S. Barbara
(Fortress)

Pza.
di
Libertà

Viale V. Veneto

Viale V. Veneto

Trieste

Viale

Bonci

XXIV

Maggio

Via

Via

M. di Scalvaia

Esterna

Via

Strada Laterina

Cimitero
Laterino
(Cemetery)

Via P. Mascagni

Via

Via d. Stalloreggi

Pian d.
Mantellini

S. Niccolò
del Carmine

Marco

Sperandie

Via d. Cerchia

N.

S.

d.

Asilo

Via

Via

Via

Massetana

di

e

B. Tirabordi

Aretina

ORTO BOTANICO

P. A.

Mattioli

Tufi

Via

d.

Cimitero Monumentale
d. Misericordia
(Cemetery)

Strada

Strada

Viale

di

V. d.

Malizia

Paradiso

Grondaie

V. d.

Nino

Bixio

G.

Via

Viale

Viale

Mazzini

D. G. Minzoni

G. Garibaldi

d'Ovile

Fonte Nuova

Via d. Montanini

Stufa Secca

Pza.
G. Matteotti

Sapienza

Archeolog.
Museum

Caterina

Basilica di
S. Domenico

Via d.
Costone

Fontebranda

Via
Sta.

Logge d.
Mercanzia

Città

Duomo
(Cathedral)

Palazzo
Patrizi

Pza.
del Duomo

Museo
d. Opera
(Museum)

Pinacoteca
Nazionale
(National Art Gallery)

Palazzo
Buonsignori

Chiesa di
S. Agostino

Sardegna

Via R. Manetti

Viale L.
Viale D. Becca

Via S. Martini

Via S. Martini

Fonte d'Ovile

Vallerozzi

Via del Comune

Banchi di Sopra

Via d. Rossi

Palazzo
Salimbeni

Chiesa di
S. Maria i. Provenzano

S. Christoforo

Università
(University)

Palazzo
Piccolomini

Il Campo

Palazzo
Pubblico

Pza.
del Mercato

Banchi
di Sotto

Via del Porrione

Via S. Mártino

Via del Sole

Via
d.

P.

Giustizia

Via S. Martini

Via L.
Memmini

Maitani

Via F. di Valdambrino

Basilica di
S. Francesco

Pza.
S. Francesco

Via

Vecchietta

Via T. di Bartolo

Boninsegna

B. Peruzzi

Via

Via

B. Peruzzi

Via
d.

Pantaneto

Via

Roma

Basilica di
S. Maria d. Servi

Pispini

Piccolomini

Via

Roma

E. S.

Via

Tozzi, the most Sienese of authors, also praised the city's radiant femininity. Even by day, the glow of rose-coloured brick warms the narrow passageways and arches. The motto of the Shell Contrada – "It's the red of the coral that burns in my heart" – could refer to the Campo, the centre of Sienese life.

For such a feminine city, Siena has a warlike reputation nourished by sieges, city-state rivalry and *Palio* battles. The average Sienese is no ethereal Botticelli nymph but dark, stocky and swarthy. Only in Sienese painting is pale theatricality the norm.

In keeping with Sienese mystique, the city's origins are shrouded in myths of wolves and martyred saints. According to legend, the city was founded by Senius, son of Remus; hence the she-wolf symbols in the oldest part of the city. Saint Ansano brought Christianity to Roman Siena and, although he was promptly tossed into a vat of hot tar and beheaded, he has left a legacy of mysticism traced through Saints Catherine and Bernardino to the present-day cult of the Madonna. The power of the church came to a dramatic end when the populace rose against the Ecclesiastical Council and established an independent republic in 1147. The 12th century was marked by emerging Sienese-Florentine rivalry in which the Florentine Guelfs usually triumphed over the Sienese Ghibellines.

Cultural superiors: In 1260 the glorious battle of Montaperti routed the Florentines and won the Sienese 10 years of cultural supremacy which saw the foundation of the university and the charitable "fraternities". The enlightened Council of the Twenty-Four, a form of power-sharing between nobles and the working class, was followed by the Council of the Nine, an oligarchy of merchants which ruled until 1335.

Although modern historians judge the "Nine" self-seeking and profligate, under their rule the finest works of art were commissioned or completed, including the Campo, the Palazzo Pubblico and Duccio's *Maestà*.

The ancient republic survived until

Campo surrounded by rose-coloured rooftops of Siena.

1529 when the reconciliation between the pope and the emperor ended the Guelf-Ghibelline feud. The occupying Spanish demolished the city towers, symbols of freedom and fratricide, and used the masonry to build the present fortress. The final blow to the republic was the long Siege of Siena by Charles V and Cosimo I in 1554.

Three companies of women fought alongside men and caused the emperor's general to exclaim, "I would rather have defeated Rome with Sienese women than with Roman soldiers." The Sienese lost despite melting down bronze bells to make cannon balls and expelling *bocche inutili* ("useless mouths") to certain death.

After the Sienese defeat, the government-in-exile survived in Montalcino until 1559, but Siena became absorbed into the Tuscan dukedom. As an untrusted member of the Tuscan empire, impoverished Siena turned in on itself until this century. In 1909, Henry James described it as "cracking, peeling, fading, crumbling, rotting".

War survivors: Soon after, the city, unlike the countryside, challenged fascist appointees. In July 1944 American and French troops surrounded Siena and forced the city to surrender. General Monsambert instructed troops not to "let any shells fall on Siena, otherwise you'll be shot". The State Archives in Palazzo Piccolomini provide a pictorial history of Siena through illuminated manuscripts and paintings. An inscription on the city gates reads, "Siena opens her heart to you wider than this door." But such openness is illusory: Siena offers hospitality but not intimacy. Its cultural and spiritual aloofness owes much to the *contrade*, the 17 city wards who represent self-sustaining cities within the Sienese empire.

Immune to influence and praise, the city takes care of its own from birth to death. The Sienese prefer to work for paternalistic local employers such as *Monte dei Paschi*, known as "the oldest bank in the world" and "the city father".

Change is anathema to the city: traditional landowning, financial specula-

Palazzo Pubblico and Torre del Mangia, Piazza del Campo.

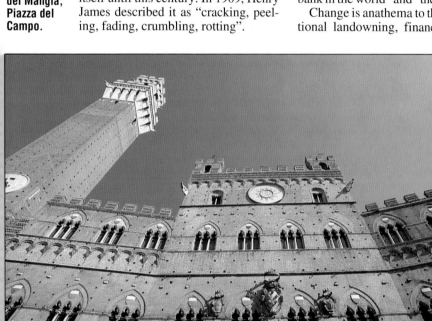

tion, trade and tourism are more appealing than new technology or industry. The city has made a virtue of conservatism; stringent medieval building regulations protect the fabric of the city; tourism is low-key; old family firms such as *Nannini*'s cake shop do a roaring trade with locals (and also produced Gianna Nannini, Italy's best-known female singer). It is a city with the psychology of a village and the grandeur of a nation.

All roads lead to the **Campo**, Siena's shell-like piazza. It is at its most theatrical in the late afternoon, after a day spent in the shadows of the city walls and inner courtyards. After so much dark, the huge pool of light draws even the most modest visitor to blunder on to centre stage.

One's eyes adjust to the redbrick piazza, a fountain depicting the Sienese wolf, and to the **Palazzo Pubblico**, the dignified Town Hall surmounted by the slender Torre del Mangia. The Town Hall, built in 1310, is a Gothic masterpiece of rose-coloured brick and silver-grey travertine. Each ogival arch is crowned by the *balzana*, Siena's black-and-white emblem representing the mystery and purity of the Madonna's life. The tower is named after the first bellringer, Mangiaguadagni, the "spendthrift" and is flanked by a chapel built as a thanksgiving after the plague.

Inside the Palazzo Pubblico is the **Museo Civico** where Simone Martini, Duccio's successor, had to create his masterpiece twice since he painted it on a wall backing on to a damp salt warehouse. His *Maestà* is a poetic evocation of the Madonna on a filigree throne.

It has a rich tapestry-like quality, not unlike the French arras, *The Lady and the Unicorn*. The muted blues, reds and ivory add a gauzy softness. Martini echoes Giotto's conception of perspective yet clothes his ethereal Madonna in diaphanous robes, concealing her spirituality in dazzling decoration.

Opposite is Martini's famous *Guidoriccio*, the haughty diamond-spangled *condottiero* reproduced on calendars and *panforte* boxes. But despite Sienese

Interior of Santa Maria dei Servi, Siena.

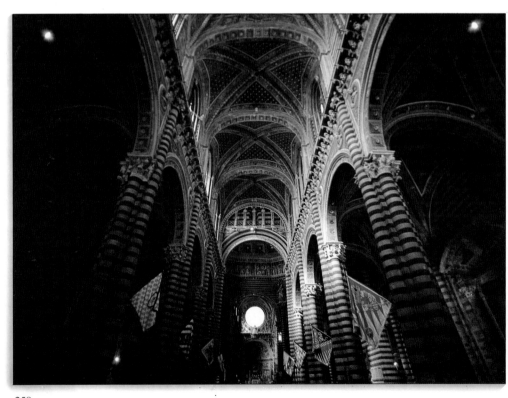

denials, this famous Trecento work is probably a Quattrocento painting concealing Martini's original. Since the Sienese Republic feared a military takeover in 1318, it would have been odd to commission a portrait of a captain for the Town Hall.

In the next room is a genuine civic masterpiece, Ambrogio Lorenzetti's *Effects of Good and Bad Government*, painted in 1338 as an idealised tribute to the Council of the Nine. The narrative realism and vivid facial expressions give the allegory emotional resonance. A wise old man symbolises the Common Good while a patchwork of neat fields, tame boar and busy hoers suggests order and prosperity. Bad Government is a desolate place, razed to the ground by a diabolical tyrant, the Sienese wolf at his feet. Since much of Bad Government is erased, Good Government triumphs – posthumously at least.

From above, the fishbone design of the Campo forms nine different shades of pink, recalling the Noveschi or "Nine". Below, the Sienese awaited news of Montaperti, the Spanish siege, and the German deportation of local Jews. In 1980 Pope John Paul II preached on the same spot where Saint Bernardino denounced witchcraft, superstition and the power of the Sienese Republic. Church and state are well matched here: the Mangia Tower and the cathedral belltower confront each other from the same height.

The **cathedral** is in Castelvecchio, the oldest part of the city. The Duomo is Siena's most controversial monument, either a symphony in black and white marble or a tasteless iced cake. It began in 1220 as a round-arched Romanesque church but soon acquired a Gothic facade festooned with pinnacles. Bands of black, white and green marble were inlaid with pink stone and topped by Giovanni Pisano's naturalistic statues.

Ruskin dismissed it as "over-striped, over-crocketed, over-gabled, a piece of costly confectionery and faithless vanity." Wagner, more attuned to its operatic intensity, burst into tears at its alien, restless beauty.

The interior is creativity run riot – Oriental abstraction, Byzantine formality, Gothic flight and pockets of Romanesque austerity. A giddy *chiaroscuro* effect is created by the black-and-white walls reaching up to the starry blue vaults.

The **floor** is even more inspiring: major Sienese craftsmen worked on the marble *pavimentazione* between 1372 and 1562. Although the oldest are marble engravings, the finest are Matteo di Giovanni's pensive Sibyls and marble mosaics by Beccafumi.

Subtle dazzler: Nicola Pisano's octagonal marble pulpit is a Gothic masterpiece: built in 1226, it is a dramatic and fluid progression from his solemn **pulpit** in Pisa Cathedral. Within the Duomo is the frescoed **Libreria Piccolomini**, the most ornate Renaissance room in Tuscany. Sienese consider the dazzling interior subtle and refined.

The present Duomo would have been the transept of the new one, a scheme devised in the Golden Age and abandoned after the 1348 plague. Beside the Gothic baptistry, the skeletal remains of the **Duomo Nuovo** are home to the **Cathedral Museum** and Pisano's original statues for the facade. In a dramatically lit room above is Duccio's *Maestà*, which was escorted from the artist's workshop to the Duomo in a torchlit procession; the largest known medieval panel painting graced the High Altar until 1506. Duccio chose Madonna blue for the Virgin's cloak to match the blue stained glass windows in the Duomo. He was inspired by French Gothic and perhaps by the Rose Windows at Chartres Cathedral.

The largest panel depicts the Madonna enthroned among saints and angels, and, since the separation of the painting, faces scenes from the Passion. Although Byzantine Gothic in style, the *Maestà* is suffused with melancholy charm. The delicate gold and red colouring is matched by Duccio's grace of line which influenced Sienese painting for the next two centuries.

The Sienese fondly believe that Giotto copied Duccio but sacrificed beauty to naturalism. The small panels around the walls do, however, reveal some of

THE PALIO

It is strange how a race lasting 90 seconds can require a year's planning, a lifetime's patience and the involvement of an entire city. In the Campo, Siena's shell-shaped square, the grey stonework is sanded over and the crenellated *palazzi* float with flags. The slender tower on the Town Hall casts a mobile shadow over the sea of exuberant Sienese and the *Palio* itself, the hand-painted silk banner which is the focus for their spiralling hysteria.

As the horses career round the San Martino bend, a few rebound off the padded walls, a jockey hits the hard track and a riderless horse wins. In just over a minute, the Campo is filled with unbearable happiness and irrational despair.

The *Palio* has raced through war, famine and plague. In the 14th century, criminals were released from prison to celebrate the festival. When the fascists were gaining ground in 1919, Siena postponed the election of a new council until after the *Palio*. In 1943, British soldiers in a Tunisian prisoner-of-war camp feared a riot when they banned Sienese prisoners from staging a *Palio*: Sienese fervour triumphed and the prisoners sang the praises of the ancient republic's throughout the night.

The *Palio* is alive and kicking, held twice a year, and attended by ministers, heads of state and royalty. Despite foreign media condemnation for the increasing violence and deaths of horses, the Sienese resist attempts to modify their ritual.

The August *Palio*, dating from the 13th century, originally took the form of a *Palio Lungo*, a bareback race the length of the city. Later, Roman and Venetian bullfights and buffalo races were adapted by the city.

The first July *Palio*, introduced after a 17th-century miracle, became known as *Palio della Tonda* since it was the first horse race held in the "round" Campo.

A Sienese adage says, "*Il Palio corre tutto l'anno*" (The *Palio* runs all year). Each *contrada* (city ward) appoints a *capitano* and two lieutenants to run the campaign. In the *Palio*, the illegal becomes legal: bribery of rival jockeys and plots with other *contrade* are commonplace. Skulduggery is motivated by traditional duty rather than by financial gain. But luck outweighs the significance of a *contrada*'s tactics, jockey or horse.

Ten out of the 17 *contrade* take part in each *Palio*, the seven who did not run in the previous *Palio* and three by lot. The horses are also chosen by lot and *contradaioli* are exultant if they have won a *bono* and desolate to be saddled with a *brocco*, literally "a sprout". Although each horse is guarded in the *contrada* stable until the race, horses are sometimes drugged or die unexpectedly during the six practice runs.

Efforts intensify when the Campo is covered with soil in readiness for the race. The words, "*C'è terra in piazza*" ("There's earth in the Campo") are a signal to remove the costumes from the museums and to finalise tactics. Superstition plays a great part: nervous *contradaioli* look for portents in shooting stars, the direction of the wind and the flight of birds. Marriages between Sienese from rival *contrade* come under great strain and "real life" is suspended. Many citizens cannot bear to watch the race in the Campo and cluster around the television set in the *contrada* square or pray in the local church.

On the eve of the race, a tense "propitiatory" dinner is held in the *contrada*. On the day, the "Blessing of the Jockey" is followed by the *Provaccia*, the dress rehearsal. Then, during a church ceremony, the *contrada* priest holds the horse's head and commands it, "*Vai e torni vincitore!*" ("Go and return victorious!"). As the procession leads into the Campo, the *Sunto* bell tolls and the flags unfurl.

After a flag-waving display, the bells are silent and the violent race lurches around the Campo three times. If a riderless horse wins, the animal is almost deified, is given the place of honour in the banquet and has its hooves painted gold.

In the victory celebrations, the winning *contrada* holds a thanksgiving service in the cathedral and supporters kiss the floor. Ask a Sienese where he is from and he will say, "*Ma sono della Lupa*" ("But I'm from the Wolf Contrada"). The first loyalty is to the city in the head, not to the city on the map.

Giotto's truthfulness and sense of perspective. The modest status of the Trecento painter was that of a master craftsman whose only reward was the devotion of the populace. As Siena's best-loved work, the *Maestà* achieves just that for its creator.

If it didn't sound too smug, the Sienese would freely admit to spiritual superiority. Apart from producing two major saints and some fine religious art, the city still venerates the Virgin. But Siena is too inter-bred for its own good: local feuds span generations; secrets cannot be kept; outsiders are frequently disparaged; *contrade* passions outweigh individual loyalty.

Pride is often indistinguishable from smugness: Sienese art and the Chigi Musical Academy are considered culture enough; the Sienese accent is naturally the "purest" in Tuscany. One of Siena's leading aristocrats even refuses to set foot in Florence.

The **Pinocateca Nazionale** houses the finest collection of Sienese "Primitives" in the suitably Gothic Palazzo Buonsignori. The early rooms are full of Madonnas, apple-cheeked, pale, remote or warmly human. The beautiful repetition of Siena's favourite theme focuses attention on the style and vivid colouring. Matteo di Giovanni's stylised Madonnas shift to Lorenzetti's affectionate *Annunciation* and to Ugolino di Nerio's radiant *Madonna*. Neroccio di Bartolomeo's *Madonna* is as truthful as a Masaccio.

As a variant, the grisly deaths of obscure saints compete with a huge medieval crucifix with a naturalistic spurt of blood. The famous landscapes and surreal Persian city attributed to Lorenzetti were probably painted by Sassetta a century later. But his *Madonna dei Carmelitani* is a sweeping cavalcade of Sienese life, as is the entire gallery.

The Sienese claim that Siena is three cities: "illustrious", "homely" and "dreamlike". Illustrious Siena is public knowledge but homely Siena belongs to the *contrade* churches, fountains and tabernacles. Fontebranda, Saint Catherine's fountain, is the oldest and

Left, full *contrada* regalia for the *Palio*. **Below**, the *Palio* race lurches round the Campo three times.

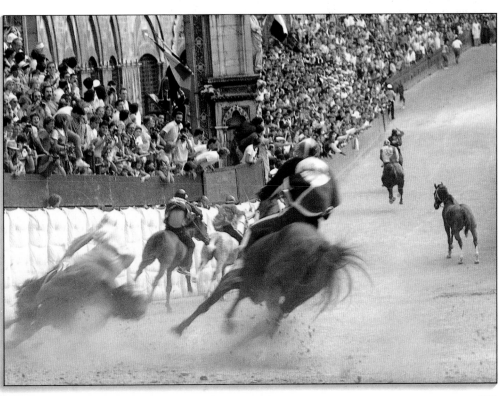

most impressive of the city's enclosed fountains.

Despite its public grandeur, much of Siena is resolutely working class. In Brucco *contrada* pockets of narrow housing, friendly shops and dignified poverty are disguised by old world charm and wishful thinking. The tiny tabernacles reflect spontaneous affection for the Madonna. Sodoma's *Madonna del Corvo* marks the spot where a crow dropped dead with the plague, thus infecting the entire city.

Dreamlike Siena embraces the cult of the Madonna and the mystique of the *Palio*. It can be sensed in the box-like *contrade* churches and in Saint Catherine's sanctuary rather than in the grander churches of San Francesco and San Domenico. The Duomo and the Campo are broad enough to accommodate all the Sienas.

But the Sienese are not borne down by the weight of the past. Siena is a sensuous city. On a drowsy summer's afternoon near the Campo, the flapping pigeons perch on a rushing fountain; the air smells of roasted chestnuts; a child eats a piece of sweet, spicy *panforte* and the Chigi choir can be heard practising. Siena is Italy's last surviving city-state, provincial and universal, a fitting capital.

Sleeping countryside: The **Chianti** is a spiritual rather than a geographical location. Its shifting borders reflect the fluctuations in Florentine and Sienese power but its soul remains where it has always been: on Florentine soil. The Sienese countryside is a bit wilder, the valleys deeper and the hills higher, but it is essentially sleepy, overly civilised Florentine Chianti.

Unlike the southern part of the province, the Chianti is not an area for artistic or architectural set-pieces. Instead, it is a place whose turbulent history has shaped a scene of utter tranquillity, a harmony of tame hills and gentle people.

In a place where nothing is essential viewing, everywhere is a glorious detour. **Castellina in Chianti** is conveniently sited on the Chiantigiana, the winding route linking Florence and Siena. Castellina surveys symmetrical *Palio* **pride.**

vineyards and wooded groves, a landscape dotted with low stone houses and late Renaissance villas.

New wine estates have been built from the ransacked remains of medieval castles. Villas have lazily domesticated the original castle or tower, but names like "La Rocca" or "La Torre" reveal the original function.

Castellina's name also reveals its medieval function as a Florentine outpost. In the late 13th century it was the first site of the Chianti League, a group of three Florentine feudal castles, each responsible for a third of the territory. The castle is now a fortified Town Hall hiding a small Etruscan museum and a warren of atmospheric back streets with half glimpsed views of the Chianti hills.

The other attraction is the *Bottega del Vino Gallo Nero*, the wine-tasting centre which gives advice on wine tours and *vendita diretta*, direct sales.

Radda in Chianti became the headquarters of the Chianti League in 1415 and retains its medieval street plan and imposing Town Hall. As in Castellina,

the spontaneous rural architecture is more rewarding. Classical Medici villas with 16th-century windows and wells compete with romantic villas, constructed magpie fashion from castles or Etruscan ruins. One 17th-century masterpiece is Villa Vistarenni, a white beacon of sophistication unimaginable in the countryside south of Siena.

The elegant loggias, the openness of the architecture, symbolise the increasing safety of the countryside and its proximity to urban Florence. In the tranquil Chianti, the country is richer and more civilised than the town. The reverse is true of the urban-inspired communes south of Siena.

Outside Radda is **Volpaia**, the most picturesque village in the Chianti. A tortuous road climbs to the medieval village with its towers, ruined castle and Brunelleschi-style church. If Chianti villages and towns have little sense of identity and few artistic treasures today, it is because they came into being with fully-fledged Florentine and Sienese identities, while military outposts like

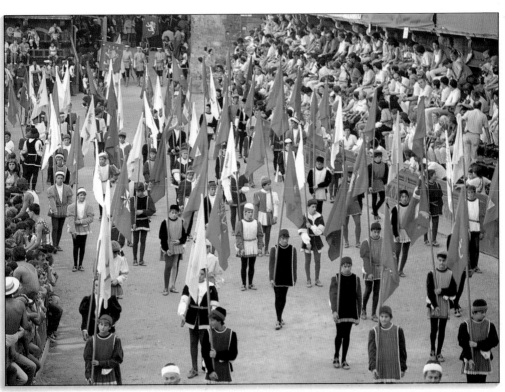

Radda had no time to develop artistically. Only the Chianti abbeys, endowed separately, had the independence to shape their own culture.

Between Radda and Gaiole is the aptly-named **Badia a Coltibuono**, Abbey of the Good Harvest, set among pines, oaks, chestnuts and vines. Since the Dissolution of the Monasteries in 1810, this medieval abbey has belonged to one family.

Although the lovely 15th-century cloisters, chapel and frescoed ceilings are only visible to guests enrolled on a Tuscan cooking course, the 12th-century walls and belltower are harmonious enough. Below the abbey are cellars filled with Chianti Classico, the abbey's traditional living.

No less famous is the aromatic chestnut blossom honey or the *vergine* olive oil, "a product of grass, flowers, pine trees, sea air, altitude, climate and soil". Much of the produce can be bought on the premises or savoured in the excellent abbey restaurant.

Gaiole in Chianti, the baby baron of

the Chianti League, is a newer riverside development in a wooded valley. It is a popular *villeggiatura*, a summer escape for hot Florentines in search of family-run hotels, home cooking and the familiar *gallo nero* (black cock) wine symbol.

History lies in wait at Meleto and Vertine, unusual castles, and Barbischio, a medieval village, is a short walk away. Tempting footpaths marked *Sentieri del Chianti* lead all the way to Siena. With vineyards rising up gentle slopes, tranquil Gaiole and sleepy Greve are traditional Chianti.

The countryside from Gaiole south to Siena and east to Arezzo is higher, wilder and wetter. The wooded peaks of the Chianti Sienese are vibrantly green and fresh with scents of thyme, rosemary and pine kernels. Deep chestnut woods provide ideal cover for wild boar, recently reintroduced.

Of the many Florentine castles in the woods, **Brolio** is the most impressive – not least because of its views over the original Chianti vineyards to Siena and Monte Amiata. On the medieval chessboard, every Florentine castle faced its Sienese shadow.

If the surviving castles are Florentine, it is because Siena lost the match and all its pieces. While Sienese Cereto and Cettamura are small heaps, Florentine Brolio and Meleto are resplendent.

As a Florentine outpost, Brolio's past spans Guelf-Ghibelline conflicts, sacking by the Sienese in 1529 and German occupation and Allied bombing in 1944. The medieval walls are the most striking feature, along with the 14th-century chapel set in lush grounds.

Brolio has long been controlled by the Ricasoli, Chianti landowners since the eighth century. Baron Bettino Ricasoli, Italian Premier in 1861, founded the modern Chianti wine industry, a business continued by the present family. The common saying, "When Brolio stirs, Siena shakes", still holds true today, not least in the wine trade.

The Chianti is a place for pottering and chance encounters, one of which is tiny **Campi di San Gusmè**, just south of Brolio. A short climb leads to a small

"Burnt sienna" of the city walls.

tower, Romanesque church and views of tumbledown castles, villas and vineyards. The tower was designed to be higher than the tallest cypresses encircling it, but, not surprisingly, the trees grew and the tower did not.

A Renaissance dolls' house: In contrast to the Chianti, towns south of Siena were never dependent on powerful Sienese and Florentine masters for their identity. The southern towns developed independently around local noblemen or industries and expressed their differences artistically. Shifting allegiances and even political domination did not mean an acceptance of new, extraneous values but only an entrenchment in local culture and traditions.

Pienza is an exquisite Renaissance dolls' house. Although created by a humanist Pope, Pius II, Pienza is too perfect to be human and too precious to be spiritual. Every fountain, piazza and painting is harmonious. Model citizens walk through streets as romantic as their names: Via dell' Amore, Via del Bacio, Via della Fortuna.

Pienza's origins go back to 1458. When E. S. Piccolomini was elected Pope, he could not resist playing God in his home village, Corsignano. He chose the noted Florentine architect, Bernardo Rossellino, to ennoble the hamlet in accordance with humanist principles.

Pius's vision knew no bounds – in that sense it was a true Renaissance vision. He held that, "In our change-loving Italy, where no ancient dynasty exists, a servant can become king." As one of 18 children from an impoverished but noble Sienese family, the future pope showed Renaissance aspirations as well as vision.

When the first masterpiece in modern town planning emerged late and over budget, the Pope reduced his fraudulent architect to tears with his words, "You did well, Bernardo, in lying to us about the expense involved in the work… Your deceit has built these glorious structures; which are praised by all except the few consumed with envy."

Bernardo was rewarded with a scarlet robe, 100 ducats and some new com-

The red earth of the Sienese landscape.

missions. The decision to build a cathedral enabled the Pope to rechristen Corsignano the village as Pienza the city, named after himself. The result is what locals call a *città d'autore*, a city inspired by one vision. After Pienza, other cities are liable to look cluttered and confused.

Symmetrical centre: Much of the symmetry lies in the cathedral square, **Piazza Pio II**, and the slightly listing cathedral adds to the charm. Despite a Renaissance facade, the interior is late Gothic and decorated with mystical paintings from the Sienese school. In one central alcove is a chilling *Assumption* by Vecchietta in which Saint Agatha holds a cup containing her breasts, torn off by the executioner.

The Cathedral's facade, the gracious arches, the well and the Palazzo Piccolomini, the Pope's home, are just as Pius left them when he set off to fight the crusades and never returned. On summer nights, impromptu concerts are often held in the ill-lit square: the tilted church, the ghostly musicians and the solidity of Pius's presence can have an unnerving effect.

Palazzo Piccolomini, now a museum, is based on the Palazzo Ruccellai in Florence. The ancient custodian is the soul of indiscretion: "Listen, he was the only one of them to die a natural death." The *palazzo* is lined with grand and homely treasures, including a library and arms collection.

Still, an image of domestic clutter prevails. In the Pope's bedroom, the intriguing book-holder, as cumbersome as a church lectern, is proof that the Pope did not read in bed. The library opens onto a tranquil loggia with Etruscan urns, hanging gardens and a panorama across the Orcia valley to Monte Amiata. It was here that the aesthetic concept of a view was first introduced to boringly functional Europe.

Critics call Pienza a Renaissance theme park; admirers liken it to an absent friend's drawing room. The "look, don't touch" element makes Pienza a precious city in both senses of the word. If overwhelmed by beauty or hunger,

Far left, Pienza, a Renaissance doll's house. **Left,** rape field in full bloom.

one can retreat to the restaurants behind the main square. Pienza is famous for its homemade cheeses, especially *pecorino* and *ricotta*. "Lucrezia Borgia" biscuits provide an antidote to a surfeit of piety.

Just outside Pienza is the **Pieve di Corsignano**, a simple but coherent Romanesque church where Pope Pius II was baptised.

Cinquecento pearls: The winding road from Pienza up to **Montepulciano** is lined with *vendita diretta* signs, offering *pecorino* and wine. If Pienza belongs to Rossellino, Montepulciano is Antonio da Sangallo's masterpiece.

Traffic is now banned from inside the city walls but just outside the walls, at the end of a long line of cypresses, lies **San Biagio**, the Renaissance building most at ease with its setting. The isolation focuses attention on the honey-coloured *travertine*, the Greek Cross design, the dome and the purity of the line. Sangallo's design skills rival Bramante's, not just in the church, the elegant well, the porticoed Canon's House, but elsewhere in the city. The airy interior has a deeply classical feel, more akin to the Roman Pantheon than to a small Tuscan church.

From San Biagio there is a short walk to **Santa Maria delle Grazie**, a 16th-century church whose Renaissance organ is still played at concerts. Although Montepulciano is also a "Pearl of the Cinquecento", it is no museum piece. After Pienza, its asymmetrical design and spontaneous development give it the architectural tension that the earlier city lacks.

Pienza's reverence of Pope Pius is surpassed by Montepulciano's devotion to Poliziano. The renowned scholar, poet and resident tutor to Lorenzo de' Medici's children was named after the Latin term for the town. The tradition of scholarship is upheld in the city's annual Renaissance Convention. Likewise, early morning buses are filled with 2,000 young Poliziano coming to receive a "humanistic education".

As a humanist, Poliziano was "bent on doing over the whole house of Italian civilisation from top to bottom". But

Church of San Biagio, Montepulciano.

Mary McCarthy's view of him as a querulous interior designer does not reflect Poliziano's deep love of the Montepulciano countryside. The spring landscape inspired Botticelli's painting *Primavera* and Poliziano's *Stanzas*. Both friends portrayed gardens of female delight in which *"Ogni bella e sicura fra tanti damigelli"*.

Fatal ecstasy: Poliziano's claims that maidens would be "safe in the shady arbours among so many young men" were probably correct. Poliziano himself is rumoured to have died in ecstasy while playing a love song on the lute to a favourite "beardless youth".

Poliziano's house is just off the main square, **Piazza Grande**, the highest part of town and the highest spot culturally. In August, the square becomes a stage for concerts and traditional Bruscello plays, originally performed by peasants on the threshing floor.

On the last Sunday in August the route is filled with sturdy *Poliziani* pushing heavy barrels uphill. The barrel race, *Bravio delle botti*, started out as a Sienese *Palio* but after numerous accidents the horse race was transformed into a pageant and an equally violent barrel race.

Florentine design has shaped the grand facades on Piazza Grande but earlier Sienese Gothic touches are present in the interiors, double arches and doorways. Both styles reflect the city's buffeting between the two city-states and the eventual supremacy of Florence. The **Palazzo Comunale** has a Florentine Michelozzo facade adorning Sienese turrets. The tower, modelled on that of Florence's Palazzo Vecchio, surveys the whole province: from Monte Amiata to Siena and even Lake Trasimeno. Once in the Palazzo, do not be deterred by the presence of a police station and the absence of a custodian: the view is legally yours in the morning.

Contessa's secret: Sangallo's **Palazzo Contucci**, on the other side of the square, is a secret. Ring the concealed bell and an elderly housekeeper or the Contessa herself will point to palatial 18th-century ceilings before alluding to the vast Contucci cellars below.

Sant'Agnese, Montepulciano.

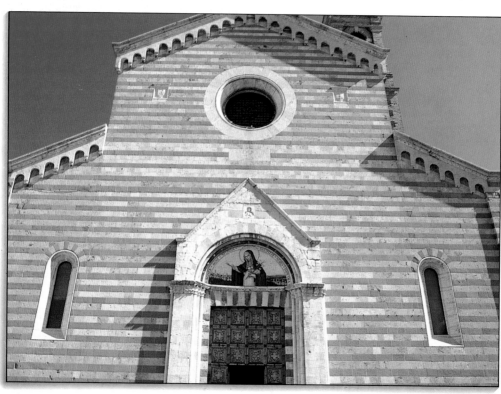

268

In the Cantina, Adamo, the wine master, will be delighted to expand on the entire noble history of the Contucci family and on his essential role on the Vino Nobile Wine Tasting Committee. Vino Nobile, a smooth red wine with a hint of violets, was "ennobled" in 1549 when Pope Paul III's sommelier proclaimed it "a most perfect wine, a wine for lords". In Montepulciano today, naive or noble-looking purchasers are often recommended the 1887 vintage. Vino Nobile is excellent with two local peasant dishes: *bruschetta*, a toasted garlic bread drenched in olive oil, or *panzanella*, a bread salad with herbs.

The Renaissance **Palazzo Bucelli** is for those with more sober tastes. It is a reminder of the city's Etruscan origins, dating back to Lars Porsena, the mythical King of the Etruscans. The Palazzo, decorated with a mosaic of Etruscan urns and pots, is a sign of what civilised Tuscans call "urban decoration" and unenlightened foreigners call theft. The Poliziani are not alone in rifling tombs for useful garden furniture.

This *palazzo* was one of the many delights Henry James missed when, after quaffing Vino Nobile "too constantly", he declared Montepulciano dirty, "parched and brown and queer and crooked". For those without a "crooked" alcoholic vision, there is a drive or walk to **Montefollonico**, a medieval village with one of the best restaurants in Italy, La Chiusa.

As well as its "Cinquecento Pearls", Siena province glories in its hidden villages, each with a separate identity and artistic treasures espied almost incidentally over the brow of a hill. This route is just one in which every village becomes more itself as time goes by.

Near Montepulciano a circular itinerary unites tiny villages once ruled by the Cacciaconti barons. Otherwise, the only link is that each tiny village considers itself civilised and the others feudal.

Petroio, set on a rocky, wooded promontory, is a grand fortified village on an old pilgrim route. It is now undergoing a revival thanks to its terracotta, examples of which adorn the city walls,

Palazzo del Comune, Montepulciano.

Palazzo Pretorio and the medieval towers. The Canon's House contains a remarkable *Madonna and Child* by Taddio di Bartolo.

Near the village is the intact **Abbadia a Sicille**, built by the Knights Templar as a refuge for knights on the way to the Holy Land. The adjoining Romanesque church is decorated with two Maltese crosses but an Olivetan coat of arms marks the abolition of the Templars.

The high road to **Castelmuzio** is dotted with *Divieto di Caccia* warnings to Sienese businessmen out to hunt boar at weekends. Quite seriously, it is advisable to wear bright clothes for walking across country in the hunting season.

Castelmuzio, set among farmland and woods, is a medieval village wrapped up in itself, its museum of Sacred Art and its direct line to San Bernardo. Narrow shops in winding streets sell honey, salami and cheese made by an ageing population of church-goers.

Once a Cacciaconti fortress, aristocratic **Montisi** commands a view over two valleys. Montisi is a feudal and feuding village, sure of its superiority over "*primitivo*" San Giovanni d'Asso in the valley. Dwellers in the Castello, or "high town", have survived many attempts to tame them over the years and also withstood German bombing raids in World War II.

Although the "low town" has a few young families and newer attitudes, the "high town" is a relic of medieval Italy. While some peasants still sell eggs individually, the distinguished Colonello rattles around in his one hundred-roomed castle and sells the noble local wine, Vino Rosso dei Cacciaconti, through his housekeeper.

The village offers intriguing alleys, views, restaurants and two tiny Romanesque churches, one decorated with a Scuola di Duccio crucifix. A few apparently stark, uninviting farmhouses conceal wonderful frescoes and the occasional private chapel.

One can return to Montepulciano via **Sinalunga**, a schizophrenic Tuscan town with a hideous "low town" but a pleasant "old town". The town's original

The abbey of Monte Oliveto Maggiore.

name, Asinalunga, echoes its shape, "the long donkey". But in the lively market, pigs not donkeys are in evidence: the entire population can be seen devouring *porchetta*, the local speciality.

The mysterious craters: Siena Province's strangest area lies to the west of these villages. From Buonconvento to Rapolano Terme is a primeval landscape. Appropriately called **Crete**, this area is a moonscape of interlocking pale clay hummocks and treeless gullies. In winter it is cold, bleak and even more crater-like. Locals speak of these infertile furrows as *maligne crete*, in the same vein as the American "Badlands". Sienese city dwellers love this barren landscape and are successfully discouraging local farmers from accepting European Union funds to flatten the land and grow wheat.

There is an extraordinary range of ill-concealed wildlife in the area: by day, wild deer roam by the Ombrone river; by night, porcupines and foxes are about in the woods. If intrepid walkers venture out in the late autumn evening they may meet a strange character with a couple of dogs, a torch and a harness. He is a truffle hunter, sniffing out truffles in the dampest ditches.

More legal are the Sardinian peasants selling cheese. Unlike many Tuscans, Sardinians are prepared to live in remote, infertile places. Sadly, the local population associate the "Sardi" with only three things: *pecorino*, horseriding and kidnapping.

Buonconvento, situated on a plain in the heart of the Crete, is a place for hunting and eating. It is also a quiet historical town, known for its *muraria*, the imposing red 14th-century walls and grand wooden gates. In 1366 Siena rebuilt the walls because, as a Sienese outpost, Buonconvento had been devastated. Sadly, few visit the Palazzo Pretorio or Pinacoteca with its pictures from the Duccio school.

The town is essentially a place for a leisurely introduction to truffles or game; or for a summer picnic in the peaceful gardens beside the town walls. Tobias Smollett, the "choleric philistine", hated Buonconvento. But then his horses had just run off, he was hungry, and he knew nothing of truffles.

In between Buonconvento and **Monte Oliveto Maggiore**, the rugged landscape is dotted with striking hill-top farmhouses. It is an empty road along which pheasants suddenly appear. Called the Accona Desert in medieval times, it retains its spiritual remoteness.

After so much pale, undulating land, the red abbey of Monte Oliveto is glimpsed through a wood of pines, oaks and olives. If the land appears to fall away from the abbey, it is not far from the truth: land erosion and frequent landslides provide a natural defence to the mystical centre.

Hermits' order: In 1313 Tolomei, a wealthy Sienese, abandoned the law for a life of prayer in the wilderness with two fellow hermits. After a vision of white-robed monks, Tolomei established an Olivetan Order under Benedictine rule. The monks followed Saint Benedict's precept that "a real monk is one who lives by his own labour".

Fortunately, a meagre diet, fervent

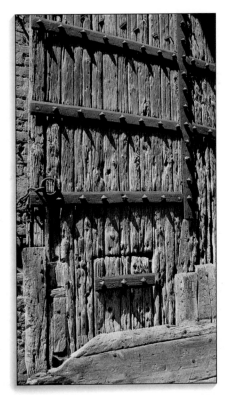

14th-century heavy timber gates at Buonconvento.

prayer and lack of conversation stimulated the monks to artistic endeavour in the form of wood carving, sculpture and manuscript design. As a noted artistic centre, the abbey invited Luca Signorelli and Il Sodoma to decorate the Renaissance style cloisters with scenes from St Benedict's life.

The moated gateway, adorned with della Robbia terracottas, leads through cypresses and meaningful *"Silenzio!"* signs to the monks' domain. To see the wonderful if over-restored frescoes is more difficult than it looks. Today's no doubt pious but very grumpy monks are still puritanical about female attire: even bare wrists need to be covered by one of the monks' stock of headscarves. Once inside the Chiostro Grande, St Benedict's life unfolds in surprisingly profane ways.

Of the two contemporaries, Signorelli had the more spiritual approach. But his loveliest work is a domestic scene portraying two monks being served food and wine by girls at an inn. St Benedict guessed that the monks had broken the monastic rule by eating outside the monastery. The fresco's expressive grace lies in the monks' absorption and in the sculptural sensuousness of one woman's neck.

However, in 1497, after only nine frescoes, Signorelli left the rest to Sodoma. The Olivetan monks' interfering ways were no match for the freedom, novelty and financial rewards dangled by Orvieto Cathedral.

Vasari adored Signorelli's spirituality as much as he loathed Sodoma's exuberance, hedonistic lifestyle and "licentious" fondness for "boys and beardless youths" which earned him his nickname in the first place. Il Sodoma's confident homosexuality helped him to flout the conventions of religious art.

One fresco originally depicted naked courtesans out to seduce the monks but the livid Abbot insisted on Sodoma "dressing" the courtesans. In his self-portrait, Sodoma has an actor's sense of his audience, a complicity shared by the pets at his feet.

Sodoma's love of what Vasari called

Fortified village of Rocca d'Orcia.

his Noah's Ark of "badgers, squirrels, apes, dwarf asses and Elba ponies" is often present but his landscapes only come to life with the temptations of the flesh. His gaze rarely focuses on the main subject but is deflected by the turn of an attractive leg, a mischievous smile, a perky badger or a soldier's buttocks. Needless to say, the inhibited monks preferred Signorelli's work to that of the man they labelled "*Il Matoccio*", imbecile or madman.

The excitement of Sodoma aside, Monte Oliveto is a spiritual retreat. The austere refectory, the library cluttered with ancient manuscripts, the marquetry work of the choir stalls are as peaceful as the hidden walks deep into the woods. A restaurant and cells are also available for overnight visitors unafraid of the monks or Sodoma's ghost.

The watery valley: The **Val d'Orcia** is a poor but beautiful rural area bordering the southern Crete. The villages have suffered from the desertion of the countryside in the 1950s and 1960s. The abandoned farmhouses used to be green oases near the barren Crete. Since the peasants had to be self-sufficient under the *Mezzadria* system, every patch of land was cultivated, from the rosemary and camomile by the house to the enclosed orchard.

Conservationists practise *Agriturismo* and developers plan leisure centres. As local politician Fabio Pellegrini said: "Beware of linking the beauty of the countryside with the living conditions of the peasants – such a harmony has never existed."

San Quirico d'Orcia is a dignified valley town still waiting for its heyday. It survived an attack by Cesare Borgia's troops in 1502 and 1944 bombardment of its formal Collegiata and city walls.

Its Romanesque **Collegiata**, made from sandstone and local travertine, has three remarkable portals. The finest is the south portal, decorated with lions and caryatids by the Giovanni Pisano school. Inside, a Sano di Pietro tryptich incorporates the town's red-and-gold coat of arms.

From San Quirico, an exciting rough walk leads to Ripa d'Orcia, Rocca

d'Orcia and Castiglione d'Orcia, three medieval fortresses.

After the turning to the shabby medieval town of Bagno Vignoni, **Ripa d'Orcia**, an enchanted castle set in cypress groves, comes into view. Although pheasants and goats are common here, locals make claims for wolves. After failing to see a wolf, the intrepid traveller clambers on to **Rocca d'Orcia**, a fortified village once owned by the warring Salimbeni clan.

The energetic can press on to **Castiglione d'Orcia** for more of the same. Wonderful views and exhaustion can be assumed. On a winter visit in 1332, Saint Catherine of Siena felt God had abandoned her to the howling winds; a sensation still true today.

Just beyond San Quirico is **Bagno Vignoni**, a tiny but energetic spa station. In the middle of a severe medieval piazza, bubbling warm water gushes into an enclosed stone pool. The hot springs were used by Romans and became public baths in medieval times. Saint Catherine perhaps bathed here on

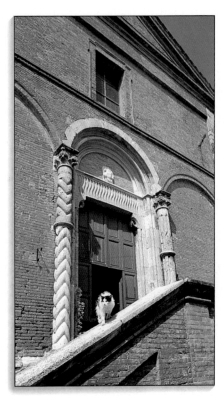

14th-century San Francesco, Chiusi.

her day off between miracles or saving the Papacy.

The new baths in Hotel Posta Marcucci are open at night on summer weekends. From the pool, all senses are fulfilled at once: the imposing Rocca d'Orcia looms above; outside the pool of light, the sound of sheep and crickets reverberates; the softness of the hot chalky water dissolves tiredness; and the smell of sulphur evaporates into the night air. The locals add the bizarre touch: while formation swimmers "dance" in time to Big Band music, spectators stare upwards for shooting stars, a feature on dark nights in mid-August. After a swim, a short *passeggiata* around the old baths shows the well-restored square at its most romantic.

The Etruscan towns: Although set among attractive low hills, **Chiusi** is an unprepossessing town, devoid of Renaissance charm. The "low town" is a commercial centre and the shabby "high town" is endearing, but overwhelmed by its glorious Etruscan past.

Then as now, the **Chiusini** were farmers, merchants and craftsmen, a spirit which predominates over artistry. Yet with a little Etruscan knowledge and much curiosity, the town is as fascinating as any in Tuscany. It boasts a complete underground city; an unrivalled collection of female cinerary urns; and the only tomb paintings in their original setting in Tuscany.

As one of the greatest city-states in the Etruscan League, Chiusi or "Kamars", controlled the area from Lago di Trasimeno to Monte Amiata. After reaching its zenith as a trading centre in the 7th century BC, Etruscan Kamars became submerged by Roman Clusium and then by medieval Chiusi.

The old city survives on three levels of civilisation: the huge Etruscan necropolis under the city hills; the Roman street grid system below the cathedral; and the medieval city above. If locals seem unimpressed by modern Chiusi, it is simply because they remember that their king, Lars Porsenna, conquered Rome in 508 BC.

The city's decline was hastened by its

Chiusi's cathedral built from Etruscan and Roman fragments.

proximity to malaria-ridden marshes. Drainage works started by Cosimo de' Medici and continued today, have created a healthier commercial climate within the grand Etruscan walls.

The **National Etruscan Museum** is a wonderfully confusing experience, concealing one of Italy's finest collections. Still, the collection as it stands attests to the vitality of Kamars and shows a distinctly female bias in the outstanding female canopic jars, cinerary urns and rounded *cippi* tombstones. The containers have Egyptian style lids resembling human or animal heads.

The Etruscans borrowed freely from the Greeks and Egyptians. The imitation Greek vases are less rational but more vigorous than the originals.

A speciality of Chiusi is *bucchero*, glossy black earthenware, often in the form of vases with figures in relief. This pottery has a sophisticated metallic finish which cannot be reproduced by modern craftsmen. Although much of the domestic pottery has a naturalness verging on the commonplace, the sarcophagi, the cinerary urns and the crouching sphynx reveal an underlying obsession with death and the appeasement of shadowy spirits.

In **Chiusi cathedral** three civilisations are visible at once: the "barbaric" Romanesque cathedral is built from Etruscan and Roman fragments; and the antique cistern beneath the belltower is from the 1st century BC. After fanciful speculation on the Etruscan galleries running beneath the town, a visit to the tombs can be arranged with the museum curator. Before this, look out for signs of "urban decoration": genuine Etruscan urns and sculptures in local gardens. The Etruscan physiognomy can also be spotted in the ironic smile or oblique glance of the bartender.

The tombs contain sarcophagi, cinerary urns and, in the case of the Monkey Tomb, rare wall paintings depicting athletic games and domestic scenes. Outside the town, ignore the two unremarkable towers, Beccati Questo and Beccati Quello, translated in Chiusi's tourist brochures as the "Get

The hot springs of Bagno Vignoni.

an Eyeful of This One" and "Get an Eyeful of That One" towers. Get a mouthful of the local fish instead.

After underground Chiusi, **Chianciano Terme** is a breath of fresh air. It has the healthiest and wealthiest climate in Tuscany: hills, spas, pine forests, and more doctors and fur coats per square metre than elsewhere in Italy. "Chianciano for a Healthy Liver," the signs into town invite, exhort or cajole.

The medieval "low town" with its good Etruscan museum and Signorelli fresco is studiously ignored by Italian visitors. A number of Etruscan tombs and temples have been discovered recently and well-marked walks lead to the sites. The "high" spa town is where Italians have flocked since Roman times to enjoy the unique powers of *Acqua Santa*: as one of the world's top spas, Chianciano is a seriously rich town.

This is the place to spot "August evacuees" relaxing in hotels, pools, parks, bars, concerts and designer shops. It is also the place for elderly matchmaking, plastic surgery or both.

Near Chianciano are some of the loveliest walks and drives in Tuscany. Many walks start from **La Foce**, a 15th-century farmhouse which overlooks the fertile Valdichiana and the desolate craters of the Val d'Orcia. There are views across an Etruscan site to Monte Amiata and Monte Cetona. Its excellent strategic position meant that its owners, the Anglo-Italian Origos, used it as the partisans' refuge during World War II.

From there, a rough track leads to Petraporciana, the partisans' hidden headquarters and to a primeval forest. This *faggeta* is full of giant oaks, cyclamens, wild orchids or snowdrops: a perfect short spring or autumn walk.

Beside La Foce is **Castelluccio**, a castle which commands the best-loved view in the province: a sinuous line of cypresses plotting an Etruscan route across the craters. When Britain's Prince Charles stayed at Villa La Foce, proud locals were not surprised to see him painting this very view.

A short walk leads to Pocce Lattaie and prehistoric caves with dripping

Romanesque abbey of Sant'Antimo.

stalagtites shaped like teats or nipples. These pagan caves were used in fertility rites and propitiatory offerings made to the gods. To tread where no prince has ever trod, be prepared to hire a guide (and a torch) from Chianciano.

Routes up to Monte Amiata: From Chianciano, an idyllic rural drive leads through Castelluccio to Sarteano and Cetona, two small medieval and Etruscan towns. These views of desolate *crete*, fortified farmhouses and hazy Monte Amiata are captured by Paolo Busato in his celebrated photographs. It is worth sacrificing a hired car to the dirt roads but the nervous can take the more direct route to Sarteano.

Castiglioncello sul Trionoro is a tiny village with a *castello*, and a church containing a Trecento Madonna. The village is set amid vast expanses of abandoned countryside in which Etruscan remains are uncovered by chance every few years.

Spilling over its double ring of city walls, **Sarteano** is a popular thermal centre that has retained its traditional

identity. The town offers Etruscan remains, a grandiose 13th-century Rocca and crumbling Renaissance *palazzi* built into the city walls. In August, Sarteano holds a famous *Giostra* or tournament.

Cetona clings on to a richly wooded hill and, with the lowest incomes in the province, is struggling to survive. The grand 18th-century houses on the plains are a relic of past prosperity. The town's star attractions are a medieval fortress, set among oleanders, and a villa owned by the fashion designer Valentino.

Although Cetona is noted for its textiles and copies of Etruscan vases, it now relies on *Agriturismo* to keep its population from leaving. A short stay in a local farm with mountain walks and *bruschetti* drenched in olive oil has much to recommend it.

The varied approaches to Monte Amiata, southern Tuscany's highest peak, are at least as good as what awaits you on arrival. The fast Pienza to Abbadia San Salvatore route allows for a detour to Siena's loveliest thermal baths, **Bagni San Filippo**. A turning to

Slopes of carefully tended vineyards.

the right shortly before Abbadia leads to a cluster of houses and orchards and the sulphurous smell indicates the thermal centre.

The winding walk down to the pool passes a pediluvium before reaching a magnificent rocky waterfall and a modern pool. Mud and massage treatments are available for those not already coated in chalky white masks. Although Italians are quite happy swimming in hot baths in the height of summer, visitors tend to collapse with exhaustion after two lengths.

The alternative route via Sarteano and **Radicofani** was the one taken by both Dickens and Montaigne to a location second only to Volterra for natural drama. While the mountain villages have sports and leisure industries to thank for their revival, the villages on the edge of Amiata are in limbo, trapped rather than enhanced by a medieval identity – and, in Radicofani's case, a medieval economy.

Sea of stones: Dickens found Radicofani "as barren, as stony, and as wild as Cornwall, in England". Perched on a craggy basalt rock 766 metres (2,513 ft) above sea level, it is the only place in Italy to possess a triple Medicea wall. The town overlooks *Il Mare di Sassi*, the "sea of stones" suitable only for very hardy sheep.

Radicofani is linked to the exploits of Ghino di Tacco, the "gentle outlaw" immortalised by Dante and Boccaccio. Exiled Ghino controlled the town from Radicofani Castle, built by Hadrian IV, the only English Pope. A fierce basalt sculpture of Ghino stands in this forbidding town of low stone houses with external stairways, blind alleys and severe facades. Although an 18th-century earthquake destroyed much of the town, enough atmosphere remains.

The drive from Radicofani to **Abbadia San Salvatore** is via Le Conie, a tortuous road known as "Amiata's sentry". For those not interested in skiing, mountain walks and disused mercury mines, Abbadia is best known for its much overrated **Abbazia** and its medieval "high town".

Interior of the abbey of Sant'Antimo.

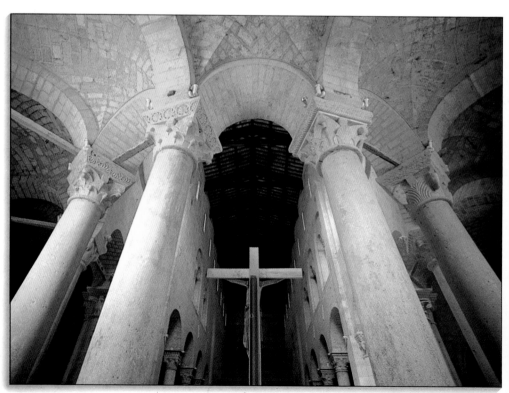

278

The Romanesque San Salvatore is all that remains of a once magnificent abbey. Unfortunately it has been heavily restored twice, once in 16th-century baroque and again in 1925. A 12th-century crucifix and the crypt with 36 columns remain relatively unspoilt. Geometric symbols, grapes, palm leaves, animals, and gordian knots decorate the pillars in this sober place.

From Abbadia, a winding road with sharp bends and sheer drops leads to the summit of **Monte Amiata**, 1,738 metres (5,700 ft) high. The wooded area around the extinct volcano has attractive walks and, since hunting is banned, there is plenty of opportunity for animal spotting. The Fosso della Cocca, a leafy tunnel, is the best place for unusual wildlife and vegetation.

Although **Castel del Piano**, set among pine forests and wild raspberries, is the oldest settlement in the area, **Piancastagnato** is a better base. Perched among chestnut groves, the town offers a newly-restored Rocca, Franciscan monastery and odd villages.

Pope Pius II, on a visit to Amiata from Pienza in 1462, wrote: "The soft spring waters run through mountain spots more beautiful than nymphs or fauns could have found". Given the sulphurous odour, the nymphs must have had colds at the time.

Quintessential Sienese: In both temperament and identity, **Montalcino** is certainly the most Sienese town in the province. Its history is a microcosm of all Sienese history. From a distance Montalcino even looks like a Sienese Trecento painting: the landscape could be a background to a saint's life; in the foreground would be the fortress and scenes of rejoicing and celebration after an historic victory.

Montalcino has been known as "the last rock of Communal freedom" since its time as the Sienese capital in exile between 1555 and 1559. After the fall of Siena, exiles gathered around Piero Strozzi and the Sienese flag. As a reward, Montalcinesi standard bearers have the place of honour in the procession preceding the *Palio* in Siena.

The magnificent 14th-century Rocca is the key to Montalcino's pride. The approach is through olive groves and the slopes famous for Brunello wine. But the asymmetrical fortress, astride a spur of land, dominates the landscape. From its gardens there is a sense of boundless space and absolute freedom.

In winter, the wind howls over the massive walls and drives visitors to a different type of fortification in the *Enoteca* bar inside. This "National Wine Library" naturally serves Brunello, the first wine in Italy to be given the DOCG *Denominazione* for excellence.

The fortress still contains the tattered flag of the old Sienese Republic. Depicting the Virgin and Child, it represents the Republic's struggle for liberty. Visiting Sienese have been known to weep on seeing the *stendardo*.

Visiting Montalcino is not a trip, it is a pilgrimage. Oddly enough, Montalcino's history has come full circle: after countless changes to its boundaries, it is now in possession of exactly the same land as in medieval times. Its liberal and left-wing traditions have also

The *fortezza* at Montalcino dominates the landscape.

survived: in the 1920s the town had a proud anti-fascist record and held out against the Germans until 1945.

Architecturally, Montalcino offers a neo-classical cathedral, a Gothic loggia, a Romanesque church and a myriad of intriguing alleys. The Duccio and della Robbia schools are well-served by the Civic and Sacred Museums. Sano di Pietro's Byzantine-style *Madonna dell' Umiltà* is particularly moving. Most significant is the Palazzo Comunale, a mass of *Fiorentinità* finished off by a Sienese tower to prove that the Sienese always surpass the Florentines.

In spring, the area is incredibly green but yellow rape seed, poppies, sunflowers and grapes soon retaliate. Before leaving, try *pici*, home-made spaghetti, and sweet *sospiri* ("sighs") in a French-style *fin de siècle* bar.

Nearby is **Sant'Antimo**, the remains of a Romanesque abbey founded by Charlemagne. If the church is closed, try the sacristan in **Castelnuove Abate**, the village up the hill. Designed in the French and Lombard style, the abbey is built from local travertine, which resembles alabaster or onyx.

But what sets Sant'Antimo apart is the interior. It has a translucent quality and, as the light changes, turns luminously golden, white and brown. Its setting, amidst cypresses in a peaceful valley, inspired Charles Tomlinson to write of the wind in the cypresses as "a continual breathing, an underwater floating of foliage" chasing its shadowy reflection against the stone tower.

Not far away, **Sant'Angelo in Colle**, a fortified hill-top village, once cast a dramatic shadow over Grosseto and other enemies. Until 1265 it was a Sienese outpost, but the tower is all that remains. Today it is a quiet medieval village with time and consideration for peaceful visitors.

Modern Siena province ends just there. As a frontier castle, Sant'Angelo looked down onto the plain which falls into Grosseto. After Siena province, Grosseto can look deceptively flat.

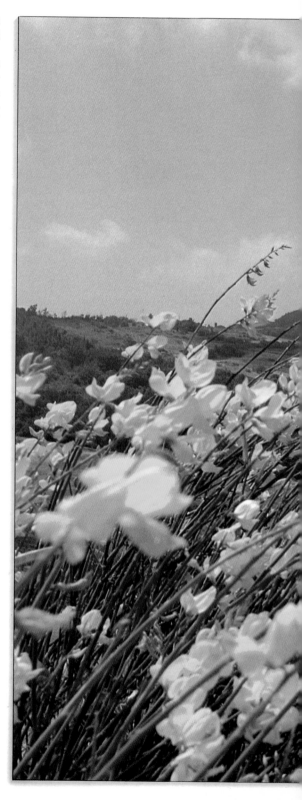

Right, the craggy *Rocca* of Radicofani, approaching Monte Amiata.

AREZZO

The landscape of the province of Arezzo is rugged with steep valleys that form a kind of backwoods hiding its towns and villages from public view. The north is a remote area of chestnut woods, vineyards and monasteries; to the south are the prosperous farms of the Valdichiana – an area which was once mainly swamps and lakes. Arezzo, the Roman Arretium, was originally an Etruscan city but in 294 BC it became a military rest station on the Via Cassia between Rome and Florence. The principal Roman site is the **amphitheatre** off the Via Margaritone, built in the 1st century BC. Now turned into a park, the huge site was much plundered to build the city walls and churches.

The view of the town from the south is quite unremarkable. The buildings run down the side of a low hill and are absorbed into the landscape while from the north and the west Arezzo looks the classic hill town, surrounded by a high wall and crowned by the **Duomo**.

The Duomo's construction, mainly from the late 13th to the early 16th centuries, was aimed at re-asserting the authority of the Church over the Commune, and it has been described as one of the most perfect expressions of Gothic architecture in Italy. The Gothic facade however is fake and dates from 1914.

Internally the effect is very similar to the North European Gothic style. There are clustered columns, pointed arches and 15th-century stained glass windows. There are also local interpretations of the Gothic style in the nave; the 14th-century marble tomb of Arezzo's patron saint, Donatus, for example. Other great works here are the 14th-century cenotaph of Guido Tarlati, which flanks the St Mary Magdalen fresco by Piero della Francesca. The **Museo del Duomo** behind the cathedral contains medieval crucifixes and Vasari frescoes.

Antiques fair: On the first Sunday of every month Arezzo holds an antique fair which is one of the largest and oldest in Italy. Stalls run around the base of the Duomo, down the cobbled main street in the old quarter, the **Corso Italia**, and into the Piazza Grande beneath the arches of Vasari's Palazzo delle Loggie.

Don't miss a visit to the **church of San Francesco** in Piazza San Francesco where you can see Piero della Francesca's fresco cycle *The Legend of the True Cross. This* is the greatest work in Arezzo, painted between 1452–66 and restored for the 500th anniversary of the artist's death in 1992. The powerful and haunting series of painting includes a 15th-century representation of Arezzo. The Quattrocento masterpiece shows great psychological depth, an understanding of perspective and a subtle manipulation of colour and mood.

The **Museo Archeologico** is stacked with some of the best examples anywhere of the red-glazed Coralline ware for which Arezzo has long been famous. In the **Museum of Medieval and Modern Art** is evidence of the goldsmith's work which has been much sought after since the Renaissance.

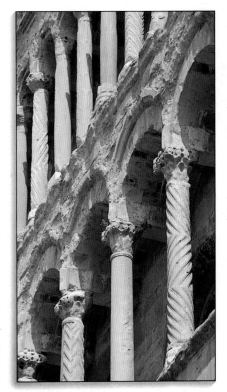

In fact, the town itself still has a large number of jewellers, though not as many as there are antique shops and furniture restorers. The antique dealers benefit from the success of the Sunday market but the restorers' tradition is sadly on the wane. Both are to be found in the vicinity of the **Piazza Grande** behind the church of **Santa Maria della Pieve**, a great Romanesque church with a Pisan-Lucchese facade.

The Piazza Grande is essentially medieval. Built around 1200 as the centre of the old city, its sloping space is flanked on two sides by 13th- and 14th-century houses and small *palazzi,* while on the third side is the apse of the *pieve* with the Palazzo Tribunale and the Palazzo della Fraternità dei Laici next to it.

On the fourth and higher side of the Piazza is Vasari's **Palazzo delle Loggie** which, when it was built in 1573, changed the entire appearance of the medieval square. The simplicity of Vasari's design creates a balance in the square which the frenetic designs of the earlier buildings could never give it.

All this is very diverting. You could, of course, sit quietly in the Biblioteca della città di Arezzo in the Via dei Pileati and read about the great intellectuals who lived in Arezzo – Maecenas, the rich friend and patron of Virgil and Horace; Petrarch; Guido d' Arezzo, the inventor of musical notation; and Giorgio Vasari, the 16th-century documenter of Italian painters' lives.

A reconstruction of Petrarch's house can be visited, as can Vasari's house, which contains some of his own frescoes and family documents.

Arezzo can be seen in one day; the hotels here are not of a very high standard, so it would be better to commute from Monte San Savino or from Cortona.

A dream town: The Upper Tiber Valley is tightly enclosed at its northern end by Alpe di Catenaia and the Alpe della Luna. According to tradition, **Sansepolcro** was built in the foothills of these Apennine peaks, near the Tiber, on the whim of two 10th-century pilgrims, Arcano and Giles, who had been inspired in a dream. Having just arrived

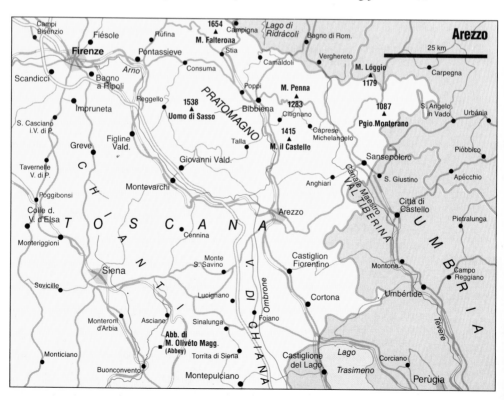

back from Palestine with relics of the Holy Sepulchre, they built a chapel on the site of the present Duomo and dedicated it to the Holy Sepulchre; the Borgo of Sansepolcro is the progeny of this.

Sansepolcro is famous for two things. It was the birthplace of Piero della Francesca, one of the greatest painters of the 15th century, and it is the source of much of Italy's pasta. Buitoni factories on the outskirts produce miles of spaghetti and macaroni, carrying the name of Sansepolcro all over the world.

The old town huddled behind crumbling ramparts is an important artistic centre. The narrow quiet streets are linked by four ancient gates, the best preserved of which is the Porta Fiorentina – though the most important one used to be the Bastione del Nord, designed in the 15th century by Buontalenti.

At the town centre, at the junction of Piazza Torre di Berta and the Via Matteotti, is the **Duomo** dedicated to St John the Evangelist. Begun in the 11th century as a monastic abbey, it was tampered with in virtually every succeeding century and today bits of it are medieval, Renaissance or baroque.

Rich interior: A wide range of excellent and indifferent artworks cover the walls of the interior including, beside the Sacristy door, a tabernacle by the della Robbia School. Perugino's *Ascension of Jesus* is also here. The Torre di Berta itself was a 12th-century tower, built at the most ancient point of the city. This was blown up by the retreating Germans in 1944.

Luckily this ruthless vandalism failed to destroy the other important buildings in this part of the town: the 16th-century Palazzo delle Laudi (the town hall) and the Palazzo Gherardi, begun in 1300, both in the Via Matteotti; and the Palazzo Pretorio opposite the Piazza Garibaldi where in the Middle Ages the citizens would gather to discuss problems affecting the community.

The survival of Piero della Francesca's greatest work, the *Resurrection* (according to Aldous Huxley, the greatest painting in the world), was under threat

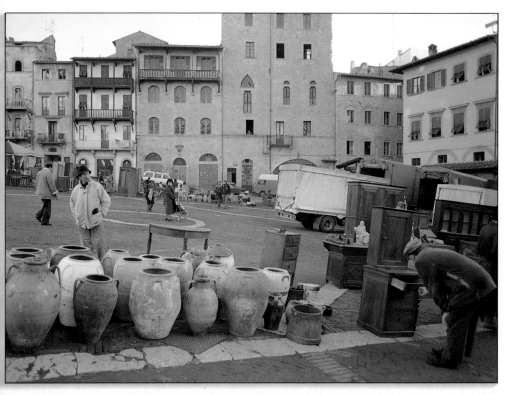

from destruction by the Allies during World War II as they bombarded Sansepolcro, believing that the Germans were still in town.

Today this intense, brooding fresco which was saved by citizens placing sandbags against it, is in the **Museo Civico** in Via degli Aggiunti. It is an early and important contribution to the search for a solution to the problem of how best to define space within a painting and to achieve the greatest harmony of its elements.

It stands opposite della Francesca's polyptych of the *Madonna della Misericordia*, another of della Francesca's most important works. In the *Resurrection* Christ and the soldiers are as rough and as rustic as della Francesca's *Madonna* in the tiny chapel of the recently restored **Madonna del Parto** outside **Monterchi**, which lies a few miles south of Sansepolcro.

The Madonna, heavily pregnant, and obviously aching after nearly nine months of carrying a child, has unbuttoned the front of her dress, while above two angels hold up the entrance to the tent in which she stands. A double row of cypresses lines the avenue from the main road to the chapel up which pregnant locals have trudged for years in order to ask the Madonna for an easy delivery. The chapel is closed on the dot of midday, so try to get there early.

Birthplace of Michelangelo: Northwest of Sansepolcro, on a steep slope above the Tiber, is the hamlet of **Caprese**, birthplace of Michelangelo. Protected by an almost complete set of walls, this clutter of rustic buildings – which includes the Buonarroti house, the old town hall where Michelangelo's father was the Florentine governor, and the tiny chapel in which Michelangelo was baptised – are interesting more for their connections than for their contents.

The town hall contains full-size reproductions of Michelangelo's works and an assortment of Michelangelo memorabilia. Outside in the garden is a sculpture park of very questionable tributes to the master from other, more recent artists.

The countryside in this region is characterised by steep rocky gorges, forests and rich pastureland. Many of the villages and hamlets here are almost inaccessible and the countryside has for a large part remained unspoilt.

At its remoter edges it cannot be much different from the day St Francis took to a lonely, desolate crag crowned with beeches on the wooded slopes of **Monte Penna** at **La Verna**, using a niche between two huge boulders as a hermitage. The mountain was given to the Franciscans as a free gift by a local devotee, Count Orlando da Chiusi di Casentino, who had been inspired by one of St Francis's sermons.

On this spot in 1224 St Francis is supposed to have received the stigmata while he was praying. Today a Franciscan sanctuary still occupies the rock and an air of solitude remains. Around a tiny piazza is a collection of monastic buildings, including one large church containing yet more terracotta sculptures by the della Robbia family, the *Annunciation* and the *Adoration of the Child*, several chapels and the conventual buildings.

On the mountain above La Verna is the spot where the saint was assailed by Satan and another where the wolf became a lamb. The journey to La Verna today from the town of **Chiusi La Verna** down below is as much of a pilgrimage as it was in the Middle Ages. A crazy twisting road drives higher up through the birch and fir forest providing a cool retreat in the summer for Florentines escaping the summer heat.

Intimations of mortality: The **Casentino** is the uppermost stretch of the Arno Valley. It is shut in by high mountains and so most access routes are tiny winding roads which have to be traversed in second gear and extremely slowly.

Sixteen kilometres (10 miles) northeast of La Verna, high in the mountains of the Casentino, is another more ancient monastery called **Camaldoli**. It was founded in 1012 by St Romuald, a former member of the Benedictine order, as a reaction to what he felt was the lax and luxurious life led by most Benedictines

Caprese, birthplace of Michelangelo.

in their monasteries. St Romuald and his followers lived here in silence and solitude. The monastery has a pharmacy in which very little has altered since the Middle Ages. An alligator hangs from the rafters and rows of dusty pots, pestles and mortars nestle up to an upright coffin with a glass lid in which is a skeleton. On the glass face of the coffin is an inscription: "In this glass you see yourself foolish mortal. Any other glass is not telling the truth."

Another 300 metres (1,000 ft) up the mountain above the monastery is the **Eremo di Camaldoli**, a hermitage consisting of nothing more than a small baroque church and eight cells, each surrounded by a high wall and a tiny garden. Here the hermits are still obeying the rules their founder laid down for them in the Dark Ages. One or two of them have been incarcerated in solitude for up to 15 years. For male visitors, a walk around the walls is permitted but a view of the hermits is not.

A brief sojourn in the loneliness of Camaldoli would easily be balanced by a visit to noisy **Bibbiena**, a typical Tuscan hill town, and one of the more important centres in the area which, unlike most other hill towns these days, is still prey to insane traffic jams.

In the church of Santa Maria del Sasso are two richly decorated panels by Giovanni della Robbia and in the church of Santa Ipolito and San Donato there is a triptych by Bicci di Lorenzo. In Via Dovizi is a rustic palace, Palazzo Dovizi, home of Cardinal Dovizi who, as Cardinal Bibbiena, became the famous secretary of Pope Leo X.

Today Bibbiena is best known for its own particular brand of salami and a lively variety of shops and bars. From the main piazza there are distant views to Camaldoli and to Poppi, the latter the gateway to an interesting district of castles and fortified towns, all of which retain traces of the barbarous quality of life lead by the inhabitants of this part of Tuscany in the late Middle Ages.

The region was continually fought over by the Guelf Florentines and the Ghibelline Aretines and a decisive bat- **Main square of Bibbiena.**

tle in 1289 which firmly established the dominance of the former over the latter is marked by a column on a site called Campaldino, just between Castel San Niccolò and Poppi.

From the latter today the views over Campaldino are of green fields, vineyards and cornfields. In 1289 the bloody battle that took place here decimated the population of the area and Dante, who was in the ranks of the Florentine army, introduced an episode from it into his *Purgatorio*. There he describes in meticulous detail the scene and the tragic death of Buonconte da Montefeltro, a fellow young Florentine.

Poppi glowers over the surrounding countryside from its hilltop perch. At its highest point is the particularly brutal-looking, and now decaying, Palazzo Pretorio, formerly a castle of the Counts Guidi, designed for them by Arnolfo di Cambio. It is not unlike the Palazzo Vecchio in Florence.

The streets of the town are lined with arcades joined by steep steps and decorated with finely carved capitals and cut stone seats. The silence of Poppi today is a reminder of the fact that young people born in remote country hill towns are constantly being drawn to the bright lights of the cities. At Poppi only old men sit about in the cafés and there is none of the ebullience and noise of Bibbiena and Arezzo.

In the distance on a hill above the village of Pratovecchio is the 11th-century **Castello di Romena**, surrounded by thickets of oak, once again a former possession of the Guidi family to whom most of the Casentino belonged. The Guidi sheltered Dante here after his expulsion from Florence at the beginning of the 14th century.

Of the 14 towers that Dante would have seen at the castle, only three now remain. **Pieve di Romena**, a stone's throw from the castle and standing on a lonely slope below the castle, is one of the most important Romanesque churches in Tuscany.

Beneath its apse, excavations have revealed the remains of an Etruscan building as well as two earlier churches.

Poppi glowering over the surrounding countryside.

Finely executed Romanesque capitals on the top of the gigantic granite columns of the nave make references to the four evangelists and to St Peter. Most notable of all is the present apse of this building which dates from 1152. The key to the church is kept by the farmer's wife, who lives in the house directly over the road.

At **Stia** is the **Castello di Porciano**, which looks down over the valley to the Castello di Romena and further on to Poppi, also in the possession of the Guidi. Whereas these monuments are all easily accessible, the fortified remains at Castel Castagnaia, with the nearby ruined Roman temple, both to the west of Stia, are harder to reach. The road peters out and a walk through rough, stony countryside is necessary in order to get to them.

Another of the Guidi castles was in the tiny village of Montemignaio. Today only a few remains of this building exist but in the village church is Ghirlandaio's *Virgin and Child with the Four Church Elders.*

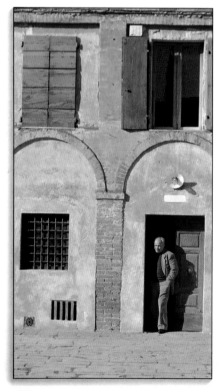

South of Bibbiena is yet another important castle at Focognano on the southwestern slope of the Pratomagno. One of the few castles in the region to have been restored is at **Chitignano**, just a few miles to the east of Focognano. The medieval remains were rebuilt in the 18th century. There are other ruined castles at Talla and Subbiano – at the latter Castelnuovo has a 15th-century tower which overlooks the main road, and is of particular interest.

Warlike bishops: The Valdarno region was the other much fought-over battle ground of the Ghibellines and the Guelfs in the Middle Ages. At the close of the 13th century pressure was exerted on the Florentines by the warlike Aretine bishops who controlled powerful and well fortified castles in the Arno valley, such as at Cennina. In an effort to resist them, the Florentines built three fortresses, which were really fortified towns, at San Giovanni Valdarno, Terranuovo and Castelfranco di Sopra.

San Giovanni Valdarno was fortified as a bulwark against the Aretines. Today it is a lively industrial centre with a prominent display of architectural and artistic wealth. The central piazza was designed by Arnolfo di Cambio while the church of Santa Maria della Grazia, in this piazza, contains Masaccio's *Virgin and Child with the Four Saints.*

Arnolfo was also responsible for the Palazzo Comunale in the middle of the piazza, and facing Santa Maria della Grazia. Just outside the town is the Renaissance monastery of Montecarlo in which is preserved the *Annunciation* by Fra Angelico.

Castelfranco di Sopra, in contrast to San Giovanni Valdarno, still retains its military character; the fortified Porta Fiorentina is as forbidding as it ever was, but these days the only thing the walls protect is an antique atmosphere. Little change has taken place here and most of the 14th-century streets and buildings have survived.

Castiglion Fibocchi defended the ancient road from the Valdarno to the Casentino and all that remains from this period is a tower and some castellated walls. The medieval nucleus spawned a

A farm worker's house.

village, little altered, which is still largely residential and the fine Renaissance residences here are as varied as those of Castelfranco di Sopra.

Etruscan heritage: Under scrutiny, the Valdarno reveals an even more ancient heritage than the comparatively recent warring of the Middle Ages. The villages of **Loro Ciuffenna** and **Cennina** bear names derived from Etruscan dialect. A more medieval rusticity is evident in their village alleyways and ruined castle fortifications. The far-distant past feels closest early in the morning when the mist covers the floor of the valley, looking like water from the height of the surrounding hills.

In prehistoric times the Arno basin was a lake, and farmers today frequently dig up fossil remains and bones of animals which have long been extinct. At **Montevarchi**, south of San Giovanni Valdarno, is the important **Accademia Valdarnese**, a museum of prehistory which houses an impressive collection of fossilised remains from the Pliocene period, discovered in this stretch of the Arno valley. The town itself contains a bizarre relic. This is a phial of the milk of the Virgin and it is kept on the altar of the Madonna del Latte. Apart from the museum and the church, there is not much to detain the traveller here, though at tiny **Galatrona** in the hills to the south of the town, above **Bucine**, is a beautiful hexagonal font in the parish church. It is covered with reliefs of the life of St John the Baptist.

Drained lake: The **Val di Chiana** is the most extensive of all the valleys in the Apennine range. The entire valley between the towns of Monte San Savino and Cortona was once covered in water. It was drained by the Etruscans and all that remains is Lake Trasimeno, just across the Tuscan border in Umbria.

By the late Middle Ages the whole area had become a swamp, and for refuge from malaria, as well as from marauding, hostile armies, the people took to the hills, barricading themselves behind high defensive walls on precipitous outcrops of rock .

Monte San Savino has been a citadel

View from Castello Conti Guidi, Poppi.

since Etruscan times, though the fortifications that survive today are medieval. In 1325 the inhabitants were unable to fend off a ruthless Aretine mob who razed the town to the ground for displaying Guelf tendencies. It was subsequently rebuilt and not much happened there until its formerly strong Jewish community was wiped out, many burnt at the stake, for resisting the French army in 1799.

Progress has hardly touched Monte San Savino; it retains medieval and Renaissance houses of which the Palazzo Comunale, with a facade by Antonio da Sangallo the Elder and a fine museum, is the most important.

The other important edifices in the town are the **Loggia del Mercato** by Sansovino and the churches of Santa Chiara and Sant' Agostino. The wild hills of the country to the northwest of the town shelter a feudal retreat, the **Castello di Gargonza**, on the west slope of Monte Palazzuolo.

This 13th-century castle, in fact a *borgo* or walled village, dominates the Chiana valley and is the centre of a vast wooded estate producing oil and wine. For nearly 400 years from 1385 a varied history shunted this castle about from one ownership to another. Dante is known to have been here in 1304 when the castle was used as a gathering point for Ghibellines from Arezzo and Florence.

Still privately owned, the walled precinct contains a number of small cell-like peasant houses which have been well-restored as a hotel complex and notable restaurant run by the Guicciardini family. Tiny stone streets, a chapel dedicated to the saints Tiburzio and Susanna, a massive baronial tower, attractive gardens and a magnificent view down to the Chiana, all make Gargonza a very pleasant retreat.

English mercenary: Another castle, originally a *borgo* as well, and at one time not unlike Gargonza in character, is the **Castello di Montecchio Vesponi**, which crowns a peak above the main road from Castiglion Fiorentino to Cortona, just south of Arezzo. The own-

Monte san Savino.

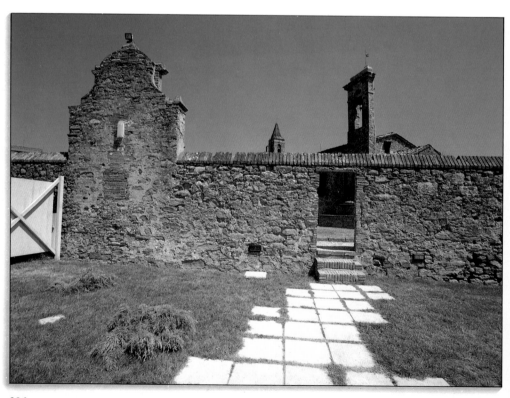

ers of this gargantuan, castellated building – which is seriously dilapidated in parts – won an award for the restoration of the 8th-century tower which stands within the enclosure.

This castle was once the property of the English *condottiero* Sir John Hawkwood, who had been hired by Florence to capture Arezzo in 1384. Montecchio was his reward. Nowadays it is only occasionally open to the public but you can always drive up to the walls and walk around the outside.

From here you can see in the distance **Castiglion Fiorentino** with its medieval girdle of walls dominated by the Cassero fortress. In this village there is an unusually high number of churches, of which no less than five are worth a visit. The most important are **Pieve San Giuliana**, which contains Signorelli's *Deposition of Christ*, and **San Francesco** which is part Romanesque and part Gothic, with a 17th-century cloister attached to one side.

Just outside the village is a strange but very fine octagonal church called Santa Maria della Consolazione. The Palazzo Comunale within the walls contains works which have been taken from all the surrounding churches – paintings, sculpture and goldsmiths work – an unbelievable quantity of treasures for such a small place.

Southeast Arezzo: The southeastern part of the province of Arezzo contains three other interesting little towns: Foiano di Chiana, Marciano di Chiana and Lucignano.

Foiana clings to the side of the hill and from afar it is a very picturesque little place. Much of it is 15th and 16th century, though traces of medieval defences can be seen around the edge of the town. The etymology of the town's name reveals a Roman origin, and just over 3 km (2 miles) to the northeast of the centre are the remains of what is believed to have been a Roman bath house, at Cisternella.

Lucignano, just south of Monte San Savino, was originally an Etruscan stronghold, though today its overriding characteristic is a very peculiar medi-

The last golden rays of the sun.

eval town plan which arranged the streets concentrically around a castle that was rebuilt in the 15th century.

With only a few exceptions the town's buildings, predominantly 13th- to 18th-century, are perfectly preserved, as is its Gothic church of San Francesco. In the 14th-century **Palazzo Comunale** are frescoes from the Sienese and Aretine schools as well as some examples of finely worked gold ornaments – evidence of the fact that the province of Arezzo has long been famous for its goldsmiths' work.

Marciano, a tiny village of great character, was also fortified in the Middle Ages and most of these fortifications still survive unchanged. Much of the castle remains and so do the walls and a gateway with a clock tower built into it. Three km (2 miles) to the southeast is the octagonal chapel of San Vittorio, designed by Vasari in 1572 to mark the spot where the Florentines defeated the Sienese in 1554.

The most important town in the province of Arezzo is **Cortona**. It sits at a height of 650 metres (2,130 ft) above the Val di Chiana, perched on a ridge on the side of Monte Sant'Egidio. Cortona is really a massive fortress, which is accessible only via a dizzy road of hairpin bends and loops.

The town is so high that it is perceptibly cooler here than in the plain below and in the evenings it is always subjected to a gentle breeze. Although the town is characteristically medieval, it was at one time a fortress belonging to the Umbrian tribe, predating even the Etruscans whose considerable relics are scattered around the Porta Colonia at the end of Via Dardano, towards the north end of the town.

The Romans colonised it, the Aretines sacked it in 1258 and in 1409 it was sold to the Florentines, which linked it from then onwards to the fortunes of the Grand Duchy of Tuscany.

The road from the plain to the city winds up through terraced olive groves scattered about with villas and farms surrounded by ilexes and cypresses, monasteries and churches. The first

Left, Castiglion Fiorentino. Right, The medieval streets of Lucignano.

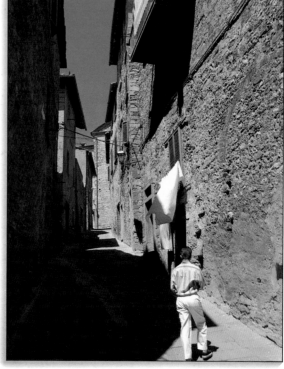

church on the way is the domed **Santa Maria della Grazia**, on the slopes beneath the town.

Beyond it is the **Porta Sant' Agostino** from which Via Guelfa leads to the Piazza Repubblica at the heart of the town. Here the 13th-century Palazzo Comunale adjoins the Palazzo Pretorio, a 13th-century mansion rebuilt in the 17th century, facing the **Piazza Signorelli**, which houses the museum of Etruscan antiquities.

It also houses some of the paintings from local churches, works by Luca Signorelli and Neri di Bicci; but it is the **Museo Diocesano** in the Piazza Duomo that houses the greatest masterpieces – Fra Angelico's *Annunciation*, a Duccio *Madonna*, a Lorenzetti *Crucifix* and Luca Signorelli's *Deposition*.

Signorelli was born in Cortona and the **Chiesa di San Niccolò** in a tiny courtyard below the Medici fortress appropriately houses his standard of *The Deposition*. The **Church of San Francesco** contains the body of St Francis of Assisi's follower and disciple, Brother Elia Coppi of Cortona who, after the death of St Francis, was responsible for sweeping away the ideal of poverty, and bringing the Franciscan Order into line with the materialistic world.

Pilgrimages: The **Basilica of Santa Margherita**, which towers over Cortona from above, contains the near perfectly preserved body of the mystic Santa Margherita who died in 1297. She was eventually received into the Third Order of St Francis. The local citizens still make pilgrimages up the winding stone-flagged streets of the town to her tomb to pray during hard times.

Cortona is predominantly medieval. Narrow streets turn into steep flights of shallow steps down which it is easy, although not desirable, to drive a small car. The overhanging houses of the Via del Gesù are quaint, even rustic, while scattered around are a number of especially fine medieval palaces: the 18th-century **Palazzo Ferreti** in the Via Nazionale, and Brunelleschi's **Palazzo Lovari** and **Palazzo Mancini** in the Via Guelfa.

The narrow steps of many villages are frequently negotiated by small cars. Following pages: Tuscan villa; the cloudy heights of Monte Senario.

INSIGHT GUIDES
Travel Tips

FOR THOSE WITH MORE THAN A PASSING INTEREST IN TIME...

Before you put your name down for a Patek Philippe watch *fig. 1*, there are a few basic things you might like to know, without knowing exactly whom to ask. In addressing such issues as accuracy, reliability and value for money, we would like to demonstrate why the watch we will make for you will be quite unlike any other watch currently produced.

"Punctuality", Louis XVIII was fond of saying, "is the politeness of kings."

We believe that in the matter of punctuality, we can rise to the occasion by making you a mechanical timepiece that will keep its rendezvous with the Gregorian calendar at the end of every century, omitting the leap-years in 2100, 2200 and 2300 and recording them in 2000 and 2400 *fig. 2*. Nevertheless, such a watch does need the occasional adjustment. Every 3333 years and 122 days you should remember to set it forward one day to the true time of the celestial clock. We suspect, however, that you are simply content to observe the politeness of kings. Be assured, therefore, that when you order your watch, we will be exploring for you the physical—if not the metaphysical— limits of precision.

Does everything have to depend on how much?

Consider, if you will, the motives of collectors who set record prices at auction to acquire a Patek Philippe. They may be paying for rarity, for looks or for micromechanical ingenuity. But we believe that behind each $500,000-plus

bid is the conviction that a Patek Philippe, even if 50 years old or older, can be expected to work perfectly for future generations.

In case your ambitions to own a Patek Philippe are somewhat discouraged by the scale of the sacrifice involved, may we hasten to point out that the watch we will make for you today will certainly be a technical improvement on the Pateks bought at auction? In keeping with our tradition of inventing new mechanical solutions for greater reliability and better time-keeping, we will bring to your watch innovations *fig. 3* inconceivable to our watchmakers who created the supreme wristwatches of 50 years ago *fig. 4*. At the same time, we will of course do our utmost to avoid placing undue strain on your financial resources.

Can it really be mine?

May we turn your thoughts to the day you take delivery of your watch? Sealed within its case is your watchmaker's tribute to the mysterious process of time. He has decorated each wheel with a chamfer carved into its hub and polished into a shining circle. Delicate ribbing flows over the plates and bridges of gold and rare alloys. Millimetric surfaces are bevelled and burnished to exactitudes measured in microns. Rubies are transformed into jewels that triumph over friction. And after many months—or even years—of work, your watchmaker stamps a small badge into the mainbridge of your watch. The Geneva Seal—the highest possible attestation of fine watchmaking *fig. 5*.

Looks that speak of inner grace *fig. 6*.

When you order your watch, you will no doubt like its outward appearance to reflect the harmony and elegance of the movement within. You may therefore find it helpful to know that we are uniquely able to cater for any special decorative needs you might like to express. For example, our engravers will delight in conjuring a subtle play of light and shadow on the gold case-back of one of our rare pocket-watches *fig. 7*. If you bring us your favourite picture, our enamellers will reproduce it in a brilliant miniature of hair-breadth detail *fig. 8*. The perfect execution of a double hobnail pattern on the bezel of a wristwatch is the pride of our casemakers and the satisfaction of our designers, while our chainsmiths will weave for you a rich brocade in gold *figs. 9 & 10*. May we also recommend the artistry of our goldsmiths and the experience of our lapidaries in the selection and setting of the finest gemstones? *figs. 11 & 12*.

How to enjoy your watch before you own it.

As you will appreciate, the very nature of our watches imposes a limit on the number we can make available. (The four Calibre 89 time-pieces we are now making will take up to nine years to complete). We cannot therefore promise instant gratification, but while you look forward to the day on which you take delivery of your Patek Philippe *fig. 13*, you will have the pleasure of reflecting that time is a universal and everlasting commodity, freely available to be enjoyed by all.

Should you require information on any particular Patek Philippe watch, or even on watchmaking in general, we would be delighted to reply to your letter of enquiry. And if you send us fig. 1: The classic face of Patek Philippe.

fig. 4: Complicated wristwatches circa 1930 (left) and 1990. The golden age of watchmaking will always be with us.

fig. 6: Your pleasure in owning a Patek Philippe is the purpose of those who made it for you.

fig. 9: Harmony of design is executed in a work of simplicity and perfection in a lady's Calatrava wristwatch.

fig. 5: The Geneva Seal is awarded only to watches which achieve the standards of horological purity laid down in the laws of Geneva. These rules define the supreme quality of watchmaking.

fig. 7: Arabesques come to life on a gold case-back.

fig. 10: The chainsmith's hands impart strength and delicacy to a tracery of gold.

fig. 11: Circles in gold: symbols of perfection in the making.

fig. 2: One of the 33 complications of the Calibre 89 astronomical clock-watch is a satellite wheel that completes one revolution every 400 years.

fig. 8: An artist working six hours a day takes about four months to complete a miniature in enamel on the case of a pocket-watch.

fig. 12: The test of a master lapidary is his ability to express the splendour of precious gemstones.

fig. 3: Recognized as the most advanced mechanical regulating device to date, Patek Philippe's Gyromax balance wheel demonstrates the equivalence of simplicity and precision.

✧

PATEK PHILIPPE
GENEVE
fig. 13: The discreet sign of those who value their time.

your card marked "book catalogue" we shall post you a catalogue of our publications. Patek Philippe, 41 rue du Rhône, 1204 Geneva, Switzerland, Tel. +41 22/310 03 66.

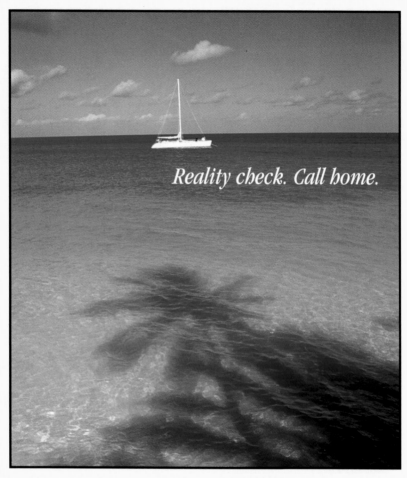

Reality check. Call home.

— *AT&T USADirect® and World Connect®. The fast, easy way to call most anywhere.* —

Take out AT&T Calling Card or your local calling card.** Lift phone. Dial AT&T Access Number for country you're calling from. Connect to English-speaking operator or voice prompt. Reach the States or over 200 countries. Talk. Say goodbye. Hang up. Resume vacation.

Austria'†††...............022-903-011	Luxembourg............................0-800-0111	**Turkey**'........................00-800-12277
Belgium'.....................0-800-100-10	**Netherlands**'.................06-022-9111	**United Kingdom**..............0500-89-0011
Czech Republic'.........00-420-00101	**Norway**..............................800-190-11	
Denmark 8001-0010	**Poland**†♦'................0◊010-480-0111	
Finland 9800-100-10	**Portugal**†........................05017-1-288	
France.................................19-0011	**Romania**'....................01-800-4288	
Germany.........................0130-0010	**Russia**'†**(Moscow)**..............155-5042	
Greece'.......................00-800-1311	**Slovak Rep.**'............00-420-00101	
Hungary'..................00◊-800-01111	**Spain**♦...................900-99-00-11	
Ireland 1-800-550-000	**Sweden** 020-795-611	
Italy '.....................................172-1011	**Switzerland**'....................155-00-11	

AT&T
Your True Choice

For a free wallet sized card of all AT&T Access Numbers, call: 1-800-241-5555.

Getting Acquainted

The Place

Tuscany (Toscana) corresponds roughly to the lands of ancient Etrutria, lying in northwest Italy between the Apennine mountains and the Ligurain and Tyrrhenean seas. Much of its 22,992 sq. km (8,876 sq. miles) is mountainous, drained by the Arno and Ombrone. The Arno, the principal river, flows through the region's capital, Florence, 80 km (50 miles) from the sea. Livorno is the main port. Tuscany also includes several islands, the largest of which is the Elba (225 sq. km/868 sq. miles).

Climate

The Tuscan climate is pleasantly mild in the spring and autumn; cool and wet in the winter, and very hot near the sea and on low-lying land in the summer with a pleasant warmth in the hills. There is very little wind except for the Tyrrhenian coastline around Marina di Pisa and Tirrenia, but surprise storms can be very heavy at any time of the year, and flooding in a number of places has caused severe damage in the past. The rainfall in Tuscany is generally higher than most other parts of Italy. The temperature is slightly lower than other areas, making it more agreeable in the summer though somewhat colder in winter.

The People

The population of Tuscany is about 3.5 million, out of a total population of 58 million in Italy. None of the cities is populous: 450,000 live in Florence, 176,000 in Livorno.

Religion

The state religion is Roman Catholicism, and even the smallest village has its church. Other denominations also hold their own services.

Culture & Customs

Italy is the world's fifth economic power on the basis of purchasing power but a report on social trends notes that since Italy became prosperous, manners and morals are changing for the worse. Still, Tuscans are generally friendly and will appreciate efforts to speak the language. Any attempt to rush or pressure them, however, will be regarded as the height of bad taste, and whatever you want will only take longer. Almost everything is done on the basis of personal favours or contacts so any personal recommendations you can muster will always come in useful.

The Economy

The typical image of Tuscany is of a gentle agricultural landscape, but there are also rugged mountains in the north which encompass the marble quarries of the Apuan Alps, the valleys of the Garfagnana and the ski resorts of the Apennines. To the south are the flat alluvial plains of Grosseto as well as metal mining and power stations. Agriculture, however, remains the mainstay of the economy with world-famous production of wine and olive oil. Tourism also plays a vital part in the local economy as visitors flock to an unrivalled centre of art and architecture.

Government

Italy is a Republic headed by a president who holds office for seven years. There are two houses of Parliament, the Chamber of Deputies, and the Senate. Power is distributed regionally among 20 regions of which Tuscany is one. Tuscany itself is divided into 10 provinces: Florence, Pistoia, Prato, Lucca, Massa-Carrara, Pisa, Livorno, Grosseto, Siena and Arezzo. The regional capital is Florence.

Planning The Trip

What To Bring

Towns like Florence, Lucca and Siena are sophisticated, so take something smart for shopping or dining out, although jackets and ties are rarely required for men. It does tend to rain unexpectedly so an essential piece of clothing is a plastic raincoat with an attached hood, large enough to cover anything worn, and light enough to be folded and carried.

Decent dress is required when visiting religious buildings; men and women are expected to have their arms covered, and shorts are frowned upon. Women often carry a headscarf as a simple headcovering. Sun hats are also recommended as protection.

Shoes need to be sturdy and comfortable, suitable for walking – especially climbing steps and on cobbled streets – if sightseeing.

Binoculars are a good idea for nature studies and architectural details.

Maps

Touring Club Italiano does a good fold-out map of the Tuscany region showing major and minor roads. The Siena and Florence Tourist Offices supply reasonable city maps.

Entry Regulations

Visa & Passport

Subjects from European Union countries require either a passport or a Visitor's Identification Card to enter Italy. A visa is not required.

Holders of passports from most other countries do not require visas for a period not exceeding three months, except for nationals of Eastern European countries, who need to obtain visas from the Italian Embassy in their own country.

THOMAS COOK MASTERCARD TRAVELLERS CHEQUES...

...HOLIDAY ESSENTIALS

Travel money from the travel experts

THOMAS COOK MASTERCARD TRAVELLERS CHEQUES ARE
WIDELY AVAILABLE THROUGHOUT THE WORLD.

INSIGHT GUIDES

COLORSET NUMBERS

Police Registration

A person may stay in Italy for three months as a tourist, but police registration is required within three days of entering Italy. If staying at a hotel, the management will attend to the formality. Although this regulation seems to be rarely observed, it is advisable that you carry a set of passport photos in case you need them for registration.

You are legally obliged to carry a piece of identity (passport, driving licence, etc.) with you at all times. This rule is often flouted but bear in mind that it would be unwise to call the police or attempt to report a problem (e.g. theft) unless you are carrying appropriate identification.

Animal Quarantine

Two certificates have to be produced for dogs and cats accompanied by travellers:
(1) A bilingual (English/Italian) Certificate of Health from a Veterinary Inspector of the Ministry of Agriculture, Fisheries and Food stating that the animal is free of any clinical signs of disease and
(2) A certificate to show the animal had been vaccinated against rabies not less than 20 days and not more than 11 months prior to the date of issue of the health certificate.

Customs Regulations

Examination of luggage, passports, currency and hand baggage takes place on both entering and leaving Italy at airports, ports and frontiers. Formalities are also carried out on trains.

Entering Italy

Registered luggage may be sent to towns with Customs Offices: examination takes place at the destination.

The following may be imported duty-free for personal use: clothing, books, camping equipment, fishing tackle, two cameras with 10 rolls of film each or 24 plates, one cine-camera with 10 rolls of film (film is expensive in Italy), one canoe or similar boat less than 5½ metres in length, sports equipment (skis, rackets etc.). One portable typewriter, one record-player with a reasonable number of records, one pram, one musical instrument, one tape recorder with a portable radio and portable television set (subject to a licence fee to be paid at the Customs), and personal jewellery (it is advisable to have jewels listed and kept with the passport to avoid problems on exit).

Items other than those listed above can be imported duty-free on condition that the owner can prove they are essential for his profession or trade (medical equipment, art material, samples, etc.). All items listed must be for personal use only and must not be sold or traded.

Professional photographers must carry an ATA Carnet (issued through the London Chamber of Commerce, 33 Queen Street, London EC4R 1BX, Tel: 0171-248 4444) for temporary importation of equipment.

Health

With Form E111 from the Department of Health and Social Security, UK visitors are entitled to reciprocal medical treatment in Italy. There are similar arrangements for other members of European Union countries. As few Italians have faith in their own state health service, it may be advisable to take out insurance for private treatment in case of accident.

Holiday insurance policies and private patients schemes give full cover during your stay abroad and are recommended for non-EU visitors.

In high summer, the weather can be very hot; sunscreen, shady hats and mosquito repellent are recommended.

See Medical Services for emergency telephone and contact numbers.

Money Matters

The monetary unit is the Italian lira (plural lire), abbreviated to Lit. (or L.). Notes are issued for 1000, 2000, 5000, 10,000, 50,000 and 100,000 lire. Coins are in denominations of 5, 10, 20, 50, 100, 200 and 500 lire. The 200 lire telephone token (*gettone*) is often used as currency in place of the 200 lire coin.

Traveller's Cheques

The use of dollar or sterling traveller's cheques is advised and all major companies' cheques are accepted, including Eurocheques, a popular option. Traveller's cheques are gradually being replaced by credit cards. Both can be used to obtain cash in any commercial bank and in exchange for goods and services in shops and hotels.

Credit Cards

Most credit cards, including Visa, Access and American Express, are accepted in hotels, restaurants and shops and for air and train tickets and cash in any bank. The American Express office in Florence is at Via Guicciardoni 13. Tel: 055-230 2256.

Exchange Rates

Exchange rates are displayed outside banks and Exchange Offices. They are also printed in daily newspapers. It is customary to get more lire for other currencies in the summer months, but the rate fluctuates according to world markets. There is one rate to buy lire and one to sell. £1 is equivalent to about L.2,500, $1 is equivalent to about L.1,600.

Banks

Working hours: 8.20am–1.30pm and at varied times between 2.35–4.30pm. Closed Saturday and Sunday.

FLORENCE

American Service Bank, Via della Vigna Nuova 2r.
Banca Commerciale Italiana, Via Strozzi 8.
Banca d'America e d'Italia, Via Strozzi 16.
Banca d'Italia, Via dell'Oriuolo 37/39.
Credito Italiano, Via Vecchietti 11.

SIENA

Banca Nazionale dell'Agricoltura, Banchi di Sopra 56-58.
Banca Nazionale del Lavoro, Piazza Tolomei 1.
Banco di Roma, Via dei Termini 37.
Cassa di Risparmio di Firenze, Piazza Tolomei.

Exchange Offices

(Only allowed to change from foreign currency into Italian lire.)
Viaggi Seti (Piazza del Campo 56) – changes notes and traveller's cheques.
Coop "Siena Hotels Promotion" (Piazza San Domenico) – changes notes, traveller's cheques and Eurocheques.
Biglietteria Stazione Ferro Viaria (railway station ticket office, Piazza Rosselli) – open day and night, including holidays. Changes notes and traveller's cheques.

Import & Export Of Currency

Foreign currency up to the value of 1 million lire may be taken out of the country. To export more than this amount, a declaration form V2 must be obtained from the Customs police when entering the country, stating the amount brought in.

Public Holidays

On Italian national holidays, all shops, banks, offices and schools are closed. Some cities celebrate their own Saint's Day, but shops and offices usually stay open.

1 January – *Capodanno* (New Year's Day)
6 January – Epiphany
Easter Monday – *Lunedi dell' Angelo*
25 April – *Anniversario della Liberazione* (Liberation Day)
1 May – *Festa del Lavoro* (Labour Day)
24 June – Saint John the Baptist – in Florence only
15 August – *Ferragosto* (Assumption of the Blessed Virgin Mary)
1 November – *Ognissanti* (All Saints' Day)
8 December – *Immacolata Concezione* (Immaculate Conception)
25 December – Christmas Day
26 December – *San Stefano* (Boxing Day)

Getting There
By Air

Tuscany is fairly well served by airports. Apart from the airport at Pisa, a short train journey from Florence, there is the new international airport of Peretola (also known as Amerigo Vespucci airport), which serves Florence. Flights to Peretola tend to be more expensive than flights to Pisa. Pisa is served by a number of charter companies, in addition to scheduled flights (e.g. Alitalia, Air France, Lufthansa and British Airways) while Peretola mainly serves business travellers.

Alitalia (AZ) and British Airways (BA) operate competitively priced flights between the UK and Pisa. In addition, a number of charter companies, notably Italy Sky Shuttle, run keenly priced flights to Pisa. Flights to Bologna and Rome are also worth considering (and are cheaper). These are quite reasonable options if your final destination is

on a direct train route from Rome/Bologna. Air UK operates daily flights to Florence from London Stansted, with Meridiana flying there from London Gatwick and Barcelona. Sabena also links Brussels and Florence Peretola.

North America: As yet, there are no direct flights between North America and Tuscany. However, British Airways runs the "Manhattan Express" which departs New York at 9pm (for London), arriving in Pisa at 4pm the following day. TWA and Air Canada are among the North American carriers who operate flights to Milan and Rome. The excellent airport train linking Fiumicino Airport (Rome) with Rome railway station (termini) and good train connections northwards to Florence mean that this is a perfectly acceptable option for visitors from the US.

Fares available on scheduled services are:
Normal fares: the most expensive but no restrictions.
Eurobudget: tickets are issued on payment. Return reservations may be left open.
Pex Fares: return only. Reservations made and tickets issued at the same time. The stay in Italy must include a Saturday night.
Superpex: the least expensive; return only. Reservations must be made at least 14 days before departure; tickets are issued at the same time. The stay in Italy must include one Saturday night.

From North America, the restrictions include a minimum week's stay and a maximum stay of 90 days.

For further information, telephone the following:
Italy's Sky Shuttle (London office). Tel: 0181-748 1333/4999; fax 0181-748 6381.
Air UK (Florence office). Tel: 055-284043.
Alitalia (Florence office). Tel: 055-27888.
Alitalia (Pisa office). Tel: 050-501570.
British Airways (Florence office). Tel: 055-218655.
TWA (Florence office). Tel: 055-230 6956.
Airport information, Florence Peretola (Amerigo Vespucci airport). Tel: 055-373498.
Airport information, Pisa (Galileo Galilei airport). Tel: 050-500707.

By Rail

Tickets: A return ticket from London to Florence costs £190, which allows for a break of journey at any intermediate station en route. It may be bought from any branch of Thomas Cook or from London Victoria Station.

Tickets for Italian railways are issued by the Italian State Railways, CIT, Marco Polo House, 3–5 Lansdowne Road, Croydon, Surrey. Tel: 0181-686 0677/5533. In the US, contact CIT, 666 Fifth Avenue, New York, NY 10103. Tel: 800-223 0230. In Canada, contact CIT, 1450 City Counsellors, Suite 750, Montreal, Quebec H3A 2E6. Tel: (514) 845 9101. These organisations will provide you with details of rail travel, including the availability of special tickets restricted to foreigners who purchase the ticket in their home country. Even if there are no special deals, Italian railways represent exceptional value, with a range of inexpensive tickets that can be bought in Tuscany.

In addition to first and second class, there are useful special tickets:
Kilometric Ticket (*Biglietto chilometrico*) allows for up to 20 trips totalling not more than 3,000 km (1,864 miles). This can be used for two months by as many as five people together or separately.
Inter Rail Ticket (*Tessera Inter Rail*) is for people under 26 and costs about £250. It allows them to travel freely for one month in the 22 countries of Europe, with a reduction of 50 percent in Italy. (The ticket gives free travel in European countries, with 30 percent discount in Britain.)

See the *Domestic Travel* (*By Rail*) section for more information on conditions and rail services.

By Road

Channel Crossing by Car: To cross the Channel to Italy, the most convenient car ferries for direct routes are from Dover and Folkstone to Calais and Boulogne; others leave from Portsmouth to Le Havre and Southampton to Cherbourg.

The AA or RAC will give up-to-date advice on Channel crossings with or without a car. The Channel Tunnel opened in 1994.

By Coach
European Coach Service: Given the cheapness of charter flights to Tuscany, this is generally a foolish option. A regular coach service is operated by National Express for a European journey from London (Victoria Coach Station, Buckingham Palace Road) via Dover – Paris – Mont Blanc – Aosta – Turin – Genoa – Milan – Venice – Bologna – Florence (via Santa Caterina da Siena) to Rome. Return fare London–Florence is about £200. Details of bookings from National Express, Victoria Coach Station, London, SW1. Tel: 0171-730 0202.

Special Facilities
The Disabled
Despite difficult cobbled streets and poor wheelchair access to many sights and hotels, many disabled people visit Florence and Tuscany. Unaccompanied visitors will experience difficulty so it is best to travel with a companion. Sources of further information are RADAR, 25 Mortimer Street, London W1M 8AB, Tel: 0171-250 3222, and the publication *Access in Florence* available from Mrs V. Saunders, 005A Office, Sherwood House, Sherwood Drive, Bletchley, Milton Keynes HK3 6AN. Tel: 01908-71131.

In the US, contact SATH, 347 5th Avenue, Suite 610, NY 10016. Tel: (212) 447-7284.

Useful Addresses
United Kingdom
Accademia Italiana, 24 Rutland Gate, London SW7 1BB. Tel: 0171-225 3474. Italian art exhibitions, events, bookshop and restaurant.

Italian Embassy: 14 Three Kings Yard, London W1Y 2EH. Tel: 0171-312 2200. General Enquiries, Commercial Office and Residence.

Italian Consulate: 38 Eaton Place, London SWIX 8AN. Tel: 0171-235 9371.

Italian Institute: 39 Belgrave Square, London SWIX 8NT. Tel: 0171-235 1461. Advises on culture, events, language and art courses in London and Italy.

Italian Trade Centre (ICE): 37 Sackville Street, London W1X 2DQ. Tel: 0171-734 2412.

Italian Chamber of Commerce: Room 418–427 Walmar House, 296 Regent Street, London W1R 5HS. Tel: 0171-637 3153.

Italian State Railways (CIT): Marco Polo House, 3–5 Lansdowne Road, Croydon, Surrey. Tel: 0181-686 0677.

Italian State Tourist Office (ENIT): 1 Princes Street, London W1R 8AY. Tel: 0171-408 1254.

Alitalia Italian Airlines: 27 Piccadilly, London W1. Tel: 0181-745 8200; Heathrow Airport: Tel: 0181-745 8400. Arrivals and departures information: Tel: 01426-914139.

Italian Sky Shuttle (Flights): 227 Shepherd's Bush Road, London W6 7AS. Tel: 0181-748 1333.

North America
Italian State Tourist Office: Store 56, Plaza 3, Place Ville Marie, Montreal, Quebec, Canada. Tel: (514) 866-7667.

Italian State Tourist Office: 630 Fifth Avenue, Suite 1565, New York, NY 10111. Tel: (212) 245-4822.

Italian State Tourist Office: 360 Post Street, Suite 801, San Francisco, California, CA 94108. Tel: (415) 392-6206.

Italian State Tourist Office: 500 N. Michigan Avenue, Chicago, Illinois, IL 60611. Tel: (312) 644-0990.

Practical Tips

Emergencies
Security & Crime
Petty crime is a problem in Italy, particularly the snatching of handbags and jewellery. Always carry valuables securely either in a money belt or handbag which can be worn strapped across the body. Cars are also vulnerable, so avoid leaving personal belongings in view and always lock your car.

Do report any thefts to the police since you will need evidence of the crime to claim insurance. Fortunately the so-called "Mosto di Firenze", who murdered eight courting couples in the 1980s, was caught in 1993 after a long search!

Medical Services
Chemists/Pharmacies: Chemists (*Farmacia*) are knowledgeable about common illnesses and sell far more medicines without prescription than in other Western countries (even so, most require a prescription). There is a list in every *Farmacia* of those open at night and on Sundays. Chemists open 24 hours (*Farmacie aperte 24 ore su 24*) in Florence are:

Farmacia Comunale 13, in Florence station. Tel: 055-289435/216761.

Farmacia Molteni, Via Calzaiuoli 7r, Florence. Tel: 055-289490/215472.

Farmacia Taverna, Piazza San Giovanni 20r. Tel: 055-211343.

In addition, you can call 110 to find out which chemists are on the night rota.

First Aid Service (*Pronto Soccorso*). A first aid service with a doctor is found at airports, railway stations and in all hospitals. *Pronto Soccorso* (*Misericordia*) in Siena can be found at Via del Porrione 49 (Tel: 0577-280028). In Florence, the *Pronto Soccorso* is:

Radio Soccorso Misericordia, Piazza Duomo, 20. Tel: 055–212222. Associazione Volontari Ospedalieri, Florence. Tel: 055-403126/234 4567. This group of volunteers will translate (free) for foreign patients.

Emergency Numbers
Medical Aid/Ambulances   116
Public Emergency Assistance
(Ambulance, Fire, Police)   113
(Replies in foreign language in main cities.)
Police Immediate Action   112

FLORENCE
Heart Emergency
(Mobile Coronary Unit). Tel: 055-214444.
Night-time and Holiday Medical Assistance. Tel: 055-477891.
Ambulances (*Misericordia*), Piazza Duomo 2. Tel: 055-212222.
Fire Brigade. Tel: 055-222222.
Lost Property Tel: 055-367943.

Tourist Medical Service, Via Lorrenzo Il Magnifico 59. Tel: 055-475 4111. 24-hour home visits, English- or French- speaking doctors.
SOS Hotline. Tel: 055-276 0382. Information on services.

ACI. Tel: 055-24861. Breakdowns (cars).

Towing Away. Tel: 055-32831. If your car is towed away, call this number for assistance.

Police Headquarters, Via Zara 2. Tel: 055-49771. This is the place to visit in the event of thefts, lost passports, etc.

Siena

Siena Hospital, Presidio Ospedaliero Maria della Scala, Piazza del Duomo. Tel: 0577-299111.

Lost Property, Comune di Siena, Via Castoro. Tel: 0577-201111.

Associazione Volontari Ospedalieri, Siena. Tel: 0577-299362. This group of volunteers will translate (free) for foreign patients.

Weights & Measures

The metric system is used for weights and measures. To convert:

	Multiply by
Centimetres to inches	0.4
Metres to feet	3.3
Metres to yards	1.1
Kilometres to miles	0.6
Gallons to litres	4.5
Kilograms to pounds	2.2

Italians refer to 100 grams as *un ettol*; 200 grams are therefore *due etti*.

Temperatures are given in Celsius (Centigrade).

Liquid measurements are in litres. One litre is 2.2 imperial pints.

Business Hours

Shops in the main cities open from Monday–Friday, 8.30am–1pm and 3.30–7.30pm. Some open on Saturday, but all shops are closed on Sunday except for a few in coastal resorts and tourist centres which open on Sundays in the summer.

Banks open from Monday–Friday 9am–1.30pm, and most of them for a short period in the afternoon.

Doing Business

Business transactions are unfortunately long-winded and bureaucratic. The *Comune* (City Council) normally monitors anything requiring legislation; most paperwork is processed by a lawyer and is issued in triplicate, with official stamps (everything must be authorised). Most public sector offices are open only in the mornings. To conduct any sort of business, make the first approach in writing a long time ahead. If possible, acquire credentials and contacts who can act as referees. The *raccommendata* is all-powerful.

Be prepared to wait in endless queues, sign several documents and receipts, and lose much time. Even withdrawing cash on a credit card or sending a parcel is a lengthy process.

In business transactions, be prepared for unorthodox methods of negotiation or settlement: payment may be required in goods or in foreign currency. If you can get anyone else to transact your business, do so – it is worth every extra lira!

Also acquire a copy of *Italy* (Cassell Business Companions), an invaluable guide to the language and business of operating in Italy.

Tipping

Allowances should be made for tipping. These are some general guidelines:

Small tips of L.100 for coffee or drinks at an ordinary bar; L.500 for sitting at a table and L.1,000 at hotel bars.

In hotels, tip doormen about L.500 for getting a taxi; chambermaids L.3–4,000 per week; the concierge L.1,000 or more according to the help given and length of stay. Other staff who carry luggage, give room service, or give help with parking or cleaning a car, L.2,000 minimum.

Tip cloakroom attendants and usherettes in a cinema or theatre L.1,000 each. Hairdressers L.3–5,000 depending on the cutting, styling or treatment given. Add 10 percent to a taxi fare.

In restaurants, the service charge of normally 15–20 percent is added to the bill which, according to law, you must have and keep until at least 100 metres from the restaurant. An extra tip is not necessary, though it is customary in cities to round up the amount, perhaps giving about five percent to the waiter who may not receive the service charge.

Media

Each large Italian town has its own newspaper. *La Stampa, Corriere della Sera*, and *La Repubblica* also have a national following. *La Nazione* is the paper favoured by most Tuscans who want to know what is happening regionally.

Television is deregulated in Italy. In addition to the state network, RAI, there are about 1,000 channels of which the main ones are Canale 5, Rete 4, Italian 1, Telemontecarlo and Video Music. There are about 500 radio stations, including many regional ones.

There are a number of useful publications for visitors to Tuscany:

Events, a monthly listings magazine in English and Italian.

Firenze Spettacolo, a monthly listings magazine in Italian, focusing on nightlife, clubs, bars and the live arts in Florence.

Toscana Qui, a serious but informative magazine (in Italian) covering such topical issues as restoration work, the arts scene, Tuscan environmental issues. Published every two months.

Firenze ieri, oggi, domani, a monthly magazine in Italian covering cultural and topical issues.

Postal Services

Main post offices in major towns are open all day, otherwise the hours are 8am to 1.30pm. Stamps are sold at post offices and tobacconists. There are letter-boxes in most main streets, at post offices and railway stations.

CAI post is a service for sending important documents world-wide in 24/48 hours.

Poste Restante

Correspondence addressed c/o Post Office with FERMO POSTA added to the name of the locality will be held for collection. Letters will be held at the local Central Post Office and will be handed over from the Fermo Posta counter on proof of identification – usually a passport – and a fee.

Telecoms

Italy has plenty of public telephones and almost every bar has a public phone, but not all can be used for long-distance calls. The phone kiosks at railway stations take coins, *gettoni* (tokens) and cards. The minimum amount of money for a call is L.200, the price of one *gettone*. Telephone cards may be purchased from a machine, which also sells *gettoni*, and the PTP (*posto* telefonico pubblico) offices. Telephone cards (schede) can be bought for the sum of L.5,000 or L.10,000 and are increasingly taking over from other forms of public telephone calls. The cards can be bought from tabacchi (tobacconists) or news kiosks.

In bars and telephone centres at stations, payment is by scatti (units) – talk first, pay later.

There is direct dialling to most countries in the world from Italy. Within the country, use a three-number code which is different for each city; when calling from outside the country, use the international code.

From the UK, dial 00-39 then the area code number, dropping the initial 0.

From Italy, dial 0044 then the area code number, dropping the initial 0.

Directories are easy to understand and give comprehensive information, or call 12 for Information from a private telephone.

Telegram, Telex & Fax

Most large hotels have a full communications service, though the more traditional have yet to install facsimile machines. Telegrams and telexes may be sent from any SIP office, post office or railway station. Only main offices and stations have fax.

INTALCABLE operates telegram services abroad, transmitting messages by cable or radio. Both internal and overseas telegrams may be dictated over the telephone.

There are photocopying machines at main railway stations such as Florence and Pisa.

Tourist Offices

General tourist information is available at the Azienda di Promozione Turistica (APT), the main Tourist Office in each provincial capital. There is a Tourist Office (Ufficio di Turismo) in most towns. In small places, the Comune holds tourist information and some commercial banks and travel agencies also publish tourist guides. The Touring Club Italiano (TCI), in almost every town, provides free information about the local area.

AREZZO PROVINCE

APT Arezzo, Piazza Risorgimento 116, 52100. Tel: 0575-23952/20839.

Cortona, Via Nazionale 70, 52044. Tel: 0575-630352.

CARRARA PROVINCE

APT Marina di Massa, Via Mazzini 21, 54037. Tel: 0585-240046/243636.
Carrara, Piazza 2 Giugno 14, 54033. Tel: 0585-70894.
Marina di Carrara, Piazza G. Menconi 6/b, 54036. Tel: 0585-632218.

GROSSETO PROVINCE

APT Grosseto, Via Monterosa 206, 58100. Tel: 0564-454510. Map in English, free on request, explaining the traditions and characteristics of the ancient villages, hermitages and convents.

FLORENCE PROVINCE

APT Firenze (Florence), Via Manzoni 16, 50121. Tel: 055-23320, Fax: 055-234 6286. This is situated slightly out of the centre (catch bus No. 19 north). Chiasso Baroncelli 17r (on a tiny alleyway behind Piazza della Signoria), Florence. Tel: 055-230 2124. This small but helpful city office is open in the spring and summer.

LIVORNO PROVINCE

APT Livorno, Piazza Cavour 6, 57100. Tel: 0586-898111.
Tourist Information Office, Central Railway Station. Tel: 0586-401193. Also the Harbour Information Office, Porto di Livorno. Tel: 0586-895320. Open in summer only.
APT Portoferraio (Elba), Calata Italia 26, 57037. Tel: 0565-914671.

LUCCA PROVINCE

APT Lucca, Piazza Guidiccioni 2, 55100. Tel: 0583-491205.
Viareggio, Railway Station. Tel: 0584-46382. Open in summer only.
Bagni di Lucca, Via Umberto I. Tel: 0583-87946.

PISA PROVINCE

APT Pisa, Via B. Croce 26, 56125. Tel: 050-40202/40096.
Central Tourist Information Office, Piazza del Duomo, Pisa. Tel: 050-560464.
Information Office, Piazza della Stazione, Pisa Centrale (Pisa central station). Tel: 050-42291.
Volterra Tourist Office, Piazza dei Priori. Tel: 0588-86150.

PISTOIA PROVINCE

APT dell'Abetone e Pistoia, Via Marconi 15, 50128. Tel: 0573-630145.
Pistoia, Corso Gramsci 110. Tel: 0573-34326.

PRATO PROVINCE

APT Prato, Via Luigi Muzzi 51, 50047. Tel: 0574-35141, Fax: 0574-607925. Prato was promoted to provincial status in 1992, in recognition of its population and status.

SIENA PROVINCE

APT Siena, Via di Città 43. Tel: 0577-42209, Fax: 0577-281041.
Tourist Office, Piazza del Campo 56, Siena. Tel: 0577-280551, Fax: 0577-270676.

Embassies

American: Lungarno Amerigo Vespucci 38, Florence. Tel: 055-239 8276.
Australian: Via Alessandria 215, Rome. Tel: 06-854 2721.
British: Palazzo Castelbarco, Lungarno Corsini 2, Florence. Tel: 055-284133/212594/287449.
German: Borgo SS Apostoli 22, Florence. Tel: 055-294722.
Netherlands: Via Cavour 81, Florence. Tel: 055-475249.

Getting Around

On Arrival

The international airport, Galileo Gallilei (Tel: 050-28088/48219) in Pisa has its own railway station. Trains take ten minutes into Pisa Centrale and 25 minutes for the 64 km (40 miles) to Florence. Car hire is available from the airport, and so are taxis.

The other international airport, Peretola, is situated in the northwestern suburb of Florence. Tel: 055-373498.

By Air

ATI is the internal airline with routes to 26 Italian cities. By leaving on a Saturday and returning by the following Sunday, there is a 30 percent discount on all Alitalia and ATI domestic services. Infants under two years, accompanied by an adult, get a 90 percent discount; over two and under 12, 50 percent discount; and from 12–21, a 30 percent discount. There are also discounts up to 30 percent if you travel at night.

By Rail

The state-subsidised railway network is a relatively cheap and convenient form of transport for travelling between major cities in Tuscany. The main Rome-Milan line is convenient for Bologna, Florence and Arezzo, while the Rome-Genoa line serves Pisa, Livorno and Grosseto. The Florence-Siena route is much faster by coach than by train.

Note that Pisa and Florence have several train stations: **Pisa Centrale** station serves Pisa city while **Pisa Aeroporto** serves the airport. (From Pisa Centrale, you can also catch Bus No. 7 to the airport.) In Florence, **Santa Maria Novella** is the main station for the city but **Rifredi** is the Florence station served by the high-speed *Pendolino* train.

Categories of trains include:

Pendolino: similar to the French TGV service, these high-speed trains provide luxurious travel between major cities. A heavy supplement (*supplemento*) is payable. The Rome-Milan service stops at Florence and Bologna; the Rome-Turin service stops at Pisa and Genoa; the Rome-Venice service stops at Florence and Bologna; and the Rome-Reggio Calabria service links Rome with the south.

Eurocity: such trains link major Italian cities with other European cities, in Germany and Switzerland, for instance. A supplement is payable.

Intercity: this fast service links major Italian cities. Buffet car. Supplement and reservations required.

Interregionali: these inter-regional trains link cities within different regions (e.g. Tuscany and Umbria) and stop fairly frequently. Some have refreshment trolleys.

Regionali: these regional trains link towns within the same region (e.g. Tuscany) and stop at every station.

The following ticketing services are available:

Booking: Reservations are mandatory for superior trains (Pendolino, Eurocity and Intercity services) and tickets should be purchased in advance. Tickets with compulsory supplements should be purchased at least three hours in advance. Buying your ticket at least five hours before travel guarantees you a free seat reservation. If you board a train without a ticket, one can be bought from a conductor, with a penalty payment of 20 percent. You can also pay the conductor directly if you wish an upgrade to first class or a *couchette* (should there be places available).

Expect long queues for tickets at major stations. For a small fee, tickets can be purchased from many travel agents as well as from railway stations.

Wagons Lits/Carrozze Letto (sleeping cars) are found on long-distance trains within Italy as well as on trains to e.g. Austria, France, Germany, Spain and Switzerland. Reservations are essential.

Although luggage trolleys are often invisible, porters (*facchini*) are available in most stations and charge L.1,500 or L.2,000 for each item of luggage.

There are a wide variety of train tickets and specials offers available:

Chilometrico: this is the best-value of the long-standing Italian ticket deals, providing a discount of over 15 percent. Valid for two months, the ticket can be used by up to five people at the same time and allows 3,000 km (1,864 miles) of travel, made on a maximum of 20 journeys. A first-class ticket costs L.316,000 while a second-class one costs L.186,000.

Group fares: groups of between 6 and 25 people can benefit from a 20 per cent discount. The group leader's ticket is free.

Youth fares: students between 12 and 26 can buy a yearly "green card" (*Carta Verde*) for L.40,000, a season ticket entitling them to a 20 percent discount.

Children's fares: children under four travel free; children between 4–12 are eligible for a 50 percent discount on all trains but must pay the full price of the

supplement on Intercity and Eurocity trains.

Pensioners' fares: the over-60s can buy a *Carta d'Argento* for L.40,000. Valid for a year, this "silver card" entitles you to a 20 percent discount on all tickets.

Booklet of Tickets (*Carnet di Biglietti*): this is a flexible scheme which varies according to distance and class travelled but allows for savings of 10 percent on short journeys (under 350 km/217 miles) and a 20 percent discount on longer journeys.

Railway Stations

The main railway stations are open 24 hours and are integrated with road and sea transport. They provide numerous services including telecommunications, left luggage, food and drink, tourist information and porters (average charge of L.2,000 per case). Most large stations have *Alberghi Diurni* (day hotels) that provide restrooms, dressing rooms, baths, showers and hairdressers for the convenience of travellers.

FLORENCE

Train information office at the ends of tracks 9 and 10. Train reservation office and a money exchange office inside the main station hall. Both open daily from 8.20am–7pm except on holidays. The left luggage counter is usually very busy. Each piece of luggage is left at your own risk, and badly packed or awkwardly shaped packages are likely to be damaged by the uncooperative staff.

There is an Air Terminal at Florence Santa Maria Novella station (near platform 5) where you can check in for Pisa airport (Tel: 055-216073) and for Rome Fiumicino airport (Tel: 055-235 2388).

In Florence, for train information Tel: 055-288785. To find out about trains going towards Rome, Tel: 055-288460. To find out about trains going towards Bologna, Milan and Venice, Tel: 055-288470. For information about trains to Siena and Pisa, Tel: 055-288480.

SIENA

The railway station is the centre for most communications. There is an information office, a 24-hour telephone bureau, telex, left luggage (and bicycles), photocopier and restaurant. Immediately outside the station is a bus ticket office and a Tourist Office.

However, Siena railway station is outside the town centre. More useful, and with faster services and a greater range of local destinations, is the coach service, with coaches leaving from Piazza San Domenico to Florence and various Tuscan towns.

LEFT LUGGAGE

The main railway stations are open 24 hours and provide numerous services including telecommunications and left luggage. The fee for luggage service is usually L.5,000 per item although the price increases every September.

By Coach

Coaches are very comfortable and often quicker, though usually more expensive, than trains. There are numerous sightseeing tours in all the main cities. Morning tours usually start at 9am and finish at 12.30pm, while afternoon tours start at 2.30pm and finish at 6.30pm. Details are available locally.

Addresses of bus/coach companies are:

ACIT, Piazza Sant'Antonio, Pisa. Tel: 050-501038. (For travel in Pisa Province.)

LAZZI, Via Mercadante 2, Florence. Tel: 055-215154, (for travel in Tuscany) and at Piazza V Emanuele II, Pisa. Tel: 46288.

SITA, Viale dei Cadorna 105, Florence. Tel: 055-483651. (For travel in Tuscany and other parts of Italy.)

Water Transport

Sea transport from Italian ports has decreased in recent years, but occasional passenger liners dock at Livorno and it is still a busy commercial port.

Yachts and small cruisers moor at Marina di Pisa, a few miles from Pisa.

Car-ferry services operate regularly to the **Island of Elba**:

Narvarma, with main offices are at Portoferraio, Viale Elba 4. Tel: 0586-916743.

Toremar, with offices in Livorno, Via Calafati, 6. Tel: 0586-22772.

Together they offer services (up to 20 a day in high season) in each direction. The first departure in the morning from Piombino is 6.15am and the last back from Portoferraio is 6.50pm. Fares range from L.15,000–44,000.

In the summer, additional services run from Livorno plus hydrofoil services between Piombino and Elba (Piombino – Cavo, 20 minutes; Piombino – Portoferraio, 40 minutes).

Public Transport
City Buses

Buses within each province are cheap and plentiful. A set amount, varying between L.1,000–2,000, is payable for one journey, each province setting its own fare level. Tickets are purchased in booklets of 10 and have to be clipped by a machine on the bus at the start of a journey. Failure to do so risks a fine of 10 times the price of the ticket, either on the spot or within a month.

In Florence, a range of tickets is available from the ATAF office (by Santa Maria Novella station). You can get a special 24-hour pass (L.5,000), a *carnet* of 10 tickets (L.12,000), or various season tickets and student reductions.

Confusingly for English-speakers, Siena's city/regional bus service is called TRA-IN.

All the times of buses within the Province are clearly displayed on a board in the APT office in Garibaldi Square, Pisa. The yellow figures indicate daily services, red means services on festivals only and white shows services on weekdays (Monday–Friday). There are buses every half an hour to Livorno and every hour to Pontedera, to change for Volterra.

Just outside Pisa Centrale Station on the left is a ticket window where they sell bus tickets.

All provincial buses are routed past the railway station in every town.

Taxis

Taxis are plentiful in all towns and tourist resorts. They wait in special taxi-ranks at railway stations and main parts of the city but can always be called by telephone. If you call a taxi by phone, the cost of the journey begins then. (In Florence, Tel: 4390 or 4798 for Radio Taxi.) Meters display the fares. A fixed starting charge varies from L.2,500–5,000.

There are extra charges for night service, Sunday and public holidays, luggage and journeys outside the town area.

In Florence, there are taxi ranks in Via Pellicceria, Piazza di San Marco and Piazza di Santa Maria Novella.

Private Transport
By Car

Italy holds one of the worst records in Europe for road accidents. Drivers in the north tend to drive very fast, regardless of the number of cars on the road or the conditions. The high level of traffic in city centres means many areas, particularly round historic sights, are closed to most vehicles.

Since Florence, Montepulciano, Pistoia and certain other historic cities have introduced partial or complete bans on driving in the city centre (at least for non-residents), it makes sense to leave the car in the car parks on the edge of the historic centre.

The state highways in Tuscany are the No.1 "Aurelia", west of Pisa, and national motorways (*autostrade*), the A11 – the "Firenze-mare" and the A12 – the "Sestri Levante-Livorno".

Driving Licence: The driver must possess a driving licence issued by countries with reciprocal agreements. Although the new EU licence does not officially require an Italian translation, it is advisable to take one. All other licences need a translation, obtainable (free) from motoring organisations and Italian Tourist Offices.

Insurance: It is strongly advised to obtain a Green Card (international motor insurance certificate) from your own insurance company at least 10 days before travelling. For minimum cover, they may be bought at ferry terminals in Britain and at the Customs Office at any border. Further comprehensive cover may be bought for "breakdown insurance" – it offers some compensation for replacement vehicles and transport home if the car breaks down.

Parking: Outside cities and towns, parking on the right-hand side of the road is always allowed, except on motorways (*autostrade*), at crossroads, on curves and near hilly ground not having full visibility. If a vehicle has stopped and is blocking the road for any reason, the driver must try to clear the road. If it is impossible, he is required to warn other vehicles by placing a special triangular danger signal at a distance of at least 50 metres behind the vehicle. All vehicles must carry these signs, which can be obtained on hire from all ACI offices at the border by paying a deposit of L.2,000.

In Florence, there is free parking outside the city with shuttle services to the centre. The Florentines consider parking meters unsightly but there are a few. Illegally parked vehicles will be fined and towed away.

Petrol Stations: In Florence, petrol stations and garages which open at night include:

AGIP, Via Antonio Pollacolo. Self-service.

Tamoil, Via Senese. Self-service.

Texaco, Viale Guidoni. Self-service.

THE ITALIAN HIGHWAY CODE

The Italian traffic rules are aligned to the Geneva Convention and Italy uses international road signs. Some slight local differences are as follows:

Road signs: ALT is a stop line painted on the road for road junctions; STOP is for a pedestrian crossing.

Right-hand drive: Vehicles must keep to the right-hand side of the road and close to the nearside kerb, even when the road is clear.

On three-lane roads, the middle lane is reserved for overtaking, which must always be signalled in advance.

Speed limits: In urban areas, the maximum speed limit for all vehicles is 50 km/h (31 mph); on country roads, up to 600cc is 80 km/h (50 mph), up to 900cc is 90 km/h (55 mph), up to 1300cc is 100 km/h (62 mph) and over 1300cc is 110 km/h (68 mph). On motorways, the speeds allowed in the same order are 90, 110, 130 and 140 (55, 68, 81 and 87 mph) maximum.

Each province declares speed restrictions. In most, the speed limits are lower at weekends and in the summer months.

Side mirrors: These are compulsory on the left-hand side of the car, for both right- and left-hand drive vehicles. Drivers may be required to have one fitted in Italy.

Seat belts: The wearing of seat belts is compulsory.

Precedence: At crossroads, motorists must give precedence to vehicles on their right, except on recently built roundabouts, when those already on the roundabout have priority.

Trams and trains always take precedence from left to right. If a motorist approaching a crossroads finds a precedence sign (triangle with point downwards) or a stop sign, he must give precedence to all vehicles coming both from right and left.

RUSH HOURS

The busiest times in the cities are between 9.30am–1pm, when most business is done. There is a lull in the afternoon until 3pm and traffic is heavy again between 4–8pm.

On country roads and motorways, heavy traffic builds up leading into the cities in the mornings and out again in the evenings around 7pm. In the summer, roads leading to the coast on Saturday mornings are especially busy; and on late Sunday afternoons, enormous queues form on routes going into the cities when people return from a day or weekend away.

MOTORWAY TOLLS

Charges for driving on motorways in Italy can be considerable. A ticket is taken from a machine on entering and payment is made at the end or at intermediate stages. For small or set amounts, coins may be thrown into a container; otherwise an attendant takes the toll and gives change. It saves time to go prepared with handfuls of coins and L.1,000–2,000 notes. Within Tuscany, there is a charge on the A11 from Florence to Pisa of L.9,000 for cars; from Florence to Lucca, L.9,500.

Access signs to the motorways, unlike those of other European countries, are in green, not blue.

For more information on tolls, charges and routes as well as traffic, contact Centro Servizi Firenze-Ovest. Tel: 055-420 0444, Fax: 055-420 3234.

ITALIAN AUTOMOBILE CLUB

The Automobile Club d'Italia (ACI), whose head office in Via Marsala, 8, 00185 Roma, Tel: 06-4998, is the equivalent of the British RAC or AA. Until December 1995, and probably on an indefinite basis, the ACI will rescue any foreign drivers who breakdown in Tuscany. Addresses in Tuscany, where drivers may obtain useful maps and road information, are:

Arezzo: Via le L. Signorelli 24a. Tel: 0575-30350, Fax: 0575-303620.

Florence: Via le Amendola, 36. Tel: 055-24861, Fax: 055-234257.

Grosseto: Via Mazzini, 105. Tel: 0564-415777, Fax: 0564-415449.

Livorno: Via G. Verdi, 32. Tel: 0586-899651, Fax: 0586-898387.

Lucca: Via Catalani, 59. Tel: 0583-582626, Fax: 0583-418058.

Massa Carrara: Aurelia Ovest 193. Tel: 0585-831941, Fax: 0585-831941.

Pisa: Via San Martino, 1. Tel: 050-47333, Fax: 050-44476.

Pistoia: Via Racciardetto, 2. Tel: 0573-32101, Fax: 0573-34377.

Siena: Via le Vittorio Veneto, 47. Tel: 0577-49001, Fax: 0577-49003.

CAR HIRE

Self-drive hire is available from major rental companies (Hertz, Avis, Europcar) in most cities and resorts with different rates and conditions. Generally the smaller firms offer cheaper rates but cars can only be booked locally. Booking from the UK, perhaps in an air-drive package, is much cheaper than hiring on arrival. Even with four or five people sharing, a self-drive car is fairly expensive.

Rates generally allow unlimited mileage and include breakdown service, maintenance, oil, seat belts but not petrol. Basic insurance is included but additional cover is available at fixed rates. Most firms require a deposit equal to the estimated cost of the hire. They often hold a credit card payment, which serves as the charge on return of the car. People travelling by air or rail can take advantage of special packages.

Cars may be hired from the airports at Pisa or Florence and at the railway station at Florence.

BREAKDOWN & ACCIDENTS

In case of a breakdown on an Italian road, dial 116 at the nearest telephone box. Tell the operator where you are, the registration number and the type of car and the nearest ACI office will be informed for immediate assistance. They are usually very efficient.

On motorways, telephones are 2 km (1 mile) apart, with special buttons to call for the police and medical assistance. Both have to be contacted if an accident involves an injury.

By Bicycle

Bicycles can be hired in Lucca at Noleggio Biciclette, Comune di Lucca, Via delle Conce. It is open from 10am–7pm; closed from October–April. On leaving an identity card – usually your passport – you may hire by the hour a sturdy, red and white bike with a large number on it. Choose one with good brakes and a stand. Prices are:
Bicycle: One hour or fraction of an hour, L.3,000; per day, L.15,000.
Tandem – I hour or fraction of an hour, L.8,000; per day, L.35,000.
Mopeds can be rented in Florence through "Sabra" at Via Degli Artisti 8. Tel: 055-576256/579609.

Where To Stay

Hotels

The quality and range of accommodation in Tuscany is extremely varied, with a choice between a city *palazzo*, grand country villa, or historic family-run hotel. Alternatively, visitors can choose to stay in a rented apartment or villa, sample an increasingly popular farm-stay holiday (*Agriturismo*) or even, in the most popular cities, a private home stay. (This is not known as bed and breakfast since breakfast is often not provided.)

The region is fairly well provided with accommodation but hotels usually need to be booked well in advance in Florence and Siena. During local summer festivals, particularly the Sienese *Palio* and Arezzo *Giostra*, rooms are scarce. The major cities differ greatly from one another in the quality of accommodation provided. Pisa, for instance, has few superior hotels while Arezzo has a distinct lack of choice. Attractive accommodation in the centre of Volterra and San Gimignano is popular so early booking is advisable.

Ratings

Italian hotels are classified according to a 1–5-star rating system. For convenience, the following hotel recommendations are listed under their near-est town and are accorded Expensive, Moderate or Inexpensive price categories. Categories refer to the price of a double room, usually with breakfast.
Inexpensive   under L.125,000.
Moderate   L.125,000–250,000.
Expensive   L.250,000–600,000.

In the Inexpensive category, hotels under about L.60,000 used to be called *pensioni* but the term is no longer used: they are now listed as hotels, usually of 1–2-star standard. Hotels in the Moderate category tend to be of 3-star standard while those in the Expensive category are 4–5-star or *deluxe*.

Many hotels with restaurants insist on a half- or full-board arrangement, particularly in the high season, including in Florence. This ploy is particularly prevalent on the islands (e.g. Elba), in seaside resorts (e.g. Forte dei Marmi), in spa resorts (e.g. Montecatini and Chianciano Terme), and where accommodation is in short supply.

Many hotels offer a choice between a room or full/half-board, in which case prices for both options are given, with the room rate referring to a double room and the full/half-board rate referring to the price per person. In the case of hotels that insist on half or full board, prices are also indicated, with the individual rate quoted. If staying out of season or contemplating a long stay, it is worth negotiating a discount (*uno sconto*).

In the case of major centres, such as Florence and Siena, hotels in neighbouring villages are listed under "Florence Environs" or "Siena Environs".

For villa and apartment rental, rural accommodation, farm stays, budget accommodation, and accommodation in private homes, see the specific categories that follow the general hotel listings.

ABETONE

Boscolungo, Via Brennero 224. Tel: 0573-60582. *Pensione* with swimming pool. Inexpensive.
Regina, Via Uccelliero 9. Tel: 0573-60007. A pleasant 19th-century villa in an attractive setting. A reasonably priced 3-star hotel. Inexpensive.

AREZZO

Continentale, Piazza G. Monaco 7. Tel: 0575-20251, Fax: 0575-350485. This 3-star hotel is centrally located and decorated in a modern, elegant style. Moderate.
Hotel Europa, Via Spinello 43. Tel: 0575-357701, Fax: 0575-357703. Conveniently near railway station.

AREZZO ENVIRONS

Gorgonza: **Castello di Gargonza**, Gargonza, Monte San Savino. Tel: 0575-847021, Fax: 0575-847054. This charming fortified village, complete with a frescoed chapel and castle walls, has been converted into a hotel with separate apartments. The converted 13th-century buildings overlook the Valdichiana. Pool and restaurant specialising in game. Moderate.

CARRARA

Hotel Michelangelo, Corso Flli. Rosselli, 3. Tel: 70-86163.

CASCINA

Hotel Villa Guelfi, Via Tosco Romagnola 941, Località Santa Anna Cascina. Tel: 050-775182, Fax: 760888. Villa in a typical Pisan 19th-century style.

CASTAGNETO CARDUCCI

La Torre, 57022 Livorno. Tel: 0565-775268. Cheap, country hotel with separate restaurant offering wild boar dishes.

CASTELLINA IN CHIANTI

Belvedere di San Leonino, Località San Leonino. Tel: 0577-740887. An imposing 15th-century country house surrounded by olives and vineyards. Decorated with antique furnishings. Pool. Inexpensive.
Salivolpi, Via Fiorentina 89, 53011 Castellina in Chianti. Tel: 0577-740484, Fax: 0577-40998. This well-restored farmhouse contains an appealing garden and uncontrived rustic decor, with the original beams, white-washed walls, terracotta tiles and decorative ironwork. Inexpensive.
Tenuta di Ricavo, Località Ricavo 53011 (5km/3 miles from Castellina in Chianti). Tel: 0577-740221, Fax: 0577-741014. Open March–October, this welcoming hotel is decorated in country tones and occupies a series of rustic houses in a medieval hamlet. Pool and good restaurant. Moderate.
Villa Casalecchi, Località Casalecchi. Tel: 0577-740240, Fax: 0577-741111. Open from March–October,

this stylish 3-star hotel is set in a 19th-century villa, surrounded by oak trees. Swimming pool and tennis courts. Moderate.

CHIANCIANO TERME

This spa town is situated in lovely countryside and makes a good base for exploring the southern Sienese countryside around Montepulciano and Pienza. Although Chianciano has an old town, the hotels, of which there are many, are modern, well-equipped and can provide invigorating thermal cures. Many hotels may expect guests to take half or full board.

Hotel Michelangelo, Via delle Piane, 53042 Siena. Tel: 0578-64004, Fax: 0578-60480. This modern 4-star hotel enjoys a fine setting, with large grounds, a pool, sauna, tennis courts and good restaurants, including a rooftop restaurant in summer. Run by Augusto, the boisterous master of ceremonies, the hotel is popular with Italians and holds such events as a barbecues, dances and bridge parties. Open April–mid-October. Moderate.

CHIUSI

Centrale Hotel, Tel: 0578-20118/0578-222043. Recently renovated and decorated. Convenient for the railway station (direct trains to Florence). Moderate.

COLLE DI VAL D'ELSA

Situated northwest of Siena, within the triangle of San Gimignano, Monteriggioni and Poggibonsi, this makes a good base for exploring Volterra and the north of Siena province.

Villa Belvedere, Località Belvedere. Tel: 0577-920966, Fax: 0557-924128. This delightful 18th-century villa is surrounded by a large park. Moderate.

ELBA

The island of Elba has few stunning hotels but offers a wide range of family accommodation and resort-type hotels beside the sea. Many will insist on half or full board. The island is especially popular with Italians and Germans.

Costa dei Gabbiani, Capoliveri. Tel: 0565-935122, Fax: 0565-925333. This vast resort complex borders a protected coastline and occupies a vast estate. Guests can choose between staying in villas, apartments or rooms. Swimming, horse-riding, golf and archery are on offer. Open all year. Moderate.

Dei Coralli, Via Degli Etruschi, Marina di Campo. Tel: 0565-976336, Fax: 0565-977748. Situated in one of Elba's most popular resorts, this 3-star hotel is 100 metres from the beach. Inexpensive.

Fabbricia, Località Magazzini, Portoferraio, Isola d'Elba. Tel: 0565-933181, Fax: 0565-933185. This 4-star hotel is situated 9km (5½ miles) from Portoferraio and is modern but decorated in island style, and set in an ancient olive grove. Beach. Moderate.

Le Acacie, Località Maregno, Capoliveri. Tel: 0565-935151, Fax: 0565-967062. This 3-star, Mediterranean-style hotel is set in an attractive part of the island. Moderate.

Associazione Albergatori, Calata Italia, 21. Tel: 0565-92754. Will help find rooms or campsite for no charge. Open daily in summer 8.30am–12.30pm, 3–7pm; winter 8.30am–12.30pm, 3–6pm.

Biodola La Hermitage. Tel: 0565-96911, Fax: 0565-969984. Bungalows in pinewoods by beach. Lively. Moderate.

FLORENCE

Hotel beds in the city centre are usually scarce so try to book ahead. Failing that, hotels can be booked at the information office in Santa Maria Novella train station. The ITA office (Informazioni Turistiche Alberghi) is situated between platforms 9 and 10 and is open 8.30am–9pm.

The cheapest hotels tend to be situated around Santa Maria Novella and the Station areas, which can become rather dodgy at night. Only in Florence can dingy hotels still get away with being situated on the top floor of a lift-free *palazzo* and closing the doors to guests at midnight. However, at the other end of the scale, the city has some of the loveliest hotels in Tuscany, with frescoed interiors or sweeping views over the city. In the upper price bracket, the essential decision is between an historic centrally located *palazzo* in the city or a beautifully appointed villa in the hills.

For villa and apartment rental, rural accommodation, farm stays, budget accommodation, and accommodation in private homes, see the specific categories that follow the general hotel listings.

If the letter **"r"** appears after numbers, it refers to *rosso* (red) and denotes a business address. Confusingly, Florentine addresses operate a dual numbering system, with "red" numbers usually denoting businesses and blue or black numbers usually denoting residential addresses.

EXPENSIVE

Croce di Malta, Via della Scala 7. Tel: 055-218351. Curious combination of mock-Renaissance and post-modern, but has the advantage of garden, pool and convenient location for the station.

Excelsior, Piazza Ognissanti 3. Tel: 055-264201, Fax: 055-210278. The grandest hotel in Florence – a lavishly furnished 19th-century building on the banks of the Arno. Celebrities and business executives stay here. Panoramic rooftop restaurant.

Grand, Piazza Ognissanti 1. Tel: 055-288781, Fax: 055-217400. Smaller than its sister hotel (the Excelsior, across the square) but almost as grand. It underwent refurbishment several years ago. Queen Victoria and other foreign royalty stayed here in the 19th century.

Grand Hotel, Villa Cora, Viale Machiavelli 18. Tel: 055-229 8451, Fax: 055-229086. Quiet, elegant hotel set in a huge park on a hill above Florence. Free limo service into the city centre.

Hotel Baglioni, Piazza Unità 6. Tel: 055-218441, Fax: 055-215695. This classic hotel retains its air of discreet elegance while providing extremely comfortable rooms. It has a following in the business community.

Hotel Regency Umbria, Piazza Massimo d'Azeglio, 3. Tel: 055-245247, Fax: 055-234 2938. A small, charming, central hotel. Gourmet restaurant.

Kraft, Via Solferino 2. Tel: 055-284273. Civilised and efficiently-run hotel in quiet location 15 minutes' walk from centre. Rooftop restaurant and swimming pool with excellent views. Popular with Americans.

Loggiati dei Servi, Piazza della SS Annunziata 3. Tel: 055-289592, Fax: 055-289595. Designed for the Servite fathers, San Gallo's gracious 16th-century *palazzo* is set on a lovely square unfairly ignored by most foreigners. Antiques adorn the vaulted interior and the small garden is a delightful surprise. This is one of Florence's most refined hotels. On a more mundane level, parking facilities are available, a luxury in the city centre.

Lungarno, Borgo Sant' Jacopo 14. Tel: 055-264211. Delightful modern hotel on south bank of the Arno. Drawings of Cocteau and Picasso feature among the owner's impressive collection of modern art. Good views of river from front rooms.

Mona Lisa, Borgo Pinti 27. Tel: 055-247 9751. A favourite among visitors to Florence. Renaissance *palazzo* with antiques, drawings and sculpture. Delightful garden.

Torre di Bellosguardo, Via Roti Michelozzi 2. Tel: 055-2298145, Fax: 055-229008. Set up in the hills, this atmospheric, quiet and roomy hotel is composed of a 14th-century tower attached to a 16th-century villa. It offers frescoed reception rooms and highly individualistic and charmingly decorated bedrooms, studded with antiques and quirky details.

Villa Medici, Via Il Prato 42. Tel: 055-238 1331, Fax: 055-238 1336. Has a swimming pool, gardens, and large airy bedrooms; convenient location near the station.

Savoy, Piazza della Repubblica 7. Tel: 055-283313. Old-established hotel in centre of shopping district. Solid, old-fashioned comforts and good service.

MODERATE

Albion, Via Il Prato 22r. Tel: 055-214171, Fax: 055-283391. Set in a stylish Neo-Gothic *palazzo*, the hotel is a showcase for modern art. Bicycles are freely available for guests.

Andrea, Piazza Indipendenza 19. Tel: 055-483890, Fax: 055-469489. Situated on a monumental square, this imposing 3-star hotel has a view of the Duomo.

Annalena, Via Romana 34. Tel: 055-222402. Elegant and spacious *palazzo* inside although the outside looks like an ordinary *pensione*. Very pleasant staff. Near Boboli Gardens.

Goldoni, Borgo Ognissanti 8. Tel: 055-2396983, Fax: 055-282576. This centrally located hotel occupies an historic *palazzo* by the river, yet not far from Santa Maria Novella.

Hermitage, Vicolo Marzio 1, Piazza del Pesce. Tel: 055-287216, Fax: 055-212208. Small, intimate and exceptionally popular hotel close to the Ponte Vecchio. Pretty rooftop terrace with views of the Arno. Some rooms very noisy.

Lungarno Hotel, Borgo San Jacopo 14. Tel: 055-264211. A modern hotel overlooking the Arno near the Ponte Vecchio.

Palazzo Benci, Via Faenza 6r. Tel: 055-213848, Fax: 055-288308. This patrician *palazzo*, traditionally the seat of the Benci family, has recently been restored but retains many original features and a tiny garden.

Pensione Quisisana and **Ponte Vecchio**, Lungarno Archibusieri 4. Tel: 055-216692/215046.

Pitti Palace, Via Barbadori 2. Tel: 055-282257. Perennial favourite with English-speaking visitors (the owner's wife is American). Pretty roof terrace and sitting rooms, convenient location just south of the Ponte Vecchio, but some bedrooms are very noisy.

Plaza Hotel Lucchesi, Lungarno della Zecca Vecchia 38. Tel: 055-264141. Comfortable, civilised and very efficiently-run hotel overlooking the Arno.

Tornabuoni Beacci, Via de' Tornabuoni 3. Tel: 055-268377. Deluxe guest house, very comfortable and very welcoming. Pretty rooftop terrace for breakfast and drinks. Half-board terms compulsory. Particularly popular with Americans.

Villa Liberty, Viale Michelangelo 40. Tel: 055-683819, Fax: 055-6812595. Set in a chic residential area of Florence, winding up towards Piazzale Michelangelo, this turn-of-the-century Tuscan villa has a homely appeal and is surrounded by a lovely garden.

Villa Belvedere, Via Benedetto Castelli 3. Tel: 055-222501, Fax: 055-223163. Exceptionally friendly and modern; south of city. Sunny rooms, pretty garden and lovely views across Florence. Swimming pool and tennis court.

INEXPENSIVE

Aprile, Via della Scala 6. Tel: 055-216237. One of the more appealing hotels near the station. A Medici palace with original frescoes and some painted ceilings. Huge range of bedrooms, some very simple.

Beacci Tornabuoni. Via de' Tornabuoni 3. Tel: 055-212645. Pleasant *pensione* in the centre of town.

Boboli, Via Romana 63. Tel: 055-229 8645. This simple but appealing 2-star hotel is conveniently situated for the Pitti Palace, Boboli Gardens and the Oltrarno.

Casci, Via Cavour 13. Tel: 055-211686, Fax: 055-239 6461. This frescoed *quattrocento palazzo* is family-run and has a welcoming atmosphere.

Centro, Via dei Ginori 17. Tel: 055-230 2901, Fax: 055-230 2902. Situated near Via Cavour and the Palazzo Medici-Riccardi, this ancient *palazzo*, once Raphael's residence, has been renovated to provide spacious, light rooms.

Cestelli, Borgo SS Apostoli 25. Tel: 055-214213. Tiny, intimate guest house in narrow medieval street. Rock-bottom prices but very simple rooms and only one with private bathroom.

Fiorino, Via Osteria del Guanto 6. Tel/Fax: 055-210579. Basic and unpretentious.

Liana, Via Alfieri 18. Tel: 055-245303. Simple hotel north of centre in former British Embassy. Quiet, pleasant but slightly faded.

Pensione Bretagna, Lungarno Corsini 6. Tel: 055-263618. A favourite with British business travellers.

Pensione La Mia Casa, Piazza Santa Maria Novella 23. Tel: 055-213061. One of the cheapest and a most attractive 17th-century *palazzo*. Popular with Americans and musicians. Near the station.

Pensione Sorelle Bandini, Santo Spirito 9-10. Tel: 055-215308. Elegant top-floor *pensione* that belies the rather scruffy entrance. Almost always full, so book at least a week in advance.

Porta Rossa, Via Porta Rossa 19. Tel: 055-287551. Large and old-fashioned, with huge spartan rooms. Favourite among the *literati*.

Rigatti, Lungarno Generale Diaz 2. Tel: 055-213022. Family-run, typically Florentine *pensione*, occupying two floors of a 15th-century *palazzo*. Lovely old furnishings and private home atmosphere. Choice of noisy rooms with a river view or quieter ones overlooking courtyard.

Splendor, Via San Gallo 30, 50129. Tel: 055-483427, Fax: 055-461276. This ancient and imposing *palazzo* near San Marco has been restored but shows signs of wear and tear. The public rooms boast frescoed ceilings, rich in stucco-work.

FLORENCE ENVIRONS

Artimino: **Paggeria Medicea**, Viale Papa Giovanni XXIII 3, 50040. Tel: 055-871 8081, Fax: 055-871 8080. Nestling between olive orchards and vineyards near Carmignano, just west of Florence, this Medicean villa has recently been restored; ironically, this grand hotel occupies the former servants' quarters. Hunting and fishing are possible options, with an adjoining hunting reserve and a lake well-stocked with fish. Expensive.

Candeli: **Villa La Massa**, Via La Massa 24, 50012. Tel: 055-651 0101, Fax: 055-651 0109. Situated 7km (4 miles) north of Florence, this cluster of beautifully converted 17th-century villas radiates elegance. In addition to a riverside restaurant, there are facilities for swimming and tennis. Expensive.

Fiesole: **Pensione Bencistà**, Via Benedetto da Maiano 4, 50014. Tel/Fax: 055-59163. This delightful 14th-century villa lives up to its name: one feels at home there. The interior of this sprawling villa is decorated with antiques and rustic furnishings, artfully assembled. There are cosy reception rooms and fine hillside views. Moderate.

Villa San Michele, Via Doccia 4, 50014. Tel: 055-59451, Fax: 055-598734. Situated in Fiesole, 4km (2½ miles) northeast of Florence, this fabulous hotel is one of the finest in Tuscany. As befits a building supposedly designed by Michelangelo, this monastery enjoys harmonious lines and heavenly views, particularly from the *loggia* (and restaurant). Spacious grounds, a pool and piano bar complete the picture. The plush suites have Jacuzzis. Deluxe/Expensive.

Galluzzo: **Relais Certosa**, Via Colle Romole 2. Tel: 055-204 7171, Fax: 055-268575. A former hunting lodge (once attached to the Carthusian monastery) has been turned into a welcoming residence, with spacious grounds and tennis courts. Expensive.

Molin del Piano: **Hotel il Trebbiolo**. Tel: 055-830 0098. Set 14km (9 miles) from Florence, this delightful 3-star hotel offers country views and good cuisine. Moderate.

Trespiano: **Villa Le Rondini**, Via Bolognese Vecchia 2224, 50139. Tel: 055-400081, Fax: 055-268212. Situated 4km (2½ miles) to the northeast of the city, this secluded villa is nota-

ble for its wonderful setting, looking over the Arno Valley. From the pool, set in an olive grove, are lovely views down over the city. The public rooms have the stilted formality that city Tuscans mistake for rusticity. The pool and restaurant are open to non-residents. A bus links the hotel with the centre. Moderate.

GAIOLE IN CHIANTI

Castello di Spaltenna, 53013. Tel: 0577-749483. Small hotel in 12th-century monastery. Typical Tuscan food in popular restaurant. With 2 Michelin stars. Moderate/Expensive.

Hotel Villa Miranda, 53013. Tel: 0577-799483. This charming villa is situated in the Sienese Chianti. It has comfortable, spacious rooms and fine vine views over Chianti countryside. Moderate.

GREVE IN CHIANTI

Villa San Giovese, Piazza Bucciarelli 5, Panzano, 50020. Tel: 055-852461, Fax: 055-852463. Situated in the Florentine Chianti, this well-restored villa offers additional rooms in a converted traditional farmhouse. Noted restaurant and wines. Closed in January and February. Moderate.

LIVORNO

Hotel Touring, Via Goldoni 61, 57100. Tel: 0586-21080. Efficient chain hotel.

Palazzo, Viale Italia 195, 57100. Tel: 0586-805371, Fax: 0586-803206. This 19th-century hotel has spacious bedrooms and public rooms and has been recently restored. Moderate.

LUCCA

Diana, Via del Molinetto 11. Tel: 0583-42202. Central location off Piazza San Martino. Inexpensive.

Hotel Cinzia, Via della Dogana 9. Tel: 0583-41323. Clean and quiet in central location. Inexpensive.

Hotel Celede, Via Giusti 27. Tel: 0583-954106. Good modern hotel outside city walls. Moderate.

Ilaria Pensione, Via del Fosso 20. Tel: 0583-47558. Reasonable bed-and-breakfast, convenient central location. Moderate.

La Luna, Via Fillungo, Angelo Corte Compagni 12, 55100. Tel: 0583-493634, Fax: 0583-490021. Family-run hotel set in the historic centre and recently restructured. Moderate.

Napoleon, Viale Europa. Tel: 0583-531141. Luxurious hotel outside city walls.

Stipino, Via Romana 95, 55100. Tel: 0583-495077, Fax: 0583-490309. This 2-star hotel is simply decorated but graced with a personal touch. Inexpensive.

Universo, Piazza Guido. Tel: 0583-43678. Large Victorian hotel where Ruskin always stayed. Expensive.

LINIGIANA

Albergo-Ristorante Roma, Via Roman 84, Comano (Massa-Carrara). Tel: 0187-484216. Inexpensive.

Golf Hotel, Via Pineta, Pontremoli (Massa-Carrara) 54027. Tel: 0187-831573. Inexpensive.

Hotel Giardinetto, Via Roma 5, Fivizzano (Massa-Carrara) 54034. Tel: 0585-92060. Inexpensive.

Hotel Ristorante Albergo, "Del Pino" Bastia di Licciana Nardi (Massa-Carrara). Tel: 0187-474084. Quiet, comfortable modern *pensione* in mountain village, surrounded by pine trees. Full board available. Inexpensive.

THE MAREMMA

Hotel Agnelli, S Quirico di Sorano. Tel: 0564-619015. Five km (3 miles) from Sorano near Vitozza. A new hotel and pizzeria.

Albergo Ristorante Pizzeria La Botte, Montorio di Sorano. Tel: 0564-638633.

Albergo Ristorante Scilla, Via del Duomo 5, Sovana. Tel: 0564-616531.

Albergo Ristorante Taverna Etrusca, Piazza del Pretorio, Sovana. Tel: 0564-616183.

MARINA DI CARRARA

Hotel Mediterraneo, Via Genova 24. Tel: 0585-635222 or 54036. Large modern hotel one block from the waterfront; near marble port so can be noisy at times. Expensive.

Hotel Miramare, Viale C. Colombo 23. Tel: 0585-634743. Expensive.

MARINA DI PISA

Albergo Manzi, Lungomare 25, 58013. Tel: 050-36593. Rooms on the sea front. Moderate.

Pensione Milena, Via Padre Agostino 14. Tel: 050-36863. Moderate.

MASSA MARITTIMA

Duca del Mare, Piazza Dante Alighieri 1/2. Tel: 0566-902284.

Hotel Cris, Via Roma 9/10, Angolo Via Cappellini. Tel: 0556-903830. In the centre of town (the only hotel in the centre). Very clean and comfortable and reasonably priced.

Il Girofalco, Via Massetana Nord 25. Tel: 0566-902177.

MASSA PISANA

This town lies between Lucca and Pisa and is a good location for touring northern Tuscany.

Villa La Principessa, Via Nuova per Pisa 1616. Tel: 0583-370037, Fax: 0583-379019. Open April–October. Exclusive mansion. Old-fashioned elegance and modern comforts. Expensive.

MONTECATINI TERME

Florio, Via Montebello 41, 51016. Tel: 0572-78632. Moderately priced hotel with own garden.

Grand Hotel Plaza e Locanda Maggiore, Piazza del Popolo 7, 51016. Tel: 0572-75831. This 4-star hotel has a wide range of facilities including swimming pool. Inexpensive.

Guhel, Via Torino 4, 51016. Tel: 0572-70010. Inexpensive.

Torreta, Viale Bustichini 63, 51016. Tel: 0572-70305. Swimming pool. Moderate.

MONSUMMANAO TERME

Grotta Giusti, Via Grotta Giusti 171, 51015. Tel: 0572-51165. Luxury hotel with swimming pool and spa facilities.

La Speranza, Via Grotta Giusti 62, 51015. Tel: 0572-51313. *Pensione* with its own well-maintained garden. Inexpensive.

PANZANO IN CHIANTI

Villa Le Barone, 50020 Florence. Tel: 055-8522. Elegant Englishness. Swimming pool.

PESCIA

Azienda Marzalla, Villa de' Rossi, Via San Moro 79, 51030 Candeglia. Tel: 0573-43748. A quiet converted farmhouse with a swimming pool in the grounds of a magnificent 17th-century villa near Pescia. Reservations essential.

Fedora, Via G. Matteotti 168, Pescia–Vellano. Tel: 0572-405517. *Pensione* in delightful mountain village about 24 km (15 miles) from Pescia.

Hotel dei Fiori, Via 8 Settembre. Tel: 0573-477871. Inexpensive.

PISA

Pisa has a number of good hotels in the Inexpensive category but a shortage of exceptional Moderate hotels and a lack of truly luxurious hotels.

Albergo "La Torre", Via C. Battisti 17. Tel: 050-21558/25220/56100. Inexpensive.

Albergho Milano, Via Mascagni. Tel: 050-23162. To the left of the station exit. Inexpensive.

Ariston, Via Maffi 42. Tel: 050-561834, Fax: 050-561891. This restrained yet welcoming 3-star hotel faces the Leaning Tower. Inexpensive.

Bologna, Via Mazzini 57. Tel: 050-502120, Fax: 050-43070. This established 2-star hotel is well-furnished. Inexpensive.

California Park Hotel, Madonna dell'Acqua (3km/1½ miles outside Pisa). Tel: 050-890726, Fax: 050-890727. Rooms are in the many small villas scattered throughout the grounds. Inexpensive.

Casa della Giovane, Via Corridoni 31. Tel: 050-22732. A 10-minute walk to the right of the station. For women only. Inexpensive.

Camping Torre Pendente, Viale delle Cascine 86. Tel: 050-561704. Good facilities, very clean and cheap. Inexpensive.

Cavalieri (CIGA). Piazza della Stazione 2. Tel: 050-43290, Fax: 050-502242. Expensive.

D'Azeglio, Piazza V Emanuele 18b. Tel: 050-500310. Expensive.

Grand Hotel Duomo, Via Santa Maria 94, 56100. Tel: 050-561894. Expensive.

Hotel Giardino, Via C. Cammeo. Tel: 050-562101. Tucked behind the corner bar and self-service restaurant at the Porta Nuova. English- and French-speaking. Inexpensive.

Hotel Kinzica, Piazza Arcivescovado 4. Tel: 050-560419. Efficient and welcoming. Moderate.

Hotel Moderno, Via Corridoni 103. Tel: 050-25021/598067. Newly built hotel 100 metres (328 ft) from the station. Inexpensive.

La Pace, Galleria B di Viale Gramsci 4, 56100. Tel: 050-29351/502266. Very clean. Moderate.

Pisa Hotel, Via Manzoni 22. Tel: 050-44551. Good service and comfort. Inexpensive.

Roma, Via Bonanno 111. Tel: 050-502532. Pleasant. Overlooking a garden. Moderate.

Royal Victoria, Lungarno Pacinotti 12. Tel: 050-502130. Has some of the best views of the Arno. Old-fashioned charm. Moderate.

Terminus e Plaza, Via Colombo 45. Tel/Fax: 050-500303. This 3-star hotel is convenient for the train station. Inexpensive.

Touring, Via Puccini 24. Tel: 050-46374, Fax: 050-502148. This well-run hotel has a classic feel. Inexpensive.

PISTOIA

Firenze, Via Curtatatone e Montanara 42, 51100. Tel: 0573-23141. Inexpensive.

Hotel Patria, Via Crispi 8, 51100 Pistoia. Tel: 0573-25187. Charming small hotel in historic centre. Parking permits available.

Il Convento, Via San Quirico 33, 51100. Tel: 0573-452651. Five km (3 miles) from town. Tranquil and comfortable.

Leon Bianco, Via Panciatichi 2, 51100. Tel/Fax: 0573-26675. Set in the *centro storico* (historic centre), this quiet and renovated hotel is a sensible choice. Inexpensive.

Milano, Viale Pacinotti 10, 51100. Tel: 0573-23061. Newly renovated and very comfortable with the added boon of a parking lot.

PORTO ERCOLE

Don Pedro, Vi Panoramica 7, 58108. Tel/Fax: 0564-033914. This 3-star family-run hotel enjoys fine views. It is open from April–October and insists on guests taking full-board. Inexpensive.

Hotel Pellicano, Località Cala Dei Santi, 58018, Grosseto. Tel: 0564-833801. Expensive, comfortable hotel (furnished with antiques) with cliff-top restaurant. Meals served on a terrace or in pinewoods. Tuscan delicacies such as wild boar pâté and marinated eel.

PORTA SAN MATTEO

Hotel La Cisterna. Tel: 0577-94028. Superb views can be enjoyed from the restaurant "La Terrazze".

Punta Ala

Golf Hotel, Via del Gualdo, 58040. Tel: 0584-922026, Fax: 0584-922688. This modern 4-star hotel is decorated in Mediterranean style and has a pool. It is open from March–October. Expensive.

Piccolo Hotel, Alleluja, 58040. Tel: 0584-922050. Very pretty, first-class hotel.

Radda In Chianti

Relais Fattoria Vignale, Via Pianigiani 8, 53107. Tel: 0577-738300, Fax: 0577-738592. Situated in the heart of Sienese wine-growing country, this is a medieval wine estate, which continues to produces quality Chianti. Open April–October. Moderate.

Radicofani

Albergo Ristorante "La Torre", Via G. Matteotti 7, 53040. Tel: 0578-55943.

Rigoli

Villa Corliano, 56017 Pisa. Tel: 050-818193. Ten km (6 miles) from Pisa. An old and imposing hotel.

San Gimignano

In and around San Gimignano there are many opportunities for rural holidays and farm stays or simply rooms in private homes. Consult the local Tourist Office or check these categories at the end of the hotel listings.

Hotel Pescille, 53037. Tel: 0577-940186. Three km (2 miles) from San Gimignano. Converted farmhouse.

La Cisterna, Piazza della Cisterna 24. Tel: 0577-940328, Fax: 0577-942080. This *trecento palazzo* is in the heart of the *centro storico*. The atmospheric fine restaurant, called La Terrazza, specialises in Tuscan cuisine. Moderate.

Le Renaie, Pancole (5km/3 miles from San Gimignano). Tel: 0577-955044, Fax: 0577-955126. This lovely *casa colonica* (traditional Tuscan farmhouse) commands the village hilltop. The interior is tastefully decorated. Inexpensive.

Villa San Paolo, Strada per Certaldo, 53037. (5km/3 miles from San Gimignano). Tel: 0577-955100, Fax: 0577-955113. This 19th-century hillside villa is decorated tastefully, with attractive rooms and terraced grounds. The hotel is closed in January and February. Moderate.

San Quirico d'Orcia

This historic town is situated between Montalcino and Pienza, south of Florence, and is popular with visitors.

Hotel Posta Marcucci, Bagno Vignoni, 53027 Siena. Tel: 0577-887112, Fax: 0577-887119. Set near the noted medieval pool, this hotel is noted for its wonderful (modern) swimming pool, with fine views of a medieval fortress from the water.

Saturnia

Terme di Saturnia Hotel, Tel: 0564-601061. Luxury hotel convenient for spa treatments.

Siena

Several of Siena's most luxurious hotels lie outside the city walls. Except for July and August (during the *Palio* festivities), it is easier to find accommodation in Siena than in Florence. For villa and apartment rental, rural accommodation, farm stays, budget accommodation, and accommodation in private homes, *see below* the specific categories that follow the hotel listings. To see the whole range of accommodation on offer in Siena and Siena Province, ask for the latest edition of *Hotel, Campeggi, Ostelli, Agriturismo*, a booklet available free from Siena Tourist Offices.

Albergo Centrale, Via Calzoleria 24. Tel: 0577-280379. Clean and spacious.

Albergo Chiusarelli, Via Curtatone 9. Tel: 0577-280562. Palm trees and genteel decay.

Albergo Tre Donzelle, Via delle Donzelle 5. Tel: 0577-280358. Good value and position.

Antica Torre, Via Fieravecchia 7. Tel/Fax: 0577-222255. This tiny, atmospheric hotel is essentially a conversion of a 17th-century tower. Inexpensive.

Cipriano (Apartment), Strada delle Tolfe 8. Tel: 0577-44322 or 49796. Serena Via Aretina 29A. Tel: 220431. Minimum stay of seven days.

Duomo, Via Stallareggi 38. Tel: 0577-289088, Fax: 0577-43043. Situated right in the heart of the historic centre, close to Siena's magnificent cathedral, this 18th-century *palazzo* has a cloistered, intimate atmosphere. Inexpensive.

Certosa di Maggiano, Via Certosa 82, 53100. Tel: 0577-288180, Fax: 0577-288189. This unique 14th-century former Carthusian monastery is the oldest in Tuscany. Now a 5-star hotel, it is adorned with antiques and boasts a prestigious restaurant. Original features lovingly restored include the chapel, cloisters and antiquarian library. Expensive.

Garden, Via Custoza 2. Tel: 0577-47056, Fax: 0577-46050. This 16th-century patrician villa is now a 3-star hotel with a formal, Italian garden and a swimming pool. Moderate.

Nuove Donzelle, Via delle Donzelle 1/3. Tel: 0577-288088. Cheap.

Palazzo Ravizza, Pian dei Mantellini 34. Tel: 0577-280462. Moderate prices. Traditional.

Park Hotel, Via Marciano 16. Tel: 0577-44803, Fax: 0577-49020. This splendid 16th-century Tuscan villa has a rarefied, exclusive atmosphere and a famous restaurant, L'Olivo. The exquisite atmosphere in this 5-star hotel is matched by rarefied prices. Expensive.

Villa Scacciapensieri, Via di Scacciapensieri 10, 53100. Tel: 0577-41441, Fax: 0577-270854. This supremely elegant villa hotel is set in lovely grounds 3km (1½ miles) north of the city. The sophisticated interior is matched by bedrooms with rural views, and by the panoramic sweep of the city from the restaurant terrace. Expensive.

Siena Environs

Sovicille: **Borgo Pretale**, Località Pretale. Tel: 0577-345401, Fax: 0577-345625. Situated in the woods, southwest of Siena, this fortified *borgo* is a renovated village divided into myriad apartments and topped by a massive medieval tower. Facilities are good but prices are high. Expensive.

Palazzo Stigliano, Località Stigliano. Tel: 0577-342081, Fax: 0578-342094. This renovated complex is a less expensive version of Borgo Pretale above and is popular with foreign families. Moderate.

Sinalunga

Locanda dell'Amorosa, 53048 Siena. Tel: 0577-679497. Lovely setting with superb restaurant. No single rooms. Expensive.

Tirrenia

Atlantico Continental Hotel, Viale Belvedere. Tel: 050-37031. A 4-star luxury-class hotel. Swimming pool, private beach and tennis court.

Bristol, Via dele Felci 38. Tel: 050-37161. This 3-star hotel is unpretentious and comfortable. Inexpensive.

Camping St Michael, Via Bigattiera. Tel: 050-33103. Quiet location, 400 metres (1,312 ft) from the sea.

Garden Hotel, Via dell'Ornello 10/a. Tel: 050-37578. Inexpensive.

Gran Hotel Golf, Via dell'Edera. Tel: 050-37545. A 4-star hotel with own golf course.

Hotel Medusa, Via degli Oleandri 37/39, 56018. Tel: 050-37162/37125. Central and quiet.

Mare e Sole, Località Calambrone, Viale del Tirreno. Tel: 050-32757. Near the sea.

Piccolo Hotel, Via del Tirreno 257. Tel: 050-37483. Inexpensive.

Pineta, Località Calambrone, Via delle Mimose. Tel: 050-37623. 100 metres from the sea.

Vittoria, Viale del Tirreno. Tel: 050-37451. Rooms and small apartments.

VOLTERRA

Etruria, Via Matteotti 32. Tel/Fax: 0588-87377. This ancient building incorporates Etruscan elements. A family atmosphere adds to its charm. Inexpensive.

Nazionale, Via dei Marchesi 11. Tel: 0588-86284, Fax: 0588-84097. This ancient *palazzo* has been a hotel since 1860. It is a charming blend of ancient and modern. Inexpensive.

San Limo, Via San Limo 26. Tel/Fax: 0588-85250. Once a monastic building, its original austerity has been softened in this successful conversion into a 4-star hotel. Moderate.

Villa Nencini, Borgo Santo Stefano 55, 56048 Pisa. Tel/Fax: 0588-86386. Attractive small hotel in 17th-century villa. Pleasant basement taverna.

Campsites

There are a number of well-run campsites in Tuscany. A list of sites with location map, **Carta d'Italia Parchi di Campeggio**, can be obtained free of charge by writing to: Centro Internazionale Prenotazioni, Federcampeggio, Casella Postale 23, 50041 Calenzano (Firenze). Tel: 055-88239.

FLORENCE

Below are some campsites in Florence. For more information on all sites in Florence, write to Federazione Italiana del Campeggia, Casella Postale 649, 50100.

Camping Michelangelo, Italiani e Stranieri, Viale Michelangelo 80, 50125. Tel: 055-681 1977. (500 tents.) Open between April and October. No. 13 bus from station. Crowded in high season. Good facilities.

Camping Villa Camerata, Viale Righi 2/4, 50137. Tel: 055-610300. Open April–October. No. 17B from station.

SIENA

Campeggio "Siena Colleverde", Strada di Scacciapensieri 37. Tel: 0577-280044. Open from end of March to end of October. Two km (1 mile) from city.

Caravan & Camper Hire

Addresses of caravan and camper hire firms in Tuscany include:

Central Camping, Via del Termine 22, Florence. Tel: 055-372336.

In the UK, contact: **Eurocamp Independent**, Edmundson House, Tatton Street, Knutsford, Cheshire, WA16 6BG. Eurocamp arranges all transport and have sites at:

Bibbona (La Capanne), open from Easter to mid-September. In the countryside, it has its own pool, bar and pizzeria.

At Fiesole, **Camping Panoramico**, Via Peramonda, 50014 Florence. Tel: 050-599069. On a terraced site, overlooking the city of Florence. Open throughout the year.

Private Home Stays

This is a fairly new development in Tuscany but is a good way of experiencing closer contact with the locals while paying modest prices. In Florence and Siena, where the system is sophisticated, the private homes are carefully graded from simple to luxurious, with prices varying accordingly. In Florence, contact AGAP (Associazione Gestori Alloggi Privati) at Via de' Neri 9, 50122 Florence. Tel: 055-284100. In Siena, request the *Affittacamere* (private lodgings) booklet of addresses from the Tourist Office (APT, Via di Città 43, Siena. Tel: 0577-42209). The list includes private accommodation in the whole of Siena Province, including San Gimignano, Montalcino and the Sienese Chianti.

Farm Stays

Farm stays (*Agriturismo*) are an excellent way of experiencing the wonderful Tuscan countryside while staying on a farm or a wine estate. Standards vary from simple, rustic accommodation at low prices to relatively luxurious surroundings, complete with private wings and swimming pool. It is best to insist on a description or a photo of the farm since many may be modern and fail to match up with the visitor's romantic image of Tuscany. Some farms, however, are genuine 16th-century wine and oil estates. There is usually the chance to buy local produce on site and meals are sometimes provided. You need to check the accommodation on offer carefully since the farms range from the provision of a few rooms to a vast number of separate self-contained apartments.

One of the best (illustrated) guides to farm stays is *Vacanza e Natura, La Guida di Terranostra*, covering the whole of Italy and revised annually. If you speak basic Italian, it is worth obtaining, thanks to its comprehensive use of pictorial symbols to explain the farms. To book a Terranostra farm in Tuscany, telephone your selection from the above book or call 055-280539. The national Terranostra organisation in Rome can also supply details of properties in Tuscany. Terranostra, Via XXIV Maggio 43, Rome. Tel: 06-468 2368/468 2370. Most local Tourist Offices also provide lists of local *Agriturismo* possibilities but pin them down as to the precise nature of the accommodation (location, size, age and atmosphere of the estate). For obvious reasons, you will normally need a car to make the most of a farm stay. The regional *Agriturismo* booking centre is Agriturist Ufficio Regionale, Piazza di San Firenze 3, 50122 Florence. Tel: 055-287838. In Siena, the booking centre is Agriturist Provinciale, Via della Sapienza 39. Tel: 0577-46194. The Italian head office is Agriturist, Corso Vittorio Emanuele 101, Rome. Tel: 06-656241.

Rural Stays

These overlap with *Agriturismo* but can include country houses or entire restored medieval villages (such as Sovicille, near Siena). In general, there is a working farm attached to the accommodation or at least the opportunity to sample or buy wine, oil and local products grown on the estate. As with farm stays, accommodation can be in simple rooms or self-contained apartments. The owners often use the profits from letting to reinvest in the restoration of the family estate or village. With rural stays, the emphasis is on country living in traditional buildings rather than in luxurious villa accommodation.

Some typical rural stays are listed in *Vacanza e Natura, La Guida di Terranostra* (see Farm Stays), while others can be booked by local Tourist Offices. Many of the owners may speak basic English, French or German but a smattering of Italian is appreciated. Always request detailed descriptions and directions. The following are typical examples:

La Ripolina, Località Pieve di Piana, 53022 Buonconvento, Siena Province. Contact Laura Cresti. Tel: 0577-282280, Fax: 0577-282954. (Correspondence address: c/o Cresti, Via del Vecchietta 156, 53100 Siena). Most of the holiday apartments are in converted farmhouses; one is actually in a fortified abbey with its 10th-century wall. Farm produce available.

Capobianco, Località Albavola, Madonna dell'Acqua, Via Vecchia Pietrasantina 11, 56017 San Giuliano Terme, Pisa Province. Contact Andrea Cosentino. Tel: 050-890671 or 055-280539. This traditional rural estate near the Pisan coast offers Tuscan dishes, farm produce, horse-riding and nature rambles.

San Savino, Val di Chio, Località Santa Lucia 89/A, 52043 Castiglion Fiorentino, Arezzo Province. Contact Maria Assunta Casagni. Tel: 0575-651000 or 055-280539. This 11th-century monastery overlooks a lake, olive groves and woods and offers several apartments (plus pool and stables).

Castles & Monasteries

Accommodation is available in a variety of castles, palaces and monasteries. Standards will vary from very simple (and cheap) to luxurious. A list of places can be obtained from the INIT (Italian State Tourist Offices abroad) or enquire at the local Tourist Office.

Villa & Apartment Rentals

Particularly recommended for Lunigiana region of northern Tuscany is "Hello Italy", a small company with a good selection of villas and houses of various sizes. The owners live locally and provide a summer "club house" for visitors, as well as very detailed information about the region. (They can also help with property hunting in the area.)

Italy Office: Hello Italy (Lunigiana Holidays), Piazza degli Archi Antich 14, Panicale, 1-54016 Licciana Nardi. Tel: 0187-474366, Fax: 0187-474013.

UK Office: East Horsely, Surrey. Tel: 01483-285002.

Prices vary enormously, depending on the season and the luxuriousness of the accommodation. In general, prices range from a simple four-person villa in the low season for about L.800,000 to a magnificent secluded villa for about L.4,000,000 in the high season. The following agencies deal with rentals:

American Agency, Via del Ponte Rossa 39r, 50129 Florence. Tel: 055-475053.

The Best in Italy, Via Ugo Foscolo 72, 50124 Florence. Tel: 055-223064, Fax: 055-2298912. The luxurious lettings agency is run by Conte Girolama Brandolini d'Adda and his wife, Contessa Simonetta, and offers villas or palazzi with pools, stables and other such luxuries.

Solemar, Via Cavour 80, 50129 Florence. Tel: 055-218112.

Casa Club, Via dei Termini 83, 53100 Siena. Tel: 0577-46484.

Budget Accommodation & Youth Hostels

A list of Youth Hostels is available from ENIT (Italian National Tourist Offices) and places can be booked through them or through local Tuscan Tourist Offices. Alternatively, contact the Associazione Italiana Alberghi per la Gioventu, Via Cavour 44, 00184 Rome. Tel: 06-4871152.

In Florence, the main youth hostels are **Europa Villa Camerata**, Viale Augusto Righi 2-4, 50137 Florence. Tel: 055-601451 and **Santa Monaca Hostel**, Via Santa Monaca 6. Tel: 050-296704/268338.

In Siena, the main youth hostel is **Ostello della Gioventu "Guido Riccio"**, Via Fiorentina 17, Località Stellino. Tel: 0577-52212. It is appealing but lies 2km (1 mile) outside the city: catch bus No. 10 or No. 15 from Piazza Matteotti and ask to be let off at Lo Stellino.

Eating Out

Breakfast is a minimal affair in Italy; most Italians grab a cappuccino or an espresso or two with a pastry (*cornetto* or *brioche*) at a local bar or cafe, usually consumed standing at the bar. Lunch is a serious business, with antipasto followed by soup or pasta (*primo*), followed by a substantial meat or fish dish (*secondo*) with vegetables (*contorni*) ordered separately. Pasta is not generally eaten as a main course. The evening meal follows a similar pattern.

IVA is VAT (a form of sales tax); it will be included in your bill. *Pane e coperto* includes bread etc. and will also be included.

What To Eat

Tuscany is known for its authentic rustic food. Some of the traditional dishes are:

Bistecca alla Fiorentina – a thick, T-bone steak grilled over charcoal, sprinkled with freshly ground black pepper and a trickle of olive oil.

Minestrone alla Fiorentina – a vegetable soup with slices of country bread.

Zuppi di fagioli alla Fiorentina – vegetable and bean soup with olive oil, flavoured with rosemary, onions, garlic, celery and tomatoes.

Il lampredotto – boiled tripe eaten in a sandwich with a green sauce.

Schiacciata alla Fiorentina – a simple cake made with flour, sugar, eggs and olive oil.

Stracotto – beef cooked for many hours in red wine.

Pappardelle alla lepre – pasta with hare sauce.

Trippa – savoury tripe cooked in onions and tomatoes.

Cacciucco alla Livornese – a stew of all kinds of fish with a very hot sauce.

Tortino di carciofi – baked artichoke omelette.

Baccalà alla Livornese – salt cod cooked in tomatoes, black olives and black pepper.

Fagioli all'uccelletto – haricot beans cooked with sausages in a sauce of tomatoes, garlic and sage.

Cinghiale di Maremma – wild boar from the Maremma region near Grosseto.

Cee – Pisan dish of young eels with olive oil, garlic and sage.

Crostini – canapés spread with chicken liver or game pâté.

Ribollita – bean stew.

Panforte di Siena – a confection made of honey, candied fruits, almonds and cloves.

Castagnaccio – chestnut cake with pine nuts and sultanas.

Ricciarelli – a very delicate biscuit of honey and almonds from Siena.

Where To Eat

Since each restaurant in Tuscany can span several price categories, the typical minimum and maximum prices (for one person) are given below:

Expensive   L.80,000 plus
Moderate   L.40,000–L.80,000
Inexpensive   L.10,000–L.40,000

For the more expensive restaurants booking is advisable, especially during the summer months.

ABETONE

La Capannina, Via Brennero, 254. Tel: 828-60562. Moderate.

AREZZO

Buca di San Francesco, Piazza San Francesco 1. Tel: 0575-23271, Fax: 0575-360588. Closed on Monday and Tuesday. Famous cellar restaurant adjoining San Francesco church, with *Trecento* frescoes and a Roman-Etruscan pavement below. Lovely medieval atmosphere matched by straightforward, rustic, tasty cuisine. Moderate.

Il Torrino, Superstrada dei Due Mari. Tel: 0575-36264. Closed on Monday. Specialities include cold meats and mushrooms. Inexpensive.

Le Tastevin, Via de' Cenci 9. Tel: 0575-28304. Closed on Friday. Set in the *centro storico*, this atmospheric restau-

rant and piano bar serves classic Tuscan cuisine, including *carpaccio* and *penne* with pepper sauce. Moderate.

Vicolo del Contento, Località Mandri, Arezzo. Tel: 0575-9149277, Fax: 0575-9149906. Closed on Monday and Tuesday. Situated 1½ km (1 mile) outside Arezzo, this restored 18th-century grange offers tasty dishes based on traditional Tuscan recipes. Moderate.

ARTIMINO

Biagio Pignatta, Paggeria Medicea, Viale Papa Giovanni XXIII. Tel: 055-8718181. Closed on Wednesday and Thursday. The restaurant occupies a lodge once belonging to Ferdinand de' Medici's major-domo and forms part of the Paggeria Medicea, a grand villa hotel. Moderate.

Ristorante La Delfina, Via della Chiesa 1. Tel: 055-871-8074. Closed Monday and Tuesday. Set in a walled medieval village (on the road to Pian di Rosello), this restaurant serves game and port with wild fennel. Moderate.

CARRARA

Bar Nuovo Punto, Via Verdi 19. Cheap local bar and restaurant with pleasant garden at the back. Good pastas and salads.

Ristorante Venanzio, Piazza Palestro 3, Colonnata (Carrara). Tel: 0595-241070. Regional cooking in a restaurant at the heart of the marble quarries.

Soldaini, Via Mazzini 11. Tel: 0585-71928. Closed on Monday. Simple yet elegant cuisine. Inexpensive.

Trattoria Cavatore, Piazza Settembre. Smart, with new light versions of Italian staples: salmon *carpaccio*, baked polenta, vegetable risotto.

CERTALDO

Osteria del Vicario, Via Rivellino 3. Tel: 0571-668228. Closed on Wednesday, also in January–mid-March. Set in Romanesque cloisters in the historic centre, this restaurant serves both Tuscan and international dishes. Moderate.

CETONA

Convento di Padre Eligio, Località Belverde. Tel: 0578-238015. Closed on Tuesday and in January. This stylish 13th-century Franciscan monastery is decorated with period furniture, paintings and antiques. Impressive, elegant cuisine using produce grown on site. Moderate.

FLORENCE

As elsewhere in the Restaurants section, prices refer to the average cost of a meal for one with wine.

EXPENSIVE

Enoteca Pinchiorri, Via Ghibellina 87. Tel: 055-242777. Closed Sunday, Monday lunch, and August. Reservations essential at "Italy's finest restaurant", as is elegant dress. Occupies a 15th-century palace with delightful courtyard for *al fresco* meals. Rated among the top restaurants of Europe. Excellent *nouvelle cuisine* and an impressive collection of wines.

Il Cestello, Hotel Excelsior, Piazza Ognissanti 3. Tel: 055-294301. Very elegant hotel restaurant with top quality Tuscan and international dishes. Popular rendezvous for business executives. Stunning views from the rooftop restaurant.

La Capannina di Sante, Piazza Ravenna. Tel: 055-688345. Closed Sunday, Monday lunch, one week in August and Christmas. One of the best fish restaurants in town, patronised by the local business community.

La Loggia, Piazzale Michelangelo 1. Tel: 055-234 2832. Closed Wednesday and two weeks in August. Popular tourist spot with superb panorama of the city.

Relais Le Jardin, Hotel Regency, Piazza Massimo d'Azeglio 3. Tel: 055-245247. Closed on Sunday. Top-notch food in exclusive hotel restaurant, overlooking a garden. Elegant dress required.

Sabatini, Via de' Panzani 9a. Tel: 055-282802/211559, Fax: 055-210293. Closed on Monday. This highly traditional restaurant was once the star Florentine haunt and although it has been overtaken by more fashionable or imaginative restaurants, it remains a sophisticated choice for classic Tuscan cuisine and sober international dishes.

MODERATE

Al Lume di Candela, Via delle Terme 23r. Tel: 055-294566. Closed on Sunday. A traditional restaurant with punctilious service.

Buca Mario, Piazza Ottaviani 16r. Tel: 055-214179. Closed Wednesday, Thursday lunch, and three weeks in July. Cellar restaurant with good home-made pasta and grilled meats. Very popular with tourists.

Cammillo, Borgo San Jacopo 57r. Tel: 055-212427. Closed Wednesday and Thursday, also part of December and January and two weeks in August. A bustling, classic trattoria with simple but robust regional dishes.

Cantinetta Antinori, Piazza Antinori 3. Tel: 055-292234. Closed at weekends. In a 15th-century *palazzo* serving typical Tuscan snacks and meals served with wines from the well-known Antinori estates. Good place for a light lunch at the bar or a fuller meal in the elegant dining room.

Cibrèo, Via dei Macci 118r. Tel: 055-234100. Closed Sunday, Monday, six weeks in August and September. One of the most popular restaurants in town amongst new-generation Florentines. Mainly *nouvelle cuisine* grafted on to Tuscan cooking. No pastas. The same food, at half the price, is served in the *Vinaria* section, just around the corner.

Coco Lezzone, Via del Parioncino 26r. Tel: 055-287178. Closed Sunday and Tuesday evening. Crowded, chaotic, white-tiled trattoria with good Tuscan cooking. Favourite haunt of locals. Where the Marchesa Frescobaldi chose to take Prince Charles to sample roast rabbit, steak, baby squid, and delicious vegetables.

Da Noi, Via Fiesolana 46r. Tel: 055-242917. Closed Sunday, Monday and August. Reservations essential. Run by former staff of Enoteca Pinchiorri (*see above*). Small and intimate with good-quality *nouvelle cuisine* and Italian dishes. No written menus but excellent English spoken.

Le Fonticine, Via Nazionale 79r. Tel: 055-282106. Closed Saturday and Sunday. Friendly, family-run restaurant near station specializing in Tuscan and Emilian dishes. Excellent home-made pastas.

Mamma Gina, Borgo San Jacopo 37r. Tel: 055-2396009. Closed on Sunday. Set in a Renaissance *palazzo*, this trattoria produces hearty Tuscan dishes.

Osteria dei Cento Poveri, Via Palazzuolo 31r. Tel: 055-218846. Closed on Tuesday and in August. A mixture of dishes from Florence and Apulia, including fish specialities. The *pugliese* dishes are particularly tasty.

Otello, Via degli Orti Oricellari 28r. Tel: 055-215819. Closed on Tuesday. Family-run restaurant with a verandah hung with plants. Classic dishes.

Traverna del Bronzino, Via delle Ruote 25r. Tel: 055-495220. Closed Sunday and three weeks in August. Spacious restaurant out of the centre. Named after the painter who lived and worked here in the 16th century. A favourite haunt for discerning Florentines.

INEXPENSIVE

Angiolini, Via Santo Spirito 36r. Tel: 055-239 8976. Closed Sunday and Monday. Bustling, typically Florentine, in the Oltrarno district. Eat mushroom pasta around the old iron stove.

Belle Donne, Via delle Belle Donne 16. Tel: 055-262609. Closed Sunday. A hole-in-the-wall restaurant near the railway station, worth visiting for simple rustic specialities.

Borgo Antico, Piazza Santa Spirito 6r. Tel: 210437. Closed Monday. A fun atmosphere and a good place for late-night pizzas.

Cantinetta dei Verrazzano, Via de' Tavolini 18-20. Tel: 055-268590. Closed on Sunday. At any time of day you can drop in here for a snack. The atmosphere is of a 19th-century coffee house. Dishes, bought separately, cost L.5–7,000 excluding wine.

Da Burde, Via Pistoiese 6. Tel: 055-317206. Closed Sunday and Tuesday and two weeks in August. Authentic Tuscan trattoria with home-made soups, pastas and puddings. No dinner served.

Da Nerbone, Mercato Centrale di San Lorenzo. Tel: 055-219949. Closed on Sunday, also closed in the evening. This authentic market eatery is as old as the market itself and the usual clientele includes local stallholders. Food is based on filling Tuscan snacks.

Garga, Via del Moro 50-52. Tel: 055-2398898. This cosy, cramped trattoria is run by an Italian-Canadian couple. Against a background of frescoed walls and cut flowers, the trendy or bohemian clientele enjoy *bistecca alla fiorentina*, fish dishes and varied trattoria fare.

Gaugin, Via degli Alfani 24r. Tel: 055-2340616. Closed on Sunday. Reputed to be the best vegetarian restaurant in Florence.

Il Caminetto, Via dello Studio 34r. Tel: 055-239 6274. Closed Wednesday and July. Hearty, simple and filling food.

I Ghibellini, Piazza San Pier Maggiore 8. Tel: 055-214424. Open Thursday–Tuesday. Quiet square; outstanding food and service.

Latini, Via dei Palchetti 6r. Tel: 055-210916. Closed Monday, Tuesday lunch. Typical Tuscan food at communal tables in noisy cellar restaurant.

Mario, Via Rosina 2r. Tel: 055-218550. Closed in the evening, and on Sunday. Typical basic Tuscan trattoria with a lively atmosphere, helped by its popularity with the local market traders. Try the *gnocchi*, tripe and *ribollita*. As a treat, try crisp *cantucci* biscuits dipped in Vin Santo, the sweet but fine Tuscan dessert wine.

Marione, Via della Spada 27r. Tel: 055-214756. Closed at weekends and from mid-July to mid-August. A simple, traditional trattoria.

Tarocchi, Via dei Renai 14r. Tel: 055-234 3912. Closed on Monday. Lively and friendly pizzeria.

Trattoria Da Za-Za, Piazza Mercato Centrale 26r. Tel: 055-215411. Open September–July Monday–Saturday, noon–3pm, 7–10pm. Excellent food, local clientele. In a riotous atmosphere are served such staples as *ribollita*, *arista* (roast pork) and bean delicacies (no pizzas).

Trattoria Le Mossacce, Via del Proconsolo 55r (between the Cathedral and the Bargello). Tel: 055-294361. Pasta dishes and basic Tuscan fare.

Vittoria, Via della Fonderia 52r. Tel: 055-225657. Closed Wednesday and August. Basic trattoria in the San Frediano district with good simply cooked fish. No meat.

Yellow Bar, Via del Proconsolo 39r. Tel: 055-211766. Popular young restaurant for pizza, pasta, salads and hamburgers.

Cafés & Ice Cream

No visit to Florence would be complete without tasting an ice cream made on the premises. Always choose ice cream parlours (*gelaterie*) with a *Produzione Propria* (home-made) sign or credentials. Alternatively, good *gelaterie* are **Perché No**, Via Tavolini 194, near the Cathedral and **Festival del Gelato**, Via del Corso 75r.

Break, Via delle Terme 17. Simple, fun and a good choice for buffet lunch.

Caffè Doney, Piazza Strozzi 16-19. Elegant premises for afternoon tea.

Giacosa, Via de' Tornabuoni 83. Closed on Monday. Up-market cafe where the young affluent eat home-made pastries, with the best cappuccino in Florence.

Giubbe Rosse, Piazza della Repubblica. Once favoured by writers and poets, and still popular, with an open air cafe and a dining room serving snacks or full meals.

Rivoire, Piazza della Signoria 5. Closed on Monday. Views of the Palazzo Vecchio and a lovely marble interior but prices are high.

Vivoli, Via Isola delle Stinche 7. Closed Sunday afternoon and Monday. Best ice cream in the world. Occasional queues. No seats but a lot of atmosphere.

GAIOLE IN CHIANTI

Badia a Coltibuono. Tel: 0577-749424, Fax: 0577-749235. Closed on Monday, as well as in January and February. Set on a glorious rural wine estate 5 km (3 miles) from Gaiole, the Badia a Coltibuono restaurant adjoins the celebrated 11th-century abbey. Specialities include *tagliatelle al porcini, tortellini* and spit-roasted meats. Moderate.

Wonderful wine and oil can be bought from the estate. Cookery courses are also on offer.

Castello di Spaltenna. Tel: 0577-749483, Fax: 0577-749269. Magnificent restaurant in a hotel converted from a fortified monastery. Dishes use fresh local ingredients and food is cooked in a wood-burning stove. Moderate.

GROSSETO

Enoteca Ombrone, Viale G Matteotti 71. Tel: 0564-22585. Superb local dishes and a spectacular cellar of olive oil; over 40 varieties to sample at table with bread rubbed with garlic. Highly recommended. It serves international dishes and such Maremman specialities as *tortelli Maremmani* and *cacciucco*. Moderate.

LIVORNO

Gennarino, Via Santa Fortunata. Tel: 0586-888093. Closed on Wednesday, and in February. Tasty fish and seafood specialities served in a stylish, classic atmosphere. Moderate.

LUCCA

Antica Locanda dell'Angelo, Via Pescheria 21. Tel/Fax: 0583-47711. Closed on Sunday evening and Monday. Discreetly elegant restaurant in keeping with its historic setting. Traditional Tuscan cuisine. Moderate.

The Antico Caffè della Mura, Piazzale V. Emanuele. Tel: 0583-834 7962. Closed on Tuesday and in January. Set on the city wall, elegant garden restaurant with white marble tables, extensive menu, with specialities like rabbit in mint sauce and risotto with petals of roses. Moderate.

Buca di Sant' Antonio, Via della Cervia 3. Tel: 0583-355881. Popular though quite expensive with excellent selection of Garfagnana specialties; *crostini'* with pheasant pâté, hare dishes, *polenta* with mushrooms. Moderate.

Giglio, Piazza del Giglio 2. Tel: 0583-494058, Fax: 0583-55881. Closed on Tuesday evening, also Wednesday and in February. Known as Lucca's best seafood restaurant, this charming spot spills out on to the piazza. It has a comfortable interior with a fine traditional fireplace, best appreciated in winter. Moderate.

Sergio, Via San Croce 44. Tel: 0583-49944. Closed on Tuesday. Adventurous local dishes, and will cater for special diets.

Solferino, San Macario in Piano (6 km/4 miles from Lucca). Tel: 0583-59118. Closed Wednesday, Thursday lunch, and two weeks in August. Rated among the best restaurants of rural Tuscany. Moderate.

Teatro, Piazza Napoleone 25. Tel: 0583-493749. Closed on Thursday. Decorated in a refined yet sober style, this restaurant serves typical local dishes, especially fish. Moderate.

MARINA DI PISA

Arsella, Via Padre Agostino. Tel: 050-36615, Fax: 35929. Closed on Tuesday and Wednesday. A seaside (hence seafood) restaurant built on wooden piles. Inexpensive.

Janett, Via Maiorca 34, Marina di Pisa. Tel: 050-36521. Fish specialities. Inexpensive.

MONTECATINI TERME

Enoteca Da Giovanni, Via Garibaldi 25. Tel: 0572-71695. Closed on Monday. Typical Tuscan dishes. Moderate.

MONTEMERANO

Caiano Montemerano, Tel: 0564-602817. New look at traditional regional dishes. Pretty restaurant with *al fresco* dining in summer. Specialises in wild mushrooms and truffles. Expensive.

Enoteca Dell'Antico Frantoio, Piazza Solferino 7. Tel: 0564-602615. Erik Banti's restaurant famous for its wine cellar, and superb food; duck breast *carpaccio*, artichoke *tagliatelle*, rabbit stuffed with ham. Moderate.

PESCIA

Cecco, Via Forti 84. Tel: 0572-477955. Asparagus, truffles and good desserts. Inexpensive.

Gambero Rosso (Collodi), Via San Gennaro. Tel: 0572-429364. Elegant Tuscan cooking in building designed by architect Giovanni Michelucci. Pancakes filled with spinach or seafood; *cannelloni* and good pasta. Inexpensive.

PIOMBINO

Centrale, Via Piazza Edison 2. Tel: 0565-221825, Fax: 220220. Closed on Saturday and in August. Tuscan specialities, notably with a wide selection of fish dishes. Moderate.

PISA

Pisa has two Michelin-rosetted restaurants serving grand cuisine:

Sergio, Lungarno Pacinotti 1. Tel: 050-580580. Closed Sunday, January and the last two weeks in July. Expensive. The smaller and slightly cheaper **Al Ristoro dei Vecchi Macelli**, Via Volturno 49. Tel: 050-20424. Closed Sunday lunch, Wednesday, one week in January and most of August. Seafood, bean soup and game in a cosy setting. Reservations advisable. Moderate.

Da Bruno, Via Bianchi 12. Tel: 050-560818). Closed Monday. Located outside the walls, it serves typical Pisan dishes such as polenta with mushrooms. Moderate.

La Mescita, Via Cavalca 2. Tel: 055-544294. Closed for lunch on Saturday, also all day Sunday and in August. A family-run trattoria with traditional Tuscan dishes. Inexpensive.

La Rota, Strada Statale 1, Via Aurelia. Tel: 055-804443, Fax: 055-803181. Closed on Tuesday. A wide choice of traditional dishes. Moderate.

Osteria dei Cavalieri, Via San Frediano 16. Tel: 055-580858. Closed for lunch on Saturday, also all day Sunday and in August. A modern restaurant located in the historic centre. Moderate.

Pergoletto, Via delle Belle Torri 36. Tel: 050-542458. Closed on Tuesday, also in August. Set in a fortified tower-house, this is a welcoming restaurant with a garden. Most typical are the grills and soups. Inexpensive.

Schiaccianoci, Via Vespucci 104a. Tel: 055-21024. Closed on Sunday evening, Monday, and in August. A cosy, welcoming, family-run restaurant. Moderate.

Trattoria Asmara, Via Cammeo 27 (at the Porta Nuova). Tel: 050-552711. Closed on Friday. The French proprietor, Jeanne, has made this into a bistro, with pretty pink tablecloths, superb food and walls covered in paintings by artists who make it their regular haunt.

PISTOIA

Cucciolo della Montagna, Via Panciatichi 4. Tel: 0573-477043. Elegant and quiet with a good selection of classic Italian and regional dishes. Moderate.

Il Ritrovio di Iccio, Via dei Fabbri 5/7. Tel: 0573-366935. Friendly restaurant in historic centre, piano music and Tuscan cooking including Roman dishes like *gran faro* (wheat broth). Moderate.

La Casa degli Amici, Via Bonellino 111. Tel/Fax: 0573-380305. Closed on Tuesday, Sunday evening and in August. Pleasant restaurant with a garden and genuine *cucina casalinga* (home cooking). Moderate.

La Limonaia, Via di Gello 9a. Tel: 0573-400453. Closed on Monday evening and all day Tuesday. Set 2 km (1 mile) from the centre of Pistoia, this appealing trattoria serves typical local dishes. Inexpensive.

Leon Rosso, Via Panciatichi 4. Tel/Fax: 0573-292230. Closed on Sunday, and in August. Small, well-run restaurant in a central location. *Gnocchi al gorgonzola* (dumplings in cheese sauce), macaroni with wild boar (*cinghiale*) and a good choice of *dolci* (desserts). Moderate.

Rafanelli, Via San Agostino, 47. Tel: 0573-532046. Serves substantial and extremely tasty Tuscan home cooking. Inexpensive.

Ristorante La Gavarina d'Oro, Via Castello Podenzana. Tel: 0187-410021. Rustic mountain restaurant specialising in *panigacci*, crisp pancakes served with creamy cheese and home-cured meats.

PORTO ERCOLE

Il Pellicano, Cala Dei Santi. Tel: 0564-833801. Meals served on a terrace or in pinewoods in a luxurious hotel-restaurant. Tuscan delicacies such as wild boar pâté and marinated eel. Expensive.

PRATO

Osvaldo Baroncelli, Via Fra Bartolomeo 13. Tel: 0574-23810. Closed on Sunday. This well-established restaurant serves inventive dishes such as chicken stuffed with pistachio, mushroom tarts and sweet pastries, drenched in honey. Moderate.

RADDA IN CHIANTI

Giulio, Via delle Conca 45. Tel: 0577-55948. Closed on Sunday, Monday, and in August. Classic Tuscan trattoria. Inexpensive.

Vignale, Fattoria Vignale, Via XX Settembre 23. Tel: 0577-738094, Fax: 0577-738730. Closed on Thursday. Set on an agricultural estate, in a converted farm-building used for olive-pressing, this restaurant serves refined Tuscan cuisine, with imaginative versions of regional dishes. Moderate.

Tastefully decorated rooms are also available in this beautiful Tuscan manor. (L.160,000–240,000 for a double room).

SIENA

Al Marsili, Via del Castoro 3. Tel: 0577-47154, Fax: 0577-47338. Closed on Monday. An elegant setting in an ancient building with the wine cellars built deep into the limestone. Sophisticated cuisine, including *gnocchi* in duck sauce. Moderate.

Castelvecchio, Via Castelvecchio 65. Tel: 0577-49586. Closed on Tuesday. Converted from ancient stables but now a typical traditional restaurant. Moderate.

Certosa di Maggiano, Via Certosa 82. Tel: 0577-288189. Converted Carthusian monastery; gourmet food served in magical setting in a cloistered courtyard overlooking Siena. Expensive.

Da Guido, Vicolo del Pettinaio. Tel: 0577-28042, Fax: 0577-271370. Closed on Wednesday and in January. A veritable Sienese institution, set in medieval premises and long popular with visiting VIPs. Traditional Sienese cuisine. Inexpensive.

Da Mugolone, Via dei Pellegrini 8. Tel: 0577-283235. Closed on Thursday and in July. Traditional ambience matched by excellent local cuisine. Moderate.

Il Barbero, Piazza del Campo 80/81. Tel: 0577-40187. Closed on Saturday. Popular self-service restaurant. Inexpensive.

Il Ghibellina, Via dei Pelligrini 26. Tel: 0577-288079. Closed on Thursday. Pleasant atmosphere with a variety of typical dishes, including ones suitable for vegetarians. Moderate.

L'Angolo, Via Garibaldi 13. Tel: 0577-289251, Fax: 0577-270646. Closed on Saturday. A formal, punctilious restaurant in the best Sienese tradition. Moderate.

La Torre, Via Salicotto 7-9. Tel: 0577-287548. Closed on Thursday and part of August. Family-run restaurant and popular young haunt below the Torre del Mangia. Inexpensive.

Le Tre Campane, Piazza L. Bonelli 5. Tel: 0577-280 6091. Closed on Tuesday. Set in a delightful spot on a square just below the Cathedral, this old-fashioned restaurant offers standard Tuscan fare. Inexpensive.

Medio Evo, Via dei Rossi 40. Tel: 0577-280315, Fax: 0577-45376. Closed on Thursday and in January. A lovely restaurant set in a 14th-century *palazzo*. Typical local dishes. Moderate.

Osteria Il Carroccio, Via Casato di Sotto 32. Tel: 0577-41165. Closed on Wednesday and in February. Well-run, tiny, quaint and highly typical trattoria serving simple local dishes. Moderate.

Osteria Le Logge, Via del Porrione 33. Tel: 0577-48013. Closed on Sunday. Set in a 19th-century grocers' shop, this charming restaurant conserves the authentic dark wood and marble interior. On the menu are duck and fennel, chicken and lemon and such exotic dishes as stuffed guinea fowl (*faraona*). There is a varied wine list, with the house olive oil and wines produced by the owners. Moderate.

Tullio ai Tre Cristi, Vicolo di Provenzano 1-7. Tel: 0577-280608.

Closed on Monday and in January. Frescoed walls add to the charming atmosphere. Inexpensive.

SINAGUNGA

Locanda dell'Amorosa, 53048 Siena. Tel: 0577-679497, Fax: 0577-678216. Superb restaurant in restored farmhouse with famous wine cellar. It is worth staying overnight in this idyllic 14th-century estate. A meal costs L.65–90,000 while a double room is L.250–450,000.

TIRRENIA

Dante e Ivana, Viale del Tirreno 207 C. Tel/Fax: 050-32549. Closed on Sunday. A big aquarium from which one chooses the fish to be cooked for dinner. Expensive.
Martini, Via dell' Edera 16. Tel: 050-37592. Closed Monday lunchtime and all day Tuesday, as well as mid-September–mid-October. Fish and seafood specialities. Moderate.

VIAREGGIO

L'Oca Bianca, Via Aurelia 312. Tel: 0584-388477. Set in an old farmstead in the north of town, this is Viareggio's finest restaurant. Only open in the evening except for weekends, when open for lunch as well. This cuisine with a personal touch is based on fish dishes such as *aragosta* (lobster). Expensive.

If feeling rich, try the gastronomic *menu degustazione* for L.90,000.
Margherita, Viale Regina Margherita 30. Tel: 0584-962553. Closed on Wednesday, also closed for lunch on Thursday, and closed in November. This Art Nouveau-style dining room is the backdrop for magnificent seafood, served with excellent wines. Expensive.
Romano, Via Mazzini 122. Tel: 0584-31382. Closed on Monday and in January. An elegant and formal yet welcoming restaurant with a charming garden. Excellent seafood, some of the best in Tuscany, creatively put together. Reservations required. Expensive.

VOLTERRA

Etruria, Piazza dei Priori 8. Tel: 0588-86064. Closed on Saturday. Local cooking especially wild boar and game dishes in season. Moderate.
Poggio, Via Matteotti 39. Tel: 0588-85257. Closed on Wednesday and in February. Set in the 15th-century

Palazzo Maffei in the heart of the historic centre, this restaurant combines rusticity and elegance. Tuscan specialities. Moderate.
Trattoria del Sacco Fiorentino, Piazza XX Settembre 18. Tel: 0588-88537. Closed on Wednesday. Set in a 17th-century *palazzo*, this restaurant is elegant yet welcoming and serves regional specialities. Moderate.

Drinking Notes

Wines: The *Denominazione di Origine Controllata* (DOC) *e Garantita* (DOCG) is a system of controlling Italian wine by EU rules similar to the French *Appellation Contrôlée*, but it does not always guarantee top quality. Chianti, the most well-known wine in Italy, and Brunello di Montalcino and Nobile di Montepulciano, all from Tuscany, have been awarded the status of DOCG. Other DOC and Vino di Tavola wines that are often of excellent quality are Vernaccia, Aleatico, Bianco Pisano di San Torp and the red and white wines from Montescudeaio. (*See Wine Wars.*)

Attractions

Culture
Archaeological Sites

Etruscan (8th–2nd century BC): There are sites at Island of Elba, Volterra, Fiesole, Arezzo, Chiusi, Vetulonia, an archaeological museum in Florence and other museums in Volterra, Chiusi, Cortona, Asciano, Grosseto and Massa Marittima.
Roman (8th century BC–5th century AD): Notable remains can be seen at Fiesole, Cosa, Roselle, Volterra and Arezzo.

Architecture

Romanesque (11th–12th century): Churches and buildings of this period are found all over Italy, mostly with regional differences, such as the Pisan-Romanesque style. Main examples in Tuscany are at Pisa, Florence, Lucca, Siena, Pistoia, and Arezzo.

Gothic (12th–14th century): The most important buildings are in Florence, Siena, Pisa, Pistoia, and Arezzo.
Renaissance (14th–16th century): Tuscany abounds in religious and secular Renaissance buildings, Florence being the most important.

Art
The most outstanding art collections of the Renaissance in Tuscany are the **Uffizi Gallery**, **Pitti Palace Gallery** and **San Marco Museum**. Works of art during the late Renaissance and mannerist periods (16th–17th century), the baroque (17th–18th century) and the neoclassical and romantic (18th–19th century), and the 20th century are exhibited at most art galleries and museums in main cities.

Things To Do
Museums and Galleries
This section includes all the sites to visit in Tuscany, with their opening hours, plus a suggested itinerary for Florence.

Take advantage of the "multi-entrance" tickets promoted by local tourist authorities, like Siena's "*Biglietto di Ingresso Cumulativo*" allowing you entry to a number of museums over a three-day period.

AREZZO

Archaeological Museum, Via Margaritone 10. Tel: 0575-20882. Open 9am–1.30pm. Closed Monday. Varied collection of Etruscan and Greek vases and sculpture.
Casa di Giorgio Vasari, Via XX Settembre 55. Tel: 0575-20295. Open Tuesday–Saturday 9am–7pm, Sunday 9am–1pm. Closed Monday. The house of Giorgio Vasari (1511–74), the painter, architect and writer, has vaulted, frescoed ceilings in small rooms. Display of paintings by mannerist artists.
Museum of Medieval and Modern Art, Via San Lorentino 8. Tel: 0575-23868. Open 9am–6.30pm, Sunday and holidays 9am–noon. Closed Monday. Works by Vasari and Spinello Aretino, follower of Giotto. Important collections of ceramics, goldsmiths' work, ivories, seals and coins.

ASCIANO

Archaeological Museum, Corso Mattcotti 46. Open 10am–12.30pm, also 4.30–6.30pm in summer.

Museum of Sacred Art, Piazza Sant'Agate. Tel: 0577-718207. Open on request. Houses 14th- and 15th-century Sienese painting, including Lorenzetti and Valdambrino.

BUONCONVENTO

Museum of Sacred Art (Museo d'Arte Sacra), Via Soccini 17. Open Tuesday–Thursday 10am–noon, Saturday 10am–noon, 4–6pm, Sunday 9am–1pm. Sienese paintings from the Trecento to the Seicento are on display in this small Buonconvento museum.

CAMALDOLI

Monastery, founded in 1012 by St Romuald. Works by Vasari and Mina da Fiesole in the 16th-century church.

CAPRESE

The birthplace of Michelangelo Buonarroti, born in 1470. Well-restored little stone house. The oldest wing of the castle, restored in modern times, has become an exhibition hall for full-sized reproductions of Michelangelo's sculpture.

CARRARA

Civic Museum of Marble, Viale XX Settembre, Località Stadio, Carrara. Tel: 0585-840561. Open 9.30am–12.30pm, 3.30–6.30pm, Sunday 9.30am–12.30pm. Entrance free.

Marble Quarries/Marble caves: The marble quarries of Colonnata and Fantiscritti are open for visitors on weekday mornings. Souvenir shop are located on site. Tours can be organised by Carrara Tourist Office (Tel: 0585-843370) or you can drive around the quarries independently.

CASTIGLION FIORENTINO

A medieval centre surrounded by walls and dominated by the Cassero fortress. The **Gothic Church of San Francesco**, the **Collegiate Church** and the **Gesù Church** are rich in art works. There is a library of paintings, tablets and priceless gold of the 12th to 15th century.

A short distance beyond the walls is the octagonal **Church of the Consolation** (Madonna della Consoazione) a frescoed Renaissance church.

CHIUSI

National Etruscan Museum, Piazza del Duomo. Tel: 0578-20177. Open 9am–1.40pm. Closed Monday. Fine collection of Etruscan remains in Chiusi. Etruscan tombs nearby that can be visited by arrangement with the custodian.

CORTONA

City Museum (Museo Civico), Palazzo Casali. Open 9am–1pm, 3–5pm. This contains a collection of Etruscan bronzes, Greek vases and medieval paintings.

Diocesan Museum, (Museo Diocesano), Il Gesù. Open 9am–1pm, 3–5pm. Inside the Jesuit church is a collection of Signorelli's greatest works.

ELBA

Villa dei Mulini, Portoferraio. Open weekdays 9am–1.30pm. The house Napoleon lived in. Library and small museum.

Villa Napoleone (Napoleon's villa) at San Martino. Open weekdays 9am–1.30pm. Has a museum and small art gallery.

EMPOLI

Pinacoteca di Sant'Andrea, Piazza della Proposiitura. Tel: 0571-76284. Open 9am–noon. Closed Monday. Good collection of Renaissance art and sculpture.

FLORENCE

A free monthly publication, *Florence Today*, is published in Italian and English and lists current exhibitions and concerts and has informative articles about museums and places of interest. In addition, obtain *Events*, a monthly magazine, and *Firenze Spettacolo*, a monthly listings magazine.

The Friends of Florentine Museums Association (Via degli Alfani 39) has 12,000 members. They arrange museum visits from 9–11pm in the summer, with orchestral recitals, to allow Florentine workers to visit museums during the tourist season, and for tourists to get a further insight into Florentine culture. In response to popular demand, the authorities have extended the opening hours of museums in summer. Many have special evening opening times. Contact the Tourist Office for details. Entry prices for museums and galleries range from L.3,000–

12,000, with the Uffizi the most expensive. State museums (such as the Uffizi) are closed on Monday while most other museums close on Tuesday or Wednesday. Get the *Biglietto Cumulativo*, a ticket which allows you to see all *Musei Comunali* (city council-run museums) on one ticket.

Archaeological Museum (Museo Archeologico), Via della Colonna 36. Tel: 055-23575. Open 9am–2pm; holidays 9am–1pm. Closed Monday.

The A. della Ragione Modern Art Collection (Raccolta d'Arte Moderna "A. della Ragione"), Piazza della Signoria 5. Tel: 055-283078. Open 10am–1pm. Closed Tuesday.

Bardini Museum and Corsi Gallery, Piazza de'Mozzi 1. Tel: 055-296749. Open 9am–2pm, holidays 8am–1pm. Closed Wednesday. **Bargello Museum** (Museo del Bargello), Via del Proconsolo 4. Tel: 055-23885. Open weekdays 9am–2pm; Sunday and holidays 9am–1pm. Closed Monday.

Collection Contini Bonacossi, Giardino di Boboli, Palazzina della Meridiana. Visits only by appointment at the ticket office of the Uffizi (Tel: 055-23885).

Fort Belvedere (Fortezza Belvedere). Venue for exhibitions, as well as various cultural events and art shows.

Gallery of the Academy (L'Academmia), Via Ricasoli 60. Tel: 055-23995. Open weekdays 9am–7pm, Sunday and holidays 9am–1pm. Closed Monday. Michelangelo's "David" exhibited here (very crowded – go in February or November to have a clear view). Alternatively, content yourself with views of the "false" Davids in Piazza della Signoria and Piazzale Michelangelo.

Ghirlandaio Refectory, Ghirlandaio's Last Supper (Cenacolo del Ghirlandaio), Borgo, Ognissanti, Piazza d'Ognissanti. Tel: 055-239 6802. Open Monday, Tuesday and Saturday only 9am–noon.

Historic Topographic Museum, "Florence as it was" (*Firenze Com' Era*) and Garden of the Oblates, Via dell' Oriuolo 4. Tel: 055-217305. Open 10am–1pm, Sunday 8am–1pm.

Historical Costume Gallery (Galleria del Costume), Giardino di Boboli, Palazzo Pitti, Piazza Pitti. Tel: 055-294279. Open 9am–2pm, holidays 9am–1pm. Closed Monday.

Historical Florentine House Museum, Palazzo Davanzati, Via Porta Rossa 13.

Tel: 055-23885. Open 9am–2pm, holidays 9am–12.15pm. Closed Monday.

Horne Museum (Museo Horne), Via de'Benci 6. Tel: 055-244661. Open 10am–1pm, 3–6pm. Closed Sunday and Tuesday.

Hospital of the Innocents (Spedale degli Innocenti), Piazza SS Annunziata 12. Tel: 243670. Open 8.30am–2pm, holidays 8am–1pm. Closed Wednesday.

Jewish Museum of Florence (Museo Ebraico), Via Farini 4. Tel: 055-245252. Open May–September Monday–Thursday 11am–1pm, Friday and Sunday 10am–1pm. Closed Saturday. The entrance price includes a visit to the synagogue.

Marino Marini Museum (Museo Marino Marini), Piazza San Pancrazio. Tel: 055-219432. Open 10am–1pm, 4–7pm. Set in a deconsecrated church, this imaginative museum displays the bold sculptures of Marino Marini, the Tuscan sculptor.

Medici Chapels (Cappelle Medicee), Piazza Madonna degli Aldobrandini. Tel: 055-23885. Open 9am–2pm, Sunday and holidays 9am–1pm. Closed Monday.

Modern Art Gallery (Galleria d'Arte Moderna), Palazzo Pitti, Piazza Pitti. Tel: 055-287096. Open 9am–2pm. Closed Monday.

Monumental or Royal Apartments (Appartamenti Monumentali), Piazza Pitti, Palazzo Pitti. Tel: 055-238 8611. Open 9am–2pm, holidays 9am–1pm. Closed Monday. The ticket is also valid for the **Palatine Gallery** and the **Silver Museum**.

Museum of San Marco (Museo di San Marco), Piazza San Marco 1. Tel: 055-23885. Open 9am–2pm except Monday.

Museum and Cloisters of Santa Maria Novella (Museo di Santa Maria Novella), Piazza Santa Maria Novella. Tel: 055-282187. Open 9am–2pm, holidays 9am–1pm. Closed Friday.

Museum of Antique Musical Instruments (Museo degli strumenti musicali antichi), Palazzo Vecchio. Visits by appointment at Ufficio Belle Arti e Musei Comunali, Via San Egidio 21. Tel: 055-217305.

Museum of Semi-precious Stone Inlaid Work (Opificio delle Pietre Dure), Via Alfani 78. Tel: 055-210102. Telephone for opening times. This is where major restoration of artistic treasures take place.

Opera di Santa Croce Museum, Piazza Santa Croce 16. Tel: 055-244619. Open 10am–12.30pm, 2.30–6.30pm. Closed Wednesday.

Opera di Santa Maria del Fiore Museum, Piazza del Duomo 9. Tel: 055-230 2885. Open 9am–7.30pm. Closed Sunday.

Palazzo Vecchio, Piazza della Signoria. Tel: 055-27681. Open 9am–7pm, holidays 8am–1pm. Closed Thursday.

Palatine Gallery, Piazza Pitti. Tel: 055-238 8611. Open 9am–2pm. Closed Monday. (Entrance ticket can also be used for the **Monumental Apartments** and the **Silver Museum**.)

Palazzo Medici Riccardi, Via Cavour 1. Tel: 055-2760. Open 9am–1pm, 3–6pm, Sunday 9am–1pm. Closed Wednesday. Admire the restored Grozzoli frescoes.

Perugino's Crucifixion (Crocifissione del Perugino), Borgo Pinti 58. Tel: 055-247 8420. Open 9am–noon, 5–7pm.

Porcelain Museum (Museo delle Porcellane), Giardino di Boboli, Palazzina del Cavaliere. Currently closed but telephone 055-212557 to check.

Refectory of Andrea del Sarto, Via San Salvi, 16. Tel: 055-677570. Open 9am–2pm. Closed Monday.

Scalzo Cloister (Chiostro dello Scalzo), Via Cavour 69. Tel: 055-238 8604. Open Tuesday and Thursday only 9am–1pm.

Refectory of Santo Spirito, Last Supper in Santo Spirito (Cenacolo di Santo Spirito), Piazza Santo Spirito 29. Tel: 055-287043. Open 9am–1pm. Closed Monday.

Silver Museum (Museo degli Argenti), Piazza Pitti, Palazzo Pitti. Tel: 055-294279. Open 9am–2pm. Closed Monday. (Ticket also valid for the **Palatine Gallery** and the **Monumental Apartments**.)

St Apollonia's Last Supper (Cenacolo di San Apollonia), Via 27 April 1. Tel: 055-287074/23885. Open 9am–2pm, holidays 9am–1pm. Closed Monday.

St Salvi's Last Supper (Cenacolo di San Salvi), Via Andrea del Sarto 16. Tel: 055-677570/23885. Open 9am–2pm, holidays 9am–1pm. Closed Monday.

Stibbert Museum (Museo Stibbert), Via Stibbert 26. Tel: 055-475520. Open 9am–1pm. Closed Thursday.

Uffizi Gallery (Galleria degli Uffizi), Loggiato degli Uffizi, 6. Tel: 055-23885. Open 9am–7pm, Sunday and holidays 9am–1pm. Closed Monday. The staff have made valiant attempts to re-open the gallery to the public after the terrorist bomb in 1993. Over 80 percent of the collection is now on view.

Vasari Corridor (Corridoio Vasariano). Viewing by appointment only. Since the bombing, which damaged the Corridor, it has been closed to the public but should re-open by 1995–96.

Scientific Museums (Musei Scienfifici)

Anthropology Museum (Museo di Antropologia), Via del Proconsolo 12. Tel: 055-239449. Open Thursday–Saturday as well as on the 1st and 3rd Sunday of the month, 9am–1pm.

Botanical Gardens (Orto Botanico), Via Micheli 3. Tel: 055-275 7402. Open Monday, Wednesday and Friday, 9am–noon.

Botanical Gardens Museum (Museo Botanico), Via La Pira 4. Tel: 055-275 7462. Open Monday, Wednesday and Friday, 9am–noon.

Geological and Paleontological Museum (Museo di Geologia e Paleontologia), Via La Pira 4. Tel: 055-238 2711. Open Monday 2pm–6pm, Tuesday–Thursday and Saturday, 9am–1pm, 1st Sunday of the month (excluding July, August, September), 9.30am–12.30pm. Closed holidays.

History of Science Museum (Istituto e Museo di Storia della Scienza), Piazza dei Giudici 1. Tel: 055-293493. Open Monday, Wednesday, Friday, 9.30am–1pm, 2–5pm.

La Specola Museum (Museo della Storia Naturale) Via Romana 17. Tel: 055-222451. **Waxworks:** Open summer Saturday 3–6pm; winter 2–5pm. **Zoology:** Open daily except Wednesday.

Museum of Mineralogy: (Museo di Mineralogia), Via La Pira 4. Tel: 275 7537. Open Monday–Friday 9am–1pm.

Prehistoric Museum (Museo di Preistoria), Via San Egido 21. Tel: 055-295159. Open 9.30am–12.30pm.

SUGGESTED ITINERARIES FOR FLORENCE

Florence's Tourist Office has produced two highly detailed walking tours, representing two different themes of the city: Medieval Florence and Brunelleschi's Florence. These booklets are free, and published in a number of different languages.

In addition, the following list is inclusive of sights listed under *Things To Do*:
(**1**) Piazza del Duomo; Baptistry; Giotto's Bell Tower; Cathedral; Cathedral Museum; Palazzo Medici-Riccardi; San Lorenzo; Laurentian Library; Medici Chapels.
(**2**) Piazza del Duomo, Orsanmichele, Via Calzaioli – garden of the Monastery of San Michele, rebuilt as a church; Piazza della Signoria; Neptune Fountain by Bartolomeo Ammannati; Palazzo Vecchio; Uffizi Gallery.
(**3**) Piazza della Repubblica; Straw Market; Ponte Vecchio – the oldest bridge in Florence; Pitti Palace – The Palatine Gallery – The Monumental or Ex-Royal Apartments – The Gallery of Modern Art – The Silver Museum; Boboli Gardens; the Brunelleschi Church of Santo Spirito; Santa Maria del Carmine with its Brancacci Chapel.
(**4**) Piazza del Duomo; Via de' Tornabuoni; Strozzi Palace; Church of Santa Trinita with the famous frescoed cycle by Domenico Ghirlandaio in the Sassetti Chapel; Palazzo Davanzati, Via Porta Rossa; Santa Maria Novella.
(**5**) Piazza del Duomo; Church and Museum of San Marco; The Accademia (Gallery of the Academy) with Michelangelo's "David"; Santissima Annunziata; Spedale degli Innocenti (Hospital of the Innocents); Archaeological Museum.
(**6**) Piazza San Firenze – Museum of Anthropology and Ethnology; House of Dante; Bargello Museum; Badia Fiorentina; Casa Buonarroti (Michelangelo's House); Church and Museum of Santa Croce; Horne Museum; Bardini Museum.

FIESOLE

Antiquarium Costantini, Via Portigiani 9. Open summer 9am–7pm; winter 10am–4pm. A collection of Greek and Etruscan objects.
Archaeological Museum (Museo Civico), Teatro Romano, Via Portigiani. Open summer 9am–7pm. This displays the finds discovered in the Roman Theatre area.
Bandini Museum (Museo Bandini), Via Duprè 1. Open 10am–1pm, 3–6pm. A collection of medieval Florentine paintings.
Primo Conti Museum, Via Duprè 18. Tel: 597095. Open 10am–1pm. Closed Sunday and Monday. Collection of water colours.

GAIOLE IN CHIANTI

Castello di Brolio (Brolio Castle). Open summer 9am–noon, 3–6pm; winter 9am–noon, 2.30–5.30pm. Closed Friday. Typical Chianti castle and wine estate.

GROSSETO

Museum of Art and Archaeology of the Maremma, Piazza Baccarini 3. Tel 27290. Closed on Wednesday. Archaeological discoveries from Roselle, Vetulonia, Populonia and Vulci. Also Sienese paintings.

LUCCA

Lucca Museum in the School of Music, Corte San Lorenzo 9. Tel: 0583-584028. Giacomo Puccini was born in Lucca and the Tourist Office has a planned tour of the places associated with him. His birthplace in Via di Poggio is now a museum in the School of Music. Open summer 1 April–30 September 10am–6pm; winter 1 October–31 March 10am–4pm. Closed Monday.

Exhibits include his Steinway piano, original manuscripts, records, photographs of costumes worn in performances. The guide – a volunteer music student – plays requested records of Puccini's music. Entrance free.
Museo Nazionale di Villa Guinigi, Via della Quarquonia, Tel 46033. Open 9am–2pm. Closed Monday. A 14th-century villa with sculptures and Renaissance paintings.

Also visit the nearby **Torre del Lago Puccini**. Puccini operas are performed in the open-air theatre in August. Telephone the Tourist Office for details, 0583-419689.

LUCIGNANO

A town built on a circular plan with streets concentrically arranged inside the walls. The 13th- to 18th-century buildings are perfectly preserved. The **Palazzo Comunale** has frescoes of the Sienese and Aretine schools. A small **museum** holds a valuable collection of gold and furnishings, with a unique gold reliquary.

MONTERCHI

Note that the **chapel** just outside the town contains Piero della Francesca's *Madonna del Parto*. Telephone 0575-70710 for opening times of the chapel.

MONTALCINO

Musei Riuniti (combined Civic, Sacred and Archeological museums), Palazzo Arcivescovile, Via Spagna 4. A collection of Sienese paintings and carved statues.
Palazzo Comunale (Town Hall). Open daily 10am–1pm, 3–6.30pm. Closed Monday.

MONTE OLIVETO

Monastero di Monte Oliveto Maggiore. Open summer 9.15am–12.15pm, 3–6pm; winter 9.15am–12.30pm, 3–5pm. 14th-century monastery with famous frescoes including the *Self Portrait* by Sodoma.

MONTICCHIELLO

Thirteenth-century **Cistercian Church** of the Saints Leonardo and Cristoforo with beautiful frescoes from the 14th and 15th centuries.

A **Fortress** or Wall was built at the same time, with 17 towers, though only a third now remain. The magnificent entrance door was blasted by the cannon fire of the army of Charles V. The elegant watchtower of Ugo Monaco, finished in 1260, was bombed by the Spanish but did not fall; it only inclined to one side.

The **Church of Monticchiello** is decorated with frescoes of the Sienese school of the 14th and 15th centuries. There is also a fine panel by Pietro Lorenzetti.

PISA

Museo dell'Opera del Duomo, Piazza Arcivescovado. Tel: 050-561820. Open winter 9am–5pm; summer 9.30am–1pm, 3–7.30pm. A display of works from the monumental structures of the Cathedral Square. Includes sculpture from the 11th–13th century; treasure and ancient robes; paintings from the 16th–18th century; wood marquetry, illuminated manuscripts, and textiles.
Museo dell Sinopie (Museum of the Sinopie), Piazza del Duomo. Tel: 050-560547. Open winter 9am–5pm; summer 9am–7pm. Medieval statues, paintings and also sketches from a fresco cycle.
Museo Nazionale di San Matteo (National Museum of Saint Matthew), Piazza San Matteo in Soarta, Lungarno Mediceo, Pisa. Tel: 050-541865. Open 9am–7pm, holidays 9am–

1.30pm. Closed Monday. On city bus No. 7. The collection includes Trecento paintings, Pisano sculptures and a Donatello bronze.

PISTOIA

Centro Marino Marini, Palazzo del Tau. Tel: 0573–30285. Closed Monday. Paintings and sculptures by contemporary artist and local son, Marino Marini (1901–80).

Museo Civico, Palazzo del Comune. Tel: 0573-3711. Closed Monday. New museum in 14th-century palace with excellent collection of Pistoian paintings and altarpieces.

PONTREMOLI

Museo delle Statue Stele, Castello Piagnaro. Tel: 831439. Open 9am–noon, 2–5pm. Closed Monday. Collection of prehistoric steles, similar to stylised menhirs but shaped to represent warriors.

PRATO

Since Prato was promoted to provincial status, many new cultural initiatives are underway. Call the Tourist Office, Tel: 0574-24112, for information about new museums.

Museo dell' Opera del Duomo, Piazza del Duomo. Tel: 0574-29339. Open Wednesday–Monday. Paintings, sculptures, and reliefs by Donatello.

Prato Museum of Contemporary Art, Viale della Repubblica 227. Tel: 0574-570620. Open 10am–7pm. Closed Tuesday. Important new museum designed by architect Italo Gamberini, for exhibitions of contemporary work.

RADICOFANI

A hilltop castle town with Gothic arches and 15th-century windows, though little remains of the medieval buildings because of many earthquakes. The parish **Church of St Peter** survived and houses several works of art including Francesco di Valdambrino's (1375–1435) wooden statue, "Madonna del Castello"; two paintings by Andrea della Robbia (1437–1528) are in each side-altar. Other works of art are in the nearby **Church of Agata**.

SAN GIMIGNANO

Some of the collections are currently being re-organised, so telephone first to check opening times. Tel: 0577-940008.

The Romanesque-Gothic **Church of Sant' Agostino** (1280–98) holds the bones of San Bartolo, the patron of the city, in an urn in a chapel dedicated to him. There is an altar by Nenedetto da Maiano (1494).

The 12th-century **Collegiate Church** (Romanesque Collegiata) has frescoes by Lippi Memmi and Domenica Ghirlandaio among others. Fine paintings by Italian masters. A fee will allow you to operate the lights for the frescoes.

Museum of Sacred Art, next to the Collegiate Church. Houses fragments from the 13th and 14th centuries, sculpture, chorals and sacred vestments. Currently closed, but telephone 0577-923125 to check.

Etruscan Museum, in the same building. Open 9.30am–12.30pm. Has a collection of oil and wine amphoras, urns of the 3rd and 2nd centuries BC, coins, bronze mirrors etc.

Palazzo del Popolo or **Palazzo Nuovo del Podestà** (1288–1323) with a fresco of the Maestà by Lippo Memmi (1317) and a collection of 16th- to 17th-century medicine bottles.

SIENA

To make the most of your time and budget, you may wish to plan your visit to Siena before setting out by using the following information. The Tourist Office can provide a list of authorised guides. Opening hours and entrance fees may vary. With one week's notice, you can visit any of the *Contrada* (district) museums that celebrate the *Palio* and the ancient city traditions. Tel: 0577-42209.

L'Accademia dei Fisiocritici (Natural History Museum), Piazza San Agostino 4. Open Monday–Friday 9am–1pm, 3–6pm. Closed at weekends and Thursday afternoons. Geological, mineralogical and zoological museum.

Duomo (Cathedral), Piazza del Duomo. Open summer 9am–7.30pm; winter 10am–1pm, 2.30–5pm. The Libreria Piccolomini, the Renaissance library inside the Cathedral, keeps the same opening hours.

Museo dell'Opera della Metropolitana (Museum of the Cathedral), Piazza del Duomo. Open 16 March–1 October, 9am–7.30pm; 1 November–31 March, 9am–1.30pm. Entrance fee L.5,000.

Palazzo Comunale (Town Hall), Piazza del Campo. Open summer 9.30am–7.45pm; winter 9.30am–1.45pm.

Closed Sunday. Inside is Simone Martini's Maestà and other famous frescoes in the medieval Council Chamber. **Pinacoteca** (National Picture Gallery), Palazzo Buonsignori, Via San Pietro 29. Open summer Tuesday–Saturday 9am–7pm, Monday 8.30am–1.30pm; winter 8.30am–1.30pm. A fabulous collection of Sienese masterpieces.

Torre del Mangia, Piazza del Campo. Open 10am–6pm. Wonderful views from the top of this famous tower.

Santuario e Casa di Santa Caterina (St Catherine's House and Sanctuary), Costa di Sant' Antonio. Open 9am–12.30pm, 3.30–6pm.

VOLTERRA

The **Art Gallery** and **Civic Museum**, Palazzo Minucci Solaini, Via dei Sarti 1. Tel: 0588-87580. Very good gallery containing Florentine Renaissance and mannerist paintings.

Museo d'Arte Sacra (The Museum of Sacred Art), Via Roma 13. Tel: 0588-86392. Free entrance. Open daily.

Museo Etrusco Guarnacci, Via Don Minzoni 15. Tel: 0588-86347. Open all year (except major holidays) 9.30am–1pm, 2.30–6pm.

Churches & Buildings

The following listings include churches, monuments, towers, archives, archaeological sites and houses associated with famous Tuscans.

FLORENCE

Battistero (Baptistry). Open Monday–Saturday 1–5pm, Sunday 9am–1pm.
Brancacci Chapel (Cappella Brancacci), Piazza del Carmine. Tel: 055-238 2195. Open daily 10am–5pm. The innovative work of Masolino and Masaccio.

Buonarroti or Michelangelo's House (Casa Buonarroti), Via Ghibellina 70. Tel: 055-241752. Open 9.30am–2.30pm. Closed on Tuesday.

Dante's House (Casa di Dante), Via Santa Margherita 1. Tel: 055-283343. Currently closed for restoration work but telephone to check.

Dome of the Cathedral (Cupola del Duomo). Open 10am–5pm. Closed on Sunday.

Duomo (Cathedral). Open summer 9am–7.30pm; winter 10am–1pm, 2.30–5pm.

Giotto's Bell Tower (Campanile di Giotto). Open daily 8.30am–7.30pm.

PISA

The main sites may be easily visited on foot or by local bus but taking a horse and carriage is a pleasant introduction to the city. Prices are negotiable (in English), but generally start around L.30,000 for a half-hour ride along the Arno, to the Piazza Cavalieri and the Piazza del Duomo. A recommended time is about two in the afternoon, when the streets are quiet and the tourist crowds are having their midday meal. Buy a joint ticket to see all the sights on the Campo dei Miracoli.

Battistero (Baptistry), Piazza Duomo. Tel: 050-560547. Open winter 9am–5pm; summer 8am–9pm. Entrance free (machines for lights and tourist information, L.300).

Campanile (Leaning Tower), situated in the Field of Miracles. Closed for repairs for the foreseeable future.

Cattedrale or Duomo (Cathedral). Tel: 050-560547. Open winter (November–February) 7.45am–12.45pm; 3–4.45pm; the rest of the year 7.45am–12.45pm, 3–6.45pm. Entrance free (machines for lights and tourist information, L.300).

Visitors may not view the interior while services are being held.

Camposanto, Piazza del Duomo. Tel: 050-560547. Open winter 9am–5pm; summer 8am–8pm. Gothic cloister with tombs and frescoes.

SIENA

See also the **Museums** and **Galleries** sections.

Archivo di Stato (State Archives), Palazzo Piccolomini, Banchi di Sotto 52. Open Monday–Saturday 9am–1pm. Closed Sunday.

Duomo (Cathedral), Piazza del Duomo. Open summer 9am–7.30pm; winter 10am–1pm, 2.30–5pm. The cathedral contains a Renaissance library and an inlaid marble floor.

Palazzo Pubblico (Town Hall), Piazza del Campo. Tel: 0577-292263. Open summer 9.30am–7.45pm; winter 8.30am–1.45pm. Entrance charge to see the state rooms and fabulously frescoed Council chamber.

Santuario e Casa di Santa Caterina (Sanctuary and House of Saint Catherine), Costa di San Antonio. Open daily 9am–12.30pm, 3.30–6pm. Catherine of Siena (1347–80), a writer who set an example by her good deeds, was proclaimed Patron Saint of

Italy by Pope Pius XII in 1939 and a Doctor of the Church by Pope Paul VI in 1970. All the places she visited, from the day of her birth, have been consecrated. The house, garden and her father's dye-works now form the "Sanctuary of St Catherine".

Torre del Mangia (Tower), Palazzo Comunale, Piazza del Campo. Open 10am–6pm. A wonderful place from which to view the city.

Oratorio di San Bernardino, Piazza San Francesco. Open 10.30am–1pm, 3–5.30pm. Bernardino of the Albizzeschi (1380–1444) became known as a talented preacher. He was the first to have the name of Jesus painted or carved, abbreviated to the initials, IHS. In Siena the monogram stands out on the facade of the Town Hall and in the "Mappamondo" hall. Sanctified by Nicholas V in 1450, he was proclaimed the "Patron Saint of Advertising" in 1959 by Pope John XXIII.

Fortezza Medicea, Viale Maccari. Open 3pm–midnight. This permanent exhibition of Italian wines occupies the former fortress cellars. This is the place to sample a wide range of Tuscan wines and have your queries fully answered about the wine-making process.

VOLTERRA

Cattedrale, Piazza del Duomo. Tel: 0588-87654. Open 7am–noon and 2.30–6pm. Entrance free.

Teatro Romano, Viale Ferrucci. Tel: 0588-86050. Open March–November. The partly reconstructed Roman theatre, lying just outside the city walls, is well worth seeing.

War Cemeteries

American War Cemetery, near Falciani (about 8 km/5 miles south of Florence, towards Siena). Tel: 202 0020. Open Monday–Friday 8am–5pm, Saturday 9.30am–5pm.

British Commonwealth War Cemetery, road No. 67 near Girone (about 7 km/4 miles east of Florence, towards Arezzo). Open 9am–5pm, Sunday 9am–1pm.

German War Cemetery, near Traversa, just beyond the Futa pass. Tel: 815248. Open 8.30am–noon, 2–7pm.

Nature Parks

If you are interested in exploring Tuscany's nature reserves, protected zones and areas of the wildest landscape,

ask a large Tourist Office for a free publication (in English and Italian), *Tuscany – Nature Tourism* (by the Regione Toscana, regional authority for Tuscany). For a complete list of all nature reserves, contact Regione Toscana, Servizio Promozione Turistica, Via di Novoli 26, 50127 Florence. Tel: 055-4383.

Parco Naturale della Maremma (Maremma Nature Reserve), extending from Principina a Mare to Talamone. Sandy bays, parkland, pine forests with a wide variety of flora and fauna. The park offers opportunities for walking, cycling, pony-trekking, canoeing, windsurfing and paragliding. The nearest train station is Grosseto, Tel: 0566-400443, but this is some distance away. Contact Grosseto Tourist Office for details (Tel: 0564-454510) or visit the Tourist Office in the park itself. Parco Naturale della Maremma, 58010 Alberese. Tel: 0564-407098.

World Wildlife Fund Bird Sanctuary, Capalbio Scalo, a few hundred metres from Lake Burano. Visits can be arranged by calling direct, Tel: 0564-898829, or by writing to the Rome section of World Wildlife Fund. There is a lake and small nature park, a favourite stop for thousands of birds migrating from the former Yugoslavia to North Africa.

Albatross, 20 Via Cavour, Grosseto, Tel: 0564-616381, has a wide choice of guided ventures, such as canoeing along the Ombrone river, trekking across the mountains, sailing along the coast, or more typically, riding from one end to the other of the park, visiting the noble ruins of San Rabano and the many towers on top of the mountains.

Villas & Gardens

FLORENCE

Times given for parks and gardens by the Tuscan authorities are rather unreliable. It is best to check with the local Tourist Office before setting off. Tel. 055-239 2124/290832.

Boboli Gardens (Giardino di Boboli), Piazza Pitti. Open summer 9am–7pm; winter 9am–4.30pm. An entrance fee of L.5,000 is charged.

Medici Villa di Careggi, Viale Pieracini 17. Open 9am–1pm. Closed weekends. Remodelled for Cosimo de Medici by Michelozzo in the 1430s.

Medici Villa di Castello, Località Castello. Tel: 055-454791. Gardens open March and October 9am–5.30pm; April–September 9am–6.30pm. Closed on Monday. Magnificent gardens with grotto by Giambologna.

Medici Villa "La Petraia", Localita Castello, Florence. Tel: 055-451208. Open 8.30am–2pm, holidays 9am–1pm. Closed on Monday. Gardens open March, April and October, 9am–5.30pm, May–September, 9am–7.30pm. Closed on Monday. 14th-century villa and gardens.

Medici Villa of Poggia a Caiano, Poggio a Caiano (a village). Open 9am–1pm, holidays 9am–noon. Closed on Monday. Magnificent villa built for Lorenzo de Medici in the 15th century, with beautiful gardens open 9am–6pm.

LUCCA

Villa Reale, Marlia, Lucca. Tel: 0583-30108. Elegant villa remodelled by Elisa Baciocchi, Napoleon's sister; stunning gardens; grottoes, fountains, lemon groves and the *Teatro di verdura*, an outdoor theatre carved from yew.

Villa Torrigiani, near Lucca, is a 16th-century villa with mannerist facade and lovely gardens.

PESCIA

Pinocchio Park, Collodi. Tel: 0572-429342 Open daily. A monument to *Pinocchio*, written in nearby Villa Garzoni.

PISA

Giardino Scotto (public garden), Lungarno Fibonacci. Open from 8am to sunset. Entrance free.

Orto Botanico (Botanical Garden), Via L. Ghini. Tel: 050-23027. Open weekdays 8am–12.30pm.

Parco Naturale di Migliarino, San Rossore-Massaciuccoli (near Pisa). Entrance at Tombolo SS1, Consorzio del Parco, Via Cesare Battisti. Tel: 050-43512.

PISTOIA

Villa Garzoni. Baroque 18th-century villa where Collodi wrote Pinocchio. Extravagant formal gardens with grottoes, maze, fountains and waterfalls.

SIENA

Orto Botanico (Botanical Garden), Via Pier Andrea Mattioli 4. Guided tours on weekdays 8am–1pm and 3–5pm.

Children's Tuscany

At first sight, Tuscany seems an adult paradise but not an obvious choice for children: Renaissance art does not have obvious appeal to bored youngsters. However, Tuscany has much to offer children of all ages, from towers to climb to medieval castles, ice creams galore and plenty of child-friendly restaurants. In addition, the region has a number of good parks, nature reserves and plenty of opportunities for riding, cycling and swimming. Much of the Tuscan coast has great appeal for children, particularly the well-equipped resorts near Viareggio and the sandy, well-organised beaches on offshore islands such as Elba.

There are also obvious children's attractions such as zoos and wildlife parks, including one based on Pinocchio.

Most cities have Luna Parks, permanent or visiting fun fairs.

Most Tuscan festivals are fun for children, especially the Lenten carnivals, the horse races, jousting, boat pageants, and all the tiny food festivals (*see Diary of Events*). Depending on the time of year, you may find a travelling circus or children's theatre, especially around Florence and Prato.

To find out what's on, particularly in summer, check the newspaper listings in *La Repubblica* or *La Nazione* as well as in *Events*, the lively Florence-based magazine.

Teenagers may well be interested in a study holiday focusing on crafts, sports, cooking or languages (*see below*).

If you read Italian, buy *Firenze Spettacolo*, a Florentine listings magazine which has a good children's section: *Città & Ragazzi*.

Boboli Gardens (*Giardini Boboli*), situated around the Pitti Palace in Florence, are fun for children to clamber around. There is an amphitheatre, strange statues and grottoes, as well as a handy cafe.

The Cascine, Florence's other main park, is popular with local families and at weekends full of children, many of whom come to see the tiny zoo.

Giardino dei Tarocchi, near Capalbio, is a bizarre garden of creations inspired by tarot cards.

Ludoteca Centrale, Piazza SS Annunziata 13, Florence. Tel: 055-247 8386. Open 9am–1pm, 3–7pm. Closed Wednesday as well as Saturday afternoon. This is a fun children's centre with games, music and audio-visual equipment designed to appeal to children under the age of six.

The Maremma is a good place for walks and wildlife spotting (*see* the section on *Villas and Gardens*).

Pinocchio Park (*Parco di Pinocchio*) at Collodi, near Pisa, is an obvious choice for children. Tel: 0572-429342. Open 8.30am–sunset.

Pistoia Zoo, Via Pieve a Celle, Pistoia. Tel: 0573-939219. A compact zoo but one of the best in the region.

Zoo Fauna Europa, just south of the town of Poppi. Tel: 0575-529079. A conservation centre for such breeds as the lynx and the Apennine wolf.

Package Holidays

The Italian State Tourist Office, 1 Princes St London W1R 8AY (Tel: 0171-408 1254) can supply free maps and brochures on a wide range of holidays and activities, and they produce a useful booklet, *La Mia Italia*, with practical information on unusual travel itineraries.

Italiatour is Alitalia's package tour operator, offering holidays on scheduled Alitalia flights from Heathrow to six Italian airports, including Pisa. For brochures and further information, write to 205 Holland Park Avenue, London W11 4XV. Tel: 0171-371 1114. Citalia also offer holidays covering the whole of Italy. Tel: 0181-686 0677.

Package deals, especially weekend breaks, are reasonable:

Magic of Italy, 227 Shepherd's Bush Road, London W6 7AS. Tel: 081-748 7575. This established company runs good-quality package tours (with a great degree of independence).

Prospect Art Tours, 454-458 Chiswick High Road, London W4 5TT. Tel: 0181-995 2151. This specialised upmarket company runs sophisticated art tours to Tuscany.

Study Holidays

LANGUAGE SCHOOLS

There are numerous language schools, mostly in Florence and Siena. The reputable ones are run by Siena and Florence universities or are organised by long-established centres, such as the British Institute.

Centro Internationale Dante Alighieri, La Lizza 10, 53100 Siena. Tel: 0577-46421.

Centro di Cultura per Stranieri dell' Università di Firenze, Via Vittorio Emanuele II 64, 50134 Florence. Tel: 055-472139.

Koinè, Via Pandolfini 27, Florence. Tel: 055-213881.

Leonardo da Vinci, Via Brunelleschi 4, Florence. Tel: 055-294247.

Machiavelli, Piazza Santo Spirito 4, Firenze. Tel: 055-296966.

As the "purest Italian language" is spoken in Siena, the **Italian Language and Culture School for Foreigners**, Piazzetta Grassi 2, Siena 53100 (Tel: 0577-49260) runs courses for foreigners and Italians who are permanent residents abroad. It is a recognised Institute of Higher Education for Language and Culture, awarding a diploma to successful students.

ART COURSES

At the **Università Internazionale dell'Arte**, Villa Il Ventaglio, Via delle Forbici 24/26, 50133 Florence. Tel: 055-570216 or 571503. Various art appreciation courses are held with specialisation in museum collections, conservation and restoration, design and graphic design.

Istituto d'Arte di Firenze, Via dell'Alloro 14r. Tel: 055-283142. Courses in drawing, design, photography, painting, watercolours, sculpture, restoration, ceramics and jewellery-making.

British Institute, Palazzo Lanfredini, Lungarno Guicciardini 9, 50125 Florence. Tel: 055-284031. Conducts art and language courses. This is the centre with the best reputation for such courses in Florence. It also has an excellent English and Italian library to which one can have temporary membership (with one section donated in 1994 by the late Harold Acton).

FASHION INSTITUTES

Centro Moda, Via Faenza 109. Tel: 055-219331/2/3.

Polimoda, Via Pisana 71. Tel: 055-717173.

MUSIC

The **Accademia Musicale Chigiana** (Chigiana Academy of Music), Via di Città 89, 53100 Siena (Tel: 0577-46152) provides proficiency courses (the classical repertoire) in July and August for young performers, both Italian and foreign.

A theoretical and practical course of jazz music is held annually at the **Seminari Nazionali Senesi**, Via Vallerozzi 77, 53100 Siena (Tel: 0577-47552). This training centre is among the most well-known for jazz music in Europe.

CERAMIC WORKSHOPS

In Sorano, an ancient medieval village of the Maremma, pottery courses of one or two weeks are held between June and September and during the Easter and Christmas holidays. Various techniques of working and firing including majolica firing, bucchero firing (ancient Etruscan technique), reduction and wood firing. Full information from:

Studio Pandora, Andrea Sola, Via della Fortezza 13, 58010 Sorano (GR). Tel: 011-877847 or 041-520 5116.

COOKING CLASSES

Italian cookery classes, from noon–3pm for three consecutive days, are given by an Italian cook with an interpreter. Lessons can be held in both English and German on request. Contact: Scuola di Arte Culinaria "Cordon Bleu", Via di Mezzo 55 red (near the Cathedral), Florence. Tel: 055-290987. Also contact Badia a Cottibuono. Tel: 0577-749424.

For further information contact the Italian Institute in London. Tel: 0171-235 1461. Florence is a prime target for foreign students, especially North Americans. Harvard and New York University are just two of the many institutions with an Italian campus in Florence.

OTHER ACTIVITIES

Spas: Tuscany has a large number of spas, in a variety of locations, catering for different ailments.

Most spas charge a daily entrance fee of around L.25,000. Extra treatments such as mudbaths cost about L.25,000 each per session. The cost of a complete cure depends on the number of treatments involved and obviously the standard of accommodation. At Montecatini Terme, for example, accommodation ranges from simple pensions to 5-star hotels.

You can see a doctor before taking a cure and some treatments such as the mudbath should only be undertaken with medical advice.

The major spas include Bagni di Lucca, Bagno Vignoni, Casciana Terme, Chianciano Terme, Monsummano, Montecatini Terme, San Carlo Terme and Terme di Saturnia.

Walking: Various areas of Tuscany are mapped routes for walkers. Some of the loveliest walks through Tuscany are in the Lunigiana moonscape or in the rolling hills of Siena Province, near Montepulciano and San Gimignano. An expensive, but highly recommended company that arranges walks is **The Alternative Travel Group Limited**, 69-71 Banbury Road, Oxford OX2 6PE. Tel: 01865-310399, Fax: 01865-310299.

These walking holidays are designed for anyone – not just serious walkers. All transport and hotel accommodation is arranged. "The Way to Assisi" is a popular walk, but there are several on offer, including gastronomic trips.

Tra cielo e terra, a trekking club based in Viareggio, Via Comparini 36/5 (Tel: 0584-391607), does a "Medieval Wayfarer", a three days' walk through Saturnia, Manciano, Sovana and Pitigliano.

Apuan Alps: The Wind Cave is a series of underground pathways with stalactites and stalagmites, rivers and waterfalls. There are four tours, taking from one to three hours. Open from 1 April to 15 October; on Bank Holidays only for the rest of the year. For group reservations, write to: Head Office, "Grotta del Vento", 55020 Fornovolasco (Lucca) or telephone, preferably the day before, 0583-763084 or 763068. There are long waits on busy days if no reservations are made.

Musia, Ballet & Opera

To keep up-to-date with events, buy *Firenze Spettacolo*, the monthly listings magazine. (Although it is in Italian, the listings themselves are quite straightforward.) Alternatively, obtain *Events*, another popular listings magazine and check the entertainment pages of *La Nazione*, the regional newspaper. If you read Italian well, then get *Toscana Qui*, and *Firenze ieri, oggi, domani.*

Concerts of popular and classical music are held regularly, often in churches or in the open air, in all towns and cities. The ORT, Orchestra della Toscana (Tel: 055-242767), and the Filarmonica di Firenze "Gioacchino Rossini" are two of Tuscany's orchestras.

The *Maggio Musicale* music festival, held from mid-May to the end of June, is a big event with top names in concert, ballet and opera performing in various venues throughout the city. Tickets are available from the Teatro Comunale, Corso Italia 16. Tel: 055-211158. Concerts, formal and informal, are held throughout the summer in cloisters, piazzas or the Boboli Gardens. The main concert hall and venue for opera and ballet is the Teatro Comunale. The opera season opens at the end of September or beginning of October. During the *Estate Fiesolina* – Fiesole's summer festival – concerts, opera, ballet and theatre are held in the Roman amphitheatre.

Classical concerts are also held in many of the city churches. To find out what Rock, Jazz and Latin American music is on offer, check in the latest issue of *Firenze Spettacolo* listings magazine.

SIENA

The Accademia Musicale Chigiana (Chigiana Academy of Music), Via di Città 89, 53100 Siena (Tel: 0577-46152) provides proficiency courses in July and August for young performers, both Italian and foreign.

Public performances of rare, unpublished and new music are held in August each year during the Sienese Music Week. They include opera, symphonic concerts and chamber orchestras plus international congresses of music studies.

A theoretical and practical course of jazz music is held annually at the Seminari Nazionali Senesi, Via Vallerozzi 77, 53100 Siena. Tel: 0577-

47552. This training centre is among the most well-known for jazz music in Europe.

PISA

In May and June, concerts are held at various annual festivals and fairs, especially during the *Gioco del Ponte* on 26 June.

Theatre

To find out what plays are on, buy *La Repubblica* newspaper on Tuesday. The main theatres are the Teatro della Pergola, Via della Pergola 18. Tel: 055-247-9651 and Teatro Niccolini, Via Ricasoli. Tel: 055-213282. Most productions are in Italian.

Movies

The cinema is well attended by Italians. There are numerous foreign films, often in English or other foreign languages with Italian subtitles.

In the summer, open-air cinemas are set up in country towns and in quiet squares of cities, such as the one in Lucca.

The main English-language cinema in Florence is the Astro, Piazza Simone, near Santa Croce, which shows films every night except Monday. Goldini Original Sound, Via dei Serragli (Tel: 055-222473) also shows foreign films in their original versions. Telephone 198 for a listing of all films being shown in Florence at any one time. In summer, occasional English-language films are shown on outdoor screens at Fort Belvedere.

Libraries

All main towns of Tuscany have reference libraries with very helpful, usually English-speaking, staff. These are free and open to anyone, as are the libraries of religious centres, universities, schools and State offices. Lending libraries exist in some towns.

FLORENCE

Medici Laurenziana Library (Biblioteca Medici Laurenziana), Piazza San Lorenzo 9. Open daily 10am–1pm. Closed Sundays. Tel: 055-210760.
American Library, Via San Gallo 10. Tel: 055-296114. Open 9am–12.30pm. Closed Saturday.
British Institute Library, Lungarno Guicciardini, 9. Tel: 055-284031. Open 9.45am–12.45pm, 3.15–7.15pm.

Closed Saturday. The library was bequeathed many books by Harold Acton.
Library of the French Institute, Piazza Ognissanti 2. Tel: 055-298902. Open 10am–1pm, 3–6pm. Closed Saturday. The Institute often organises showings of French films.
Library of the Dutch University Institute, Via Torricelli 5. Tel: 055-221612. Open 9am–1pm, 2–6pm. Closed Saturday.

SAN GIMIGNANO

In the Communal Library are 18th-century manuscripts, civic documents etc. In the Medical Library are herbalists' and medical books of the 17th and 18th centuries.

SIENA

Libreria Piccolomini (Piccolomini Library), inside the Cathedral. Open summer 9am–7.30pm; winter 10am–1pm, 2.30–5pm.

Diary Of Events

AREZZO

First Sunday in September: Saracens' Joust (*Giostra del Saraceno*). Mounted knights representing the four districts of the city attack the wooden effigy of a Turk. A procession is held before the event.
First Sunday of every month: An antique fair is held in the square.

CORTONA

July/August: The Cortona Summer Festival offers a full artistic programme.
15 August: *Sagra della Bistecca* (Feast of the Beefsteak).
September: An exhibition of antique furniture is held during this month.

FLORENCE

February/March: *Carnevale*, the Lenten festival. Almost as dramatic as the Venice Carnival.
May and June: *Maggio Musicale Fiorentino* – performance of opera, ballet and concerts; much patronised by the Florentines themselves.
24 and 28 June: *Calcio in Costume* (*Calcio Fiorentino*) – football in medieval costume in Piazza della Signoria.
Easter Day (*Lo Scoppio del Carro*): The burning of a "carriage" (float) and the emergence of a dove among the crowds. Fireworks display.

Ascension Day: Festival of the crickets in Cascine Park. Sale of crickets and sweets.

7 September: Night festival of the *Rificolone* (lanterns). A procession of carts, lanterns and singers.

LUCCA

September: *Luminaria di Santa Croce*, a religious procession.

LUCIGNANO

Last two Sundays in May: *Maggiolata Lucignanese*, a Lucignano festival that takes place in May, includes a procession of carts decorated with allegorical scenes in flowers.

MASSA MARITTIMA

Sunday following May 20 and the **second Sunday in August**: Twice a year the *Balestro del Girifalco* (crossbow competition with mechanical falcon) and flag-wavers recall the ancient republic.

MONTICCHIELLO

Last 15 days of July: Each year *Il Teatro Povero* (the Poor Theatre) presents a drama written and acted by everyone about the local history and the culture of the farmer.

PIENZA

August/September: Each year, "A meeting with a Master of Art" takes place in the council chamber (1500) of the Town Hall, Pienza. Many famous artists have displayed their work.

First Sunday of September: The *Fiera del Cacio* (Sheep Cheese Fair) is held, as Pienza is considered the supreme centre for sheep cheese production.

PISA

May and **June**: Concerts are held at various annual festivals and fairs, but especially during the *Gioco del Ponte* on 26 June.

PISTOIA

25 July: A traditional festival – the *Giostra dell' Orso* or Joust of the Bear is held in Piazza del Duomo. The "bear" is made of wood and a mock battle takes place between the "bear" and 12 knights in costume.

SIENA

28–30 April: The Feast of St Catherine.
July 2 and **16 August**: The *Palio* (traditional horse race) takes place. For tickets and hotel bookings, write to the Tourist Office six months in advance. Visits may be made to the Museums of the 17 *Contrade* (districts) of Siena by giving at least one week's advance notice. (The Tourist Office will also supply a list of museums.) Each district has its own church and museum and celebrates the festival of its patron saint.

August: Sienese Music Week. Public performances of rare, unpublished and new music are held in August including opera, symphonic concerts and chamber orchestras plus international congresses of music studies.

VIAREGGIO

February: *Carnevale*, the best in Italy, with elaborately decorated floats paraded along the seafront.

VOLTERRA

July/August: Crossbow tournâment (*torneo di tiro con la balestra*) in Piazza dei Priori.
Last Monday in September: Regional bird fair (*fiera regionale degli uccelli*).
September: National Festival of Choral Groups (*festivale nazionale dei gruppi corali*).

Nightlife

Italians enjoy playing and listening to music: violin players stroll round restaurants, small orchestras and bands play at gatherings in preference to taped music. Summer discos are set up in resorts, usually dancing takes place outside a restaurant or rustic bar. Increasingly popular are displays of traditional flag-waving ceremonies and peasant dancing.

All the cities have a wide variety of music and entertainment, but nightclubs often do not stay in business, so it is advisable to ask your hotel for the name of a recommended place to go. To keep up with the ever-changing Tuscan scene, get *Firenze Spettacolo*, the listings magazine, or buy a copy of *La Repubblica* newspaper on Tuesday.

Bars/Piano Music/Live Music

Most places are closed on Monday.
Be Bop, Via dei Servi 76c. Cocktail bar; live music: jazz, blues, country. Entrance free.
Caffè, Piazza Pitti 9. Tel: 051-296241. Chic, refined and exclusive atmosphere. It is a cosy spot to chat to friends, both during the morning and evening.
Caffèdeco, Piazza della Libertà 45. Closed Monday. Designed in Art Deco style, this stylish bar is popular with jazz-lovers.
Caffè Donatello, Piazza Donatello. Opens at 7pm for cocktails, drinks and dinner; from 10pm live music, performances, poetry, cabaret, rock 'n' roll.
Caffè Voltaire, Via della Scala 9r (near Santa Maria Novella). This is a Florentine "open space", with a changing programme of live entertainment from blues to poetry, salsa to samba.
Chapeau, Via Verdi 57-59r. Tel: 298738.
Chiodo Fisso Club, Via Dante Alighieri 16r. Tel: 051-238 1290. A well-established club, with live music every night.
Dolce Vita, Piazza del Carmine. This is an extremely fashionable bar in the bohemian Oltrarno quarter, across the river.
Meccanò Meccanò, Piazzale delle Cascine. Tel: 055-331371. This huge late-night spot has a piano bar, disco and restaurant. Themed music, different every night.
Riflessi d'Epoca, Via dei Renai 13. This club tends to be a venue for jazz bands and has a laid-back, smoky atmosphere.
Tabasco (Gay), Piazza Santa Cecilia 3. Tel: 213000. Men only.

Discos

FLORENCE

Jackie O', Via dell'Erta Canina 24b. Tel: 234 2442 Generally for thirty somethings.
Space Electronic, Via Palazzuolo 37. Tel: 055-293082. Has lasers and videos and is usual hang-out of foreign teenagers and would-be Latin lovers.
Tropicana, Parco Le Cascine. A big nightclub set in the Cascine Park. It tries to create a hot Latin American sound and encourages excess.
Villa Laser, Lungarno, Colombo. Tel: 051-676912. Closed Monday. Nightclub popular with celebrities. Check the nature of the function/music before turning up.

SIENA

Jet Set, Via Paneanto 13. Tel: 288378.
Club Enoteca, Fortezza Medicea. Tel: 285466.
Tom Cat, Via dei Termini. Tel: 280152.

Shopping

What To Buy

The quality of goods in Italy is very high and prices reasonable. Some suggested purchases are:

Fashions: Dresses, hats, linen, shoes, gloves, silk ties and shirts, knitwear, boutique goods (including classic fashion from top designers), jewellery.

Leather goods: handbags, beauty-cases, boxes, luggage, fine shoes, wallets, belts.

Cloth: silk, linen, wool, cotton.

Handicrafts: Lace, tablecloths; pottery and ceramics; gold and silver ware; alabaster and marble objects; woodwork; straw and raffia goods; glass and crystal work; art books and reproductions; marbled paper; rustic household goods; prints; antiques; reproduction furniture; Tuscan impressionist and modern paintings.

Alcohol: Wines: regional red wines; spirits; liqueurs and aperitifs: Grappa, Strega, Campari, Cinzano, Martini, Carpano.

Food: olive oil; bottled vegetables; herbs.

Duty-Free Goods

Used personal effects may be imported and exported without formality.

The import of narcotics, weapons and pirated materials is forbidden. Certain items (e.g. alcoholic drinks, tobacco, perfume) are limited as to the amount one may take in or out, and these amounts vary for those coming from within the EU, other European countries or outside Europe. This can seem confusing, particularly since the amounts also vary depending on whether the goods were bought duty-paid (i.e. in Italy) or duty-free (i.e. at the airport, on a ship or on a plane).

For EU citizens, provided goods obtained in the European Union are for your personal use, there is no further tax to be paid. European Union law sets out recommended guide levels and if you bring in more than the amounts in the guide levels you must be able to show that the goods are for your personal use. The guide levels for **duty-paid** goods are:

800 cigarettes **or** 400 cigarillos **or** 200 cigars **or** 1 kg tobacco; 10 litres spirits **and** 20 litres intermediate products (such as port and sherry) **and** 90 litres wine (of which not more than 60 litres sparkling) **and** 110 litres beer; gifts up to £71.

Duty-free: 200 cigarettes **or** 100 cigarillos **or** 50 cigars **or** 250 g tobacco; 2 litres still table wine **and** 1 litre spirits; 60 ml perfume and 250 ml toilet water; gifts up to £71.

For citizens outside the EU, the duty-free allowances remain:

200 cigarettes **or** 50 cigars **or** 250 g of smoking tobacco; 1 litre of alcohol **or** 2 litres of fortified or sparkling wine **and** gifts worth up to £136.

If planning to import or export large quantities of goods, or goods of exceptionally high value, contact the Italian Consulate and your own customs authorities beforehand to check on any special regulations which may apply.

Note that different regulations apply to all types of commerical import and export. For further information, contact the Italian Consulate in your own country or your own customs authorities.

Clothes/Shoe Sizes Guide

WOMEN'S DRESSES/SUITS

American	Continental	British
6	38/34N	8/30
8	40/36N	10/32
10	42/38N	12/34
12	44/40N	14/36
14	46/42N	16/38
16	48/44N	18/40

WOMEN'S SHOES

American	Continental	British
4½	36	3
5½	37	4
6½	38	5
7½	39	6
8½	40	7
9½	41	8
10½	42	9

MEN'S SUITS

American	Continental	British
34	44	34
—	46	36
38	48	38
—	50	40
42	52	42
—	54	44
46	56	46

MEN'S SHIRTS

American	Continental	British
14	36	14
14½	37	14½
15	38	15
15½	39	15½
16	40	16
16½	41	16½
17	42	17

MEN'S SHOES

American	Continental	British
6½	—	6
7½	40	7
8½	41	8
9½	42	9
10½	43	10
11½	44	11

Shopping Areas

Chain stores such as La Rinascente, Upim and Standa can be found in most towns in Tuscany. Foreign languages are spoken in most shops in cities, large towns and tourist resorts.

Open-air markets are held usually once or twice a week in almost all tourist resorts.

Supermarkets are found in most of the tourist resorts and in all towns. Baby food can be bought everywhere at chemists (*farmacie*), supermarkets and grocers.

Tobacconists are licensed to sell postage stamps, *schede* (telephone cards), salt and candles besides cigarettes and tobacco.

Florence

MARKETS

Straw Market (Mercato del Porcellino). Hand-embroidered work, Florentine straw, leather goods, wooden objects, flowers.

Flea Market (Mercato delle Pulci), Piazza dei Ciompi. Objects from the past – basically junk, but great fun.

San Ambrogi (Piazza Ghiberti). Vegetables, fruit, food, flowers, clothes.

San Lorenzo Market (Mercato di San Lorenzo), Piazza San Lorenzo. Vegetables, fruit, food.

Cascine Market (Mercato delle Cascine). Tuesdays only. Produce, household goods, clothing. This market is popular with Florentines.

SHOPS

Despite tourism, consumerism and high labour costs, Florence still has a reputation as a city with high standards of craftsmanship in many spheres, from leather-work to silver jewellery, from ceramics to hand-marbled paper. If you wish to visit craftsmen at work, consult the Tourist Office and ask for their booklets on crafts, including *From Craftsmanship to Art,* (*Tra Artigianato ed Arte*). Although a bit out of date, it lists the main craftsmen still practising in Florence. For example, the Santa Croce leather school, Piazza Santa Croce and Via Giuseppe 5r, is a popular place for visitors to watch the skilled Florentine leather-workers.

SHOES

Ferragamo, Via de' Tornabuoni 16. Italy's most prestigious shoemaker's, providing hand-tooled shoes of all descriptions and beautifully crafted ready-to-wear collections. The Ferragamo boast that once one has worn their shoes, nothing else feels good enough.

Cresti, Via Roma 9r. These are also beautifully crafted shoes, but available at much lower prices.

Francesco, Via di Santo Spirito 62r. This is the place to have unpretentious hand-made shoes tooled in classic designs, made by a traditional craftsman.

JEWELLERY

The Ponte Vecchio is the main place visitors first espy Florentine jewellery. Although the setting is atmospheric, most of the craftsmen work in very different conditions. There is still a flourishing jewellery trade in Florence (particularly in Oltrarno, on the south side of the river) but most gold jewellery is made in Arezzo nowadays.

However, the following traditional goldsmiths and silversmiths remain:

Fulvio Casamonti, Piazza del Carmine 1. Silversmith.

Marzio Casprini, Via dei Serragli 56. Silversmith.

Giovanni Barone, Piazza Duomo 36r. Goldsmith.

Gatto Bianco, Borgo SS Apostoli 12r. Goldsmith.

Exclusive Jewellery:

Torrini, Piazza del Duomo 10r. Tel: 055-284457.

Buccellati, Via de' Tornabuoni 71r. Tel: 055-239 6579.

MARBLED PAPER

This marbled paper is closely associated with Florence and many of the designs echo ancient themes or Medici crests. Visit the following:

Giulio Giannini e Figlio, Piazza Pitti 37r. This is the longest established marbled paper shop.

Il Papiro, Via Cavour. These marbled paper designs are on display in Il Pario's three Florentine branches.

LEATHER

Leather goods are, of course, the best buy in the city. Quality ranges from the beautifully tooled creations of local artisans to shoddy goods aimed at undiscerning tourists. For top of the range quality (and prices), start with the designer boutiques in the Via de' Tornabuoni or shops in streets around the Piazza della Repubblica.

Raspini at Via Roma 25-29 has superb leather shops, bags and coats as well as high quality fashions. For more down-to-earth prices, head for the **market** of **San Lorenzo** northwest of the Duomo, where numerous street stalls sell shoes, bags, belts, wallets (as well as cheap woollen sweaters, silk ties and scarves).

BOUTIQUES

Florence is a high-spot for fashion, and the centre is full of top designer boutiques. The most elegant street is the Via de' Tornabuoni where Gucci, Ferragamo, Versace, Valentino and other big names in fashion have their outlets.

Other exclusive streets are the Via Calzaiuoli and Via Roma (both of which have a stunning range of leather goods), Via della Vigna Nuova and Via del Parione.

Alex, Via della Vigna Nuova 19. Tel: 055-214952.

Atelier Alta Moda, Paola Quadretti, Via del Sole 17r. This is an imaginative designer boutique run by a young Florentine designer.

Emilio Pucci, Via de' Pucci 6. Tel: 055-283061/2 and at Via della Vigna Nuova 97.

Enrico Coveri, Via de' Tornabuoni 81. Tel: 055-211263.

Ferragamo, Palazzo Spini-Feroni, Via de' Tornabuoni 2. Tel: 055-292123. These famous Florentine shoemakers have now branched out into accessories and clothes.

Gianni Versace, Via de' Tornabuoni 13. Tel: 055-296167.

Giorgio Armani, Via della Vigna Nuova 51r. Tel: 055-219041.

Gucci, Via de' Tornabuoni 73. Tel: 055-264011. This international Florentine firm has developed a tighter, more sophisticated range in recent years but the belts and handbags are still their trademark.

Lietta Cavalli, Via della Vigna Nuova 45. Tel: 055-298572.

Raspini, Via Roma 25–29. Tel: 055-213077.

Valentino, Via della Vigna Nuova 47r. Tel: 055-282485.

Zanobetti, Via Calimale 22. Tel: 055-210646.

FABRICS

Antico Setificio, Via L. Bartolini 4. Tel: 055-213861. This wonderful craft shop specialises in fabrics produced along traditional lines, especially silk, and is run by Alessandro, Emilio Pucci's son. Silk is woven on 18th-century looms.

Casa dei Tessuti, Via de' Pecori, 20–24. Tel: 055-215961. Charming silks, linens and woollens.

BOOKSHOPS

The **Paperback Exchange**, Via Fiesolana 31r, in the Santa Croce district, is no ordinary bookshop. For a start, it stocks just about every book ever written on Florence currently in print, and many that are no longer published. In addition, it operates a system whereby you get a credit of 25 to 40 percent of the original price of any book you trade in which can be used to buy books from their vast stock of quality secondhand English and American paperbacks. The shop is run by enthusiasts who know everything there is to know about Florence and books.

After Dark, Via del Moro 86r. Tel: 055-294203. English bookshop.

Feltrinelli International, Via Vavour 12/20. Tel: 055-219524. This is the most comprehensive and respected bookshop in Florence.

Seeber, Via de' Tornabuoni 70r. Tel: 055-215697. The shop has a good selection of books in English and Italian.

SUPERMARKETS

Consorzio Agrario, Piazza San Firenze 5r.
Standa, Via Pietrapiana 42/44.
Coop, Via Nazionale 32r.
Conrad, Via L. Alamanni 2r.

Pescia

Flower Market: The huge flower market is now housed in a new, specially designed building. The market begins early, so try to get there by 7am. For details, contact the Pescia Tourist Office, Mercato dei Fiori, Via Amendola 28. Tel: 0572-476897.

Siena

Siena is known for its **confectionery**, a type of bread, *panforte*, made from a sweet dough, flavoured with vanilla and candied citrus fruits, covered with almonds. The most famous maker of such specialities is Panforte Nannini at Piazza Matteotti 21, Piazza del Monte 95/99 and Bar Pasticceria Nannini at Banchi di Sopra 24. (The owner's daughter is Italy's best-known female rock singer).

Pan co' Santi is another Sienese cake made with raisins and nuts, traditionally eaten on All Saints' Day. *Cavallucci* are small biscuits with chopped nuts and *Copate* are biscuits made of soft nougat with wafers on each side.

Giogi Leonardo & Co. at Antica Siena, Piazza del Campo 28, Tel: 0577-46496, sells beautiful blue and yellow **porcelain**.

Local production of wrought **iron** and **copper**, ceramics, crystal and stained glass provide a wide choice for visitors.

The Province of Siena produces a variety of good **wines** including Chianti, Brunello di Montalcino, and Nobile di Montepulciano. The Permanent Italian Wine Exhibition in Fortezza Medicea, Tel: 0577-288497, was set up for the display and sale of regional wines. Visitors can discover and appreciate a wide variety of Italian wines. Wine traders may purchase and export their selections.

Shopping Hours

Food, vegetable and general stores mostly open from 8.30am–6pm, closing from 1–4pm in the afternoon. Supermarkets, departmental stores and city shops open at about 9am until 1pm, then from 3.30–7.30 or 8pm.

Some shops are closed on Monday morning or all day Monday, others on Saturday afternoon or all day Saturday. Everything closes on Sunday except tourist shops in resorts or tourist centres. Shops are also closed on public holidays and some saints days.

Export

For the exportation of antiques and modern art objects, an application must be presented to the Export Department of the Italian Ministry of Education. If the request is granted, a tax in accordance with the value of the items must be paid.

Sports

Participant

It is possible to play any popular sport either at private clubs or at municipal centres under the National Olympic Committee (CONI). There are tennis courts at most resorts, and swimming, scuba diving, windsurfing and boating on the coast. In villages, bowls (*boccie*) and cards are popular. Gambling, often for high stakes, is widespread, though illegal except in approved casinos and betting shops.

Golf

There are **golf** courses in Tuscany at: **Florence**: Golf Club Ugolino, 50015 Grassina. Tel: 055-230 1096. 18 holes, a course set in an olive grove. **Tirrenia**: Cosmopolitan Golf and Country Club. Tel: 050-33085. Nine holes. **Punta Ala**: Tel: 0564-922121. 18 holes.

Fishing

Sea sport fishing may be practised both from the shore and from a boat. In some ports, a special permit is required from the Harbourmaster's Office. Only those over 16 are allowed to use underwater guns and such equipment. When submerged, an underwater fisherman is required to indicate the fact with a float bearing a red flag with a yellow diagonal stripe, and must operate within a radius of 50 metres (164 ft) of the support barge or the float bearing the flag. Fishing is prohibited at within 500 metres (1,640 ft) of a beach used by bathers and 50 metres (164 ft) of fishing installations and ships at anchor.

Freshwater fishing in rivers and lakes for trout, grayling, char, chub, carp, tench, pike, perch, roach, etc. is generally satisfactory. Foreigners need a temporary membership of FIPS (Federazione Italiana della Pesca Sportiva) and a Government licence issued by the Provincial Administration. A licence for rod-fishing with or without a reel costs about £1.50 and is valid for one year. Every provincial town has an office to give advice and notice of restrictions on fishing-times and places.

Watersports

At all Tuscan sea resorts, it is possible to water-ski and row with hired boats. **Yacht chartering** facilities are available in Marina di Pisa and Tirrenia.

Warning: Sharks have occasionally been sighted off the Tuscan coast and a diver has been killed by a 20-ft (6-metre) shark...so beware!

Swimming Pools

Most luxury hotels have swimming pools and there are public pools in most towns. If you wish to use a particular pool but are not a hotel guest, it is worth calling to ask if you can use it (for a fee). The following pools are in Florence:

Piscina Costoli, Viale Paoli, Campo di Marte. Tel: 050-669744. This is in the north of the city.
Piscina Comunale Bellariva, Lungarno Colombo 6. Tel: 050-677521. Open-air.
Piscina Le Pavoniere, Viale degli Olmi (Parco delle Cascine). Tel: 050-367506. Set in the Cascine Park, this is one of the most appealing pools.

Skiing

Tuscany has a major ski resort at Abetone in the Apennines, north of Pistoia.

The skiing area extends over four valleys and 30 km (19 miles) of trails. Tourist information on ski passes, pistes, etc. from Azienda Autonoma Soggiorno e Turismo, Abetone. Tel: 0573-60231.

Hunting & Shooting

Shooting birds and animals is a popular sport in Italy but not encouraged by the Tourist Boards. There are strict rules on the importation and use of firearms. Information may be obtained from the Federazione Italiana Caccia, Viale Tiziano 70, Rome. Tel: 06-394871.

The Maremma and the Volterra are areas of wild boar hunting and there are several reserves for shooting pheasant.

Horse-riding

In Siena, the Club Ippico Senese, Località Pian del Lago (Tel: 53277), has horse-riding. There are also over 40 Centres of the National Association of Equestrian Tourism (ANTE) where it is possible to spend your holiday on horseback. For further information, write to: ANTE, Largo Messico 13, Rome or to the Federazione Italiana Sport Equestri, Viale Tiziano 70, Rome. Tel: 06-390228.

If you'd like to go riding in the Florence area, contact the Country Riding Club, Via di Grioli, Badia a Settimo, Scandicci (just southwest of the city). Tel: 055-790277.

Sport Centres

Circolo Tennis Siena, Località Vico Alto. Tel: 0578-44925/283397.
Piscina Comunale (swimming), Piazza G. Amendola. Tel: 0578-47496.
Tiro a Segno Nazionale (target shooting), Viale Sclavo. Tel: 0578-52417.

Spectator

The main spectator sports in Tuscany are football, horse racing and speed cycling which culminates in the Grand Tour of Italy. All important events are watched avidly on television.

In Florence, there is a race course in the Cascine Park, Ippodromo le Cascine. Tel: 055-360598.

Language

General

Pronunciation is claimed by all Italians to be simple: you pronounce as you read. This is approximately true. A couple of important rules for English speakers: **c** before **e** or **i** is pronounce **ch** e.g. *ciao, mi dispiace, la coincidenza*. **Ch** before **i** or **e** is pronounced as **k** e.g. *la chiesa*.

Nouns are either masculine (**il**, plural **i**) or feminine (**la**, plural **le**). Plurals of nouns are most often formed by changing an **o** to an **i** and an **a** to an **e** e.g. *il panino*: i *panini*; *la chiesa*: *le chiese*.

There is, of course, rather more to the language than that, but you can get a surprisingly long way in making friends with a mastery of a few basic phrases.

It is well worth buying a good phrase book or dictionary, but the following basics will help you get started.

Basics

hello (Good day)/*buon giorno*
good evening/*buona sera*
good night/*buona notte*
goodbye/*arrivederci*
hi/goodbye (familiar)/*ciao*
yes/*sì*
no/*no*
thank you/*grazie*
you're welcome/*prego*
all right, OK/*va bene*
please/*per favore* or *per piacere*
excuse me (get attention)/*scusi* (singular), *scusate* (plural)
excuse me (in a crowd)/*permesso*
Can you show me...?/*Puo indicarmi...?*
can you help me?/*puo aiutarmi, per piacere?*
I'm lost/*mi sono perso*
sorry/*mi dispiace*
I don't understand/*non capisco*
I am English/American/*sono inglese/ americano/*
Irish/Canadian/*irlandese/canadese*
Do you speak English?/*Parla inglese?*

Where is the lavatory?/*Dovè il bagno?*
gentlemen/*Signori/Uomini*
ladies/*Signore/Donne*

Questions & Answers

I'd like .../*vorrei ...*
I'd like that one, please./*Vorrei quello lì, per favore.*
Is there/do you have ...?/*C'è (un) ...?*
yes, of course/*sì, certo*
no, we don't /*no, non c'è*
(Also used to mean: s/he is not here)

Transport

airport/*l'aeroporto*
aeroplane/*l'aereo*
arrivals/*arrivi*
boat/*la barca*
bus/*il bus*
bus station/*autostazione*
connection/*la coincidenza*
departures/*le partenze*
ferry/*il traghetto*
ferry terminal/*stazione marittima*
flight/*il volo*
hydrofoil/*l'aliscafo*
left luggage/*il deposito bagagli*
no smoking/*vietato fumare*
platform/*il binario*
port/*il porto*
railway station/*stazione ferrovia*
return ticket/*un biglietto di andata e ritorno*
single ticket/*un biglietto di andata sola*
sleeping car/*la carrozza letti*
station/*la stazione*
stop/*la fermata*
taxi/*il taxi*
train/*il treno*
What time does the train leave?/ *Quando parte il treno?*
What time does the train arrive?/ *Quando arriva il treno?*

Days of the Week

Monday/*Lunedi*
Tuesday/*Martedi*
Wednesday/*Mercoledi*
Thursday/*Giovedi*
Friday/*Venerdi*
Saturday/*Sabato*
Sunday/*Domenica*

Months

January/*Gennaio*
February/*Febbraio*
March/*Marzo*
April/*Aprile*
May/*Maggio*
June/*Giugno*

July/*Luglio*
August/*Agosto*
September/*Settembre*
October/*Ottobre*
November/*Novembre*
December/*Dicembre*

Numbers

0/*zero*
1/*uno*
2/*due*
3/*tre*
4/*quattro*
5/*cinque*
6 /*sei*
7/*sette*
8/*otto*
9/*nove*
10/*dieci*
11/*undici*
12/*dodici*
13/*tredici*
14/*quattordici*
15/*quindici*
16/*sedici*
17/*diciassette*
18/*diciotto*
19/*diciannove*
20/*venti*
21/*ventuno*
30/*trenta*
40/*quaranta*
50/*cinquanta*
60/*sessanta*
70/*settanta*
80/*ottanta*
90/*novanta*
100/*ottanta*
200/*duecento*
1,000/*mille*
2,000/*duemila*
3,000/*tremila*
4,000/*quattromila*
5,000/*cinquemila*
1,000,000/*un milione*

For Sightseeing

abbey, monastery/*abbazia, badia, convento*
frescoes/*affreschi*
tickets/*biglietti*
library/*biblioteca*
chapel/*capella*
house/*casa*
castle/*castella*
church/*chiesa*
cloisters/*chiostro*
closed/*chiuso*
city/*città*
courtyard/*cortile*
cathedral/*cuomo*

district (in the city)*contrada, rione*
district (in the country)/*località*
fair, regatta, etc./*fiera*
gardens/*giardini*
seashore promenade/*lungomare*
(bank of the River Arno)/(*Lungarno*)
market/*mercato*
walls/*mura*
nave/*navata*
works/*opere*
panel, altarpiece/*pala*
palace, grand house/*palazzo*
walk, stroll/*passeggiata*
storey/floor/*piano*
picture gallery/*pinacoteca*
picture/*quadro*
feudal castle/*rocca*
ruins/*Rovine, ruderi*
sacristy, vestry/*sagrestia*
stairs, ladder/*scala*
excavations/*scavi*
beach/*spiaggia*
treasure/*tesoro*
tower/*torre*
belltower/*campanile*

Road Signs

no entry/*enso vietato*
no entry for/*vietato ingresso*
vehicles/*veicoli*
parking permitted (times given)/*sosta autorizzata*
no parking/*sosta vietata*
closed to/*vietato transito*
heavy vehicles/*autocarri*
level crossing/*passaggio a livello*
slow down/*rallentare*
bend/*svolta*
crossroads/*incrocio*
exit or way out/*uscita*
entrance or way in/*entrata*
road works ahead/*lavori in Corso*

Directions

right/*a destra*
left/*a sinistra*
straight on/*sempre diritto*
far away/*lontano*
nearby/*vicino*
opposite/*di fronte*
next to/*accanto a*
traffic lights/*il semaforo*
junction/*l'incrocio, il bivio*
building/*il palazzo*
turn left/*gira a sinistra*
Where is ...?/*Dov'è ...?*
Where are ...?/*Dove sono...?*
Where is the nearest...?/*Dov'è ...più vicino?*
bank/petrol station/bus/*la banca/la benzinaio/la fermata di autobus*

hotel/garage/*l'albergo/il garage*
Can you show me where I am on the map?/*Può indicarmi sulla cartina dove mi trovo?*

Further Reading

General

The Italian State Tourist Office: *Italy Traveller's Handbook* (updated yearly). Italian Touring Club Regional Guides and maps from Stanfords, Long Acre, London WC2E 9LP. Tel: 0171-836 1321.

An excellent selection of books and maps on Italy is available from The Travel Bookshop, 13 Blenheim Crescent, London W11 2EE. Tel: 0171-229 5260. Also from The Travellers Bookshop, 25 Cecil Court, London WC2N 4EZ. Tel: 0171-836 9132.

Background

A Room with a View, by E.M. Forster. Penguin.
The Architecture of the Italian Renaissance, by Peter Murray. Thames and Hudson.
Autobiography, by Benvenuto Cellini. Penguin Classics.
A Concise Encyclopedia of the Italian Renaissance, edited by J.R. Hale. Thames and Hudson.
The Civilization of the Renaissance in Italy, by Jacob Burckhardt. Phaidon Press.
D.H. Lawrence and Italy, by D.H. Lawrence. Penguin.
Etruscan Places, by D.H. Lawrence. Olive Press.
The Florentine Renaissance and *The Flowering of the Renaissance* by Vincent Cronin. Fontana
The High Renaissance and *The Late Renaissance and Mannerism*, by Linda Murray. Thames and Hudson
Italians, by David Willey. BBC Publications.
Italian Hours, by Henry James. Century Hutchinson.
Italian Wines, by Maureen Ashley. Sainsbury's.
The Italians, by Luigi Barzini. Hamish Hamilton.
The Italian Painters of the Renaissance, by Bernard Berenson. Phaidon Press.

The Italian World, by John Julius Norwich. Thames and Hudson.
Lives of the Artists, by Giorgio Vasari. Vols. 1 & 2. Penguin Classics.
Love and War in the Apennines, by Eric Newby. Picador.
The Love of Italy, by Jonathan Keates. Octopus.
The Merchant of Prato, by Iris Origo. Penguin.
Pictures from Italy, by Charles Dickens. Granville Publishing.
The Stones of Florence, by Mary McCarthy. Penguin.

Tuscany

Companion Guide to Tuscany, by Archibald Lyall. Collins.
The Etruscans, by Gabriele Cateni. Regione Lazio.
Florence Explored, by Rupert Scott. The Bodley Head.
A Guide to Tuscany, by James Bentley. Penguin.
Machiavelli, by Anglo Sydney. Paladin.
Painter's Florence, by Barbara Whelpton Johnson.
The Rise and Fall of the House of Medici, by Christopher Hibbert. Penguin.
Siena: A City and its History, by Judith Hook. Hamish Hamilton.
Traveller's Guide to Elba, by Christopher Serpell and Jane Serpell. Jonathan Cape.
Tuscany, an Anthology, by Laura Raison. Cadogan Books.
The Villas of Tuscany, by Harold Acton. Thames and Hudson.

Tuscany (In Italian)

Domenica Dove (itineraries in Tuscany), by Giorgo Battini. Bonechi Editore.
Guerra in Val d'Orcia (An account of the war in Tuscany), by Iris Origo. Bompiani.
Le Più Belle Passeggiate nella Nostra Terra (walks in Tuscany), by La Nazione.

Other Insight Guides

Apa Publications has a comprehensive selection of books on this region. They include Insight Guides to *Italy, Florence, Rome, Bay of Naples, Venice, Umbria, South Tyrol, Sardinia* and *Sicily*, and Insight Pocket Guides to *Tuscany, Florence, Milan, Rome, Venice, Sardinia* and *Sicily*.

Index

347